ILLINOIS 1858 CAMPAIGN

22339

11676998

☆ LINCOLN–DOUGLAS DEBATE
★ DOUGLAS SPEECH
☆ LINCOLN SPEECH
✪ LINCOLN & DOUGLAS SPOKE ON DIFFERENT DAYS
——— RAILROADS
0   25 MILES

(For a map of The Expansion of the United States as Referred to in the Lincoln-Douglas Debates, see back endpapers.)

Mitchell Shostak

The AMERICAN CONSCIENCE

The AMERICAN

The Drama of the

HORIZON PRESS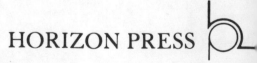

CONSCIENCE

Lincoln-Douglas Debates

SAUL SIGELSCHIFFER

New York

To my wife Rita, and my daughter Tamar,
and to the memory of my parents

PREFACE

The clash between Abraham Lincoln and Stephen A. Douglas is an epic of American history, illustrative of the struggle of the national conscience over slavery. The light in which the debates reveal the two antagonists dissolves the stereotyped images held of them. Lincoln emerges as a tough political campaigner and shrewd stump speaker rather than the Christlike figure into which he has been canonized, while Douglas is not a villain — the foil to Lincoln — but a brilliant and attractive personality, who contributed much to the development of the nation. Drama springs from the relationship of the two men, whose lives were intertwined throughout their careers, bringing them into confrontations other than the debates of 1858.

For many years I was intrigued by the Lincoln-Douglas debates though in print the text is repetitious and tedious reading. I found, however, that there was no book that told their complete story. There were articles and treatises which dealt with one or more aspects, and biographies and general historical works which gave accounts of them. But it was apparent that the whole was greater than the sum of its parts.

It is a wonderfully dramatic story. To render it adequately in its full drama it is necessary to bring together its elements — to present the story within a story of Lincoln and Douglas, to trace the development of the thinking of the two opponents, to show why each debate took the turn it did, to let the orators speak for themselves through typical passages, to provide the requisite background for understanding allusions and situations that might otherwise be incomprehensible, and to describe the aftermath which led to the nation's greatest crisis — the Civil War. It is a story for both the scholar and the general reader.

I wish to express my appreciation for use of facilities and for various courtesies and services to the New York Public Library, the Yonkers Public Library (with thanks to Miss Grace Malone and Mrs. Beatrice O'Connell), the Mt. Vernon Public Library, the Illinois Historical Library, the Newberry Library, the Library of Congress, Mrs. Jane Bowman of the Historical Society of Quincy and Adams County, and Curtis Wynn of the Galesburg Public Library.

For help generously extended I thank Dean Hermann R. Muelder and Professor Alfred Watts Newcombe of Knox College, I.O. Karraker of Jonesboro, and C.C. Tisler of Ottawa. I am also indebted to Professor Allan Nevins for information he sent me in answer to an inquiry. My friends, Abraham Ponemon, formerly director of English of the Board of Education of the City of New York, and John Stahr read parts of the manuscript and offered excellent suggestions. Professor Abraham Hurwitz of Yeshiva University and his wife, Ann, maintained a devoted interest and faith in my work. My secretary, Mrs. Lillian Modell, did a magnificent job of typing the manuscript.

I am especially grateful to Dr. Irving S. Cohen, Chairman of Social Studies in the New York City high schools, for reading the entire manuscript and giving me invaluable advice. His unfailing encouragement carried me over difficult moments. I am also grateful to Jeremy Tarcher whose counsel benefitted me greatly. To Ben Raeburn, editor par excellence, and his associate, Mrs. Laura Vajda, I make a bow for their imaginative handling of the process of transforming a manuscript into a book. Last, and with much love, I thank my wife, Rita, for being my best critic and constant, patient aide.

— SAUL SIGELSCIFFER

Mount Vernon, New York

CONTENTS

ILLUSTRATIONS

PART I

The Controversy

It is an irony of history that slavery was brought to the New World simultaneously with the arrival of those who fled the Old World to seek freedom.

Yet the true instincts of America found expression in the Declaration of Independence, which proclaimed that all men were created equal. For that reason the conscience of America could not rest with the paradox of liberty and slavery living side by side.

The voice of conscience, small at first, grew louder as the eighteenth century drew to a close. Soon the paradox was mooted in the home, on the farm, in the streets, in the press, in the churches and in the halls of government.

Slavery became the center of controversy, enmeshed in the intricacies of the Constitution and the laws of the states. Public figures argued the pros and cons, often incapable of seeing, or purposely evading, the simple issue of humanity, locked as it was into the question of race.

In this struggle of conscience, the high point was provided by the Lincoln-Douglas debates.

CHAPTER 1

American Paradox

When the founding fathers met to form the government of the United States in 1787, they faced a dilemma. To justify their fight for freedom from Great Britain, the thirteen colonies had subscribed to the Declaration of Independence. This revolutionary document stated that all men were "created equal" and were entitled to "liberty." If the new government was to be faithful to the Revolution, its Constitution would have to incorporate the principles of the Declaration of Independence.

Yet Negro slavery existed in six of the newly independent states in the South. Originally all thirteen colonies had been slaveholding, but after the War of Independence, Massachusetts had abolished slavery, and her six northern sister states had made a start toward freedom by providing for gradual emancipation to be completed at various times in the future.

How were the fathers to reconcile the fine words of the Declaration of Independence with the existence of slavery among them? The dilemma was not satisfactorily resolved. In an effort to placate conflicting interests, the framers wrote contradictions into the Constitution which were to lead to conflict between the free and slave states, and eventually to civil war.

One contradiction concerned the recognition of slavery. Article I, section 9 gave Congress the power to abolish the slave trade (not slavery) after the year 1808. Article IV, section 2 required the return of fugitive slaves.

Another inconsistency was reflected in terminology. The language of the Constitution avoided the words "slave" and "slavery" and employed instead the phrase "person held to service or labor." Yet the inferior status of such "persons" was fixed by Article I, section 2, which counted them as only three-fifths of white persons for purposes of taxation and Congressional representation.

THE INTENT OF THE FATHERS

These contradictions cast doubt upon the intent of the founders of the country. Did they mean to recognize slavery as a permanent institution, or did they look to its eventual extinction?

This question assumed importance with the expansion of the United States and the admission of new territories into the Union. Were these new areas to be slave or free? By the 1850's the problem had reached proportions which threatened the existence of the nation. It was this controversy which was the subject of the debates between Lincoln and Douglas in 1858.

Douglas maintained that the founding fathers had envisioned a republic composed permanently of free and slave states. Each newly acquired territory, therefore, should be permitted to choose which status it preferred. This he called the theory of "popular sovereignty." Lincoln, on the other hand, believed that the founders anticipated the future abolition of slavery, which could never take place unless territories were kept free until subsequently admitted as free states.

The question remained unsettled until February, 1860 when, as we shall see, Lincoln literally dug up the answer by considerable original research and presented it in a speech at Cooper Union in New York City. This speech not only laid the question to rest for all time but helped him win the Republican nomination for President.

Some idea of the difficulty of assessing the intent of the founders of the Republic may be seen from the case of Thomas Jefferson. It would seem that there could be no doubt regarding the attitude of the author of the Declaration of Independence. Yet the position of no other great revolutionary figure was more ambiguous.

Throughout his life Jefferson remained a slaveholder. Unlike George Washington, who provided for the manumission of all of his slaves at his death, Jefferson freed only a few. Neither was he identified, as were his associates Benjamin Franklin, John Jay and Alexander Hamilton, with the abolition societies which began springing up toward the latter quarter of the eighteenth century.

How, then, did this aspect of Jefferson's life accord with his assertion that "all men are created equal" and are entitled to liberty? Did it mean that he did not intend to include Negroes in the Declaration of Independence? Were Jefferson's words mere empty phraseology? His position requires careful examination.

The chief justification for the enslavement of the Negro was the belief that he was inferior. Jefferson concurred in this belief to a large extent, but he was troubled by doubts. It appeared to him that Negroes were equal to whites in memory, but "in reason much inferior . . . and in imagination . . . dull." He therefore felt that scientific study of the question was necessary. "The opinion that they are inferior must be hazarded with great diffidence," he wrote. "To justify a general conclusion, requires many observations."[1]

However, Jefferson was emphatic in his denunciation of slavery and advocated its abolition by law. He has left many expressions of his strong feeling on the subject. In his "Notes on Virginia," written in 1781, he said:

> Can the liberties of a nation be thought secure when we have removed their only firm basis, a conviction in the minds of the people that these liberties are the gift of God? That they are not to be violated but with his wrath? Indeed I tremble for my country when I reflect that God is just; that his justice cannot sleep forever; that considering numbers, nature and natural means only, a revolution of the wheel of fortune, an exchange of situation is among possible events . . . The Almighty has no attribute which can take side with us in such a contest.[2]

As early as 1774, he wrote: "The abolition of domestic slavery is the great object of desire in the colonies."[3] The best approach, he was convinced, was through the prohibition of the slave trade. As a result of his influence, Virginia and Maryland abolished the slave traffic during the War of Independence. In 1779 he also submitted an elaborate plan of emancipation to the Virginia legislature. This provided for the education of the freedmen at the public expense in "tillage, arts or sciences," and then their colonization in some suitable region. But the measure did not receive serious consideration, and Jefferson never brought it up again. As he later pointed out in his autobiography, "the public mind would not ... bear the proposition."[4]

In advocating colonization after emancipation, Jefferson was motivated by the peculiar nature of slavery in America. Distinct from previous forms of it elsewhere and at other times in history, it was based exclusively on color. The former slave would always bear the ineradicable mark of servitude on his person. It was therefore essential, according to Jefferson, that he be removed beyond the reach of admixture.[5] In his autobiography, written toward the close of his life in 1821, the Sage of Monticello summed up his thinking:

> Nothing is more certainly written in the book of fate, than that these people are to be free; nor is it less certain that the two races, equally free, cannot live in the same government. Nature, habit, opinion have drawn indelible lines of distinction between them. It is still in our power to direct the process of emancipation and deportation, peaceably, and in such slow degree, as that the evil will wear off insensibly.[6]

Nothing that Jefferson said or did, however, had a profounder practical impact on the slavery question than its interdiction in the Northwest Territory. He was responsible for the Ordinance of 1787 which was drawn up to govern the huge areas north and west of the Ohio River acquired from England in the War of Independence. One of its provisions read: "There shall be neither slavery nor involuntary servitude, in the said territory, otherwise than in punishment of crimes, whereof the party shall be duly convicted." This legislation not only saved for freedom the states of Ohio, Indiana, Illinois, Michigan and Wisconsin, but also served as the prototype for all subsequent efforts to keep slavery out of newly acquired territories. It was naturally a subject which figured prominently in the debates between Lincoln and Douglas. It is interesting to note that the language of the provision was employed almost without change in the Thirteenth Amendment to the Constitution adopted at the close of the Civil War.

Jefferson was thus a controversial and paradoxical figure. Both North and South found in him justification for their beliefs and principles either in precept or example.

ANTI-SLAVERY ACTIVITY STIRS THE NEW WORLD

As the eighteenth century drew to a close, it seemed that slavery was slowly dying. The intellectual elements of the South regarded it as an evil, contrary to Christianity and the doctrine of natural rights, to be tolerated temporarily only out of necessity or expedience. Patrick Henry of Virginia, who had spoken the famous words "Give me liberty or give me death," expressed the prevalent view; he considered slavery "as repugnant to humanity as it is inconsistent with the Bible and destructive of liberty." In spite of these convictions, he was "drawn along by the general inconvenience of living without them [the slaves]."[7] Nevertheless, manumissions were fairly common and represented a hopeful trend for the future.

In other areas of the New World, slavery was gradually losing ground. In 1793 the island of Haiti, whose population ratio of blacks to whites was proportionately sixteen to one, became free as a concomitant of the French Revolution. Unfortunately, one of the tragedies resulting from the constant unrest on that island was the massacre of the white population in Santo Domingo in 1804 — at the memory of which event the South never ceased to shudder. The revolutions of the other Latin-American colonies from Spain brought with them, in most cases, the early abolition of slavery in the new republics.

This wave of emancipation was followed by the abolition of slavery in all British possessions. English soil itself had always been free. Any doubt about it had been settled in 1771 by the decision of Lord Mansfield in Somersett's Case. A Negro, James Somersett, had been brought from Virginia to England. He successfully resisted return to Virginia by claiming that his presence on free soil had made him free.

The case of Somersett paralleled that of Dred Scott in 1857, with the difference that Dred Scott was not granted freedom. This was the case which shook the United States to its foundations and formed one of the leading subjects of controversy in the Lincoln-Douglas debates.

The movement to abolish slavery in the British colonies was

sparked by the English Anti-Slavery Society, which came into existence in 1823. It achieved its goal in 1833 with a law providing for an appropriation of £20,000,000 for gradual, compensated emancipation.

These gains on the New World scene had a strong impact in the United States. Anti-slavery societies began to spread. Even in the South there were estimated to be about a hundred, most of them in border states. One of the high-minded southern men of this period was James G. Birney, a former slaveholder of Alabama, who joined the anti-slavery movement, helped to organize it politically, and ran for President as the candidate of the new Liberty Party in 1840 and 1844.

The general attitude of religious bodies was expressed by a unanimous resolution of the assembly of the Presbyterian Church in 1818. It condemned slavery as "a gross violation of the most sacred and precious rights of human nature, and utterly inconsistent with the law of God, which requires us to love our neighbor as ourselves."[8]

The anti-slavery impulse was also expressed in the formation of the American Colonization Society in 1817. Influenced by Jefferson's thinking, it reflected the desire to solve the race problem by removing Negroes to other lands. Prominent men like Daniel Webster and Henry Clay and later Abraham Lincoln, supported the movement, which undertook to send free Negroes to Africa and to establish a civilized, Christian republic there. It was thus that Liberia was founded and became a republic in 1847. However, in spite of the best efforts of the Society only a few hundred Negroes trickled into Africa each year. It was estimated that up to 1854 only about 10,000 freedmen were colonized. At this rate the reduction in numbers was too infinitesmal to counteract the increase from slave-breeding and slave-smuggling.[9]

The invention of the cotton gin in 1793 by the young Yankee, Eli Whitney, changed the course of events. It solved the vexing problem which faced every cotton plantation: the tedious process of separating the seeds from the fibre of the cotton boll by hand. With this economic change, the attitude toward slavery changed.

Whitney's invention coincided with the inventions of spinning and weaving machinery in England, which revolutionized the manufacture of cotton cloth. The hunger of these new

industries for raw cotton was now satisfied by the southern
states. By 1860 the South was supplying 80% of England's
cotton, thus making the prosperity of that country's manufac-
turing and working classes dependent upon it. The budding
mills of New England likewise looked to the South. In the
1850's the South's cotton production composed seven-eighths
of the world supply and was 56% of the total of all United
States exports. The southerners' boast that "Cotton is King"
was true.

The phenomenal rise of this new monarch changed the
South's thinking about slavery. Slowly the idea that it was a
temporary phenomenon was replaced by the conviction that
it was a great good and should be perpetuated.[10] Southerners
began to regard slavery as their "peculiar institution" to be
defended as a benefit not only to slaveholder and slave, but
also to many other populations, such as the English and the
workers and manufacturers of the North, whose welfare was
bound up with it.

This conviction was strengthened by an increase in the value
of slaves. When, in accordance with Constitutional provision,
the slave trade was legally ended in 1808 by act of Congress
and the supply from abroad was cut, the price of slaves began
to rise. To meet the need for plantation labor, slave smuggling
was winked at. Only a few decades were to elapse before a
demand for the legal reopening of the African slave trade was
revived. This was a subject to which Lincoln made many
references in the debates.

The demand for cotton also increased the demand for land.
Cotton culture was a wasteful economy because planters did
not diversify their crops. In their insatiable desire for quick
profits, they planted the one crop and thus rapidly exhausted
the soil. It was therefore necessary to obtain fresh lands. The
planters turned to the virgin soil of the West and Southwest.
This desire to gain new territories for slavery became a focus
of struggle between the forces of slavery and freedom and was
the nub of the Lincoln-Douglas debates. The growing slavocracy
also dreamed of the annexation of Cuba, Mexico and Central
America to form part of a huge slave empire.

The first clash between the pro- and anti-slavery forces occurred in 1819 when Missouri applied for admission as a slave
state. This territory was part of the tremendous area known as

Louisiana, whose purchase from France in 1803 for $15,000,000 had been authorized by President Jefferson. A fiery debate ensued because Missouri was strategic territory. It was a geographical extension of the region of the Ohio River states which had been dedicated to freedom by the Northwest Ordinance. Besides, it was important as a channel for immigration to the West and could determine whether that area would be slave or free.

Another consideration assumed importance. Alabama had just been admitted as a slave state, thus equalizing the balance of power in the Senate, with eleven free and eleven slave states. Control of the Senate was vital to the South. In population, that section of the country was losing ground. From an equality in numbers at the inception of the Republic, the North had gained a majority of 600,000 in a total of 10,000,000. The approaching census of 1820 would give the North a preponderance of thirty in the House of Representatives. It would obviously be detrimental to the interests of the South if the North controlled the Senate also.

A compromise was therefore agreed upon. Maine, which was also seeking admission, was to come in as a free state and Missouri as a slave state. In addition, slavery was to be "forever prohibited" in the Louisiana Territory north of 36° 30', which was the southern boundary of Missouri and corresponded roughly with the line of the Ohio River.

Congress adjourned, however, before final action was taken. When it reconvened, it was discovered that Missouri's constitution, in addition to providing for slavery, also contained a clause forbidding the entrance of free Negroes into the state. The debate was thereupon reopened with renewed vehemence, and the compromise seemed about to be shattered. It was at this juncture that Henry Clay stepped into the role of pacificator. Missouri was admitted on condition that she expunge her exclusion of free Negroes. The crisis passed and excitement subsided.

But the struggle allowed a peep into a Pandora's box which stirred dark misgivings in both North and South. From his retreat in Monticello, the aged Jefferson wrote:

> This momentous question, like a fire bell in the night, awakened and filled me with terror. I considered it at once

as the knell of the Union. It is hushed, indeed, for the moment. But this is a reprieve only, not a final sentence. A
geographical line, coinciding with a marked principle, moral
and political, once conceived and held up to the angry passions of men, will never be obliterated; and every new irritation will mark it deeper and deeper.[11]

He feared that the result would be a separation of the
sections:

> I have been among the most sanguine in believing that our
> Union would be of long duration. I now doubt it much. . .
> My only comfort and confidence is, that I shall not live to
> see this; and I envy not the present generation the throwing
> away the fruits of their fathers' sacrifices of life and fortune,
> and of rendering desperate the experiment which was to
> decide ultimately whether man is capable of self-govern-
> ment.[12]

Arguments over the Missouri Compromise would occupy a
large place in the debates between Lincoln and Douglas.

GARRISON, THE GOAD

The triumph of the cotton gin over humanitarianism engendered deep guilt feelings in the South which were fanned into
hysteria by two events in 1831. The first was a slave insurrection
in Southhampton, Virginia, led by a fanatical Negro preacher
named Nat Turner. About sixty white persons, chiefly women
and children, were killed in cold blood. There had been
sporadic insurrections in other southern states in the past, but
none made a deeper impression on the public mind than this,
which stirred dread memories of the fearful massacre in Santo
Domingo. So profound was its effect that it precipitated proposals for a general emancipation at the 1831-32 session of the
Virginia legislature. Nothing came of them, however.

The second, and far more important, event was the appearance of radical abolitionism. On January 1, 1831, there appeared in Boston the first issue of a weekly journal which for
thirty-five years was to engender more frenzy in the South than
probably any other single agency. It was *The Liberator,* one of
whose editors was William Lloyd Garrison.

Since abolitionism was a subject which came up frequently
in the debates between Lincoln and Douglas, it is important

to understand the reaction to it not only in the South but also in the North.

Garrison's solution to the slavery problem was simple. "Gradualism" was a delusion, ultimate emancipation a snare, and colonization a folly. He would cut the Gordian knot with one stroke. Immediate abolition, regardless of the consequences! Slavery was wrong and should not be temporized with. It was a cancer and should be excised without delay. No need to be concerned with problems of adjustment. The future would take care of itself.

"I will be as harsh as truth and as uncompromising as justice," he said. "I am in earnest — I will not equivocate — I will not excuse — I will not retreat a single inch — and I will be heard."[13] He asserted that the Constitution was one of the chief bulwarks of slavery and characterized it as a "covenant with death, and an agreement with hell."[14] He advocated the dissolution of the Union, taking as his motto "No union with slave-holders."[15] On July 4, 1854, at an abolitionist meeting near Boston, he burned a copy of the Constitution to dramatize his views.

But besides attacking the government, he also castigated the churches for not taking an active part in destroying slavery. To respectable elements in society, therefore, Garrison was a dangerous anarchist. The word "abolitionist" acquired a new and opprobrious meaning. The alarmed South placed a price on Garrison's head, and one furious governor declared that abolitionists should be put to death without benefit of clergy.[16]

A similar reaction occurred in the North. In 1835 Garrison was dragged by a mob through the streets of Boston with a rope around his neck and barely escaped with his life. Another editor, Elijah Lovejoy of Alton, Illinois, was not so fortunate. In 1837 he was killed while repelling an attack on his press.

In fanatical reaction to abolitionism, the southern states passed a host of more severe laws against the Negro. The death penalty was provided in more cases of crimes by slaves, and the movements and occupations of free Negroes were restricted. By the late '50's many states not only had laws against manumission but also provided that free Negroes emigrate or return to slavery.

The aroused South also blamed the abolitionists for every manifestation of unrest and trouble which disturbed the social structure of the country, such as the new socialist movement, feminism, the polygamy of the Mormons, and the attendant evils of industrialism. In turn, it defended slavery with greater pugnacity and intolerance, proudly justifying the institution as the only stable force in a world of confusing and disruptive changes.

Garrison's extremism threw a shadow on the moderates of the anti-slavery movement, who believed in accomplishing their purpose by legal and constitutional means.

In 1832 Garrison founded the New England Anti-Slavery Society, and the next year aided in the formation of the American Anti-Slavery Society, whose purpose was to operate on a national, rather than a local, scale. It was not long, however, before a split occurred within the organization.

In 1837 James G. Birney became secretary of the American Anti-Slavery Society. Under his leadership, the moderates decided to enter the political arena. They formed the Liberty Party and entered the national elections of 1840 and 1844 with Birney as their candidate for President. Garrison disapproved of this action and remained aloof. He was opposed to any participation in government which, he maintained, was an instrument of force and was, therefore, evil. Moral agitation, he claimed, was the only solution to public problems. He would not vote and counselled his followers not to vote.

The differences between the extremists and the moderates were not always clear to the public. To avoid the ill repute of the word "abolitionist," the moderates preferred to be known as anti-slavery men or Free Soilers. For a politician to be known as an abolitionist was an almost certain guarantee of defeat. During the course of the debates in the Senate campaign of 1858, Douglas constantly tried to fasten the odium of abolitionism on Lincoln, and the latter was forced to defend against the charge.

MORAL CONFUSION

Despite the suspicion attaching to Garrison, public opinion in the North gradually swung to the anti-slavery cause. The conscience of the North could not regard with equanimity, indifference or mere irritation, the indictments against slavery. In addition to violating the moral tenets of religion and the concept of natural rights, slavery was charged with encouraging brutality, debasing the white population, separating slave families by sale, and denying education and religious instruction to slaves. Most serious was the charge of miscegenation; in many instances slaveholders descended to the practice of selling their own children born of union with slaves. Southern defenders denounced these charges as exaggerations based on isolated cases and claimed that the slave was economically better off than workers in the North and in other parts of the world.

In 1844 there occurred an event which provided one of the glaring paradoxes of slavery — a split in the churches. Southern clergymen could not accept the position that slavery was evil and un-Christian. There had always been a tendency to justify slavery on biblical grounds, even among some northern clergymen. The southern Methodists now withdrew from the national church and formed their own Methodist Episcopal Church South. A similar schism soon followed in the Baptist and Presbyterian churches. With the religious bodies of both North and South quoting scripture to arrive at opposite conclusions, the moral question became muddied and confused. This was one of the crucial points of the Lincoln-Douglas debates.

While the controversy raged on many other fronts besides the religious, the main struggle took place on the political front, for here lay control of the government. As if by instinct, the South, that is, the slave-holding aristocracy, prepared for the contest which was eventually to split the nation in two.

The slavocracy was small, but closely knit and single of purpose. According to the census of 1850, there were 347,525 slaveholders. Including their families, they constituted no more than one-fourth of the total white population of 6,000,000 in the South. Yet for close to a half-century this small group dominated the social and political life of the South, and for three decades was to wield a disproportionate influence in the politics of the country.

Environment and training had brought this situation about. Isolated from society in their miniature empires, the southern planters were lords and masters of their domains, brooking no interference with their will or desires. Living by a rigid and peculiar code of their own, they were prone to settle differences by violence. To satisfy their "honor," they resorted to the gun, the whip and the cane, while the feud and the duel were not uncommon occurrences even though prohibited by law. One of the incidents that fanned anti-slavery feeling in the North was the brutal caning of Senator Charles Sumner of Massachusetts by Congressman Preston Brooks of South Carolina in 1856. It was an incident to which Lincoln referred in the debates.

As the leisure class, the planters were well-educated and devoted themselves to "gentlemanly" pursuits and the professions. They thus had the time and the inclination for politics, which was an expected and an accepted career for a planter. Perpetuation in office was a natural result. This contrasted with the situation in the North, where the energies of men were directed into industrial and commercial channels. Politics was but one of many challenging activities, and rotation, rather than perpetuation in office, was the rule. In their desire to preserve their peculiar institution, the small group of slaveholders, already in control of the South, now set itself to dominate the federal government.

Their main strategy proceeded along obvious lines. It was to maintain and perpetuate the balance of power in the Senate in view of the fact that control of the lower house of Congress was assured to the North as a result of the constant increase of population into the free areas of immigration. To accomplish this goal, more slave territory was necessary for the creation of new slave states. This was to lead to demands for the annexation of Mexico, Cuba and Central America.

Another aspect of their policy was to attract northern men to their cause by rewards of political support and appointment to public office. In the decade before the Civil War such "northern men with southern principles"[17] preponderated in public office, including the presidency. This policy led eventually to southern control of the Democratic Party, the rise of the anti-slavery Liberty and Free Soil Parties, the disintegration of the Whig Party, and the emergence of the Republican Party.

At this point it is well to understand the role of the Whig Party because of the constant reference to it in the debates. The party had been formed in the early 1830's in opposition to Democratic President Jackson and his policies. Its leading figures were Henry Clay of Kentucky, and John Quincy Adams and Daniel Webster of Massachusetts. The party was the successor to the Old Federalist and National Republican parties, which believed in strong central power. It espoused Clay's "American System" that was designed to build up the country's economic structure by a protective tariff, which appealed to the industrialists of the North, while it also favored internal improvements in the form of roads and canals, which appealed to the planters of the South. Lincoln, conservative in outlook and an admirer of Clay, was a Whig.

In the 1850's the party began to disintegrate over the slavery issue. The southern Whigs moved into the Democratic Party, but the conservative northern Whigs, who were opposed to slavery, were confused and uncertain where to turn. Many had no liking for the anti-slavery parties, which they considered too radical, though some, with deep convictions, eventually joined the new Republican Party as Lincoln did. In Illinois, these Old Line Whigs were strong enough to hold the balance of power, and Lincoln and Douglas each labored hard to win them to his side.

It was logical for the slavocracy to look to the Democratic Party to champion its cause. Since the time of Jefferson, the party had stood for the theory of states' rights, or a strict construction of the Constitution. The controversy between the "strict" constructionists and the "loose" constructionists, who favored strong federal power, resulted from the fact that the precise relationship between the states and the union had never been clear. Nor was it clear whether the federal bond which held the states together was permanent and irrevocable.

Jefferson had put the theory of states' rights into political form in 1798. In association with James Madison, he drew up the Kentucky and Virginia resolutions, which asserted that the Constitution was a compact or treaty among sovereign states that had delegated certain specific powers to the federal government, and had thus authorized it to act merely as their agent. When the federal government exceeded its powers, the states had a right to disavow such unwarranted use of authority.

Though neither Jefferson nor Madison intended the resolutions to weaken the actual operations of government, dangerous implications were inherent in the doctrine. It remained for Senator John C. Calhoun of South Carolina to expound its ultimate logical consequences of secession and disunion. In 1828, under the leadership of Henry Clay, Congress passed a high protective tariff, which the South derisively labelled the "Tariff of Abominations." In opposition to it, Calhoun drew up the "South Carolina Exposition and Protest," which elaborated upon the "compact" theory of Jefferson and called for nullification of the tariff.

His arguments bore fruit in 1832 when South Carolina passed an ordinance of nullification, declaring the tariff unconstitutional and threatening secession if the United States attempted to enforce the payment of tariff duties. Only a "Compromise Tariff," enacted under the influence of Clay in 1833, led South Carolina to repeal its nullification ordinance and averted an actual test of strength with the federal government.

Thus, four implications flowed from the states' rights theory: limitation of the federal powers to those specifically set forth in the Constitution, non-extension of the federal powers because of possible interference with the powers of the states, nullification and secession. After the brush with the national government on nullification, the South confined its defense of slavery to the first two courses which amounted to a policy of "hands off" by the federal government. The ultimate course of secession always hung as a threat in the background.

To the statesmen of the South, the principle of "hands off" became a sacred doctrine. Scrupulously followed, it meant that the federal government was powerless to keep slavery out of the territories. This was the position ultimately taken by the Democratic Party under the leadership of Douglas.

However, Calhoun, the South's leading theorist and spokesman, abandoned this for a more radical theory. Seeking even greater support for slavery, he claimed that it was the duty of the federal government to protect slave property in all territories of the United States. Because it called for the active intervention of the federal government, and thus the scrapping of states' rights, this position amounted to a complete reversal of the traditional role of the Democratic Party. It was so far in advance of the thinking of the South that it received little support at first. But the Supreme Court decision in the Dred Scott Case in 1857 upheld this extreme view and made it into a new sacred doctrine for the South. Its effect, however, was to divide the Democratic Party into northern and southern factions, thus assuring the election of Lincoln to the presidency.

THE PROBLEM OF TEXAS

The acquisition of new territory accelerated the struggle on the political front and engendered the series of events which led to the Lincoln-Douglas debates.

It started with Texas. Under the leadership of Sam Houston, Texas acquired independence from Mexico in 1836. It was generally suspected throughout the country that the purpose of Houston's venture was to win new slave territory for the Union. This would fulfill the hopes of the South. Four or five slave states could be created from the vast area of Texas and would compensate for the new free states which would enter the Union from the Louisiana Territory north of the Missouri Compromise line. Except for a small remaining area, the land south of the 36° 30′ line, dedicated to slavery, had already been exhausted with the admission of Louisiana, Missouri and Arkansas. The line-up in the Senate now stood at thirteen to thirteen. If the balance of power was not to be tipped against the South, the annexation of Texas was essential.

Texas herself applied for annexation almost immediately after winning independence, but Democratic President Jackson, whose term of office was expiring, merely extended recognition to the Lone Star State. Efforts by the southern bloc to push matters further were unsuccessful. Martin Van Buren, Jackson's heir and successor, was a northern man not imbued with southern principles, while the following election of 1840 brought the Whigs into power with old war hero "Tippecanoe" Harrison. Annexation had to await a more propitious moment.

This occurred as a result of the election of 1844. Nominating James K. Polk of Tennessee, the Democrats adopted a bold expansionist platform. They took as their slogan "Reannexation of Texas and Reoccupation of Oregon." It was a shrewd appeal for the fulfillment of the nation's "manifest destiny," which aimed at extending its boundaries to the Pacific coast. It also coupled southern ambitions with the popular urge for western settlement. The implications of the slogan were that Texas was originally part of the United States and that Oregon had originally been settled by Americans. Oregon, extending from the fortieth to the fifty-fourth parallel, was occupied jointly by Britain and the United States by mutual agreement. The "Whole of Oregon or None" and "Fifty-four forty or fight" now became campaign slogans which aroused martial enthusiasm for expansion.

The Whigs nominated the popular Clay, but their platform was silent on expansion. In an ill-fated moment, Clay wrote a letter which equivocated on the issue of Texas, and lost enough anti-slavery votes in New York to candidate Birney and the new Liberty Party to give that state and the election to Polk.

The victorious Democrats thereupon proceeded to annex Texas. In December 1845, she was admitted as a slave state with the agreement that four additional states might be formed out of her territory. It was also agreed that the Missouri Compromise line be extended to her territory, a proposal advanced by Stephen A. Douglas, then the chairman of the Committee on Territories of the House of Representatives. In addition, the United States consented to handle the adjustment of disputes involving the boundary between Texas and Mexico.

The question of the Texas boundary precipitated war with Mexico. It was also to provide considerable ammunition to Douglas for future attacks on Lincoln.

Mexico had never recognized the independence of Texas, and there had always been the possibility that she would reassert her claim to it by force. Upon the annexation of Texas, Mexico severed relations with the United States. The situation was a volatile one, which could easily lead to war. It was not enhanced by the attitude of the South, which began to cast envious eyes on the remaining Mexican territories in the southwest. Some extremists even wanted Mexico itself.

President Polk was receptive to these ambitions, but he determined to obtain the territories by peaceful means if he could. He tried, but failed; Mexico was deaf to any offer of purchase.

The only recourse was war, but it was necessary to provoke Mexico into it and the boundary question offered the opportunity. Texas claimed that her southern boundary was the Rio Grande River, even though the Nueces River farther north had been so regarded when Texas was a province of Mexico. Polk ordered General Zachary Taylor to occupy the disputed territory between the Nueces and the Rio Grande. As a countermeasure the Mexican army crossed the Rio Grande. A skirmish followed between minor forces.

This was all that Polk needed. On May 11, 1846 he sent a message to Congress asserting that "after reiterated menaces, Mexico has passed the boundary of the United States, has invaded our territory and shed American blood upon American soil. . . War exists, and, notwithstanding all our efforts to avoid it, exists by the act of Mexico alone." Congress responded by declaring war and by authorizing the enlistment of men and the appropriation of money.

The war was one-sided. In a little over a year Mexico capitulated. In February 1848 hostilities were terminated by the Treaty of Guadalupe-Hidalgo. Mexico recognized the title of the United States to Texas as far as the Rio Grande, and ceded the huge areas of California and New Mexico, which touched the Pacific Ocean. In the course of the negotiations Mexico sought to provide that the ceded territory remain free of slavery, but this proposal was rejected.

Though the war had been generally popular because of the Mexican "attack," there had nevertheless been significant opposition to it. The Whigs viewed it as a "southern conspiracy." In Congress they had no choice but to support the war once it had started by voting for appropriations of money and supplies, but they lost few opportunities to blame the President for starting it.

PARTY LINES CRACK

The greatest repercussions arose, however, with respect to the territories that were certain to be acquired. In August 1846, David Wilmot, a Democrat from Pennsylvania, introduced a proviso to a Congressional bill for appropriations reading: "Provided, that as an express and fundamental condition to the acquisition of any territory from the Republic of Mexico by the United States . . . neither Slavery nor involuntary servitude shall ever exist in any part of said Territory, except for crime, whereof the party shall be first duly convicted."

The voting on the proviso shattered party lines. Congressmen voted according to their views on the slavery question. Southern Democrats and Whigs voted against the proviso, but northern Democrats and Whigs, forming a majority, passed it in the House of Representatives. Congressman Douglas was one of the northern Democrats who voted against it, advocating as he had done in the case of Texas, the extension of the Missouri Compromise line (this time to the Pacific Ocean). As expected, the proviso was defeated in the Senate where the balance of power favored the South. The proviso was brought up again in February 1847 and suffered a similar fate. It continued to reappear at various times in various forms with the same result.

Abraham Lincoln, who had been elected to Congress, naturally supported the Whig position. He later said that he voted for the Wilmot Proviso "about forty times." He went further and submitted a series of resolutions attacking the President's statement that it was on American soil that American blood had been shed. He wanted the spot identified. These "Spot Resolutions," as they were mockingly called, made Lincoln unpopular back home and subsequently forced him into temporary political oblivion. We shall see Douglas, during the course of the debates, addressing him as "Spot" Lincoln, and ridiculing as often as possible his wartime record as a Congressman.

As a result of the war, the area of the United States reached from ocean to ocean. There now remained the question of what to do with the newly acquired territories. Were they to be slave or free? There were four possible answers:

1. Extend the Missouri Compromise Line of 36°30′ to the Pacific, as Douglas had advocated.

2. Exclude slavery in accordance with the doctrine of the Northwest Territory and the Wilmot Proviso.

3. Allow slavery in accordance with the Calhoun theory that slaves were property entitled to the protection of the Constitution.

4. Let the decision as to slavery be decided by the people of the territory, with Congress keeping hands off.

The last approach was summed up effectively by Senator Lewis Cass of Michigan. Cass wrote a letter to A. O. P. Nicholson, a Tennessee lawyer, editor and politician, in December 1847, in which he expounded the doctrine of "popular sovereignty," which was later to be championed by and identified with Stephen A. Douglas:

> The theory of our Government presupposes that its various members . . . are sovereign within their boundaries, except in those cases where they have surrendered to the General Government a portion of their rights. . . Local institutions . . . are left to local authority. . .

Congress has no right to say there shall be Slavery in New York, or that there shall be no Slavery in Georgia; nor is there any other human power, but the people of those States which can change the relations existing therein. . .

It [the power of the government] should be limited to the creation of proper governments for new countries . . . and to the necessary provisions for their eventual admission into the Union; leaving, in the meantime, to the people inhabiting them, to regulate their internal concerns in their own way.

They are just as capable of doing so as the people of the States; and they can do so, at any rate as soon as their political independence is recognized by admission into the Union. During this temporary condition, it is hardly expedient to call into exercise a doubtful and invidious authority which questions the intelligence of a respectable portion of our citizens . . . an authority which would give to Congress despotic power, uncontrolled by the Constitution, over most important sections of our common country.[18]

The Nicholson letter received much publicity and stamped Cass as a northern man with southern principles. He received as his reward the Democratic nomination for President in 1848.

The Whigs, hoping to repeat their victory of 1840 by running a war hero, nominated "Old Rough and Ready" Zach Taylor to oppose Cass.

Both parties preferred to avoid the touchy issue of what to do with the Mexican territories. Their platforms mentioned no word on the subject. The question of Oregon fortunately had been settled. A treaty with Britain fixed the boundary at 49°, and in August 1848, Oregon was organized as free territory.

But the issue with reference to the remaining territories refused to be ignored. Bolters from the Whig and Democratic ranks joined with elements from the Liberty Party to form the Free Soil Party. Their platform was moderate and reflected a change in strategy to accompany the change in the political situation. Unlike the Liberty Party platform, which sought abolition of slavery in the states and in the District of Columbia, and advocated repeal of the Fugitive Slave clause of the Constitution, the Free Soil platform concerned itself with the non-extension of slavery into the territories. "No more slave states and no more slave territory," it declared. "Let the soil of our extensive domains be kept free for the hardy pioneers of our own land, and the oppressed and banished of other lands."[19]

The Free Soilers nominated as their candidate former President Martin Van Buren. Whereas in 1840 and 1844 the Liberty Party had polled 7,000 and 62,000 votes respectively, this time the Free Soil Party received close to 300,000 votes, drawing away enough Democratic support in New York to swing the election to Taylor.

There was no mistaking the significance of the election. It revealed the growing strength of the political anti-slavery movement. Mounting defections from the two major parties would result within eight years in the creation of the new Republican Party, whose principles would be taken almost bodily from the Free Soil platform.

Soon after the election, the march of events made it impossible to delay the question of the territories. California was knocking at the door for admission. The '49 gold rush had swelled its population to the number sufficient by law for admission as a state before it had acquired even the status of an organized territory. It had adopted a constitution excluding slavery and would thus come in as a free state. Since Iowa in 1846 and Wisconsin in 1848 had been admitted as free states, the admission of California would swing the balance of power to the North, sixteen to fifteen.

To complicate the problem, other aspects of the slavery question obtruded themselves. Slavery existed in Washington, D.C., a constant reproach and reminder that the capital itself was the chief symbol of the nation's paradox. Strong pressure existed for abolition within this federal territory.

On the part of the South, there was pressure for a change in the Fugitive Slave Law. This law, in conformity with the Constitution, had been passed in 1793, leaving enforcement chiefly in the hands of state officials. The free states had always been hostile to the law. Their officers usually found ways of avoiding its enforcement and had thus, in effect, practically nullified it.

Though the number of escaping slaves was small, this flouting of the law was a sore point with the South. Especially irritating and insulting was the open invitation to slaves to escape through the "underground railroad," which had been set up by the abolitionists for the purpose of smuggling fugitives into the free states and then aiding them to reach Canada. The

South wanted a new Fugitive Slave Law which would be enforced by federal, and not by state, authorities.

CLAY'S NEW COMPROMISE

The only solution to the conflict of interests was compromise. Again the magic of Clay, the "Great Pacificator," was necessary. His proposals were: Let California come in as a free state. Let the remainder of the Mexican cession be organized as territories without any restrictions by Congress, allowing popular sovereignty to rule. Let the slave trade, but not slavery, be abolished in the District of Columbia, and finally, enact a more effective Fugitive Slave Law to be enforced by federal authority.

For nine months, from January to September 1850, a battle over the compromise raged in Congress. Strong support from Daniel Webster and Stephen A. Douglas finally turned the scale in its favor. For Douglas, who was now chairman of the Committee on Territories of the Senate, as he had formerly been of the House, this meant the abandonment of the Missouri Compromise line, of which he had been so staunch an advocate, in favor of popular sovereignty. This action later forced him to defend himself against the abuse of his constituents. But in the struggle with Lincoln for the votes of the Old Line Whigs, he would point to the example of Webster, the eminent Whig, who put party aside to join with him in saving the country.

The country breathed a sigh of relief when the Compromise of 1850, known as "Clay's Omnibus," became law. The South had its Fugitive Slave Law, and the North the abolition of the slave trade in the District of Columbia. But most important, provision had been made for all the territory under the jurisdiction of the United States. It seemed that the vexing slavery question at last was ended. Unless a new wave of expansionism should add other acquisitions, there was no more territory to fight over. The solution seemed to be final.

A calm followed the Compromise of 1850, but it was deceptive. Strong elements in both sections of the country were dissatisfied. In the North there was opposition to the Fugitive Slave Law even among the moderates. Several states passed Personal Liberty Acts which sought to nullify the new law. By local statutes, administrative measures and judicial proceedings, the efforts of federal officials to restore escaped slaves to their southern owners were thwarted.

An atmosphere of disquiet prevailed in the South. The South felt uneasy about the large areas of still unsettled Louisiana territory that were committed to the North by the Missouri Compromise. The previous year John C. Calhoun had drawn up an "Address of the Southern Delegates in Congress to their Constituents" in which he expressed the fear that the attempt "by the North to monopolize all the territories to the exclusion of the South" would someday give the North control of three-fourths of all the states, sufficient for the passage of an amendment to the Constitution emancipating the slaves.[20]

This fear strengthened the conviction among the slaveholders that additional new territories to the south must be acquired to counterbalance the future advantages of the North. Previous attempts during Polk's administration to purchase Cuba and to interfere in Nicaragua and Yucatan had been unsuccessful. A further blow to the expansionist schemes of the South occurred during the Whig administration when, in 1850, the United States concluded the Clayton-Bulwer Treaty with Great Britain, by which both powers agreed to refrain from colonizing any part of Central America. Agitation in the South for the acquisition of Latin American territory never ceased, however, and presented a danger to the peace of the Republic.

Despite these disturbing undercurrents, the country settled into the belief that the Compromise of 1850 had provided a final settlement of the slavery problem and needed only the passage of time to make it effective. This belief was encouraged and strengthened by the leaders of the two major parties and echoed by the press.

The election of 1852 reflected this crystallization of public opinion. Both parties accepted the compromise and averred in their platforms that they would resist any further agitation on the slavery question. With no other issue of major importance, the Democrats won an overwhelming victory, and rode back into power with their dark horse candidate, Franklin Pierce, of New Hampshire. The temper of the country was also illustrated in the decline of the vote of the Free Soil Party, which polled only 156,000 out of 3,000,000 votes.

In his inaugural address, the new President said: "I fervently

trust that the question is at rest, and that no sectional or
ambitious or fanatical excitement may again threaten the dura-
bility of our institutions."[21]

DOUGLAS DESTROYS THE MISSOURI COMPROMISE

The final settlement lasted four years. It was shattered by
an explosion of volcanic proportions that shook the country
to its foundations. The hand that applied the match to the
powder keg was that of Stephen A. Douglas. When the smoke
cleared, the Whig Party was dead, the Democratic Party hope-
lessly split and the Republican party born.

The blow fell unexpectedly. As chairman of the Committee
on Territories, Douglas had for several years been anxious to
organize the remainder of the Louisiana territory, especially
that part known as Nebraska. This vast area lay to the west
and northwest of the state of Missouri and, inasmuch as it was
located above 36°30', was destined to become free soil. Douglas
wanted a railroad to the Pacific, which would tie the Far West
to the East. Settlers were beginning to enter the Nebraska
territory. It was necessary to extinguish Indian titles and to
bring order to the development of the territory.

Just before the close of the Thirty-Second Congress, in
February 1853, Douglas introduced the first bill for the organization of the Nebraska territory. It was brought in too late to
be passed, but approval was expected when the new Congress
met in December.

The language of the bill assumed that the Missouri Compromise Line was in force. It was supported by Senator David
Atchison of Missouri, one of the most aggressive of the southern
clique, who was also President pro tempore of the Senate.
Between the final session of the old Congress and the opening
of the new, however, things began to change. Atchison consulted with other Missouri slaveholders. They sensed grave
danger to their interests. Iowa to the north and Illinois to the
east were free. The creation of a free state to the west would
hem Missouri in and eventually doom slavery, ruining all the
slaveholders financially. Besides, with sixteen free states opposed to fifteen slave states, the balance of power was against
the South. If a new slave state could be created, the balance of
power would be restored. Atchison therefore pledged that he

would oppose any bill which did not allow slaveholders to enter the territory with their human property on an equal footing with other settlers. This action, of course, would vitiate the Missouri Compromise.

In January 1854 Douglas again brought in a Nebraska bill. This time, as the result of southern pressure, it incorporated the principle of popular sovereignty. But it was not enough. The southern clique, led by Atchison and Senator Archibald Dixon of Kentucky, Clay's Whig successor, pressed for outright repeal of the Missouri Compromise. Another group, whose prime interest was a Pacific railroad over a northern route, pressed for the formation of two territories instead of one, because they felt that it would enhance the development of the northern area and thus increase its chances of capturing the railroad. Douglas therefore agreed to change the bill to provide for the repeal of the Compromise and also to organize two territories, Kansas and Nebraska.

To make sure of its passage, Douglas demanded presidential support. Pierce, who was completely under southern domination, consented and with his own hand wrote out the crucial language of the bill which referred to the Missouri Compromise as follows:

> ... which being inconsistent with the principle of non-intervention by Congress with slavery in the States and Territories, as recognized by the legislation of 1850 (commonly called the Compromise measures) is hereby declared inoperative and void; it being the true intent and meaning of this act not to legislate slavery into any Territory or State, nor to exclude it therefrom, but to leave the people thereof perfectly free to form and regulate their domestic institutions in their own way, subject only to the Constitution.[22]

The debate over the bill was long and rancorous. James Ford Rhodes termed it "the most momentous measure that passed Congress from the day senators and representatives first met to the outbreak of the civil war."[23] The Democrats enjoyed tremendous majorities in both houses, and the bill passed easily enough in the Senate, but it had to be forced through the House. There, even though the Democrats had a majority of more than two to one, the vote was only 113 to 110.

In the Senate the battle against it was fought by the triumvirate of Salmon Chase of Ohio, Charles Sumner of Massachusetts and William Seward of New York. In order to prove that the "true intent" of the act was to allow slavery into the territory, Chase fathered an amendment to it couched in positive terms giving the people the power to exclude slavery if they wished. The amendment, however, was defeated. Chase prophetically declared that the act would "light up a fire in the country which may, perhaps, consume those who kindle it."[24]

The explosion in Congress was followed by mighty blasts throughout the North. Indignant meetings were held. Demonstrations were staged. Editorials thundered denunciations. State legislatures passed resolutions. Petitions were drawn up. A memorial of protest was signed by more than 3,000 New England ministers. Excitement rose to such fury that Douglas later declared that he could travel from Boston to Chicago by the light of his burning effigies. Once again, as in 1850, when he reached home, he was forced to defend his course against the abuse of his constituents. And Lincoln, who had been out of politics since 1849, because of his unpopular stand against the Mexican War while in Congress, was back on the political scene.

The elections of 1854 told an ominous story for the Democratic Party. Anti-slavery Democrats had begun to align themselves with Free Soilers. They were joined by many northern Whigs who felt their party incapable of taking a strong stand against slavery. A new party was in the making. In some states this alignment had already adopted the title "Republican." In others it went simply under the name "Anti-Nebraska." In the South the opposite phenomenon occurred. The pro-slavery Whigs deserted and went over to the Democrats.

With the exception of a few diehard "Old Liners," who stuck to the party label, the Whig Party was dead. Its demise was aided by the sudden appearance of another new party, the American Party. This was a hodgepodge of former secret "native American" societies, which had arisen as a result of the recent large Irish and German immigration. Their program was anti-Catholic and anti-immigrant: "Americans must rule America . . . native-born citizens should be selected for all State, Federal and municipal offices." These societies had been dubbed "Know-Nothings," because their members had been instructed to answer, "I know nothing" to all questions about the societies' purposes. They were now out in the open as a full-fledged political party.

When the elections were over, the Congressional results were as follows:

33rd Congress (December 1853)		34th Congress (to meet December 1855)	
Whigs	71	Anti-Nebraskans	108
Free Soilers	3	Know-Nothings	40
Democrats	154	Democrats	75

It was a grim portent for the presidential election of 1856.

THE STRUGGLE FOR KANSAS

The Kansas-Nebraska Act shifted the scene of battle to Kansas itself. Here popular sovereignty was to be given its chance. If the flow of population was peaceable and the organization of the territory orderly, perhaps it would work. The advantages, however, would be with the North. According to the census of 1850 the population of the free states was 13,000,000 as compared with 9,000,000 for the slave states, of whom 3,000,000 were slaves. The North thus had an edge of more than two to one in the white population. Besides, the free population was more mobile. It was difficult for a slaveholder to tear up stakes and move his slaves and property to a new location. In any population race the North was certain to win.

The country sensed, however, that the method of decision would not be pacific. It was not expected that the slavocracy would submit to the processes of democracy and the arbitrament of the ballot. Its very existence depended on force, fear and fraud. It could be expected to stop at nothing to maintain itself and to assure its survival.

Settlers began trickling into the territory early. The slaveholding element came chiefly from across the border of Missouri, and for the first few months outnumbered the settlers from the free states. In October 1854, however, with the arrival of emigrant trains from the North, the tide began to turn.

This aroused the resentment and fear of the slaveholders. A struggle ensued for political control of the territory. In March 1855 an election was held for a territorial legislature. Armed bands, termed "border ruffians" by Horace Greeley, editor of the *New York Tribune,* crossed over from Missouri to intimidate the Free Soil voters and to vote illegally themselves.

The result was that, with the exception of one man, the entire legislature was pro-slavery. This "bogus legislature" met during July and August, and enacted a code of laws incorporating verbatim the Revised Statutes of Missouri, with their severe provisions for the protection of slavery, and adding drastic provisions of its own. It also designated Lecompton as the territorial capital.

The Free Soil settlers did not submit to these outrages tamely. In September 1855 they held a convention of their own at which they repudiated the bogus legislature and announced that they would take no part in any future election provided by its laws. In October they met at Topeka to draw up a constitution of their own. It contained provisions against slavery but also against the admission of free Negroes, and provided for elections to be held in January 1856 for a legislature, state officers and a representative in Congress.

The supporters of the pro-slavery government responded by forming a "Law and Order Party," denouncing the Free State Party as revolutionary and treasonable and branding the Topeka Constitution as subversive.

Thus the issue was joined. It required only an incident to touch off a bloody conflict. This occurred when a young Free State settler was murdered. Raids, forays and killings followed on both sides. In May 1856 the "militia" of the pro-slavery group attacked the town of Lawrence, citadel of the Free Staters. Only one man was killed and a few houses were burned and pillaged. But the "sack of Lawrence" sent a ripple of horror and anger throughout the North. Four days later a group of men under the leadership of the inspired fanatic, John Brown, went to Pottawatomie Creek, dragged five pro-slavery men from their beds in dead of night and murdered them in cold blood. Reprisal led to reprisal, and civil war raged full scale in "bleeding Kansas." Popular sovereignty had received a baptism of blood.

When the Free State elections were over in January 1856, Kansas had two governments. To President Pierce this was intolerable. In a special message to Congress, he denounced the Topeka Constitution and its government as insurrectionary and threatened force to back up the pro-slavery government.

The House, controlled by the anti-Nebraskans, reacted by setting up a committee to go to Kansas and investigate the situation.

As the excitement over Kansas grew, a new incident of sensational character stunned the country and threw it into a fresh turmoil. On May 19 and 20, Senator Charles Sumner, of Massachusetts, delivered an address on the "Crime Against Kansas."[25] It was a polished, but highly violent tirade against slavery. In the course of it he directed a personal attack against elderly Senator A. P. Butler, of South Carolina. The South was incensed at the insult to one of its venerable political figures, and hot southern blood reached the boiling point.

Preston Brooks, a young Congressman from South Carolina, who was also a nephew to Senator Butler, determined to avenge the family and southern honor. Brooks enjoyed a good reputation in Washington; he was handsome in appearance, courteous in manner and highly competent in debate. A frank statement of his that the cotton gin had changed the attitude of the South toward slavery was widely quoted. Lincoln himself subsequently referred to it in the Jonesboro debate. Two days after his speech, Sumner was sitting at his desk in the Senate chamber at the close of the session. Brooks approached him unexpectedly, and before he could rise from his seat, beat him so severely upon the head with his cane that Sumner was rendered unconscious.

The effect on the nation was electrifying. The North sprang to the defense of Sumner, the South to the defense of Brooks. Press, pulpit and meetings echoed denunciations of the "cowardly" act of a member of the southern chivalry, or rang out praises for the just retribution of a foul insult uttered by a northern Abolitionist. So great was the feeling of horror and revulsion in the North that several state legislatures passed resolutions of condemnation. So great was the elation in the South that Brooks was feted as a hero wherever he went and was presented with canes as testimonials to his honor and courage. It was an incident Lincoln would have occasion to mention in the debates.

The country was in a dangerous state. Its existence seemed threatened. The coming national election was therefore of special importance.

The first party in the field was the "Know-Nothing," or

American National Party. It nominated former President Fillmore, hoping to attract voters who hated immigrants and Catholics, and looked to Fillmore to steer a middle course for the preservation of the Union.

In February the organization of the new Republican Party, composed of anti-Nebraskans and former Free Soilers, began to coalesce on a national scale. At their convention in June they cast about for a candidate who would appear less radical to the public on the slavery issue than Seward, Sumner or Chase. They found him in Colonel John C. Fremont, well-known for his brilliant efforts in the exploration of the West and the conquest of California. For the purpose of picking up the Whig vote, William L. Dayton, an Old Line Whig, was nominated for Vice-President. The Republican platform, modelled after that of the Free Soilers, declared against the repeal of the Missouri Compromise and the extension of slavery into the territories, and called for the admission of Kansas as a free state.

THE CINCINNATI PLATFORM

The Democrats held their convention in Cincinnati. The chief candidates were Douglas, Pierce and James Buchanan, of Pennsylvania, the ambassador to England. The chances of both Douglas and Pierce were doubtful because of their identification with the difficulties in Kansas, while Buchanan was free of any such taint. By the sixteenth ballot Buchanan had a majority but not the necessary two-thirds to ensure nomination. Douglas, who was second in the running, thereupon sent a message withdrawing in favor of Buchanan for the sake of party harmony. This was regarded as a very magnanimous gesture, inasmuch as both men had been strong rivals for the nomination in 1852 and had killed each other off. John C. Breckenridge, of Kentucky, was selected as the vice-presidential candidate.

The Democratic platform supported the principle of the Kansas-Nebraska Act as the "only sound and safe solution of the slavery question," and emphasized the "non-interference of Congress with Slavery in the Territories or in the District of Columbia."

This statement was to assume tremendous importance within

the next two years as the course of events changed rapidly and unexpectedly. In the debates with Lincoln, Douglas frequently referred to the Cincinnati Platform and also, in view of a subsequent about-face, to Buchanan's unqualified support of it. In his letter accepting the nomination, Buchanan praised the Kansas-Nebraska law. "This legislation," he said, "is founded upon principles as ancient as free government itself, and in accordance with them has simply declared that the people of a territory, like those of a state, shall decide for themselves whether slavery shall or shall not exist within their limits."

With the eyes of the country on Kansas, the Administration had to do something to restore order there in order to help the Democratic campaign. Pierce appointed General John W. Geary as governor of the territory. Two previous governors had proved ineffective. Perhaps a military man like Geary would do better. In July, however, the House investigating committee which had gone to Kansas brought in its report. It presented factual proof of the false registrations and fraudulent returns by means of which the pro-slavery minority had imposed an unconstitutional and unlawful authority over the territory.

This was excellent campaign material for the Republicans. Their chances looked good, and as the campaign progressed, threats of secession in the event of a Republican victory came constantly from southern leaders.

Alarmed by the trend of events was a remnant of the Whig Party, especially a large group in New England which had strong commercial interests allied to the southern economy. They viewed with dismay the threats to the Union, to peace and to their economic position. Unable to commit themselves to either major party as so many of their associates had done, they determined on an independent course.

In September they met in Baltimore and endorsed the candidacy of Fillmore, without accepting the platform of the "Know-Nothing" Party. Their platform was Fillmore himself. They declared that they had "no new principles to announce," and called upon the country "to support a candidate pledged to neither of the geographical sections now arrayed in political antagonism."

The election depended on the outcome in Pennsylvania,

Indiana and Illinois. To the Republican slogan "Free Speech, Free Press, Free Soil, Free Men, Fremont and Victory," the Democrats countered with the cry "Buchanan, Breckinridge, and Free Kansas" and "Kansas will bleed no longer." Besides thus befogging the public mind on the Kansas issue, the Democrats poured large sums of money into the three doubtful states. These tactics, plus the effect of the Whig vote, brought these states into the Democratic column and with them came victory.

Ignoring the closeness of the vote, the slavocracy chose to view the election as a rebuke to the anti-slavery forces. As a result of what they considered a showdown battle, they were encouraged to believe that they were winning the struggle for men's minds and had put the abolitionists on the run.

On the ideological front, they moved to the offensive. They attacked the cherished shibboleths of the North. One of their Congressmen had declared: "It is a misnomer to speak of our institution as peculiar; ours is the general system of the world and the free system is the peculiar one."[26] Considering the fact that there were few areas in the world which were free, this statment was true. A northern Senator, John Pettit of Indiana, echoing this evaluation, paraphrased the Declaration of Independence and termed equality "a self-evident lie."[27]

Senator James Hammond, of South Carolina, expounded what became known as the "mudsill theory." It was impossible "to build a house in the air," he said. Just as it was necessary to sink sills into the mud to support the structure, so every society needed a class of mudsills upon which progress and development depended. In the South, it was the slaves; in the North, it was the supposedly free laboring class. Had the North abolished slavery? "Aye, the *name* but not the *thing*; all the powers of earth canot abolish that."[28]

These aggressive arguments, however, were rationalizations of a deep-seated fear — fear of emancipation. This was something which every southerner carried in his conscious or subconscious mind. The brilliant and perceptive John C. Calhoun had expressed it openly in the "Address of the Southern Delegates in Congress to their Constituents." He drew a picture that made Southerners shudder:

> To destroy the existing relation between the free and servile races at the South would lead to consequences unparalleled in history: They cannot be separated, and cannot live to-

gether in peace, or harmony, or to their mutual advantage, except in their present relation. Under any other, wretchedness, and misery, and desolation would overspread the whole South. . .

They would not stop at emancipation. Another step would be taken — to raise them to a political and social equality with their former owners, by giving them the right of voting and holding public offices under the Federal Government. . .

When once raised to an equality, they would become the fast political associates of the North, acting and voting with them on all questions, and by this political union between them, holding the white race at the South in complete subjection. The blacks, and the profligate whites that might unite with them, would become the principal recipients of federal offices and patronage, and would, in consequence, be raised above the whites of the South in the political and social scale.

We would, in a word, change conditions with them — a degradation greater than has ever yet fallen to the lot of a free and enlightened people, and one from which we could not escape, should emancipation take place, but by fleeing the homes of ourselves and ancestors, and by abandoning our country to our former slaves, to become the permanent abode of disorder, anarchy, poverty, misery and wretchedness.[29]

Did non-slaveholders of the South share this fear with the oligarchy? Were their interests the same? Again Calhoun supplied the answer. He told the Senate: "With us the two great divisions of society are not the rich and poor, but white and black; and all the former, the poor as well as the rich, belong to the upper classes, and are respected and treated as equals."[30]

THE CASE OF DRED SCOTT

Regardless of arguments or fears, the slavocracy determined to use its recently confirmed control of the governmental machinery to consolidate its position. Up to this point the political struggle had centered in Congress and the White House. Now it moved into the majestic chambers of the Supreme Court of the United States.

A case was pending about which so many leaks and rumors had occurred that it had lost its judicial character and had assumed a political one. The press indulged freely in specula-

tion and gossip and made predictions as to how the issues would
be decided and how the judges would vote.

This was the case of Dred Scott vs. Sanford,[31] which was to
have more explosive reverberations throughout the country
than even the Kansas-Nebraska Act. It was also to supply considerable fuel for the Lincoln-Douglas controversy.

The case had been brought on appeal to the Supreme Court
toward the close of 1854, after having been tried first in the
State Courts of Missouri and then in the Federal District Court.
Dred Scott was a slave who had been sold by his owner, Captain
Peter Blow of St. Louis, to an army surgeon, Dr. John Emerson.
During the years 1834-38 he accompanied Dr. Emerson as his
household servant to Rock Island in Illinois and to Fort Snell-
ing in Wisconsin Territory. Both of these areas were free soil.
He was then brought back to St. Louis. On Dr. Emerson's
death, he became the property of the widow. In 1846 Scott
brought suit against Mrs. Emerson in the Missouri courts on
the grounds that residence in free territory had made him free.

It is not clear how the case was started, or who were the
prime movers in the proceedings that dragged through the
courts for more than ten years. Several people were involved
who were of both pro- and anti-slavery leanings, and because of
this, charges were made later by each side that the other had
instigated the case.

In 1850 Mrs. Emerson married a Massachusetts physician,
Dr. Calvin Chaffee, an abolitionist. Obviously for purposes of
litigation, she arranged to transfer ownership to her brother,
John Sanford of New York. This diversity of citizenship enabled the case to be brought into the United States courts, and
thence on appeal to the Supreme Court.

The point to be decided was whether Dred Scott was a
citizen. Only a citizen could bring suit in the federal courts; a
slave could not. The important question therefore was: Did
Scott's residence in the free state of Illinois and in the free territory of Wisconsin make him free and therefore a citizen? If
not, the Supreme Court did not have jurisdiction, and Dred
Scott had to be remanded to slavery.

But implicit in the question was the constitutionality of the
Missouri Compromise. The main reason for maneuvering the
case into the Supreme Court was the desire to obtain a ruling
on this question. It was true that the compromise had been

repealed by the Kansas-Nebraska Act, but that very act showed that Congress could still legislate on slavery in the territories. Now the opportunity presented itself to determine whether Congress actually possessed such power. If it did not, not only was the Missouri Compromise unconstitutional, but slavery could not be kept out of the territories, and popular sovereignty was dead.

The makeup of the court seemed to presage what the ruling would be. There were seven Democratic justices, five of whom (Chief Justice Taney and Associate Justices Campbell, Catron, Daniel and Wayne) were from the South, and two (Grier and Nelson) from the North. Grier was a friend and neighbor of Buchanan. Only McLean of Ohio, who had been a candidate for the Republican nomination in opposition to Fremont, and Curtis of Massachusetts, a Whig, were regarded as being in opposition. In any crucial decision on slavery, the court could be expected to stand six to three, and possibly seven to two.

The southern leaders lost no opportunity to put pressure on the judges. A judicial victory would remove slavery from the realm of political action and graft it irrevocably into the constitutional structure of the nation. A heavy correspondence passed between leaders and judges. There was even an exchange of letters between President-elect Buchanan and Justices Catron and Grier. Less than two weeks before his inauguration, Buchanan received a letter from Grier which read:

> Your letter came to hand this morning. I have taken the liberty to show it, in confidence, to our mutual friends, Judge Wayne and the Chief Justice. We fully appreciate, and concur in your views as to the desirableness at this time of having an expression of the opinion of the Court on this troublesome question. With their concurrence, I will give you in confidence the history of the case before us, with the probable result. . . There will therefore be six, if not seven (perhaps Nelson will remain neutral) who will decide the Compromise law of 1820 to be of non-effect.[32]

Grier even disclosed that the decision would be handed down on March 6. On March 4, in his inaugural address, Buchanan referred to the problem of slavery in the territories in these words:

> It is a judicial question, which legitimately belongs to the

Supreme Court of the United States, before whom it is now pending, and will, it is understood, be speedily and finally settled. To their decision, in common with all good citizens, I shall cheerfully submit, whatever this may be.

On March 6 the court, by a vote of seven to two, duly rendered its decision. Chief Justice Taney delivered the majority opinion:

... The question is simply this: Can a negro,* whose ancestors were imported into this country, and sold as slaves, become a member of the political community formed and brought into existence by the Constitution of the United States, and as such, become entitled to all the rights, and privileges, and immunities, guaranteed by that instrument to the citizen? . . .

We think they [the negroes] are not, and that they are not included, and were not intended to be included, under the word "citizens" in the Constitution, and can therefore claim none of the rights and privileges which that instrument provides for and secures to citizens of the United States. On the contrary, they were at that time considered as a subordinate and inferior class of beings, who had been subjugated by the dominant race, and, whether emancipated or not, yet remain subject to their authority, and had no rights or privileges but such as those who held the power and the government might choose to grant them.

They had for more than a century before been regarded as beings of an inferior order, and altogether unfit to associate with the white race, either in social or political relations; and so far inferior, that they had no rights which the white man was bound to respect; and that the negro might justly and lawfully be reduced to slavery for his benefit. . . It was regarded as an axiom in morals as well as in politics, which no one thought of disputing, or supposed to be open to dispute. . .

The general words [of the Declaration of Independence] would seem to embrace the whole human family; and if they were used in a similar instrument at this day, would be so understood. But it is too clear for dispute, that the enslaved African race were not intended to be included, and formed no part of the people who framed and adopted this Declara-

*The term "Negro" was not capitalized in the writing of that era. All quotations following, therefore, will give the spelling as originally written.

tion; for if the language, as understood in that day, would embrace them, the conduct of the distinguished men who framed the Declaration of Independence would have been utterly and flagrantly inconsistent with principles they asserted. . .

Yet the men who framed this Declaration were great men . . . incapable of asserting principles inconsistent with those on which they were acting. They perfectly understood the meaning of the language they used, and how it would be understood by others; and they knew that it would not, in any part of the civilized world, be supposed to embrace the negro race, which, by common consent, had been excluded from civilized government and the family of nations, and doomed in slavery. . .[33]

Taney then went on to declare that the Missouri Compromise "is not warranted by the Constitution, and is therefore void." Congress could deprive no one of his property without due process of law, and "the right of property in a slave is distinctly and expressly affirmed in the Constitution." Since Congress itself could not exercise such power, it could not authorize a territorial government to exercise it.

Justice Daniel, in a concurring opinion, was even more emphatic:

The same instrument, which imparts to Congress its very existence, and its very functions, guarantees to the slaveholder the title to his property, and gives him the right to reclaim his property throughout the country; and, further, the only private property which the Constitution has *specifically recognized,* and has imposed it as a direct obligation both on the States and the federal government to protect and *enforce,* is the property of a master in his slave: no other right of property is placed by the Constitution on the same high ground, nor shielded by a similar guarantee.[34]

In his dissenting opinion, Justice Curtis said:

In five of the thirteen original States colored persons then possessed the elective franchise, and were among those by whom the Constitution was ordained and established. If so, it is not true in point of fact that the Constitution was made exclusively by the white race, and that it was made exclusively for the white race is in my opinion not only an assumption not warranted by anything in the Constitution, but contradicted by its opening declaration that it was ordained and established by the people of the United States for themselves and their posterity; and as free colored persons were then citizens of at least five States, and so in every sense part of the people of the United States, they were among those for whom and whose posterity the Constitution was ordained and established.[35]

Justice McLean in his dissent stated:

> Our independence was a great epoch in the history of freedom. . . Many of the States on the adoption of the Constitution, or shortly afterwards, took measures to abolish slavery within their respective jurisdictions. . . But . . . why confine our view to colored slavery? On the same principles white men were made slaves. All slavery has its origin in power and is against right.[36]

We shall find the concepts and the phraseology of the majority and minority opinions cropping up frequently in the course of the debates.

CONSPIRACY?

Bitter denunciation greeted the decision in the North. Indignation meetings, resolutions of state legislatures, sermons from the pulpit and editorials in the press protested and stormed. Editor William Cullen Bryant of the *New York Evening Post* wrote that slavery was no longer the South's peculiar institution, but a federal institution, and that "wherever our flag floats, it is the flag of slavery."[37]

He asserted that the decision was the result of a conspiracy, a charge which was echoed throughout the North. The rumors and leaks which preceded the decision, and the inaugural statement by Buchanan two days before the decision was rendered, seemed substantiation of the charge. Senator Seward carried it to the floor of the Senate. Just prior to the administering of the oath of office at the inaugural ceremony, he said, the Chief Justice and the President-elect had engaged in dishonorable "whisperings."[38] Lincoln also charged conspiracy, and became involved in several sharp exchanges with Douglas over the allegation.

The South received the decision with jubilation. But the

effect on the Democratic Party was to prove disastrous. The northern Democrats headed by Douglas were put in an untenable position. They were faced with the prospect of concurring in an astonishing reversal of accepted Democratic principles. States' rights and limitation of federal power had always been cardinal Democratic tenets and had therefore offered some justifiable ground for insisting that Congress keep its hands off the territories. Now, according to the decision, Congress was charged with the duty to protect slavery in the territories. It was a complete triumph for Calhoun's doctrine.

In order to save his position of leadership of the northern Democrats, who were faced with the choice of capitulating to the southern wing or of defecting to the Republican Party, Douglas attempted to rationalize his position by claiming that, though slavery could theoretically go into any territory, it could not exist there unless it was sustained by local law. Hostile regulations could render the right to hold slaves a nullity. This position even found some support among practical-minded southerners, like James L. Orr, of South Carolina, later to be Speaker of the House of Representatives, who said:

> In every slaveholding community of this Union, we have local legislation and local police regulation appertaining to that institution, without which the institution would . . . be valueless. . . Without them the slave-holder could not enforce his rights. . .
>
> . . . . . .
>
> The legislative authority of a Territory is invested with a discretion to vote for or against laws. We think they ought to pass laws in every Territory . . . to protect slave property. But if they decline to pass such laws, the power was invested in the Territorial legislature, and exercised by them, to prohibit it.[39]

The weakness and inconsistency of this straddle were later to figure prominently in the debates and to be bared in all their nakedness as the Freeport doctrine.

The final act in the drama of popular sovereignty was now to be played and to serve as a prologue for the Lincoln-Douglas debates. The theme was a constitution for Kansas. Since the Topeka Constitution of the Free Staters had no chance of Administration or Congressional approval, the Committee on

Territories of the Senate in June 1856 had considered two bills designed to provide for fair elections and for the submission of a constitution to the vote of the people. One bill had been offered by Douglas and the other by Senator Robert Toombs of Georgia. At a Democratic caucus in Douglas' home, it was decided to sponsor the Toombs Bill as a party measure. When it came out of committee, however, the provision for submitting the constitution to ratification by the people was missing.

Because of this, the bill was defeated in the House after prior passage in the Senate. But the omission of a ratification clause stirred such strong repercussions that they carried into the great debates and provided almost the entire subject of controversy of the fourth debate at Charleston.

In January 1857 the pro-slavery legislature of Kansas took matters into its own hands. It provided for a constitutional convention to be elected in June and to meet at Lecompton in the fall. The Free Staters boycotted the election, with the result that the delegates to the constitutional convention were all pro-slavery. However, for the elections for a new legislature in October, the Free Staters turned out in full force and won. The situation was now both anomalous and farcical. Pro-slavery delegates were to draw up a constitution for a territory, the majority of whose population was clearly anti-slavery.

Under the leadership of John Calhoun, former surveyor of Illinois and employer of Abraham Lincoln (not to be confused with John C. Calhoun of South Carolina), the convention did as it was expected to do. It drew up a pro-slavery constitution. For the sake of appearances, it provided for a popular referendum. But there was a catch in it. The vote was to be not on the entire constitution, but merely on the "constitution with slavery" or the "constitution without slavery." The latter choice contained a provision that "the rights of property in slaves now in the Territory, shall in no manner be interfered with." The complete abolition of slavery was therefore impossible.

THE TROUBLESOME LECOMPTON CONSTITUTION

This comic performance was greeted with disgust and protest by the Republicans. It also placed the northern Democrats in an embarrassing position. What had happened to their popular sovereignty? Furthermore, what was Douglas going to do about it?

The Little Giant was equal to the occasion. On December 2 he returned to Washington for the opening of Congress. The next day he went to see the President. A stormy session ensued. Douglas urged the President not to support the constitution in his forthcoming message to Congress. If he did, he said, he would denounce it the moment the message was read.

Buchanan, however, had already made up his mind, and he was not to be moved. Angered by Douglas' ultimatum, he reminded him of the fate of Talmadge and Rives, two men whom President Andrew Jackson had broken for party insurgency. "Mr. Douglas," he said, "I desire you to remember that no Democrat ever yet differed with an administration of his own choice without being crushed." Douglas received this sally with scorn. To him Buchanan was no Jackson. "Mr. President," he flashed back, "I wish you to remember that General Jackson is dead." With that, he strode from the room.[40]

A few days later Buchanan delivered his message. The next day Douglas rose to speak. The galleries were crowded in anticipation. Trying to avoid an open difference with the President, Douglas attacked the Lecompton scheme as inconsistent with Democratic promises:

> Why force this Constitution down the throats of the people of Kansas in opposition to their wishes and in violation of our pledges? . .
>
> I will stand on the great principle of popular sovereignty. . . If Kansas wants a slave-state constitution, she has a right to it; if she wants a free-state constitution, she has a right to it. It is none of my business which way the Slavery clause is decided. I care not whether it is voted down or voted up. . .
>
> The people want a fair vote. They never will be satisfied without it. . . But if this Constitution is to be forced down our throats, in violation of the fundamental principle of free government, under a mode of submission that is a mockery and insult, I will resist it to the last.[41]

The full portent of the speech was not lost on the country. The brewing rift between the two wings of the Democratic Party had broken out into the open. The Republicans welcomed Douglas' aid in the all-out battle against Lecompton.

There was even talk that Douglas, like other prominent Democrats before him, such as Chase and Sumner, might desert his
party and enter the Republican fold. Horace Greeley and his
New York Tribune were ready to support Douglas in his forthcoming campaign for reelection to the Senate on the ground
that all anti-Lecomptonites should be given aid in their fight
against the Administration.[42] Even Garrison's *Liberator* had
words of praise for him.[43] Gossip had it that Douglas had also
been heard talking of a Constitutional Union party, composed
of Republicans and Union Democrats, to save the nation from
the southern extremists and the danger of secession. He would
be a strong candidate for the presidency on such a platform.

The referendum on the Lecompton Constitution was set for
December 21. As a countermove, the newly-elected Free State
legislature had met on December 7 and provided for a referendum on the entire constitution to be held on January 4. The
results were again farcical. The constitution with its pro-slavery
clause was voted in on December 21 by 6,000 votes, 3,000 of
which were found to be fraudulent. On January 4 the entire
constitution was voted down by 10,000 votes.

Despite these results, the President urged Congressional
approval of the Lecompton Constitution and immediate admission of Kansas as a state, even though her population fell far
short of the 93,000 required.

The Democrats had majorities in both houses, but to make
sure of support, the Administration decided to use the whip
and patronage to keep hesitant members in line. Postmasters
especially felt its heavy hand. The Administration press, especially the Washington *Union,* also engaged in a campaign of
violent denunciation of the anti-Lecomptonites. Douglas naturally was the object of the bitterest attacks, which were stimu-
lated by the fact that he had once voted against the editor of
the *Union* for the office of Public Printer.

The Administration won its victory in the Senate. An amend-
ment to the Lecompton bill by the venerable Senator John J.
Crittenden of Kentucky, Old Line Whig and colleague of
Henry Clay, providing for a vote on the entire constitution
by the people of Kansas, was defeated. But in the House the
Administration received a setback. An amendment similar to
Crittenden's, offered by Representative Montgomery, of Penn-

sylvania, was passed by a combination of Republicans and anti-Lecompton Democrats.

To save face for the Administration, a committee of conference of the two houses presented a bill by Congressman William H. English, of Indiana. It provided for submission of the entire constitution to the people with a reward for its acceptance. Kansas would be admitted immediately as a state, with liberal grants of land and a percentage of the proceeds of the sale of other tracts of land — a tempting economic lure for a struggling pioneer community. Because it offered the possibility for Kansans to vote on the entire constitution, many of its opponents wavered and the bill passed both houses. Douglas also wavered momentarily, but decided to stick with the anti-Lecomptonites to the end, thus forfeiting any possibility of reconciliation with the Administration.

In August the Lecompton Constitution was resubmitted to the people of Kansas with the provisions of the English Bill, and was rejected by a vote of approximately 12,000 to 2,000.

The Lecompton Constitution and the English Bill received considerable attention in the Lincoln-Douglas debates. Two questions which challenged the contestants in the discussion were: Should a state be admitted into the Union before it had the requisite legal population? Did the decision depend on whether it would come in as a slave or a free state? But these questions proved to be theoretical. The answers were supplied during the Civil War. Kansas remained a territory until 1861, when in due course it was admitted into the Union as a free state.

As a result of his stirring fight against the Lecompton Constitution, Douglas received a hero's welcome on his return to Chicago in July, where he was to open his campaign for re-election to the Senate. Gone were the memories of his hostile receptions of 1850 and 1854.

He knew, however, what a difficult fight lay ahead of him. The Administration in its vindictiveness would use every weapon at its command to defeat him. It was determined to ruin him politically and to wrest the state's party machinery from his grasp. But more than that, the Republicans had nominated their best man to contest the field against him. That man was Abraham Lincoln.

PART II
The Antagonists

The contestants who engaged in the memorable battle of the hustings before the people of Illinois seemed handpicked by fate.

There was much that was similar in their backgrounds. Both had migrated to the new state in its early days, and both had struggled against poverty and hardship to the eminence of leadership of a political party. Both also possessed the strong qualities of intellect and personality and the power of the spoken word, which were able to sway men's minds and to hold men's allegiance.

They were fantastically opposite, however, in appearance and temperament. Each had something of the grotesque in his physical makeup which, instead of repelling, attracted the public. The striking contrast between them, as much as the cause of combat, stirred the interest and imagination of their auditors, and until the present day has exercised a fascination for all who love a rousing contest.

Since the biblical struggle between David and Goliath, few personal encounters have been as fateful to a nation as to the combatants themselves.

CHAPTER 2

"I Never Dodge a Question": Stephen A. Douglas

When Stephen Douglas was twenty-five years of age, he began an autobiography. He was already one of the most prominent politicians in Illinois, because in the short span of five years since he had settled in the state, his career had been meteoric. He thus had a good deal to write about.

"I this day commence this memorandum or journal of passing events," he wrote on September 1, 1838, "for the purpose of refreshing my mind in future upon subjects that might otherwise be forgotten."[1] Contrary to the usual custom of autobiographies, Douglas' emphasis was on the future, rather than the past. Though he had already gone far, the future had much more in store for him, for it caught him up swiftly and within a short space of time lifted him to the dizzy heights of national eminence. Before another ten years had passed, he was being mentioned for the presidency.

Douglas never wrote another line of his autobiography after that day in 1838.[2] He was too busy with the exciting present and the gleaming prospects for the future. His was the stirring and fabulous story of the boy who went West and made good.

The Little Giant was born in Brandon, Vermont, on April 23, 1813. His father, a physician, was the scion of an old New England family which had originally come from Scotland. His grandfather had served as a soldier during the Revolution, from Valley Forge to the surrender of Cornwallis at Yorktown.

Stephen was only a baby of three months when his father died. His mother took him and his older sister to live with her bachelor brother on the family farm nearby. Here the boy grew up, working on the farm in summer and attending the district school in winter. At the age of fifteen he wanted to enter an academy to prepare for college, but his uncle, who controlled the family's finances, was just as opposed to losing a good farm hand as to encouraging "educational improvement," so the youngster decided to learn a trade and become independent. He had had enough of an uncle who, he felt, was exploiting him.

He bade farewell to his mother and sister, so the story goes, and walked the fourteen miles to Middlebury, where he apprenticed himself to a cabinetmaker. When he later became famous, he often referred jocularly to his early experience, as he did in the first debate with Lincoln at Ottawa, as having qualified him for making cabinets, bureaus and secretaries.

Douglas, however, was a frail, slender lad, slightly over five feet in height. Though he loved cabinetmaking, he worked at it for only two years, supposedly because it proved too exacting for his health. More likely, he had saved enough money to continue his education. He therefore returned home to enter the academy at Brandon. His mother remarried shortly thereafter, and when she and her husband settled in Canandaigua, New York, he entered the academy there and subsequently took up the study of law in the office of one of the leading lawyers.

It was in these early years that Douglas was attracted to the Democratic Party. Even while he was a cabinetmaker, he had been interested in reading political works and had become a worshiper of Andrew Jackson. Heated arguments with his Whig employer, strengthened his attachment to the "party of the people." At the academy he was recognized as an outstanding debater and as one of the best informed students on political matters. In the campaign for the reelection of General Jackson to the presidency in 1832, the young Douglas took an active part and organized a band of "Jackson boys" to help win votes.

In June 1833, when he was twenty years old, Douglas decided to seek his fortune in the new West. His mother could not support him for the seven years of legal and classical studies necessary to become a lawyer in the state of New York. In some parts of the West, like Illinois, there were no requirements for admission to the bar, and in Ohio only one year of study was required.

So with $300 in his pocket, "the last of his patrimony," he set out for Cleveland, which was then only a small village, where he had a relative. He was offered the opportunity of continuing his studies in a law office and was prepared to settle down to work and study, when he suddenly fell ill with malaria. Confined to bed for four months with the fever, he frequently despaired of recovery.

When he was well enough to move around, his physicians advised him to return home. Life in the West might prove too hard for a sickly youngster. But Douglas would not think of it. Instead, though he had only $40 left, he determined to push farther on. He went to Cincinnati, Ohio, to Louisville, Kentucky, and then to St. Louis, Missouri, hoping to find some means of employment, preferably school teaching, until he could fully regain his health and again take up the study of law. But he was unsuccessful everywhere, and with his funds almost depleted, he resolved to go to Jacksonville, Illinois, of which, according to one source, he had read a charming description in a book of travels. He might have been drawn there because it bore the name of his idol, or more probably, because his funds were so low that he could go no further.

He arrived in Jacksonville in November with a little more than a dollar in his pocket. The young stranger, only five feet four inches in height, with his pale face and wasted form, looked like a stripling. He could obtain no employment, and was forced to sell a few of his remaining possessions to sustain himself. He was fortunate, however, in making the acquaintance of General Murray McConnell, one of the prominent citizens of Jacksonville. McConnell lent him several old law books, a favor for which Douglas never ceased to be grateful. Toward the end of the month Douglas left Jacksonville for Winchester to try his luck there. He had heard that there was a possibility of organizing a school and the money he might earn would help to tide him over the winter. Once again he had to walk to his destination, this time by night.

Now luck was with him. The second day after his arrival, an auction was held in the town square and Douglas was hired as clerk to keep a record of the transactions. He was paid $2.50 a day for the two days that the auction lasted. More important, Douglas made friends who helped him to set up a school with forty pupils, each paying $3 for a quarter of a year. At the end of the quarter, Douglas returned to Jacksonville to open a law office. In March 1834 he was admitted to the bar.

THE YOUNG POLITICIAN

From that moment on, his rise was rapid. Taking an active interest in the politics of Morgan County, in which Jacksonville was situated, he was elected State's Attorney by the legislature in February 1835 over John J. Hardin, one of the outstanding lawyers and public figures in the state. Young though he was, he began to show great organizing ability, and his influence on Democratic policies was so great that in 1836 he succeeded in getting the party to adopt the convention system for the selection of candidates for public office. Previously, as many as ten or fifteen candidates would run for an office, each relying on his own personal popularity and efforts to win. The convention plan limited the number of Democratic candidates to one for each office. It proved its success when five of the six Democratic candidates were elected to the legislature from Morgan County, he himself being one of the successful aspirants. Thereafter the Whigs were forced to adopt the convention system also.

In April 1837, newly elected President Martin Van Buren appointed Douglas to the post of Register of the Land Office at Springfield, and the young leader thereupon resigned from the legislature to take up his new duties. It was while serving in this position that Douglas acquired his grasp of public land policy, on which he became so expert later in his career. The office itself also brought him a large income, which was the basis of a subsequent fortune. It was politics, rather than money, that attracted him, however, so in November, when he was selected by a Democratic convention to be the candidate for Congress in the election to be held in August 1838, he gave up his post.

His opponent was John T. Stuart, Abraham Lincoln's law partner. In March, both men started off together to make a thorough canvass of the district which covered a large area of the state. For five months they traveled together, sharing the hardships of the road, a test of endurance which the frail young Douglas surmounted with surprising robustness. In a disputed vote, Stuart won by a slim majority.

The luster of Douglas' name was not diminished by this setback, however. His reputation was now well established throughout the state as an orator of force and brilliance. He was one of the chief men in the Democratic Party and generally acknowledged as the foremost expounder of its principles. His position in politics was assured.

He had already entered into a law partnership and had announced his intention to devote himself entirely to the practice of law when he was called back to the political arena. In January 1839, the recently elected Democratic governor, Thomas Carlin, appointed John A. McClernand Secretary of State, but the Senate, controlled by the Whigs, refused to act in confirmation or rejection of the appointment. The effect of this action was to retain the Whig incumbent in office. The matter was taken to the Supreme Court of the state, and Douglas served as one of a group of counsel to argue the case for the governor's right of removal and appointment. The court, however, also under Whig control, ruled against the governor.

The decision spurred the Democrats to revise the makeup of the court. Their efforts came to a head during the presidential campaign of 1840.

The Constitution of Illinois provided that free white male inhabitants over the age of twenty-one could vote in all elections. Nothing was said about naturalization. But the rush of immigration into the state posed a threat to the Whigs. Most of the new immigrants were Irish, and they voted Democratic. Fearful that this "alien" vote, which had never been questioned before, would perpetuate the Democrats in office, the Whigs decided to challenge it.

The matter came up for adjudication before the State Supreme Court. If the Whig claim was successful, a severe blow would be dealt to the Democratic Party. Douglas was selected to serve among counsel for the "alien" side. After argument, the case was held over until June. When court reconvened, Douglas sought a postponement until the fall. His plan was to forestall another unfavorable decision by the Whigs from the bench which would prevent the aliens from voting in the election. He, therefore, found some technical clerical errors in the court record and succeeded in obtaining an adjournment until the following term in November.

The strategy was successful. In the intervening election, with the alien vote undisturbed, not only did the Democrats carry the state legislature, but the state itself was one of seven that remained loyally in the Democratic column in the Van Buren debacle to "Tippecanoe" Harrison. This was a telling tribute to the effectiveness of the Democratic organization. Since Douglas had been chairman of the Democratic State Committee, he emerged from the campaign with enhanced prestige.

When the legislature met in December, the Democrats got busy. The Whig Secretary of State did not wait for the legislature to unseat him, but wisely resigned, and in January 1841 Douglas was appointed to the post. He held it, however, only a month, because in the meantime the Supreme Court had rendered its decision in the "alien" case in favor of the Whigs, and the legislature retaliated by passing an act in February increasing the number of judges from four to nine.

This was enough to reverse the decision. Douglas was one of the new judges elected and, of course, voted with the new majority. Thus within seven years of his admission to the bar he was on the bench, the youngest Supreme Court judge in Illinois history.

The "packing" of the court and the elevation of Douglas to one of the packed judgeships supplied Lincoln with effective and telling ammunition in the course of the debates.

Despite the questionable circumstances of his election, Douglas did well as a judge. One of the ablest Whig lawyers was quoted as saying: "Damn that little squatty Democrat — he is the very best and most acute Judge in all this Democratic State."[3] The Supreme Court judges also served as circuit judges. Douglas' duties as a circuit judge of the Quincy district brought him into contact with the Mormons who had settled at Nauvoo, in the western part of the state. His fairness won him popularity with this persecuted sect. From them he learned the word "Danite," which he later applied as a term of opprobrium to the adherents of Buchanan who sought to bring about his defeat for reelection in 1858.[4] The Danite Band was a fanatical secret organization of Mormons pledged to support their prophet, Joseph Smith, regardless of law or accepted morality.[5] It derived its name from the biblical prophecy of Jacob regarding one of his sons: "Dan shall be a serpent in the way."[6] We shall find Douglas using this term frequently in the course of the debates.

TO WASHINGTON

Douglas' meteoric rise continued uninterrupted. In 1843 he was elected to Congress where he remained by reelection for the next four years. He distinguished himself early, for in January 1844 he made a speech urging an appropriation to repay Andrew Jackson the $1,000 fine a federal district judge had imposed upon him after the battle of New Orleans. It was a vindication of the general's right to impose martial law which the judge had declared to be in contempt of court. The subject of clearing the old general's name had come up in the House before but without success. Douglas, however, gave it a new impetus and the bill was passed.

Douglas' reputation was made. "Old Hickory" himself expressed his gratitude when, as a member of a Democratic convention held in Nashville, Tennessee, several months later, the young Congressman visited the general at his home, the Hermitage. "I felt convinced in my own mind that I was not guilty of such a heinous offense," Douglas' idol said, "but I could never make out a legal justification of my course, nor has it ever been done, Sir, until you, on the floor of Congress, at the late session, established it beyond the possibility of cavil or doubt."[7]

In the presidential election of 1844, Douglas enthusiastically supported the dark horse Democratic nominee, James K. Polk, and the party platform of the "reannexation of Texas and the reoccupation of Oregon." Full recognition of his ability as a legislator and orator, and of his championing of "manifest destiny," came when he was chosen by the Twenty-Ninth Congress as chairman of the Committee on Territories. The committee lost no time in pressing the bill admitting Texas into the Union. As for Oregon, his position was extreme. He was one of the few who stood by "Fifty-four forty or fight" to the end. In one of his speeches he said:

While I would not violate the laws of nations, nor treaty

stipulations, nor in any manner tarnish the national honor, I would exert all legal and honorable means to drive Great Britain, and the last vestiges of royal authority, from the continent of North America, and extend the limits of the Republic from ocean to ocean. I would make this an ocean-bound republic, and have no more disputes about boundaries or red lines upon maps.[8]

When the war with Mexico broke out, Douglas was among the staunchest defenders of the justice of the American cause. To the detractors of the President he gave eloquent answer:

Patriots may differ as to the expediency of a declaration of war, or the wisdom of a course of policy which may probably lead to such a result, but honor and duty forbid divided counsels after our country has been invaded, and American blood has been shed on American soil by a treacherous foe...

Aside from the insults to our flag, the indignity to the nation, and the injury to our commerce, it is estimated that not less than ten millions of dollars are due to our citizens for these and many other outrages which Mexico has committed within the last fifteen years. When pressed by our government for adjustment and remuneration, she has resorted to all manner of expedients to procrastinate and delay.[9]

He pointed out, too, that Britain and France had taken armed action against Mexico for lesser reasons and received satisfaction:

Thus we find that remuneration and satisfaction were made to England and France for the same injuries of which we complain, where their subjects and our citizens were common sufferers. Still the wrongs of our citizens are unredressed, and the indignity to the honor and flag of the country unavenged. Our wrongs were tenfold greater than theirs in number, enormity, and amount.

Their complaints have been heard in tones of thunder from the mouths of their cannon, and have been adjusted according to the terms dictated by the injured parties. The forebearance of our government to enforce our rights by the same efficient measures which they employed has been considered as evidence of our imbecility, which gave impunity to the past and license to future aggressions. Hence we find that while Great Britain and France, by the energy and efficiency with which they have enforced their rights, have commanded the respect of Mexico and reestablished their amicable relations, the United States, by an ill-advised magnanimity and forbearance toward a weak and imbecile neighbor, has forfeited her respect, and lost all the advantages of that friendly intercourse to which our natural position entitles us.

Under the operation of these causes, our commerce with Mexico has dwindled down by degrees from nine millions of dollars per annum to a mere nominal sum, while that of France and Engand has steadily increased, until they have secured a monopoly of the trade and almost a controlling influence over the councils of that wretched country.[10]

Not content with defending the administration, he went to the attack, a characteristic of his style in debate:

The facts which I have briefly recited are accessible to, if not within the knowledge of, every gentleman who feels an interest in examining them. Their authenticity does not depend upon the weight of my authority. They are to be found in full and in detail in the public documents on our tables and in our libraries. With a knowledge of the facts, or, at least, professing to know them, gentlemen have the hardihood to tell us that the President has unwisely and unnecessarily precipitated the country into an unjust and unholy war.

They express great sympathy for Mexico; profess to regard her an injured and persecuted nation — the victim of American injustice and aggression. They have no sympathy for the widows and orphans whose husbands and fathers have been robbed and murdered by the Mexican authorities; no sympathy with our own countrymen who have dragged out miserable lives within the walls of her dungeons, without crime and without trial; no indignation at the outrages upon our commerce and shipping and the insults to our national flag. . .[11]

It was no wonder that Douglas' magnificence in debate catapulted him to the very top of both Democratic and Congressional leadership. He did not fear to cross swords with the ablest and most accomplished speakers. Even the former President, John Quincy Adams, who was now serving in the House, and who was known as "Old Man Eloquent," suffered discomfiture at his hands.

When Adams opposed the Little Giant's attempt to prove

American title to the territory bounded by the Rio Grande, Douglas presented a dispatch written to the Spanish minister by Adams in 1819 when he was Secretary of State, in which he had set forth the claims of the United States to that area. Adams' embarrassment was as evident as was Douglas' triumph. There were few who cared to tangle with the Little Giant after that.

Douglas was now ready for the Senate. During the summer and fall of 1846 he made an active campaign for the seat. In December, the Democrats in the legislature nominated him for the post, and early in 1847 he was elected. Thus, before he was thirty-five years old, he became the acknowledged leader of the Democratic Party in his state. He also became the key Congressional figure in directing the expansion of the United States, for soon after taking his seat in December 1847, the Senate honored him by organizing a Committee on Territories, which it had not had before, and making him its chairman.

Before he entered the Senate, however, Douglas succumbed to romance. In April 1847 he married Martha Denny Martin of North Carolina. The bride's father, Colonel Robert Martin, owned plantations in Mississippi as well as in his home state. As a wedding gift he presented his son-in-law with a deed to the Mississippi plantation, which, with its slaves and equipment, was worth about $100,000. Douglas declined the gift, saying he was a northern man and had no experience with that kind of property.

When the colonel died the next year, the plantation was willed to his daughter in terms which respected his son-in-law's views. "In giving to my dear daughter full and complete control over my slaves in Mississippi, I make to her one dying request," the will said, "that is, that if she leaves no children, to make provision before she dies to have all these Negroes, together with their increase, sent to Liberia, or some other colony in Africa. I would remind my dear daughter that her husband does not desire to own this kind of property. . ."[12]

Douglas, however, was named manager of the estate with a fifth of the net income as a management fee. Because of this he was later charged with and forced to deny the ownership of slaves.[13]

PROPHET OF "MANIFEST DESTINY"

Besides his absorption with the problems of the admission of the new territories acquired from Mexico, Douglas was prominent in pushing programs for the economic growth and development of the West and of the country as a whole. Even as a Congressman he had been interested in the improvement of the Illinois River as a connecting link between the Great Lakes and the Gulf of Mexico via the Mississippi River.

A program of internal improvements, encouraged by the federal government, was one side of the coin, the other side of which was the doctrine of "manifest destiny." He believed in the greatness of the country and the inevitability of its expansion. His vision of the future revealed the attributes of the far-sighted statesman. It was reflected in connection with his unflinching stand on Oregon: "The great point at issue between us and Great Britain is for the freedom of the Pacific Ocean, for the trade of China and Japan, of the East Indies, and for the maritime ascendency on all these waters."

He was also later to oppose the Clayton-Bulwer Treaty because it tied the hands of the United States in regard to the acquisition of isthmus rights to a canal to the Pacific Ocean. In the course of a debate, he said:

> You may make as many treaties as you please to fetter the limbs of this giant republic, and she will burst them all from her, and her course will be onward to a limit which I will not venture to prescribe. . .
>
> What is the use of your guarantee that you will never erect any fortifications in Central America; never annex, occupy, or colonize any portion of that country? How do you know that you can avoid doing it? If you make the canal, I ask you if American citizens will not settle along its line; whether they will not build up towns at each terminus; whether they will not spread over that country, and convert it into an American state; whether American principles and American institutions will not be firmly planted there?
>
> And I ask you how many years you think will pass away before you will find the same necessity to extend your laws over your own kindred that you found in the case of Texas? How long will it be before that day arrives? . . . So certain as

this republic exists, so certain as we remain a united people,
so certain as the laws of progress which have raised us from
a mere handful to a mighty nation shall continue to govern
our action, just so certain are these events to be worked out,
and you will be compelled to extend your protection in that
direction. . .

I am not desirous of hastening the day. I am not impatient
of the time when it shall be realized. I do not wish to give
any additional impulse to our progress. We are going fast
enough. But I wish our policy, our laws, our institutions,
should keep up with the advance in science, in the mechanic
arts, in agriculture, and in every thing that tends to make
us a great and powerful nation.

Let us look the future in the face, and let us prepare to
meet that which can not be avoided. Hence I was unwilling
to adopt that clause in the treaty guaranteeing that neither
party would ever annex, colonize, or occupy any portion of
Central America.[14]

It was because of his efforts that Congress granted the necessary land and concessions for the building of the Illinois Central
Railroad. This railroad united the northern and southern
sections of Illinois and, from its junction at the Ohio River,
united with another railroad reaching to the gulf. It was this
passion for promoting the economic, as well as the territorial,
expansion of the country that subsequently complicated his
plans for the organization of the Nebraska territory.

While in the House, Douglas had voted against the Wilmot
Proviso, and proposed instead the extension of the Missouri
Compromise Line to the Pacific Ocean, just as it had been
extended to Texas previously. This proposal was defeated by
northern votes. In the Senate he followed the same policy, again
proposing the extension of the Missouri Line to the Pacific,
when the organization of the Oregon territory was being considered. He had already reached the conviction that the inhabitants of a territory should decide whether they wanted slavery
or not, in accordance with the Cass doctrine as expounded in
the Nicholson letter, but he was willing to accept the Missouri
Line as a ready and simple method of adjustment of the slavery
question for new territories. He therefore resisted all attempts
to rule out slavery completely in these territories. In these
efforts he was embarrassed by resolutions of the Illinois legisla-

ture instructing him and his colleagues to support the Wilmot
Proviso. It was probably because of this contretemps that he
was impelled in a speech in Springfield in October 1849 to say
of the Missouri Compromise:

> It has received the sanction of all parties in every section
> of the Union. It had its origin in the hearts of all patriotic
> men who desired to preserve and perpetuate the blessings of
> our glorious Union. All the evidences of public opinion seem
> to indicate that this Compromise has become canonized in
> the hearts of the American people as a sacred thing, which no
> ruthless hand would be reckless enough to disturb.[15]

This statement was to plague him in the course of the debates
with Lincoln.

Following the adoption of the Compromise of 1850, Douglas
himself gave a summary of his change of position on the Missouri Compromise in a speech in the Senate on December 23,
1851:

> My preference for the Missouri Compromise was predicated
> on the assumption that the whole people of the United States
> would be more easily reconciled to that measure than to any
> other mode of adjustment; and this assumption rested upon
> the fact that the Missouri Compromise had been the means
> of an amicable settlement of a fearful controversy in 1821,
> which had been acquiesced in cheerfully and cordially by
> the people for more than a quarter of a century, and which
> all parties and sections of the Union professed to respect and
> cherish as a fair, just, and honorable adjustment. I could
> discover no reason for the application of the Missouri Line to
> all the territory owned by the United States in 1821 that
> would not apply with equal force to its extension to the Rio
> Grande and also to the Pacific, so soon as we should acquire
> the country.
>
> In accordance with these views, I brought forward the
> Missouri Compromise at the session of 1844–45 as applicable
> to Texas, and had the satisfaction to see it adopted. Subse-
> quently, after the war with Mexico had commenced, and
> when, in August, 1846, Mr. Wilmot first introduced his pro-
> viso, I proposed to extend the Missouri Compromise to the
> Pacific as a substitute for the Wilmot Proviso. . .
>
> California and New Mexico having been acquired without
> any condition or stipulation in respect to slavery, the question

arose as to what kind of territorial governments should be established for those countries. . . I brought forward my original proposition to extend the Missouri Compromise to the Pacific in the same sense and with the same understanding with which it was originally adopted. This proposition met the approbation of the Senate, and passed this body by a large majority, but was instantly rejected in the House of Representatives by a still larger majority. . .

At the opening of the next session, upon consultation with the friends of the measure, it was generally conceded — with, perhaps, here and there an individual exception — that there was no hope left for the Missouri Compromise, and consequently some other plan of adjustment must be devised. I was reluctant to give up the Missouri Compromise, having been the first to bring it forward, and having struggled for it in both houses of Congress for about five years.[16]

LITTLE GIANT MAGNIFICENT

When Douglas abandoned the Missouri Compromise for popular sovereignty and also supported the Fugitive Slave Law in pushing the Compromise of 1850, he placed himself in serious jeopardy with the electorate. After the passage of the Compromise, Douglas set out for Chicago where he found a hostile constituency. On October 19 the city council passed resolutions denouncing the Compromise and the Fugitive Slave Law as violations of the law of God and of the Constitution. It termed those who had supported the measures as "fit only to be ranked with the traitors, Benedict Arnold and Judas Iscariot. . . ."[17] and called upon the city police not to render any assistance for the arrest of fugitive slaves. A public mass meeting was called for the following evening to ratify the resolutions.

At this point Douglas displayed his mettle, revealing to the fullest extent the force of personality and the courage which made him truly a giant. He came to the mass meeting at which 2,500 had gathered, and from the rostrum announced that he would appear the next evening to defend every measure of the Compromise and to show that he was right and the people were wrong. He issued an invitation to everyone to be present.

The next evening a crowd of 4,000 citizens, most of them hostile, confronted Douglas. Point by point he took up the measures of the Compromise, inviting questions freely from the audience. "Is there any other objection?" he would ask. Or he would say, "I thank the gentleman for calling my attention to this point," or "That is the very question I was anxious someone should propound, because I was desirous of an opportunity of answering it," or "I will answer that question with a great deal of pleasure." It must have been a thrilling scene, indeed — one man, standing alone, opposed to a tremendous mob, and meeting all comers.[18]

The hisses and catcalls soon turned into applause. It was a striking demonstration of Douglas' remarkable way with an audience and of his brilliant powers of persuasion. When he finished, the meeting which had come to condemn, paid a tribute of praise in a series of resolutions, the last one of which read: "Resolved, that we, the people of Chicago, repudiate the resolutions passed by the Common Council of Chicago upon the subject of the Fugitive Slave Law."[19] The next night the city council met again, and repealed its own resolutions by a vote of twelve to one. It was a magnificent and memorable triumph for the Little Giant.

One section of his speech, dealing with the "higher law," is of particular interest to the reader today, apart from its eloquence, because it reveals how difficult it was for the average man of the time to resolve the problem of the morality of slavery. Only the clear thinking and lucid reasoning of a Lincoln could break through the fog of doubt and confusion.

To a question from the audience about whether the clause in the Constitution providing for the surrender of fugitive slaves was not in violation of the law of God, Douglas replied:

> We should all recognize, respect, and revere the divine law. But we should bear in mind that the law of God, as revealed to us, is intended to operate on our consciences, and insure the performance of our duties as individuals and Christians. The divine law does not prescribe the form of government under which we shall live, and the character of our political and civil institutions. Revelation has not furnished us with a Constitution — a code of international law — and a system of civil and municipal jurisprudence. It has not determined the right of persons and property, much less the peculiar privileges which shall be awarded to each class of persons under any particular form of government. God has created man in His own image, and endowed him with the right of self-

government, so soon as he shall evince the requisite intelligence, virtue, and capacity to assert and enjoy the privilege.

The history of the world furnishes few examples where any considerable portion of the human race have shown themselves sufficiently enlightened and civilized to exercise the rights and enjoy the blessings of freedom. In Asia and Africa we find nothing but ignorance, superstition, and despotism. Large portions of Europe and America can scarcely lay claim to civilization and Christianity; and a still smaller portion have demonstrated their capacity for self-government.

Is all this contrary to the laws of God? And if so, who is responsible? The civilized world have always held that when any race of men have shown themselves so degraded, by ignorance, superstition, cruelty, and barbarism, as to be utterly incapable of governing themselves, they must, in the nature of things, be governed by others, by such laws as are deemed applicable to their condition. It is upon this principle alone that England justifies the form of government she has established in the Indies, and for some of her other colonies — that Russia justifies herself in holding her serfs as slaves, and selling them as a part of the land on which they live — that our Pilgrim Fathers justified themselves in reducing the negro and Indian to servitude, and selling them as property — that we, in Illinois and most of the free states, justify ourselves in denying the negro and the Indian the privilege of voting, and all other political rights — and that many of the states of the Union justify themselves in depriving the white man of the right of the elective franchise, unless he is fortunate enough to own a certain amount of property.

These things certainly violate the principle of absolute equality among men, when considered as component parts of a political society or government, and so do many provisions of the Constitution of the United States, as well as the several states of the Union. In fact, no government ever existed on earth in which there was a perfect equality in all things among those composing it and governed by it. . . . If inequality in the form and principles of government is therefore to be deemed a violation of the laws of God, and punishable as such, who is to escape? Under this principle all Christendom is doomed, and no pagan can hope for mercy! . . . Who can assert that God has prescribed the form and principles of government, and the character of the political, municipal, and domestic institutions of men on earth?

This doctrine would annihilate the fundamental principle

upon which our political system rests. Our forefathers held
that the people had an inherent right to establish such Constitution and laws for the government of themselves and their
posterity as they should deem best calculated to insure the
protection of life, liberty, and the pursuit of happiness, and
that the same might be altered and changed as experience
should satisfy them to be necessary and proper. Upon this
principle the Constitution of the United States was formed,
and our glorious Union established. . .

If the Constitution of the United States is to be repudiated
upon the ground that it is repugnant to the divine law, where
are the friends of freedom and Christianity to look for another and a better? Who is to be the prophet to reveal the will
of God, and establish a theocracy for us? Is he to be found in
the ranks of Northern abolitionism or of Southern disunion;
or is the Common Council of the city of Chicago to have the
distinguished honor of furnishing the chosen one? . . .[20]

On this occasion Douglas also expounded his popular sovereignty doctrine in terms which he was to repeat in the debates
with Lincoln:

These measures are predicated on the great fundamental
principle that every people ought to possess the right of
forming and regulating their own internal concerns and
domestic institutions in their own way. It was supposed that
those of our fellow-citizens who emigrated to the shores of
the Pacific and to our other Territories were as capable of
self-government as their neighbors and kindred whom they
left behind them; and there was no reason for believing that
they have lost any of their intelligence or patriotism by the
wayside, while crossing the Istmus or the Plains. . . To
question their competency to do this was to deny their capacity for self-government. If they have the requisite intelligence
and honesty to be intrusted with the enactment of laws for
the government of white men, I know of no reason why
they should not be deemed competent to legislate for the
negro. . .[21]

The Little Giant could justly say with pride when speaking
about his Chicago experience on the Senate floor, "I never
dodge a question. I never shrink from any responsibility which
my position and duty justly devolve upon me. I never hesitate

to give an unpopular vote, or to meet an indignant community, when I know I am right."[22]

Most important of all, the Little Giant believed in the finality of the Compromise of 1850. In the same speech he declared:

> I have determined never to make another speech upon the slavery question; and I will now add the hope that the necessity for it will never exist. . . So long as our opponents do not agitate for repeal or modification, why should we agitate for any purpose? We claim that the Compromise is a final settlement. Is a final settlement open to discussion and agitation and controversy by its friends? What manner of settlement is that which does not settle the difficulty and quiet the dispute?[23]

AN "AMERICAN SOVEREIGN" ABROAD

Douglas was in his thirty-ninth year when the campaign for the presidency got under way in 1852, and he was a strong candidate for the Democratic nomination. His supporters made a serious blunder, however. They hailed him as the representative of Young America, before whom the "old fogies," such as Cass, Buchanan and Butler, should defer. The latter were "statesmen of a previous generation" and were branded as "senile." In their recklessness, the partisans of the Little Giant used such terms as "old clothes-horses" and "charlatans" to describe his rivals, and their press rang with similar offensive epithets. This kind of campaign did Douglas little good and laid the foundation for later enmities, such as Buchanan's. The result was that the rivals cancelled each other out, and the nomination went to Franklin Pierce, the dark horse.

At the turn of the year Douglas suffered a severe blow in the death of his wife, which left him a widower with two young sons. Partly to assuage his grief, he left at the close of the Congressional session for a trip to Europe. Though feted by the royal courts, the Little Giant was proud to display the manners and habiliments of American democracy. He refused an audience with the Queen of England because he would have had to don court dress. The story is told that when his landlady requested him to cease smoking in his apartments because that privilege was reserved for royalty, he drew himself up to his full small height and stared her down with "Madam,

I am an American sovereign." The landlady, crushed, retired deferentially, full of apology and embarrassment.[24] In Russia he was received by the Czar at a review of the Imperial Army and was the only American ever so honored. In accordance with his wishes he wore the dress in which he would be admitted into the presence of the President of the United States.[25]

Douglas returned from Europe in time for the opening of Congress in December 1853. Shortly thereafter he brought in his Kansas-Nebraska bill. There had been some interesting preliminary maneuvers. At several meetings of the Committee on Territories and at caucuses of the Democratic leaders the serious differences between the northern and southern Democrats had been discussed. The radical southern element maintained that the Missouri Compromise was invalid. There was no reason why slaves as property could not be taken into the federal territories. Douglas agreed that the principle of the Compromise of 1850 superseded the Missouri Compromise, but insisted that the establishment or prohibition of slavery was a matter of local law to be decided by the people of the territory.

To prevent an open rupture it was agreed by all to abide by the determination of the Supreme Court as to whether Congress had any power over slavery which could be delegated to the people of a territory. This agreement was later to be held against Douglas by the South when he did not accept all of the implications of the Dred Scott decision.

Pending a ruling of the court it was agreed that the Kansas-Nebraska bill should be drafted along the lines of the Compromise of 1850 with its popular sovereignty provisions. To all intents and purposes this was a virtual repeal of the Missouri Compromise anyway, although it did not state so in explicit language.

Douglas' plans were upset, however, when Senator Dixon, of Kentucky, decided to offer an amendment to the bill repealing the Missouri Compromise outright. Dixon was a Whig, but party alignments were already breaking, and his attitude was summed up when he said, "Upon the question of slavery I know no Whiggery and no Democracy."[26]

The amendment caught Douglas by surprise. He tried to remonstrate privately with Dixon, but ended up agreeing with him. In arriving at this decision he was probably spurred on by the clique of southern radicals and especially by Atchison.

This firebrand later declared that he had told Douglas that he would be glad to step down as President pro tempore of the Senate if he could become chairman of the Committee on Territories in order to introduce a Nebraska bill which would repeal the Missouri Compromise. When Dixon succeeded in convincing Douglas that explicit, rather than implicit, repeal was the correct course, Douglas is said to have exclaimed, "By God, sir, you are right. I will incorporate it in my bill, though I know that it will raise a hell of a storm."[27]

Years later, in writing about the incident, Dixon attributed the following words to Douglas: "I shall be assailed by demagogues and fanatics in the North without stint. Every opprobrious epithet will be applied to me. . . . It is more than probable that I may become permanently odious among those whose friendship and esteem I have heretofore possessed. This proceeding may end my political career."[28]

Whether or not Douglas used the flowery words that Dixon wrote, or the more laconic phraseology about the storm that would be raised, his predictions about the consequences of his action were amply fulfilled.

What prompted Douglas to take this fateful and, as it later developed, fatal step? Did he sincerely believe in the soundness of popular sovereignty as a solution to the slavery problem? Was it because he desired to remove the vexing question from politics and from the legislative halls of Congress by transferring it to the settlers who would be directly affected by it? Was it because he was ambitious for the presidency and wished to be assured of southern support? Or was it because he expected the South would now drop its claims for a southern or central route for the Pacific railroad with St. Louis or New Orleans as the terminus, in favor of the northern route whose terminus would be his home city, Chicago? It was probably a combination of all these elements.

He might also have been motivated by the desire that no one else should get the credit for a measure of such importance, especially since he, as chairman of the committee, was charged with the duty of promoting the organization of new territories. Perhaps, too, he saw this as an opportunity to unify the Democratic Party.

After all, both factions of the party wanted repeal of the Missouri Compromise, though for different reasons. The southern radicals wanted it in order to break down a formidable barrier against settling in territory from which they were barred. Douglas, on the other hand, representing the northern faction, wanted the repeal because he counted on the local population to decide slavery's fate. Hostile local law, he believed, would destroy it. Therefore, for the sake of party harmony, let the Missouri Compromise be repealed, but let the Supreme Court eventually interpret what the rights of slavery were under the Constitution.

The motive most persistently attributed to Douglas is that he capitulated to the southern radicals because he was looking ahead to the nomination for the presidency in 1856 and needed their support. This charge was contained bluntly in an "Appeal of the Independent Democrats in Congress to the People of the United States," which appeared on January 19, 1854. It was drawn up by Senator Chase, and signed by him, Senator Sumner and four abolitionists in the House. It was a highly emotional document, in which the Nebraska Bill was arraigned as a "criminal betrayal," "an enormous crime," and a "manifest falsification of the truth of history." It asked: "Will the people permit their dearest interests to be thus made the mere hazards of a presidential game?"[29]

A letter which Douglas wrote in November 1853, just two months before he introduced the Nebraska Bill, to the editor of the *Illinois State Register,* who was his staunch supporter, throws some light on his plans:

> I see many of the newspapers are holding me up as a candidate for the next Presidency. I do not wish to occupy that position. I do not think I will be willing to have my name used. I think such a state of things will exist that I shall not desire the nomination. Yet I do not intend to do any act which will deprive me of the control of my own action. I shall remain entirely non-committal and hold myself at liberty to do whatever my duty to my principles and my friends may require when the time for action arrives. Our first duty is to the cause — the fate of individual politicians is of minor consequence. The party is in a distracted condition and it requires all our wisdom, prudence and energy to consolidate its power and perpetuate its principles. Let us leave the Presidency out of view for at least two years to come.[30]

The ambiguity in the letter was typical of the shrewd politician. Though Douglas disclaimed that he wanted the presidency, he was careful to keep the door open by indicating that it was premature to talk about it. In the meantime he would be the instrument to unite the party through the Kansas-Nebraska Bill, and then he would be "at liberty" to accept the nomination.

Against Chase and Sumner's charges in their "Appeal" that he was bartering the interests of the country for the presidency, Douglas defended himself in customary vigorous fashion. On January 30, 1854 he answered the charges by maintaining the soundness of popular sovereignty and, therefore, of the Nebraska Bill:

> Let me ask you, where have you succeeded in excluding slavery by an act of Congress from one inch of the American soil? You may tell me that you did it in the Northwest Territory by the Ordinance of 1787. I will show you by the history of the country that you did not accomplish any such thing. You prohibited slavery there by law, but you did not exclude it in fact. Illinois was a part of the Northwest Territory. . . . Yet, when Illinois was organized into a Territorial government, it established and protected slavery, and maintained it in spite of your Ordinance and in defiance of its express prohibition. It is a curious fact, that, so long as Congress said the Territory of Illinois should not have slavery, she actually had it; and on the very day when you withdrew your Congressional prohibition the people of Illinois, of their own free will and accord, provided for a system of emancipation. . .[31]
>
> It was the policy of the fathers of the republic to prescribe a line of demarkation between free Territories and slaveholding Territories. . .[32]
>
> I do not like, I never did like, the system of legislation on our part, by which a geographical line, in violation of the laws of nature and climate and soil, and of the laws of God, should be run to establish institutions for a people contrary to their wishes; yet, out of a regard for the peace and quiet of the country, out of respect for past pledges, and out of a desire to adhere faithfully to all compromises, I sustained the Missouri Compromise so long as it was in force, and advocated its extension to the Pacific Ocean.
>
> Now, when that has been abandoned, when it has been superseded, when a great principle of self-government has been substituted for it, I choose to cling to that principle,

and abide in good faith, not only by the letter, but by the spirit of the last compromise.[33]

On March 3 Douglas made another speech in which he carried the attack to Chase and Sumner:

> If these gentlemen have entire confidence in the correctness of their own position, why do they not . . . controvert the soundness of this great principle of popular sovereignty. . .
>
> The opponents of the bill tell us . . . that their great desire is peace and harmony; and they complain bitterly that I should have disturbed the repose of the country by the introduction of this measure. Let me ask these professed friends of peace and avowed enemies of agitation, how the issue could have been avoided? They tell me that I should have let the question alone — that is, that I should have left Nebraska unorganized, the people unprotected, and the Indian barrier in existence, until the swelling tide of emigration should burst through, and accomplish by violence what it is the part of wisdom and statesmanship to direct and regulate by law. . .
>
> How long could you maintain that Indian barrier, and restrain the onward march of civilization, Christianity, and free government by a barbarian wall? Do you suppose that you could keep that vast country a howling wilderness in all time to come, roamed over by hostile savages, cutting off all safe communication between our Atlantic and Pacific possessions? . . .
>
> You must decide upon what principles the territories shall be organized; in other words, whether the people shall be allowed to regulate their domestic institutions in their own way, according to the provisions of this bill, or whether the opposite doctrine of Congressional interference is to prevail. . . The Missouri Compromise was interference; the Compromise of 1850 was non-interference. . . The Committee on Territories were compelled to act on this subject. I, as their chairman, was bound to meet the question. I choose to take the responsibility, regardless of consequences personal to myself. . . We were compelled to take our position upon the doctrine either of intervention or non-intervention. We chose the latter. . . The principle was right, and it was the principle adopted in 1850, to which the two great political parties of the country were solemnly pledged. . .
>
> When the people of the North shall all be rallied under one banner, and the whole South marshaled under an-

other banner, and each section excited to frenzy and madness
by hostility to the institutions of the other, then the patriot
may well tremble for the perpetuity of the Union. Withdraw
the slavery question from the political arena, and remove it
to the states and territories, each to decide for itself, such a
catastrophe can never happen.[34]

In closing his speech he appealed to both North and South
to support his cherished doctrine and envisioned its final acceptance by both sections:

Now, I wish to say to our southern friends, that if they desire to see this great principle carried out, now is their time to
rally around it, to cherish it, preserve it, make it the rule of
action in all future time. If they fail to do it now, and thereby
allow the doctrine of interference to prevail, upon their
heads the consequence of that interference must rest. To our
northern friends, on the other hand, I desire to say, that from
this day henceforward, they must rebuke the slander which
has been uttered against the South, that they desire to legislate slavery into the territories. . . I say frankly that, in my
opinion, this measure will be as popular at the North as at
the South, when its provisions and principles shall have been
fully developed and become well understood.[35]

The course of events revealed Douglas to be a poor prophet.
Not only did the Kansas-Nebraska Act prove unpopular in the
North, but after the Dred Scott decision it was rejected by the
South. The slaveholders became thoroughly disenchanted with
Douglas' popular sovereignty and with non-interference of the
federal government with slavery. They wanted assured protec-
tion of their human property and began to demand that Con-
gress enact a slave code for the territories.

CHICAGO DEBACLE

In spite of unmistakable evidences of their hostility toward
the Kansas-Nebraska Act, Douglas was confident that he could
convince the people of the North of its soundness. He had
already forced the support of the Illinois legislature. Of the
seventy Democrats in that body, only three had originally been
in favor of the bill. But on instructions from Douglas, their
party boss, that backing it was a party necessity, all swallowed
their repugnance, did an about-face, and voted resolutions

endorsing it. Only John M. Palmer, Norman B. Judd and Burton C. Cook refused to go along. These diehards subsequently aided in the formation of the Republican Party in Illinois.

Douglas' confidence was expressed in a speech before the Union Democratic Club of New York in June: "I hear men now say that they are willing to acquiesce in it. . . . It is not sufficient that they shall not seek to disturb Nebraska and Kansas, but they must acquiesce also in the principle."[36] After the adjournment of Congress he proceeded to Chicago to face his constituents. All along the way he met with abuse. In many places he was burned in effigy. In one Ohio village he was presented with thirty pieces of silver in token of his "Judas" role.

Chicago prepared to receive him on Saturday, September 1. That night, it had been announced, he would address the people. In the afternoon, flags began to appear at half-mast on buildings and boats, and church bells tolled in sign of mourning. Early in the evening crowds began to gather in the square. By eight o'clock the mob was estimated to number between 5,000 and 8,000 persons.

When Douglas rose to speak, he was greeted by an ominous silence. Then boos, hisses and catcalls began to drown him out. For almost four hours he was heckled. Try as he would, he could not get the crowd to listen to him. His temper grew short, while that of the crowd grew ugly. Finally, he was forced to admit defeat. He pulled his watch from his pocket, looked at it under the gaslight, and taking advantage of a momentary lull, bellowed: "Abolitionists of Chicago! It is now Sunday morning. I'll go to church, and you may go to Hell."[37] It was a debacle as complete as had been his triumph four years before.

Douglas' prospects for the presidential nomination appeared shattered. Not only that. The wave of anti-Nebraska sentiment was such that the loss by his follower and colleague, James Shields, of his seat in the United States Senate to Lyman Trumbull presaged difficulty in the matter of his own reelection in 1858. Not even an intensive speaking tour throughout the state, in which he crossed swords with Lincoln on several occasions, could reverse the swell of anger and indignation against him. The omens were indeed bad, because two years later another close friend and supporter, Congressman William A. Richardson, who had helped push the Nebraska Bill through the House of Representatives, was defeated for Governor by William Bissell, the candidate of the newly born Republican Party.

Shortly after the presidential election of 1856, Washington buzzed with the exciting news of Douglas' impending marriage to Adele Cutts. Miss Cutts, twenty-two years younger than the Senator, was the acknowledged belle of the capital. Though her father was an obscure government clerk, she came of distinguished lineage, being the great-niece of Dolly Madison. The wedding, which took place on Thanksgiving Day, was the talk of society. The nation's most powerful Senator was united with the city's most beautiful woman.

The second Mrs. Douglas was genuinely admired and highly regarded by both sexes. She was as charming and gracious as she was beautiful. It was no wonder that with such a personality she should cause the Republicans to complain in 1858 that her tour of the state with Douglas during the senatorial campaign was devastating to Lincoln's chances. She was the Little Giant's "secret weapon."

Events continued to move rapidly for Douglas. Within a few months came the bombshell of the Dred Scott decision. The northern Democrats were troubled. What became of popular sovereignty if, according to the decision, settlers had no right to exclude slavery from a territory? Three years before, in Democratic caucus over the Kansas-Nebraska bill, Douglas had pledged to let the Supreme Court decide the fate of slavery and to abide by the decision. How could he now stand by the Supreme Court and at the same time defend popular sovereignty?

But Douglas was equal to the occasion. With adroit political skill he tried to reconcile both. On June 12, 1857, he presented his views to the electorate in a speech at Springfield. These were the views he would carry into the debates with Lincoln the following year. First he upheld the court:

> Whoever resists the final decision of the highest judicial
> tribunal, aims a deadly blow to our whole republican system
> of government — a blow which, if successful, would place all
> our rights and liberties at the mercy of passion, anarchy and
> violence. I repeat, therefore, that if resistance to the decisions
> of the Supreme Court of the United States, in a matter like
> the points decided in the Dred Scott case . . . shall be forced

upon the country as a political issue, it will become a distinct and naked issue between the friends and the enemies of the Constitution. . .[38]

Then he showed how the court's decision and popular sovereignty were compatible:

The Missouri Compromise Act was unconstitutional and void before it was repealed by the Nebraska Act, and consequently did not and could not have the legal effect of extinguishing a master's right to his slave in that territory. While the right continues in full force under the guaranty of the Constitution, and cannot be divested or alienated by an act of Congress, it necessarily remains a barren and worthless right, unless sustained, protected and enforced by appropriate police regulations and local legislation, prescribing adequate remedies for its violation. These regulations and remedies must necessarily depend entirely upon the will and wishes of the people of the territory, as they can only be prescribed by the local legislatures. Hence the great principle of popular sovereignty and self-government is sustained and firmly established by the authority of this decision.[39]

Lincoln and the Republicans were quick to see the incompatibility. What Douglas was advocating in effect was nullification of the Dred Scott decision by local option. The full extent of Douglas' heresy would be exploited in the joint debates the following year when Lincoln was to frame his famous interrogatory at Freeport to make sure that the true significance of Douglas' stand would not be lost on the South. Because of it he was to forfeit southern support for the presidential nomination in 1860 and, as the candidate of the northern wing of the disrupted Democratic Party, to lose the presidency itself to Lincoln.

Further on in his speech Douglas justified the reasons for the court's decision. Here he entered moral ground, and also the *raison d'être* of the Union — ground on which Lincoln was to grapple with him to a finish:

We are told . . . that that decision is cruel — is inhuman and infamous, and should neither be respected nor obeyed. What is the objection to that decision? Simply that the negro is not a citizen. What is the object of making him a citizen? Of course to give him the rights, privileges and immunities of a citizen, it being the great fundamental law in our Government, that under the law, citizens are equal in their rights and privileges. . .

I submit to you, fellow citizens, whether any man can pronounce the decision inhuman and infamous, without resorting to that great principle, which, carried out, puts the negro on an equality with other citizens. . . For instance, did you ever hear any of them make a public speech in which he did not quote the Declaration of Independence, that "we hold all men are born free and equal," and then appeal to you to know whether slavery could be justified or palliated by any man who believed in the Declaration of Independence? Do they not argue that by this instrument negroes were declared to be born equal to white men; and hence, any man who is opposed to carrying out that great principle of theirs, of negro equality with the white man, is opposed to the Declaration of Independence?

Passing from that to the formation of the Constitution of the United States, you will find that instrument was framed, and adopted, and put into operation with the immortal Washington at the head, by twelve slaveholding States and one free State, or one State about to become free. In view of these facts, I submit to you whether any man can assert that the founders of our institutions intended to put the negro and the white man on an equality in the system of government which they adopted? If the signers of the Declaration had intended to declare the negro equal to the white man, would not they, on that very day, have abolished slavery in every one of the States of the Union in order to have conformed with that Declaration? . . . But no vindication is needed from me of those immortal men who drafted, and signed, and proclaimed to the world the Declaration of Independence. They did what they professed. They had reference to the white man, and to him only, when they declared all men were created equal.

They were in a struggle with Great Britain. The principle they were asserting was that a British subject, born on American soil was equal to a British subject born in England — that a British subject here was entitled to all the rights, and privileges, and immunities, under the British Constitution, that a British subject in England enjoyed; that their rights were inalienable, and hence that Parliament, whose power was omnipotent, had no power to alienate them.

They did not mean the negroes and Indians — they did

not say we white men and negroes were born equal; but they were speaking of the race of people who colonized America, who ruled America, and who were declaring the liberties of Americans, when they proclaimed the self-evident truth that those men were born free and equal. . .

At that day the negro was looked upon as being of an inferior race. All history had proved that in no part of the world, or of the world's history, had the negro ever shown himself capable of self-government, and it was not the intention of the founders of the Government to violate the great law of God, which made the distinction between the white and the black man. . .

The Supreme Court of the United States have decided that, under the Constitution, a negro is not and cannot be a citizen. The Republican Abolition party pronounce that decision cruel, inhuman and infamous, and appeal to the American people to disregard and refuse to obey it. Let us join issue with them, and put ourselves upon the country for trial.[40]

Two weeks later Lincoln replied to the speech, in a prelude to their debates of the following year.

ANTI-LECOMPTON HERO

The uproar over the Dred Scott decision was soon followed by the crisis over the Lecompton Constitution. Previously Douglas had supported the Administration's partisan policy in Kansas. Now he was forced to the wall. Would he continue to support the party or would he stand by his doctrine of popular sovereignty? He faced the choice of disgrace in Washington or the loss of his constituency in Illinois.

With his own reelection to the Senate at stake, he decided to sustain himself at home. In December 1857 he made his sensational speech in the Senate against the Lecompton Constitution and precipitated the irrevocable break with the Administration. It was in the course of this speech that he made the famous statement which has since been associated with his name and which was to plague him in the future debates with Lincoln: "It is none of my business which way the slavery clause is decided. I care not whether it is voted down or voted up. . . ."

In the course of the Lecompton debate questions embarrassing to the Little Giant were raised over the ill-fated Toombs Bill of June 1856. Numerous charges and countercharges flew back and forth across the Senate floor. It was brought out that a Democratic caucus held in Douglas' home had decided to sponsor the bill as a party measure, and that the bill originally contained a provision for ratification of a constitution by the people of Kansas. However, when the Committee on Territories finally reported the bill, the provision for ratification was missing.

Senator Bigler, of Pennsylvania, one of the Administration stalwarts, disclosed what had happened in committee:

> It was held, by those most intelligent on the subject, that in view of all the difficulties surrounding that Territory, (and) the danger of any experiment at that time of a popular vote, it would be better that there should be no such provision in the Toombs Bill; and it was my understanding, in all the discourse I had, that that convention would make a constitution and send it here without submitting it to the popular vote.[41]

Enraged at the innuendo that he had obviously been among those who had agreed to exclude the referendum, Douglas called upon Bigler to assert whether he had ever been "privately or publicly, in my own house or any other, in favor of a constitution without its being submitted to the people?"[42] To this inquiry Bigler answered in the negative. Despite Bigler's denial, it was unclear how the "submission" provision of the Toombs Bill had been eliminated without Douglas' knowledge.

In support of Douglas' position, however, the record showed that when the bill containing the new provision specifically excluding ratification by the people reached the floor of the Senate, the Little Giant had moved to strike it out, and that his motion had carried. This left the bill without any provision for or against submission to a referendum. According to Douglas, the bill was thus in the same category as all previous bills for the admission of new territories, none of which carried a specific provision for ratification. He declared that approval of a constitution by the people was a fair construction to be placed on this bill as was the case in previous bills.

Nevertheless, the fact remained that Douglas, as chairman of the Committee on Territories, had submitted the Toombs

Bill to the Senate with its original provision for popular ratification of a constitution omitted. On this point Lincoln subjected the Little Giant to withering attack at the Charleston debate.

But to the people of Illinois, these incidents were remote and unimportant. Thrilled by his fight against the Lecompton Constitution, they restored Douglas to the hero's pedestal which he had formerly occupied. When he returned to Illinois in July 1858 to face the opposition of Lincoln and of the Administration's henchmen, the champion of popular sovereignty met a tumultuous reception.

The Little Giant was now ready for the toughest battle of his career. As he made his preparations for the Senate campaign, Illinois stirred with excitement at the prospect of the greatest political contest in its history.

CHAPTER 3

"There Is Not Much of Me": Abraham Lincoln

If there had been no slavery issue, Abraham Lincoln would not have become President of the United States. He would not have debated with Douglas and thus attracted the national attention which subsequently won him the nomination. He would have been just another country lawyer and frustrated politician, unknown to history.

Those who see the hand of Providence in the affairs of men have ample justification for regarding Lincoln as "the instrument of God," chosen to destroy slavery and to give the Union "a new birth of freedom." For years on the remote prairies of Illinois he pondered the riddle of slavery, and at the right moment he emerged from obscurity to play his role.

This is the central fact of his story. All other facets of his life take their meaning from it. Yet so fascinated have men been by this story, that every circumstance of his life — no matter how insignificant or trivial — has been investigated. The hunger to know as much as possible about him seems insatiable. It is probably true that more has been written about Abraham Lincoln than any other man.

The purpose of this brief biography is to sketch only those phases of his life which have some bearing on the Negro problem, or which aid in a better understanding of the debates. Lincoln's own words will form the basis of the narrative.

Lincoln wrote two short autobiographies. The first he did in

December 1859, more than a year after the debates, at the solicitation of Jesse W. Fell, an old friend and associate, for the purpose of furthering his presidential possibilities. Apologetically, he wrote to Fell: "There is not much of it, for the reason, I suppose, that there is not much of me."[1]

In June 1860, shortly after his nomination for the presidency, Lincoln wrote the other autobiography, this time in the third person, for John L. Scripps, who was to prepare a campaign biography. This was considerably more lengthy, and contained many items which Lincoln considered would be of interest to the public. It is from this account that extracts are taken to serve as pegs for our story.

Lincoln begins his autobiography by telling of his birth in Kentucky, and how, when he was eight years old, his father moved the family to Indiana. *This removal was partly on account of slavery.**

In this reference to slavery we find a statement of what must have been among Lincoln's earliest reactions to this problem. The poorer non-slaveholding farmers in the slave states found the atmosphere of slavery uncongenial to their labors and social status. They were looked down upon by the slaveholders. Those who had ambition and drive usually emigrated to areas where they were treated as social equals and where there were unlimited opportunities for improvement of their economic position. It was from personal experience, therefore, that, in his speech at Peoria, Illinois in October 1854, attacking the Kansas-Nebraska Act and popular sovereignty, Lincoln said:

> Whether slavery shall go into Nebraska, or other new territories, is not a matter of exclusive concern to the people who may go there. The whole nation is interested that the best use shall be made of these territories. We want them for the homes of free white people. This they cannot be, to any considerable extent, if slavery shall be planted within them. Slave States are places for poor white people to remove FROM: not to remove TO. New free States are the places for poor people to go to and better their condition. For this use, the nation needs these territories.[2]

*Lincoln's own words appear in italics. All quotations from this campaign autobiography are found in Roy P. Basler, ed., *The Collected Works of Abraham Lincoln* IV, 60-67.

When Lincoln was nineteen, he made his first trip on a flat-boat to New Orleans with a cargo. He and another man were the sole crew. *One night they were attacked by seven negroes* [along the sugar coast] *with intent to kill and rob them. They were hurt some in the melee, but succeeded in driving the negroes from the boat.*

This was the first of Lincoln's two experiences conveying a flatboat down the Mississippi River. His objective recital of it indicates that his encounter with the Negroes did not affect his attitude toward them adversely. He probably considered it one of the hazards of the trip.

EGYPT

In March 1830 the Lincoln family *left the old homestead in Indiana and came to Illinois.* The following winter was the *winter of the very celebrated "deep snow."*

The "winter of the deep snow" was engraved into the memories of the early settlers of northern and central Illinois. To preserve their own lives and the lives of their cattle, they organized caravans of eight to ten wagons to go to Cairo in the southern part of the state to purchase grain and seed. "We are the sons of Jacob going to Egypt to buy corn," they said.[3]

For this reason the lower part of Illinois was thereafter known as Egypt. It was aptly named. Cairo was situated in the fertile delta where the Ohio River met the Mississippi. Nearby were two settlements named Karnak and Thebes. In addition to the fact that the second debate was held in that area, Egypt was to be mentioned frequently in the course of the debates.

Lincoln made a second trip to New Orleans in 1831, starting from Sangamon County, where he was to spend the early years of his manhood. There is no doubt that Lincoln saw enough of slavery in New Orleans, including the wretched slave pens with their recently smuggled Negroes, to leave an indelible impress on his mind.

On his return from New Orleans, Lincoln settled in New Salem in Sangamon County. In 1832 the Black Hawk War broke out. Lincoln fondly recalls the experience: *Abraham joined a volunteer company and, to his own surprise, was elected captain of it. He says he has not since had any success in life which gave him so much satisfaction.*

It is interesting to note that, despite his satisfaction, Lincoln never used the title of captain. This is especially striking because, as Nicolay and Hay point out, this was a country "where military titles were conferred with ludicrous profusion, and borne with absurd complacency."[4]

It was in the course of his service in the Black Hawk War that Lincoln made friends with Major John T. Stuart who became Lincoln's first law partner. Stuart was impressed with Lincoln's personality, for it was his popularity with the men that led to his election as captain.

Returning from the campaign, Lincoln was without funds or work. *Strangely enough, a man offered to sell, and did sell, to Abraham and another as poor as himself, an old stock of goods upon credit. They opened as merchants. . . They did nothing but get deeper and deeper in debt. . . The store winked out.*

However, the surveyor of Sangamon County came to his rescue *and offered to depute to Abraham [a] portion of his work. . . He accepted, procured a compass and chain, and went at it. This . . . kept body and soul together.*

Stores in pioneer communities sold all kinds of groceries. They also sold liquor in bulk for consumption off the premises. If a tavern license was obtained, liquor could be sold by the drink for consumption on the premises. As a result, a kind of opprobrium was attached to the term "grocery."

It seems that the store owned by Lincoln and his partner had such a license. But Lincoln himself, contrary to the habits of the frontier, was a teetotaler, and opposed individual drinking on the premises. This was undoubtedly one of the reasons why the partnership soon dissolved and the store "winked out."

In the first of the debates at Ottawa, Douglas twitted Lincoln for having been a "flourishing grocery-keeper," and hit below the belt by accusing him of being able to "ruin more liquor than all the boys of the town together." Lincoln made a humorous rejoinder to this charge.

At Freeport, the scene of the next debate, he also told a humorous surveying story, which had particular point for the crowd, because they knew that Old Abe had once been a surveyor. The surveyor of Sangamon County referred to in the autobiography was none other than John Calhoun, who later turned up as the leader of the pro-slavery forces in Kansas.

Lincoln's popularity in New Salem was reflected in his election to the legislature in 1834 *by the highest vote cast for any candidate,* as he proudly states. Major Stuart was also elected, and during the canvass he encouraged Lincoln to study law.

After the election, reads the autobiography, *he borrowed books of Stuart, took them home with him, and went at it in good earnest.* Lincoln was reelected in 1836, 1838 and 1840. He obtained his law license in 1836 and in 1837 removed to Springfield to practice, *his old friend Stuart taking him into partnership.*

Lincoln ran for office as a Whig. In forming a partnership with Stuart, he became associated with one of the most prominent Whig politicians in Illinois. One incident in the campaign for reelection in 1836 is worthy of notice. Lincoln wrote a letter to the *Sangamo Journal* setting forth his political views, in which he said in part: "I go for all sharing the privileges of the government, who assist in bearing its burthens. Consequently I go for admitting all whites to the right of suffrage, who pay taxes or bear arms (by no means excluding females)."[5] In this statement he was echoing the provision of the Illinois Constitution which permitted all white males of six months residence to vote, thus excluding free Negroes. The statement is of interest in showing that Lincoln shared the general northern attitude on civil rights for the Negro. Yet on woman suffrage he was siding with the radicals of the time.

While he was serving in the legislature, he was instrumental in having the capital removed from Vandalia to Springfield in Sangamon County, his home county. It was a good indication of his talents as a politician.

Lincoln was a great admirer of Henry Clay, the Whig, just as Douglas was of Andrew Jackson, the Democrat. Clay's attitude toward slavery had a deep influence on Lincoln's thinking.

Like Jefferson, Clay was a paradox. He condemned slavery, and twice was in the forefront of attempts to abolish it in Kentucky, the first time in 1799 as a young man, and the second toward the close of his life in 1849. In the fifty years between he helped found the American Colonization Society. Yet during his lifetime he manumitted only seven of the more than fifty slaves he had acquired.

In a eulogy delivered in the State House at Springfield

shortly after Clay's death in 1852, Lincoln summarized the Great Pacificator's position on slavery:

> He ever was on principle and in feeling, opposed to slavery. The very earliest, and one of the latest public efforts of his life . . . were . . . made in favor of gradual emancipation of the slave in Kentucky.
>
> He did not perceive, that on a question of human right, the negroes were to be excepted from the human race. And yet Mr. Clay was the owner of slaves. Cast into life where slavery was already widely spread and deeply seated, he did not perceive, as I think no wise man has perceived, how it could be at once eradicated, without producing a greater evil, even to the cause of human liberty itself. His feeling and his judgment, therefore, ever led him to oppose both extremes of opinion on the subject.[6]

This was Lincoln's own view as stated in his Peoria speech two years later:

> If all earthly power were given me, I should not know what to do, as to the existing institution. My first impulse would be to free all the slaves, and send them to Liberia. . . But a moment's reflection would convince me . . . that its sudden execution is impossible.[7]

This opposition to radical solutions, despite the strong aversion to slavery, was not the only similarity in the thinking of the two men. Lincoln reflected another Clay concept in his belief that new territories should be free. Clay had once said:

> I look upon it as a great evil; and deeply lament that we have derived it . . . from our ancestors. . . If a state of nature existed and we were about to lay the foundations of society, no man would be more strongly opposed than I should be, to incorporating the institution of slavery among its elements.[8]

It was in the newly acquired territories that the foundations of society could be started anew, and for that reason should be untouched by slavery. Though to Lincoln, as to Clay, the problem might be too difficult and too complex for solution where slavery already existed, hope for the future lay in the virgin areas annexed by the nation.

Just as Clay was a member of the American Colonization

Society, so was Lincoln a member of the Illinois Colonization
Society. In 1827, in a speech to his society, Clay spoke of the
purpose of colonization:

> There is a moral fitness in the idea of returning to Africa
> her children, whose ancestors have been torn from her by the
> ruthless hand of fraud and violence. Transplanted in a for-
> eign land, they will carry back to their native soil the rich
> fruits of religion, civilization, law and liberty . . . to trans-
> form an original crime, into a signal blessing to that most
> unfortunate portion of the globe.[9]

In his eulogy on Clay, Lincoln echoed this thought:

> If as the friends of colonization hope, the present and com-
> ing generations of our countrymen shall by any means, suc-
> ceed in freeing our land from the dangerous presence of
> slavery; and, at the same time, in restoring the captive people
> to their long-lost father-land, with bright prospects for the
> future; and this too, so gradually, that neither races nor in-
> dividuals shall have suffered by the change, it will indeed be
> a glorious consummation.[10]

Clay's oratory, too, made a profound impression on Lincoln.
He frequently quoted from Clay's eloquent denunciations of
slavery, especially when addressing Whig audiences in the debates with Douglas. There is no doubt that Clay's lofty sentiments inspired some of Lincoln's finest oratorical efforts.

Two passages which he was fond of quoting came from Clay's
1827 speech before the American Colonization Society:

> We are reproached with doing mischief by the agitation
> of this question. . . What would they, who thus reproach
> us, have done? If they would repress all tendencies towards
> liberty, and ultimate emancipation, they must do more than
> put down the benevolent efforts of this society. They must
> go back to the era of our liberty and independence, and
> muzzle the cannon which thunders its annual joyous return.
> . . . They must blow out the moral lights around us, and
> extinguish that greatest torch of all which America presents
> to a benighted world — pointing the way to their rights, their
> liberties, and their happiness.
> And when they have achieved those purposes their work
> will be yet incomplete. They must penetrate the human soul,
> and eradicate the light of reason and the love of liberty.

Then and not till then, when universal darkness and despair prevail, can you perpetuate slavery, and repress all sympathy, and all humane, and benevolent efforts among free men, in behalf of the unhappy portion of our race doomed to bondage.[11]

Mild and conservative as Lincoln's views were, they nevertheless ran counter to the general feeling in Illinois in the 1830's. Public hostility to the abolitionist movement was reflected in the legislature.

This body had received memorials from the states of Virginia, Alabama, Mississippi, New York and Connecticut in opposition to the abolitionists, and had responded by drawing up resolutions declaring its disapproval of the formation of abolition societies, its agreement that the right of property in slaves was sacred to the slaveholding states, and its belief that the general government could not abolish slavery in the District of Columbia against the consent of its citizens.

Lincoln, in association with another member, drew up a protest against these resolutions in March 1837, as he proudly stated in his autobiography, but although it was inoffensively worded, no other members had the courage to sign it. Because it is an early expression of Lincoln's independent views, it is worth quoting:

Resolutions upon the subject of domestic slavery having passed both branches of the General Assembly at its present session, the undersigned hereby protest against the passage of the same.

They believe that the institution of slavery is founded on both injustice and bad policy, but that the promulgation of Abolition doctrines tends rather to increase than abate its evils.

They believe that the Congress of the United States has no power under the Constitution to interfere with the institution of slavery in the different States.

They believe that the Congress of the United States has the power, under the Constitution to abolish slavery in the District of Columbia, but that the power ought not to be exercised unless at the request of the people of the District.

Dan Stone
A. Lincoln
Representatives from the County of Sangamon.[12]

Lincoln could be deservedly proud of his protest, because the temper of the populace was turning ugly. In a few short months a mob was to murder abolitionist Elijah Lovejoy at Alton and throw his printing press into the Mississippi River.

Eleven years later, when in Congress, Lincoln did introduce a bill to abolish slavery in the federal capital, but it was lost in the legislative maze. It remained for the Compromise of 1850 to do away with only the slave traffic in the District of Columbia.

Lovejoy's murder occurred in November 1837, and in January 1838 Lincoln again demonstrated his courage in standing up for his opinions. He was invited to give an address before the Young Men's Lyceum of Springfield. His topic was "The Perpetuation of Our Political Institutions," and he used the occasion to assail mob rule as dangerous to the orderly processes of government. The love for the Constitution and the laws, which he bore throughout his life, and which determined in many ways his solution of the slavery problem, is reflected in this speech. The position he would later take toward the Dred Scott decision is also foreshadowed here.

Though the oratory appears somewhat florid in places, the speech was restrained in comparison with the excesses to which the frontier communities were accustomed. A number of passages are marked by a simple eloquence which, having matured over the years, characterized his later style.

After pointing out that our ancestors left us a "goodly land" and a "political edifice of liberty and equal rights" he asked whence the dangers to this legacy might arise:

> I answer . . . it must spring up amongst us. It cannot come from abroad. If destruction be our lot, we must ourselves be its author and finisher. As a nation of freemen, we must live through all time, or die by suicide. . .
>
> There is, even now, something of ill-omen amongst us. I mean the increasing disregard for law which pervades the country; the growing disposition to substitute the wild and furious passions, in lieu of the sober judgment of Courts; and the worse than savage mobs, for the executive ministers of justice. . .
>
> By the operation of this mobocratic spirit, which all must admit, is now abroad in the land, the strongest bulwark of any Government, and particularly of those constituted like

ours, may effectually be broken down and destroyed — I mean
the attachment of the people. Whenever this effect shall be
produced among us; whenever the vicious portion of population shall be permitted to gather in bands of hundreds and
thousands, and burn churches, ravage and rob provision-
stores, throw printing presses into rivers, shoot editors, and
hang and burn obnoxious persons at pleasure, and with impunity; depend on it, this Government cannot last. . .

The question recurs, "How shall we fortify against it?"
The answer is simple. Let every American, every lover of
liberty, every well wisher to his posterity, swear by the
blood of the Revolution, never to violate in the least particular, the laws of the country; and never to tolerate their
violation by others. As the patriots of seventy-six did to the
support of the Declaration of Independence, so to the support of the Constitution and laws, let every American pledge
his life, his property, and his sacred honor; — let every man
remember that to violate the law is to trample on the blood
of his father, and to tear the charter of his own, and his
children's liberty.

Let reverence for the laws, be breathed by every American
mother, to the lisping babe that prattles on her lap — let it be
taught in schools, in seminaries, and in colleges; let it be
written in Primers, spelling books, and in almanacs; — let it
be preached from the pulpit, proclaimed in legislative halls,
and enforced in courts of justice. . . In short, let it become
the political religion of the nation.[13]

CONCLUSIONS ON SLAVERY

Thus, early in his career, the general outlines of Lincoln's
position on slavery were clear. Though his thinking matured
and deepened over the years, his position underwent no fundamental change. His views remained remarkably consistent,
and he carried them into the presidency. They may be summarized as follows:

1. Slavery was morally wrong.
2. The federal government had the right to act against slavery
   in territory under its jurisdiction. Therefore, slavery
   should not be extended to the territories.
3. Because of the restrictions of the Constitution, the federal
   government had no right to interfere with slavery in the
   states where it existed.

4. Because of the provision in the Constitution, the recovery of fugitive slaves would have to be enforced.
5. Abolitionism and violence were bad because they were destructive of the Constitution and of the rule of law.
6. The only legal way to get rid of slavery in the states where it existed was by gradual emancipation through compensation.
7. Free Negroes should be colonized outside of the United States.

At this point, let Lincoln himself through his third person autobiography take up the story:

In 1838 and 1840, Mr. Lincoln's party voted for him as Speaker, but being in the minority he was not elected. After 1840 he declined a reelection to the legislature. He was on the Harrison electoral ticket in 1840, and on that of Clay in 1844, and spent much time and labor in both these canvasses. In November, 1842, he was married to Mary, daughter of Robert S. Todd, of Lexington, Kentucky.

The early years in Springfield were busy and wonderful ones for Lincoln. He made many friends, the most intimate being Joshua F. Speed, who came from a slaveholding family in Louisville, Kentucky, and ran a large general store in Springfield. Another close friend was James Matheny, who subsequently was best man at his wedding to Mary Todd. As a law associate of Stuart and as a legislator, he also moved in influential circles, meeting the leading figures of the state, both Democratic and Whig, men like Orville H. Browning, John J. Hardin, Sidney Breese, William Bissel, Edward D. Baker, Richard Yates, Norman B. Judd, Archibald Williams, John Wentworth, Elihu Washburne, Simeon Francis, editor of the *Sangamo Journal,* Ninian W. Edwards, who became his brother-in-law, and, of course, Stephen A. Douglas. The fact that his party voted for him as Speaker of the legislative assembly is evidence of the high opinion in which he was held.

Lincoln's romance with Mary Todd began during the winter of 1839–40 and flowered into an engagement. Their marriage was set for January 1, 1841, but Lincoln got cold feet and the engagement was broken. He fell into a mood of deep depression, and in order to restore his mental health through a change of scene, Joshua Speed invited him to visit with his family in Louisville. Lincoln spent the latter part of August and early September in the hospitable Speed household, returning to Springfield in better spirits and with his perspective recovered.

His trip to Louisville was not without its effect on Lincoln's reaction to slavery. Shortly after his return he wrote a chatty letter to Speed's sister, Mary, in which he recounted an experience on board the riverboat taking him and her brother, Joshua, back to Illinois:

> A fine example was presented on board the boat for contemplating the effect of condition upon human happiness. A gentleman had purchased twelve negroes in different parts of Kentucky, and was taking them to a farm in the South. They were chained six and six together. A small iron clevis was around the left wrist of each, and this fastened to the main chain by a shorter one at a convenient distance from the others; so that the negroes were strung together precisely like so many fish upon a trot-line.
>
> In this condition, they were being separated forever from the scenes of their childhood, their friends, their fathers and mothers, and brothers and sisters, and many of them, from their wives and children, and going into perpetual slavery where the lash of the master is proverbially more ruthless and unrelenting than any other where; and yet amid all these distressing circumstances, as we would think them, they were the most cheerful and apparently happy creatures on board. One whose offence for which he had been sold was an over-fondness for his wife, played the fiddle almost continually; and the others danced, sung, cracked jokes, and played various games with cards from day to day. How true is it that "God tempers the wind to the shorn lamb," or in other words, that he renders the worst of human conditions tolerable, while he permits the best, to be nothing better than tolerable.[14]

The impression caused by this incident was obviously a very strong one, because fourteen years later Lincoln recalled it to his friend, Speed, in a letter:

> You suggest that in political action now, you and I would differ. I suppose we would; not quite as much, however, as you think. You know I dislike slavery; and you fully admit the abstract wrong of it. So far there is no cause of difference.

But you say that sooner than yield your legal right to the slave — especially at the bidding of those who are not themselves interested, you would see the Union dissolved.

I am not aware that any one is bidding you to yield that right; very certainly I am not. I leave that matter entirely to yourself. I also acknowledge your rights and my obligations under the Constitution, in regard to your slaves. I confess I hate to see the poor creatures hunted down, and caught, and carried back to their stripes, and unrewarded toils; but I bite my lip and keep quiet.

In 1841 you and I had together a tedious low-water trip, on a Steam Boat from Louisville to St. Louis. You may remember, as I well do, that from Louisville to the mouth of the Ohio, there were, on board, ten or a dozen slaves, shackled together with irons. That sight was a continued torment to me; and I see something like it every time I touch the Ohio, or any other slave-border. It is hardly fair for you to assume, that I have no interest in a thing which has, and continually exercises, the power of making me miserable. You ought rather to appreciate how much the great body of the Northern people do crucify their feelings, in order to maintain their loyalty to the Constitution and the Union.[15]

Lincoln, like Douglas, had married the daughter of a southern slaveholder. This, in addition to his previous contacts with slavery and the fact that he was southern-born, gave him an intimate knowledge of the southern point of view. He was, therefore, less prone to condemn, and more inclined to reason, which was not usually the case with northern anti-slavery men. He was patient and understanding, without excusing or indulging the southern position. His utterances thus possessed a sobering quality which had a more telling and lasting effect than effusive oratorical denunciations. In his speech at Peoria in 1854 against the Kansas-Nebraska Act, which has already been mentioned, he picked apart the southern arguments with calm, but withering analysis:

I think I have no prejudice against the Southern people. They are just what we would be in their situation. If slavery did not now exist amongst them, they would not introduce it. If it did now exist amongst us, we should not instantly give it up. — This I believe of the masses north and south. — Doubtless there are individuals on both sides, who would not hold slaves under any circumstances; and others who would gladly introduce slavery anew, if it were out of existence. We know that some southern men do free their slaves, go north, and become tip-top abolitionists; while some northern ones go south, and become most cruel slave-masters.

When southern people tell us they are no more responsible for the origin of slavery than we; I acknowledge the fact. When it is said that the institution exists, and that it is very difficult to get rid of it, in any satisfactory way, I can understand and appreciate the saying. I surely will not blame them for not doing what I should not know how to do myself. If all earthly power were given me, I should not know what to do, as to the existing institution.

My first impulse would be to free all the slaves, and send them to Liberia, — to their own native land. But a moment's reflection would convince me, that whatever of high hope . . . there may be in this, in the long run, its sudden execution is impossible. If they were all landed there in a day, they would all perish in the next ten days; and there are not surplus shipping and surplus money enough in the world to carry them there in many times ten days.

What then? Free them all, and keep them among us as underlings? Is it quite certain that this betters their condition? I think I would not hold one in slavery, at any rate; yet the point is not clear enough to me to denounce people upon. What next? — Free them, and make them politically and socially our equals? My own feelings will not admit of this; and if mine would, we well know that those of the great mass of white people will not. Whether this feeling accords with justice and sound judgment, is not the sole question, if indeed, it is any part of it. A universal feeling, whether well or ill-founded, cannot be safely disregarded. We cannot, then, make them equals. It does seem to me that systems of gradual emancipation might be adopted; but for their tardiness in this, I will not undertake to judge our brethren of the south.

When they remind us of their constitutional rights, I acknowledge them, not grudgingly, but fully, and fairly; and I would give them any legislation for the reclaiming of their fugitives, which should not, in its stringency, be more likely to carry a free man into slavery, than our ordinary criminal laws are to hang an innocent one. . .

Equal justice to the South, it is said, requires us to consent to the extending of slavery to new countries. That is to say, inasmuch as you do not object to my taking my hog to Nebraska, therefore I must not object to you taking your

slave. Now, I admit this is perfectly logical, if there is no difference between hogs and negroes. But while you thus require me to deny the humanity of the negro, I wish to ask
whether you of the south yourselves, have ever been willing
to do as much? . .

In 1820 you joined the north, almost unanimously, in declaring the African slave trade piracy, and in annexing to it
the punishment of death. Why did you do this? If you did
not feel that it was wrong, why did you join in providing
that men should be hung for it? The practice was no more
than bringing wild negroes from Africa, to sell to such as
would buy them. But you never thought of hanging men for
catching and selling wild horses, wild buffaloes or wild bears.

Again, you have amongst you, a sneaking individual . . .
known as the "SLAVE-DEALER." He watches your necessi-
ties, and crawls up to buy your slave, at a speculating price.
If you cannot help it, you sell to him; but if you can help it,
you drive him from your door. You despise him utterly. You
do not recognize him as a friend, or even as an honest man.
Your children must not play with his; they may rollick freely
with the little negroes, but not with the "slave-dealer's" children. If you are obliged to deal with him, you try to get
through the job without so much as touching him. It is
common with you to join hands with the men you meet; but
with the slave-dealer you avoid the ceremony—instinctively
shrinking from the snaky contact. If he grows rich and retires
from business, you still remember him, and still keep up the
ban of non-intercourse upon him and his family. Now why
is this? You do not so treat the man who deals in corn, cattle
or tobacco.

And yet again, there are in the United States and territories, including the District of Columbia, 433,643 free
blacks. At $500 per head they are worth over two hundred
millions of dollars. How comes this vast amount of property
to be running about without owners? We do not see free
horses or free cattle running at large. How is this? All these
free blacks are the descendants of slaves, or have been slaves
themselves, and they would be slaves now, but for SOME-
THING which has operated on their white owners, inducing
them, at vast pecuniary sacrifices, to liberate them. What is
that SOMETHING? Is there any mistaking it? In all these
cases it is your sense of justice, and human sympathy, continually telling you, that the poor negro has some natural right

to himself—that those who deny it, and make mere merchandise of him, deserve kickings, contempt, and death.

And now, why will you ask us to deny the humanity of the slave? And estimate him only as the equal of the hog? Why ask us to do what you will not do yourselves? Why ask us to do for nothing, what two hundred million dollars could not induce you to do?[16]

BILLY HERNDON, JUNIOR LAW PARTNER

Even though Lincoln refused reelection to the legislature, he still remained prominent in politics. He was ambitious for a seat in Congress. In April 1841 his partnership with Stuart was dissolved, and shortly thereafter he formed a new partnership with Judge Stephen T. Logan, who was recognized as one of the finest and most successful lawyers in the state. In Lincoln's first two law associations, he was the junior partner, whose political ambitions had to defer to the interests of the senior. Stuart was more politician than lawyer and was elected to Congress shortly before the Lincoln partnership was dissolved. Logan was exact and methodical and demanded scrupulous attention to the details of legal practice. The Logan partnership lasted until the autumn of 1844, when it, too, was dissolved. Lincoln then entered into a third partnership, with William H. Herndon, which lasted until his death.

In the association with Billy Herndon, Lincoln was the senior partner. It was an ideal relationship for both. Billy was a worshipper of Lincoln. He was content to take care of the office end of the partnership, and he had no personal political ambitions. He was completely devoted to Lincoln's interests and to promoting his political advancement. Competent, and pleasing in manner, he had a "hail-fellow-well-met" personality, and could hold his liquor with the best of the hard-drinking frontier folk. These qualities were an asset in politics.

Herndon was a Whig, but though maintaining his membership in the Whig Party, he was also an abolitionist, engaging in constant correspondence with the leading lights of the movement, such as Theodore Parker, Sumner, Greeley, Phillips and Garrison. He bought all the literature dealing with slavery that he could lay his hands on, both abolitionist and southern. Lincoln read the literature and discussed it with Herndon.

In his biography of Lincoln, Herndon writes that he was never conscious of having made an impression on his partner as a result of their discussions. He thought Lincoln too conservative, while the latter considered Billy "too rampant and spontaneous."[17] For all that, when the Republican Party was being organized in Illinois in 1854, Herndon himself steered Lincoln away from affiliating with it, because as he put it, "Strong as I was in the faith, yet I doubted the propriety of Lincoln's taking any stand yet. As I viewed it . . . it would not do for him to occupy at that time such advanced ground as we were taking."[18] Lincoln was indeed fortunate in having such an astute political adviser. Within two years, when the time was ripe, he did join the Republican Party.

In the summer of 1841, shortly after he had formed the partnership with Logan, Lincoln argued the first of two cases in his career involving claims to slaves. A Negro girl named Nance had been sold by one Cromwell to Bailey for a promissory note. Cromwell tried to collect on the note, and Bailey hired Lincoln to represent him on the appeal to the Supreme Court. Lincoln argued that a person domiciled in free Illinois could not be the subject of sale and that, therefore, the note was illegal. Judge Sidney Breese, who presided, agreed with this position, and rendered the decision in favor of Lincoln's client.

As a staunch Whig, Lincoln was sorely disappointed by the defeat of Henry Clay for the presidency in 1844. He expressed his bitterness at the role of the "Liberty" men in bringing this about in a letter to Williamson Durley in October 1845. Durley, a Whig himself, had nevertheless voted with the Liberty Party. In the letter, Lincoln defined his position toward the extension of slavery:

> If the Whig abolitionists of New York had voted with us last fall, Mr. Clay would now be President, Whig principles in the ascendant, and Texas not annexed; whereas by the division, all that either had at stake in the contest, was lost. . .
>
> I think annexation an evil. I hold it to be a paramount duty of us in the free states . . . to let the slavery of the other states alone; while, on the other hand, I hold it to be equally clear, that we should never knowingly lend ourselves directly

or indirectly, to prevent that slavery from dying a natural death—to find new places for it to live in, when it can no longer exist in the old.[19]

In 1846 he was elected to the lower House of Congress, and served one term only, commencing in December, 1847, and ending with the inauguration of General Taylor, in March 1849. Mr. Lincoln was not a candidate for reelection. This was determined upon and declared before he went to Washington, in accordance with an understanding among Whig friends, by which Colonel Hardin and Colonel Baker had each previously served a single term in this same district.

In 1848, during his term in Congress, he advocated General Taylor's nomination for the presidency, in opposition to all others, and also took an active part for his election after his nomination, speaking a few times in Maryland, near Washington, several times in Massachusetts, and canvassing quite fully his own district in Illinois, which was followed by a majority in the district of over 1,500 for General Taylor.

Shortly before he took his seat in Congress, Lincoln was involved in his second slave case, but this time he was on the other side of the fence. He was retained as one of counsel in behalf of Robert Matson of Kentucky who brought his slaves seasonally to a farm he owned in Illinois in order to gather the crops, and then returned them to Kentucky. A family of his slaves, who learned that they might be sold down the river on their return, took refuge with sympathetic whites, and Matson tried to get them back.

Lincoln was also approached to represent the slaves, which he indicated he would have liked to do, but he had already committed himself to Matson's attorneys, and it was too late. It appears that his heart was not in the case, however,[20] because in his argument he himself raised the question on which the case hinged: Were the slaves in transitu, that is, passing through the state, or were they domiciled by consent of their owner, even for an indefinite period? In the former event, they kept their status as slaves, but in the latter event, they were emancipated. The court decided that the latter was the situation, and ordered the slaves freed. Matson hurriedly left the state and Lincoln never got his fee. One of the lawyers who defended the Negroes was Orlando B. Ficklin, a Democrat, who was to be a colleague of Lincoln in Congress and also to figure in a diverting incident in the Charleston debate.

Lincoln was the only Whig Congressman from Illinois. The congressional district, in which Sangamon County and the city of Springfield were located, was the only district where a Whig had a chance for election to Congress. So it was "turnabout is fair play" for the aspirants, and this time it was Lincoln's turn. He was, therefore, regarded in Washington as the head of the party in Illinois, just as Stephen A. Douglas in the Senate was regarded as the chief of the Democrats.

Serving in the House at the same time were Joshua Giddings of Ohio, the abolitionist; Democrats Andrew Johnson of Tennessee, who was later to become Lincoln's Vice-President; David Wilmot of Pennsylvania; former President, John Quincy Adams; the two Whigs from Georgia, Alexander H. Stephens and Robert Toombs, the former of whom was to become Vice-President, and the latter Secretary of State of the Confederacy; and George Ashmun of Massachusetts, who was to become chairman of the Republican National Convention in 1860. In the Senate were the giant figures of Webster, Calhoun, Benton, Cass, Crittenden, Jefferson Davis and Douglas. When Adams, the "Old Man Eloquent," was stricken and died on the floor of the House, Lincoln was named to the committee of arrangements for the funeral.

Many years later, after Lincoln's death, Stephens wrote: "I knew Mr. Lincoln well and intimately, and we were both ardent supporters of General Taylor for president in 1848. Mr. Lincoln, Toombs . . . myself and others formed the first Congressional Taylor Club, known as 'The Young Indians,' and organized the Taylor movement, which resulted in his nomination." Though Clay was a hero to the Whigs and deserved a second chance to run, Lincoln was among those who felt that a war hero at the head of the national ticket would assure victory to the party. Shrewd, practical politics, indeed. His support of Taylor, rather than of Clay, for the Whig nomination, was the subject of a sarcastic attack by Douglas in the Alton debate.

The bolt of Whig leaders to the Free Soil Party, which threatened Taylor's candidacy, was especially serious in Massachusetts, so there was a demand for Whig speakers to fight the defection. Lincoln was one of those invited. He was glad to accept, remembering the effect on the fortunes of Clay as a result of the votes of the Liberty Party. In September he spoke at several cities, including Worcester and Boston. In the latter city he appeared on the same platform with William H. Seward. Accounts of the time indicate that Lincoln made an excellent impression.

Though Lincoln participated in the debates in Congress and was well-liked by his colleagues for his unique personality, his career as a legislator was undistinguished. However, he sponsored two measures which attracted attention and had unexpected repercussions. One dealt with slavery in the District of Columbia and the other with the Mexican War.

Since slavery had become a supreme subject of discussion and debate, bills were constantly coming up for its abolition or the abolition of the slave trade in the District of Columbia. Lincoln had voted against the more radical of these. In January 1849 he prepared a bill of his own which reflected the consistency and conservatism of his views. It prohibited the bringing of slaves into the district or the selling of them out of it, and provided that children born of slave mothers after January 1, 1850 should be free. It also provided that owners who wished to emancipate their slaves should be reimbursed out of the national treasury. In order to win southern support, the bill included a section for the capture and return of fugitive slaves, inasmuch as the Fugitive Slave Law then in force did not apply to the District of Columbia.

Lincoln introduced his bill as an amendment to a resolution instructing the Committee on the District of Columbia to bring in a bill abolishing slavery in the District. It was debated, but there were other resolutions and amendments on the subject, and the session closed in March without anything being done about it.

Lincoln's abortive bill obtained a mixed reception from the anti-slavery wing. Joshua Giddings, who with Lincoln and several other Whig Congressmen boarded together at the same "mess," wrote in his diary:

> This evening our whole mess remained in the dining-room after tea, and conversed upon the subject of Mr. Lincoln's bill to abolish slavery. It was approved by all; I believe it as good as we could get at this time, and am willing to pay for slaves in order to save them from the Southern market, as I

suppose every man in the District would sell his slaves if he
saw that slavery was to be abolished.[21]

Wendell Phillips, however, who was one of the foremost
abolitionists of the time, was infuriated by the section providing for the apprehension of fugitive slaves. Years later he denounced Lincoln as "that slave hound from Illinois."[22]

THE "SPOT" RESOLUTIONS

Lincoln's second measure, dealing with the Mexican War,
plunged him into trouble which plagued him for years, especially in the Douglas debates. His autobiography explains the
background.

*All the battles of the Mexican War had been fought before
Mr. Lincoln took his seat in Congress, but the American army
was still in Mexico, and the treaty of peace was not fully and
formally ratified till the June afterward. Much has been said
of his course in Congress in regard to this war.... He voted
for all the supply measures that came up, and for all the measures in any way favorable to the officers, soldiers, and their
families... He also voted ... that the war was unnecessarily
and unconstitutionally begun by the President of the United
States.*

*Mr. Lincoln's reasons for the opinion expressed by this vote
were briefly that the President had sent General Taylor into
an inhabited part of the country belonging to Mexico, and not
to the United States, and thereby had provoked the first act of
hostility, in fact the commencement of the war; that the place,
being the country bordering on the east bank of the Rio
Grande, was inhabited by native Mexicans, born there under
the Mexican government, and had never submitted to, nor
been conquered by, Texas or the United States, nor transferred
to either by treaty...*

*Mr. Lincoln thought the act of sending an armed force
among the Mexicans was unnecessary, inasmuch as Mexico was
in no way molesting or menacing the United States or the
people thereof; and that it was unconstitutional, because the
power of levying war is vested in Congress, and not in the
President.*

Lincoln was very sensitive about his position on the Mexican
War. His recital in justification of this part of his career is

quite lengthy. His was the typical Whig Congressional position, but it was not popular with the folks back home. Though the Whigs voted supplies for the army, patriotic feeling ran too high to condone labelling the war an unjust one and placing the blame for it on the Administration.

Lincoln, therefore, ran afoul of his constituency when he presented what subsequently became known as the "Spot" resolutions:

RESOLUTIONS IN THE UNITED STATES HOUSE OF REPRESENTATIVES
DECEMBER 22, 1847

WHEREAS the President of the United States, in his message of May 11, 1846, has declared that "the Mexican Government, . . after a long-continued series of menaces, has at last invaded *our territory* and shed the blood of our fellow-citizens on our own soil:". . .

And whereas this House is desirous to obtain a full knowledge of all the facts which go to establish whether the particular spot on which the blood of our citizens was so shed was or was not at that time *our own soil*: Therefore,

Resolved By the House of Representatives, That the President of the United States be respectfully requested to inform this House—. . .

Whether the spot is or is not within the territory which was wrested from Spain by the Mexican revolution.

Whether that spot is or is not within a settlement of people, which settlement had existed ever since long before the Texas revolution, and until its inhabitants fled before the approach of the United States army. . .[23]

On January 12, he followed with a speech on the floor of the House attacking the Administration's justification of the war.

The shrewd Herndon accurately gauged the sentiment at home and wrote Lincoln that he had made a mistake. Besides, he himself was in favor of the war. Lincoln was distressed by his partner's reaction and took pains to justify his position. In one of his letters he wrote:

Washington, February 1, 1848

Dear William:

Your letter of the 19th ultimo was received last night, and for which I am much obliged. The only thing in it that I wish to talk to you at once about is that because of my vote

. . . you fear that you and I disagree about the war. I regret this, not because of any fear we shall remain disagreed after you have read this letter, but because if you misunderstand I fear other good friends may also. That vote affirms that the war was unnecessarily and unconstitutionally commenced by the President; and I will stake my life that if you had been in my place you would have voted just as I did. Would you have voted what you felt and knew to be a lie? I know you would not. Would you have gone out of the House—skulked the vote? I expect not. If you had skulked one vote, you would have had to skulk many more before the end of the session. . . No man can be silent if he would. You are compelled to speak; and your only alternative is to tell the truth or a lie. I cannot doubt which you would do. . .[24]

It was just as well that Lincoln did not stand for reelection. The Whigs were unpopular in Illinois. In spite of the boasted 1,500 majority in Lincoln's district, Taylor lost the state, and Judge Logan, whose turn it was to run for Congress in the Whig district, went down to defeat.

The "Spot" resolutions left their mark on Lincoln. He was thereafter referred to as "Spot" Lincoln whenever his adversaries mentioned his record on the Mexican War. Douglas was to take full advantage of this defect in Lincoln's armor in the course of the debates.

Upon his return from Congress he went to the practice of the law with greater earnestness than ever before. . . In 1854 his profession had almost superseded the thought of politics in his mind, when the repeal of the Missouri Compromise aroused him as he had never been before.

The five years from 1849 to 1854 were a plateau in Lincoln's life, a period in which his thoughts were maturing quietly and he was being made ready for his entrance on the stage of history. Evidences of his deep thinking on the subjects of slavery and of government are preserved in several fragments of notes. One fragment attributed to the summer of July 1854 reads as follows:

If A. can prove, however conclusively, that he may, of right, enslave B.—why may not B. snatch the same argument, and prove equally, that he may enslave A?

You say A. is white, and B. is black. It is *color*, then; the lighter, having the right to enslave the darker? Take care.

By this rule, you are to be slave to the first man you meet, with a fairer skin than your own.

You do not mean *color* exactly? You mean the whites are *intellectually* the superiors of the blacks; and, therefore have the right to enslave them? Take care again. By this rule, you are to be slave to the first man you meet, with an intellect superior to your own.

But, say you, it is a question of *interest;* and, if you can make it your *interest,* you have the right to enslave another. Very well. And if he can make it his interest, he has the right to enslave you.

Although volume upon volume is written to prove slavery a very good thing, we never hear of the man who wishes to take the good of it *by being a slave* himself.

Most *governments* have been based on the denial of the equal rights of men; . . *ours* began by affirming those rights. *They* said, some men are too *ignorant* and *vicious* to share in government. Possibly so, said we; and, by your system, we would always keep them ignorant, and vicious. We proposed to give *all* a chance; and we expected the weak to grow stronger, the ignorant, wiser; and all better, and happier together.[25]

An unsigned editorial on the repeal of the Missouri Compromise by the Kansas-Nebraska Act, appearing in the *Illinois State Journal* on September 11, is attributed to Lincoln. It reveals his uncanny ability to see to the heart of a problem and reduce it to its bare essentials through simple and homely analogy. The Journal had previously appeared as the *Sangamo Journal.* Its editor, Simeon Francis, was a good friend of Lincoln's and the latter contributed many articles and editorials to the paper. After first quoting the language of the Act — "it being the true intent and meaning of this act not to legislate slavery into any territory or State, nor to exclude it therefrom, but to leave the people thereof perfectly free to form and regulate their domestic institutions in their own way" — the editorial goes on:

To illustrate the case—Abraham Lincoln has a fine meadow, containing beautiful springs of water, and well fenced, which John Calhoun had agreed with Abraham (originally owning the land in common) should be his, and the agreement had been consummated in the most solemn manner,

regarded by both as sacred. John Calhoun, however, in the
course of time, had become owner of an extensive herd of
cattle—the prairie grass had become dried up and there was
no convenient water to be had. John Calhoun then looks
with a longing eye on Lincoln's meadow, and goes to it and
throws down the fences, and exposes it to the ravages of his
starving and famishing cattle.

"You rascal," says Lincoln, "what have you done? What
do you do this for?"—"Oh," replies Calhoun, "everything is
right. I have taken down your fence; but nothing more. . .
It is my true intent and meaning not to drive my cattle into
your meadow, nor to exclude them therefrom, but to leave
them perfectly free to form their own notions of the feed, and
to direct their movements in their own way!"

Now would not the man who committed this outrage be
deemed both a knave and a fool,—a knave in removing the
restrictive fence, which he had solemnly pledged himself to
sustain;—and a fool in supposing that there could be one
man found in the country to believe that he had not pulled
down the fence for the purpose of opening the meadow for
his cattle?[26]

The John Calhoun referred to in the editorial was, of course,
the former surveyor of Sangamon County, who had gone to
Kansas as a leader of the pro-slavery forces.

*In the autumn of that year he took the stump with no
broader practical aim or object than to secure, if possible, the
re-election of Hon. Richard Yates to Congress. His speeches at
once attracted a more marked attention than they had ever
before done. As the canvass proceeded he was drawn to different
parts of the State. . . He did not abandon the law, but gave
his attention by turns to that and politics. The State agricultural fair was at Springfield that year, and Douglas was announced to speak there.*

The State Fair at Springfield took place in October, a month
after Douglas' debacle in Chicago, when he first tried to justify
the Kansas-Nebraska Act to the people of Illinois. Douglas
spoke on October 3; Lincoln replied the next day, and Douglas
followed with a rebuttal.

This was practically the same speech made by Lincoln several
days later at Peoria, to which reference has been made previously. It was the speech that precipitated him into public life
once again. He had prepared and written it out carefully, but

only an abstract of it had been published after he had spoken at Springfield. It was not given to the press until after its delivery at Peoria. Shorthand reporting was rare at the time. It was only in 1858, when the importance of the great debates attracted nation-wide attention, that shorthand reporting was regularly employed in Illinois.

At Peoria, as at Springfield and several other towns, the rivals shared the same platform. If Lincoln was in town, as he was at Springfield, it was generally expected that he would answer Douglas. At other times, Lincoln would receive calls from places where Douglas was to speak. Thus, though these exchanges were not formally arranged debates, they were dress rehearsals for the great battle between them four years later.

Such exchanges were customary. The code of the West required challenges in sports and contests to be accepted, especially by the champion. Political debate became the substitute for the ruder athletic sports, such as shooting matches, wrestling and horse races. "To refuse any contest, to plead any privilege, would be instant loss of prestige," according to Nicolay and Hay.[27] Douglas recognized this at Springfield when he said: "I will mention that it is understood by some gentlemen that Mr. Lincoln of this city is expected to answer me. If this is the understanding, I wish that Mr. Lincoln would step forward and let us arrange some plan upon which to carry out the discussion."[28]

Lincoln was not present at the moment, but the next day when he spoke, Douglas was there, occupying a seat just in front of him. When Douglas subsequently made his rejoinder, he explained: "My friend Mr. Lincoln expressly invited me to stay and hear him speak today, as he heard me yesterday, and to answer and defend myself as best I could. I here thank him for his courteous offer."[29]

When the rivals clashed again at Peoria on October 16, the *Illinois State Journal* reported the exchange as follows:

> When Senator Douglas closed . . . the crowd began to call for LINCOLN, who, as Judge Douglas had announced was, by agreement, to answer him, Mr. Lincoln took the stand and said—
> "I do not arise to speak now, if I can stipulate with the audience to meet me here at half past 6 or 7 o'clock. It is now

several minutes past five, and Judge Douglas has spoken over
three hours. If you hear me at all, I wish you to hear me
thro'. It will take me as long as it has taken him. That will
carry us beyond eight o'clock at night. Now every one of you
who can remain that long can just as well get his supper,
meet me at seven, and remain one hour or two later.

"The judge has already informed you that he is to have
an hour to reply to me. I doubt not but you have been a
little surprised to learn that I have consented to give one of
his high reputation and known ability, this advantage of me.
Indeed, my consenting to it, though reluctant, was not
wholly unselfish, for I suspected if it were understood, that
the judge was entirely done, you democrats would leave and
not hear me; but by giving him the close, I felt confident
you would stay for the fun of hearing him skin me."

The audience signified their assent to the arrangement,
and adjourned to 7 o'clock P.M.[30]

THE SPRINGFIELD-PEORIA SPEECH

The Springfield-Peoria speech is one of Lincoln's greatest.
It reflects Lincoln's matured, powerful style, and the close
reasoning that caused Douglas to say four years later, when
he learned that Lincoln was to oppose him for Senator that
the Republicans had chosen the most formidable foe that
could be sent against him.

The speech may be considered Lincoln's first step to the
presidency, for thereafter he was to be increasingly recognized
as the soundest and most redoubtable exponent of the case
against slavery. The impression it made may be judged from
what Horace White wrote several years later of its effect on
him. White was a reporter for the Chicago *Evening Journal*
who subsequently covered the Douglas debates for the Chicago
Tribune.

I have never heard anything . . . either by Mr. Lincoln, or
by anybody, that I would put on a higher plane of oratory.
All the strings that play upon the human heart and understanding were touched with masterly skill and force, while
beyond and above all skill was the overwhelming conviction
pressed upon the audience that the speaker himself was
charged with an irresistible and inspiring duty to his fellow
men. This conscientious impulse drove his arguments
through the heads of his hearers down into their bosoms. . .

> It seemed to me, when this speech was finished as though I had had a very feeble conception of the wickedness of the Kansas-Nebraska Bill. I was filled, as never before, with the sense of my own duty and responsibility as a citizen toward the aggressions of the slave power.[31]

The Peoria speech therefore merits more attention than has been given it in most studies of Lincoln.

Douglas had defended the Kansas-Nebraska Act by stating that it had merely confirmed the repeal of the principle of the Missouri Compromise previously repudiated by the Compromise of 1850. Lincoln proved that the Missouri Compromise involved no principle; that it was a specific measure to meet a specific situation:

> That [the Missouri Compromise's] terms limit it to the country purchased from France, is undenied and undeniable. It could have no principle beyond the intention of those who made it. They did not intend to extend the line to country which they did not own. If they intended to extend it, in the event of acquiring additional territory, why did they not say so? It was just as easy to say, that "in all the country west of the Mississippi, which we now own, or may hereafter acquire there shall never be slavery," as to say what they did say. . .
>
> Another fact showing the specific character of the Missouri law—showing that the line was not intended as a universal dividing line between free and slave territory north of which slavery could never go—is the fact that by that very law, Missouri came in as a slave State, north of the line. If that law contained any prospective principle . . . the South could fairly contend that inasmuch as they got one slave state north of the line at the inception of the law, they have the right to have another given them north of it occasionally—in the indefinite westward extension of the line. This demonstrates the absurdity of attempting to deduce a prospective principle from the Missouri Compromise Line. . . .[32]

Lincoln denied that by providing for popular sovereignty in the territories of Utah and New Mexico, the Compromise of 1850 established a new principle applicable to Kansas and Nebraska:

> I insist this provision was made for Utah and New Mexico,

and for no other place whatever. It had no more direct reference to Nebraska than it had to the territories of the moon. But, they say, it had reference to Nebraska, in principle. Let us see. The North consented to this provision, not because they considered it right in itself; but because they were compensated—paid for it.—They, at the same time, got California into the Union as a free State. . . Also, they got the slave trade abolished in the District of Columbia. For all these desirable objects the North could afford to yield something and they did yield to the South the Utah and New Mexico provision. . .

Now can it be pretended that the principle of this arrangement requires us to permit the same provision to be applied to Nebraska, without any equivalent at all? Give us another free State; . . give us another step toward the destruction of slavery in the District, and you present us a similar case. But ask us not to repeat, for nothing, what you paid for in the first instance. If you wish the thing again, pay again. That is the principle of the compromises of '50, if indeed they had any principles beyond their specific terms—it was the system of equivalents.[33]

In an analysis of the meaning of self-government, Lincoln laid bare the speciousness of popular sovereignty with devastating effect:

One great argument in support of the repeal of the Missouri Compromise . . . is "the sacred right of self-government" . . .

The doctrine of self-government is right—absolutely and eternally right—but it has no just application, as here attempted. Or perhaps I should rather say that whether it has such application depends upon whether a negro is not or is a man. If he is not a man, why in that case, he who is a man may, as a matter of self-government, do just as he pleases with him. But if the negro is a man, is it not to that extent a total destruction of self-government, to say that he too shall not govern himself? When the white man governs himself that is self-government; but when he governs himself, and also governs another man, that is more than self-government —that is despotism. If the negro is a man, why then my ancient faith teaches me that "all men are created equal," and that there can be no moral right in connection with one man's making a slave of another.

Judge Douglas frequently, with bitter irony and sarcasm, paraphrases our argument by saying: "The white people of Nebraska are good enough to govern themselves but they are not good enough to govern a few miserable negros!!"

Well I doubt not that the people of Nebraska are, and will continue to be as good as the average of people elsewhere. I do not say the contrary. What I do say is, that no man is good enough to govern another man, without that other's consent. I say this is the leading principle—the sheet anchor of American republicanism. . .[34]

There are constitutional relations between the slave and free States, which are degrading to the latter. . . In the control of the government—the management of the partnership affairs—they have greatly the advantage of us. By the constitution . . . each has a number of Representatives, in proportion to the number of its people. . . But in ascertaining the number of the people, for this purpose, five slaves are counted as being equal to three whites. The slaves do not vote; they are only counted and so used as to swell the influence of the white people's votes.

The practical effect of this is more aptly shown by a comparison of the States of South Carolina and Maine. South Carolina has six representatives, and so has Maine. . . Thus in the control of the government, the two States are equals precisely. But how are they in the number of their white people? Maine has 581,813—while South Carolina has 274,567. Maine has twice as many as South Carolina, and 32,679 over. —Thus each white man in South Carolina is more than the double of any man in Maine. This is all because South Carolina, besides her free people, has 384,984 slaves. The South Carolinian has precisely the same advantage over the white man in every other free State, as well as in Maine. He is more than the double of any one of us in this crowd. . .

Now all this is manifestly unfair; yet I do not mention it to complain of it, in so far as it is already settled. It is in the Constitution; and I do not, for that cause, or any other cause, propose to destroy, or alter, or disregard the Constitution. . .

But when I am told I must leave it altogether to OTHER PEOPLE to say whether new partners are to be bred up and brought into the firm, on the same degrading terms against me, I respectfully demur. I insist, that whether I shall be a whole man, or only the half of one, in comparison with others, is a question in which I am somewhat concerned; and one which no other man can have a sacred right of deciding for me.

If I am wrong in this — if it really be a sacred right of self-government, in the man who shall go to Nebraska, to decide whether he will be the EQUAL of me or the DOUBLE of me, then, after he shall have exercised that right, and thereby shall have reduced me to a still smaller fraction of a man than I already am, I should like for some gentleman, deeply skilled in the mysteries of sacred rights, to provide himself with a microscope, and peep about, and find out, if he can, what has become of my sacred rights! — They will surely be too small for detection with the naked eye.

Finally, I insist that if there is ANYTHING which it is the duty of the WHOLE PEOPLE to never entrust to any hands but their own, that thing is the preservation and perpetuity, of their own liberties, and institutions. And if they shall think as I do, that the extension of slavery endangers them, more than any, or all other causes, how recreant to themselves, if they submit the question, and with it, the fate of their country, to a mere handful of men, bent only on temporary self-interest.[35]

Lincoln exposed the folly of popular sovereignty as a solution either of the slavery question or of the problem of Nebraska:

Wherever slavery is, it has been first introduced without law. The oldest laws we find concerning it, are not laws introducing it; but regulating it, as an already existing thing. A white man takes his slave to Nebraska now; who will inform the negro that he is free? — Who will take him before the court to test the question of his freedom? In ignorance of his legal emancipation, he is kept chopping, splitting and plowing. Others are brought, and move on in the same track. At last if ever the time for voting comes, on the question of slavery, the institution already in fact exists in the country, and cannot well be removed. The facts of its presence, and the difficulty of its removal, will carry the vote in its favor.

Keep it out until a vote is taken, and a vote in favor of it, can not be got in any population of forty thousand, on earth, who have been drawn together by the ordinary motives of emigration and settlement. To get slaves into the country simultaneously with the whites, in the incipient stages of settlement, is the precise stake played for, and won in this Nebraska measure. . .[36]

The people are to decide the question of slavery for themselves; but WHEN they are to decide, or HOW they are to decide; or whether, when the question is once decided, it is to remain so, or is to be subject to an indefinite succession of new trials, the law does not say. Is it to be decided by the first dozen settlers who arrive there? or is it to await the arrival of a hundred? Is it to be decided by a vote of the people? or a vote of the legislature? or, indeed, by a vote of any sort? To these questions, the law gives no answer...

Some Yankees, in the east, are sending emigrants to Nebraska to exclude slavery from it; and, so far as I can judge, they expect the question to be decided by voting, in some way or other. But the Missourians are awake too. They are within a stone's throw of the contested ground. They hold meetings, and pass resolutions, in which not the slightest allusion to voting is made. They resolve that slavery already exists in the territory; that more shall go there; that they, remaining in Missouri, will protect it; and that abolitionists shall be hung, or driven away. Through all this, bowie-knives and six-shooters are seen plainly enough; but never a glimpse of the ballot-box...

Is it not probable that the contest will come to blows, and bloodshed? Could there be a more apt invention to bring about collision and violence, on the slavery question, than this Nebraska project is?[37]

Lincoln's arguments were most effective when he touched the moral issue. As a conservative lawyer who revered the Constitution and the law, he felt honor bound to make the necessary concessions to the legalities of slavery. However, while a law, though bad, had to be obeyed, he opposed extending its effect or investing it with moral sanction.

This difference was not so clearly understood that it could be accepted by most people. As mentioned earlier, the slavery problem was muddied by the disagreement prevalent in the various church pulpits on the moral issue. It was further confused by the intertwined, seemingly insuperable, implicit social and political factors. Most contemporary orators, carried away by fervor, were given to extreme solutions, which violated or disregarded important aspects of the problem. Someone, somewhere had to be able to clarify it and reduce it to an essential element which the ordinary man could grasp.

This it was Lincoln's unique genius to do. He had the gift

of drawing careful distinctions, stripping away the troublesome layers of concomitant factors from the main issue, and
revealing a single, uncomplicated point easily comprehended
by his auditors. The arguments he presented were not necessarily new or original, but his reasoning and presentation were.

Thus, he reduced the moral aspect of slavery to the prime
requisite of unqualified acceptance of the Negro as a human
being who was entitled to his liberty, without complicating
the issue by questions of political and social status. This is
the concept which, in the course of the next few years and
especially in the debates with Douglas, he would repeat to
different audiences at different places.

In the Peoria speech he presented this idea as part of a lofty
concept of the role of the United States among the nations
of the world:

> Let it not be said I am contending for the establishment
> of political and social equality between the whites and
> blacks. . . I am not now combating the argument of neces-
> sity, arising from the fact that the blacks are already amongst
> us; but I am combating what is set up as MORAL argu-
> ment for allowing them to be taken where they have never
> yet been — arguing against the EXTENSION of a bad thing,
> which where it already exists we must of necessity, manage
> as we best can. . .[38]
>
> I particularly object to the NEW position which the
> avowed principle of this Nebraska law gives to slavery in the
> body politic. I object to it because it assumes that there can
> be MORAL RIGHT in the enslaving of one man by
> another. . . I object to it because the fathers of the republic
> eschewed, and rejected it. The argument of "Necessity" was
> the only argument they ever admitted in favor of slavery.
> They found the institution existing among us, which they
> could not help. . .
>
> Thus we see, the plain unmistakable spirit of that age,
> towards slavery, was hostility to the PRINCIPLE, and tol-
> eration, ONLY BY NECESSITY.
>
> But now it is to be transformed into a "sacred right."
> Nebraska . . . places it on the high road to extension and
> perpetuity. . . Henceforth it is to be the chief jewel of the
> nation—the very figurehead of the ship of State.
>
> Little by little, but steadily as man's march to the grave,
> we have been giving up the OLD for the NEW faith. Near

eighty years ago we began declaring that all men are created equal; but now from that beginning we have run down to the other declaration, that for SOME men to enslave OTHERS is a "sacred right of self-government." These principles can not stand together. They are as opposite as God and mammon; and whoever holds to the one must despise the other. . .[39]

Senator Douglas remarked . . . that he had always considered this government was made for the white people and not for the negroes. Why, in point of mere fact, I think so too. But in this remark of the Judge, there is a significance, which I think is the key to the great mistake which he has made in this Nebraska measure. It shows that the Judge has no very vivid impression that the negro is a human; and consequently has no idea that there can be any moral question in legislating about him.

In his view, the question of whether a new country shall be slave or free, is a matter of as utter indifference, as it is whether his neighbor shall plant his farm with tobacco, or stock it with horned cattle. . .[40]

This declared indifference, but, as I must think, covert real zeal for the spread of slavery, I can not but hate. I hate it because of the monstrous injustice of slavery itself. I hate it because it deprives our republican example of its just influence in the world — enables the enemies of free institutions with plausibility, to taunt us as hypocrites — causes the real friends of freedom to doubt our sincerity, and especially because it forces so many really good men amongst ourselves into an open war with the very fundamental principles of civil liberty — criticizing the Declaration of Independence, and insisting that there is no right principle of action but self-interest. . .[41]

Let no one be deceived. The spirit of seventy-six and the spirit of Nebraska, are utter antagonisms; and the former is being rapidly displaced by the latter.

Fellow-countrymen — Americans south, as well as north, shall we make no effort to arrest this? . . . Is there no danger to liberty itself, in discarding the earliest practice, the first precept of our ancient faith? In our greedy chase to make profit of the negro, let us beware, lest we "cancel and tear to pieces" even the white man's charter of freedom.

Our Republican robe is soiled, and trailed in the dust. Let us re-purify it. Let us turn and wash it white, in the spirit, if not the blood, of the Revolution. Let us turn

slavery from its claims of "moral right" back upon its existing legal rights, and its arguments of "necessity." — Let us
return it to the position our fathers gave it; and there let it
rest in peace. Let us re-adopt the Declaration of Independence, and with it, the practices, and policy, which harmonize
with it. Let north and south — let all Americans — let all
lovers of liberty everywhere — join in the great and good
work. If we do this, we shall not only have saved the Union;
but we shall have so saved it, as to make, and to keep it,
forever worthy of the saving. We shall have so saved it, that
the succeeding millions of free happy people the world over,
shall rise up, and call us blessed, to the latest generations.[42]

AVOIDING THE REPUBLICAN LABEL

It was also at the State Fair at Springfield on October 4
that the first attempt was made to set up a Republican organization in the state. The leading movers were the abolitionists, chief among whom were Owen Lovejoy, the murdered
Elijah's brother, and Ichabod Codding, who was a well-known
temperance lecturer. The idea was to fuse the abolitionists,
the Free Soilers, the anti-Nebraska Democrats, and the Whigs
into one organization. Herndon was in the thick of it. The
fusionists had announced an organization meeting for that afternoon, but since Lincoln was replying to Douglas at that time,
they postponed their meeting for the evening.

Herndon knew that they planned to get Lincoln to speak
for them. That was dangerous. The abolitionists were still in
bad repute. While Lincoln must not alienate them, he must
avoid open identification with them, at least for the present.
Herndon therefore convinced his partner that it was best for
him to have some pressing business in nearby Tazewell County
and shun the meeting. Lincoln took the advice, dutifully
hitched his horse and buggy, and left town.

After fiery speeches the meeting organized a Republican
State Central Committee, of which the absent Lincoln was
nevertheless chosen a member, and drew up a series of resolutions, which we shall meet in the Lincoln-Douglas debates
as the Codding resolutions. The most objectionable feature
of the resolutions, to which Lincoln, of course, could not sub-
scribe, was a demand for the repeal of the Fugitive Slave Law.
Lincoln learned that he had been made a member of the Com-

mittee when, a little more than a month later, he received
a notice to appear at a meeting. This was his response:

I. Codding, Esq   Springfield,
Dear Sir   Novr. 27, 1854
    . . . I have been perplexed some to understand why my
name was placed on that committee. I was not consulted on
the subject; nor was I apprized of the appointment, until I
discovered it by accident two or three weeks afterwards. I
suppose my opposition to the principle of slavery is as strong
as that of any member of the Republican party; but I had
also supposed that the extent to which I feel authorized to
carry that opposition, practically was not at all satisfactory
to that party. . .

                                         Yours truly, A. Lincoln[43]

The fall elections resulted in a Democratic setback in Illinois
as well as throughout the North. Anti-Nebraska men carried
the state legislature, and it was a certainty that, if united, they
would elect an anti-Nebraska man to the United States Senate
in place of Douglas' henchman, James Shields. Lincoln's blood
was up now, for he scented his chance. He immediately began
to line up support.

When the legislature met in February 1855 to choose a
Senator, Lincoln was just short of a majority. The three former
Democratic stalwarts, Norman B. Judd, Burton C. Cook and
John M. Palmer, who had bolted the party on the Nebraska
issue, as well as two other anti-Nebraska men, supported Lyman
Trumbull, the most prominent of the Democratic rebels. These
five men held the balance of power. On successive ballots they
stuck with Trumbull. Since, as Democrats, they had always
been in control, they were reluctant to switch to a Whig and
vote for Lincoln.

Suddenly a new factor entered into the voting. The regular
Democrats began to back Governor Joel A. Matteson, instead
of Shields. Matteson had not committed himself on the Kansas-
Nebraska Act and was personally very popular. It seemed
very likely that he would be able to draw off the rebellious
Democrats from Trumbull. Lincoln saw the danger. If Illinois
was to have an anti-Nebraska Senator, it would have to be
Trumbull and not himself. He therefore instructed those who

still supported him to switch to Trumbull. The deadlock was broken, and Trumbull was elected.

The Democrats were furious. They charged that Lincoln and Trumbull had made a deal, that in return for his support now, Trumbull was to back Lincoln for Senator in 1858 when Douglas' term would expire. Douglas hurled this charge frequently at Lincoln in the course of their debates in order to portray himself as the victim of a plot.

Lincoln's defeat left him melancholy and dejected. He wanted the Senatorship badly. But he did not remain depressed very long. The next day he wrote a letter to Elihu Washburne, in which he said:

> I regret my defeat moderately, but I am not nervous about it. I could have headed off every combination and been elected, had it not been for Matteson's double game — and his defeat now gives me more pleasure than my own gives me pain. On the whole, it is perhaps as well for our general cause that Trumbull is elected. The Nebraska men confess that they hate it worse than anything that could have happened. It is a great consolation to see them worse whipped than I am. I tell them it is their own fault — that they had abundant opportunity to choose between him and me, which they declined, and instead forced it on me to decide between him and Matteson.[44]

Thereafter Lincoln returned to his law practice, but he also maintained an active interest in the political stew which was brewing. Owen Lovejoy was still intent on getting him to join the "fusionists," but Lincoln remained cautious. He was worried about the role of the Know-Nothings, who still formed a powerful force. In a letter to Lovejoy in August 1855, he wrote:

> Knownothingism has not yet entirely tumbled to pieces. . . . Until we can get the elements of this organization, there is not sufficient materials to successfully combat the Nebraska democracy with. We can not get them so long as they cling to a hope of success under their own organization. About us here, they are mostly my old political and personal friends; and I have hoped their organization would die out without the painful necessity of my taking an open stand against them. Of their principles I think little better than I do of those of the slavery extensionists. Indeed I do not perceive

how any one professing to be sensitive to the wrongs of the negroes, can join in a league to degrade a class of white men.

I have no objection to "fuse" with anybody provided I can fuse on ground which I think is right.[45]

About the same time, he wrote two other letters which give an insight into his state of mind. The first, to Judge George Robertson of Kentucky, is prophetic as to the ultimate course of the slavery problem and is suggestive of the language of the famous "house divided" speech which he was to make at the opening of the campaign against Douglas:

I think that there is no peaceful extinction of slavery in prospect for us. . .

When we were the political slaves of King George, and wanted to be free, we called the maxim that "all men are created equal" a self-evident truth; but now when we have grown fat, and have lost all dread of being slaves ourselves, we have become so greedy to be MASTERS that we call the same maxim "a self-evident lie." The fourth of July has not quite dwindled away; it is still a great day — *for burning FIRE-CRACKERS*!!! . . .

So far as peaceful, voluntary emancipation is concerned, the condition of the negro slave in America . . . is now fixed, and hopeless of change for the better. . . . The Autocrat of all the Russias will resign his crown, and proclaim his subjects free republicans, sooner than will our American masters voluntarily give up their slaves.

Our political problem now is "Can we, as a nation, continue together *permanently — forever* half slave, and half free?" The problem is too mighty for me. May God, in his mercy superintend the solution.[46]

The second letter, to his friend Joshua Speed, has already been mentioned in connection with the trip they had together on the river boat fourteen years before. In it he revealed his hesitation at the brink before taking the plunge into Republicanism a few months later.

You inquire where I now stand. That is a disputed point — I think I am a Whig; but others say there are no Whigs, and that I am an abolitionist. When I was at Washington I voted for the Wilmot Proviso as good as forty times, and I never heard of any one attempting to unwhig me for that. I now do no more than oppose the *extension* of slavery.

I am not a Know-Nothing. That is certain. How could I be? How can any one who abhors the oppression of negroes, be in favor of degrading classes of white people? Our progress in degeneracy appears to me to be pretty rapid. As a nation, we began by declaring that *"all men are created equal."* We now practically read it *"all men are created equal, except negroes."* When the Know-Nothings get control, it will read *"all men are created equal, except negroes, and foreigners, and catholics."* When it comes to this I should prefer emigrating to some country where they make no pretence of loving liberty — to Russia, for instance, where despotism can be taken pure, and without the base alloy of hypocrisy.[47]

FUSING THE REPUBLICAN PARTY

Lincoln took the plunge on Washington's birthday 1856. Ever since the first efforts at organization at Springfield in October 1854, groups of anti-Nebraska men had been meeting all over the state and adopting resolutions, very often of a radical nature. Now on February 22 a group of newspaper editors, including some avowed Republicans, met at Decatur to organize the state for the coming presidential election. Lincoln was there among them. He was now out in the open, clearly identified with the radicals. His purpose, however, was to unify the diverse anti-Nebraska elements through a policy of moderation. As a result of his influence, extreme statements were missing from the platform which emphasized opposition to the extension of slavery. A call was issued for an anti-Nebraska convention to be held in Bloomington on May 29.

As the time for the convention drew near, the tempo of political events began to increase. Kansas was bleeding, and Preston Brooks committed his assault on Senator Sumner. Lincoln was fearful that not many moderates would show up, but as it turned out, all shades of anti-slavery opinion made an appearance. There were Old Line Whigs, Democrats, Free Soilers, Know-Nothings, and Abolitionists, who presented a striking contrast of former antagonisms. When Lincoln saw Norman B. Judd step off the train, he remarked to a companion: "That's the best sign yet. Judd is a trimmer."[48] It was now certain that a new party would emerge.

The convention adopted a platform drawn up by the conservative Old Line Whig, Orville H. Browning, which was based on the proceedings at Decatur. Unlike the Codding resolutions adopted in Springfield two years before, it avoided mention of repeal of the Fugitive Slave Law, but affirmed the power of Congress to prohibit slavery in the territories, denounced the repeal of the Missouri Compromise, and upheld the right of the voters of Kansas to reject slavery.

The new party, however, hesitated to call itself Republican. The Republican Party, recently organized on a national scale, was already being called "Black." This was an odious term in Illinois. Its partisan press therefore referred to it as the "Anti-Nebraska State Convention" or the "People's Convention." But there was no doubt that the new party would support the presidential candidate soon to be nominated by the Republicans. So the Illinois Democrats promptly stigmatized it as the "Black Republican Party."

Lincoln, who remained in the background, was instrumental in drawing up the state ticket, headed by William H. Bissell, a former Democrat and hero of the Mexican War, for governor. There was much oratory in the course of the proceedings, but at the end there were calls for Lincoln to speak.

Lincoln knew that he would be called on to close the convention. He knew his words must weld the still potentially discordant elements into a strong organization. He did so with a tongue of fire. The audience was transfixed. Reporters were so carried away that they forgot to take notes. This became Lincoln's "lost speech," termed by tradition his greatest oratorical effort. Joseph Medill, of the *Chicago Tribune,* who was present, thus described his reactions: "The thrilling scene in that old Bloomington hall forty years ago arises in my mind as vividly as the day after its enactment. . . I never witnessed such a scene before or since. The convention went fairly wild."[49]

Lincoln never wrote out the speech even when invited to do so. Perhaps he was not unwilling to let the speech be lost. Medill had this to say about it:

> My belief is that, after Mr. Lincoln cooled down, he was rather pleased that his speech had not been reported, as it was too radical in expression on the slavery question for the digestion of central and southern Illinois at that time, and that he preferred to let it stand as a remembrance in the minds of his audience. But be that as it may, the effect of it

was such on his hearers that he bounded to the leadership
of the new Republican party of Illinois, and no man afterwards ever thought of disputing that position with him.[50]

Horace White, however, did not believe that the speech
was lost. He thought that Lincoln repeated the substance of
it at various times during the campaign of 1856. This is probably so, but it could not have been repeated in the same way
or with the same effect. Henry C. Whitney, an attorney who
was present at Bloomington, wrote out what he thought to
be the substance of the speech many years later, and it is included in some editions of Lincoln's speeches.[51]

THE REPLY TO DOUGLAS ON DRED SCOTT

In the canvass of 1856 Mr. Lincoln made over fifty speeches.
. . .

With these words Lincoln neared the completion of his campaign biography, evidently assuming that his record as a public
figure from this time on was well known and documented. In
the canvass referred to, he stumped the state for Fremont and
Dayton, and of course, for the entire Republican ticket.
Though Buchanan carried the state by 9,000 votes, the Republicans won the governorship by 4,700 votes and elected
their state ticket. The state victory established the strength of
the party, and was an encouraging harbinger for future elections.

Soon after Buchanan's inauguration came the bombshell of
the Dred Scott decision. Douglas' support of the decision before the people of Illinois was made on June 12, 1857 at
Springfield. Two weeks later at the same place, Lincoln made
a reply, as was expected of him as the acknowledged leader of
the Republican Party. It brings us close to the debates of
1858 because so many of the arguments he employs reappear
in the later duel with Douglas. Like the Peoria speech, it reveals the further flowering of his style: the ability to delineate
clear moral choices, the close reasoning which could strip a
seemingly logical argument to shreds, and the unpretentious
eloquence which had its inspiration in an abiding faith in
man and a sublime concept of the nation's institutions. First
he took up the matter of resistance to the decision:

We believe, as much as Judge Douglas . . . in obedience to, and respect for, the judicial department of government. . . . But we think the Dred Scott decision is erroneous. We know the court that made it, has often overruled its own decisions, and we shall do what we can to have it overrule this. We offer no resistance to it. . .

But Judge Douglas considers this view awful. Hear him: "If resistance to the decisions of the Supreme Court of the United States, in a matter like the points decided in the Dred Scott case, . . shall be forced upon the country as a political issue, it will become a distinct and naked issue between the friends and enemies of the Constitution."

Why, this same Supreme Court once decided a national bank to be constitutional; but General Jackson, as President of the United States, disregarded the decision, and vetoed a bill for a re-charter. . .

Again and again have I heard Judge Douglas denounce that bank decision, and applaud General Jackson for disregarding it. It would be interesting for him to look over his recent speech, and see how exactly his fierce philippics against us for resisting Supreme Court decisions, fall upon his own head. It will call to his mind a long and fierce political war in this country . . . in which he fought in the ranks of the enemies of the Constitution.[52]

Next Lincoln examined Chief Justice Taney's interpretation of the Declaration of Independence. This section of his speech contains a passage which, for beauty of imagery, is unmatched in the annals of oratory.

Taney had said that the words of the Declaration "would seem to include the entire human family, and if they were used in a similar instrument at this day would be so understood." Said Lincoln:

In those days, our Declaration of Independence was held sacred by all, and thought to include all; but now, to aid in making the bondage of the negro universal and eternal, it is assailed, and sneered at, and construed, and hawked at, and torn, till, if its framers could rise from their graves, they could not at all recognize it.

All the powers of earth seem rapidly combining against him [the negro]. Mammon is after him; ambition follows, and philosophy follows, and the Theology of the day is fast

joining the cry. They have him in his prison house; they have
searched his person, and left no prying instrument with him.
One after another they have closed the heavy iron doors upon
him, and now they have him, as it were bolted in with a lock
of a hundred keys, which can never be unlocked without the
concurrence of every key; the keys in the hands of a hundred
different men, and they scattered to a hundred different and
distant places; and they stand musing as to what invention,
in all the dominions of mind and matter, can be produced to
make the impossibility of his escape more complete. . .

Chief Justice Taney, in his opinion in the Dred Scott case,
admits that the language of the Declaration is broad enough
to include the whole human family, but he and Judge Douglas argue that the authors of that instrument did not intend
to include negroes, by the fact that they did not at once,
actually place them on an equality with the whites. Now this
grave argument comes to just nothing at all, by the other fact,
that they did not at once, or ever afterwards, actually place
all white people on an equality with one another. . .

I think the authors of that notable instrument intended to
include all men, but they did not intend to declare all men
equal in all respects. They did not mean to say all were
equal in color, size, intellect, moral developments, or social
capacity. They defined with tolerable distinctness, in what respects they did consider all men created equal — equal in
"certain inalienable rights, among which are life, liberty,
and the pursuit of happiness". . . They did not mean to
assert the obvious untruth, that all were then actually enjoying that equality, nor yet, that they were about to confer it
immediately upon them. . . They meant simply to declare
the right, so that the enforcement of it might follow as fast
as circumstances should permit.[53]

They meant to set up a standard maxim for free society,
which could be familiar to all, and revered by all; constantly
looked to, constantly labored for, and even though never
perfectly attained, constantly approximated, and thereby
constantly spreading and deepening its influence, and augmenting the happiness and value of life to all people of all
colors everywhere. The assertion that "all men are created
equal" was of no practical use in effecting our separation
from Great Britain; and it was placed in the Declaration,
not for that, but for future use. Its authors meant it to be,
thank God, it is now proving itself, a stumbling block to
those who in after times might seek to turn a free people

back into the hateful paths of despotism. They knew the proneness of prosperity to breed tyrants, and they meant when such should reappear in this fair land and commence their vocation they should find left for them at least one hard nut to crack.

Now let us hear Judge Douglas' view of the same subject, as I find it in the printed report of his late speech. Here it is:[54]

And Lincoln proceeded to quote Douglas' assertion that the Declaration referred only to "British subjects on this continent being equal to British subjects . . . in Great Britain."

My good friends, read that carefully over some leisure hour, and ponder well upon it — see what a mere wreck — mangled ruin — it makes of our once glorious Declaration...

Why, according to this, not only negroes but white people outside of Great Britain and America are not spoken of in that instrument. The English, Irish, and Scotch, along with white Americans, were included to be sure, but the French, Germans and other white people of the world are all gone to pot along with the Judge's inferior races.

I had thought the Declaration promised something better than the condition of British subjects; but no, it only meant that we should be equal to them in their own oppressed and unequal condition. According to that, it gave no promise that having kicked off the King and Lords of Great Britain, we should not at once be saddled with a King and Lords of our own.

I had thought the Declaration contemplated the progressive improvement in the condition of all men everywhere; but no, it merely "was adopted for the purpose of justifying the colonists in the eyes of the civilized world in withdrawing their allegiance from the British crown, and dissolving their connection with the mother country." Why, that object having been effected some eighty years ago, the Declaration is of no practical use now — mere rubbish — old wadding left to rot on the battlefield after the victory is won.

I understand you are preparing to celebrate the "Fourth," tomorrow week. What for? The doings of that day had no reference to the present; and quite half of you are not even descendants of those who were referred to at that day. But I suppose you will celebrate; and will even go so far as to read the Declaration. Suppose after you read it once in the old fashioned way, you read it once more with Judge Douglas'

version. It will then run thus: "We hold these truths to be
self-evident that all British subjects who were on this continent eighty-one years ago were created equal to all British
subjects born and then residing in Great Britain."

And now I appeal to all — to Democrats as well as others, —
are you really willing that the Declaration shall be thus frit-
tered away? — thus left no more at most, than an interesting
memorial of the dead past? thus shorn of its vitality, and
practical value; and left without the germ or even suggestion
of the individual rights of man in it?[55]

With far-seeing eye Lincoln discerned the struggle which
loomed for the senatorship the following year, and laid bare
the chief argument on which Douglas would rely to win reelection:

> There is a natural disgust in the minds of nearly all white
> people, to the idea of an indiscriminate amalgamation of the
> white and black races; and Judge Douglas evidently is basing
> his chief hope upon the chances of his being able to appro-
> priate the benefit of this disgust to himself. If he can, by
> much drumming and repeating, fasten the odium of that
> idea upon his adversaries, he thinks he can struggle through
> the storm. He therefore clings to this hope, as a drowning
> man to the last plank. . .
>
> He finds the Republicans insisting that the Declaration of
> Independence includes ALL MEN, black as well as white;
> and forthwith he boldly denies that it includes negroes at all,
> and proceeds to argue gravely that all who contend it does,
> do so only because they want to vote, and eat, and sleep, and
> marry with negroes! . . .
>
> Now I protest against the counterfeit logic which concludes
> that, because I do not want a black woman for a slave I must
> necessarily want her for a wife. I need not have her for
> either, I can just leave her alone. In some respects she cer-
> tainly is not my equal; but in her natural right to eat the
> bread she earns with her own hands without asking leave
> of any one else, she is my equal, and the equal of all others.[56]

This brought Lincoln to Douglas' argument that freedom
for the slave meant miscegenation, and that slavery was the
only way to preserve the purity of the white race:

> Judge Douglas is especially horrified at the thought of the
> mixing of blood by the white and black races. . . On this

point we fully agree with the Judge; and when he shall show that his policy is better adapted to prevent amalgamation than ours we shall drop ours, and adopt his. Let us see. In 1850 there were in the United States 405,751 mulattoes. Very few of these are the offspring of whites and free blacks; nearly all have sprung from black slaves and white masters. . .

Among the free states those which make the colored man the nearest to equal the white, have proportionably . . . the least of amalgamation. In New Hampshire, the state which goes farthest toward equality between the races, there are just 184 mulattoes, while there are in Virginia — how many do you think? — 79,775, being 23,126 more than in all the free states together.

These statistics show that slavery is the greatest source of amalgamation; and next to it, not the elevation, but the degradation of the free blacks. Yet Judge Douglas dreads the slightest restraints on the spread of slavery, and the slightest human recognition of the negro, as tending horribly to amalgamation.[57]

The Dred Scott speech was Lincoln's last great effort before the opening of the campaign of 1858. In the ensuing time Douglas had his falling out with Buchanan over the Lecompton Constitution and was attracting Republican support because of his opposition to the administration. Even Seward was reported favorable to the Little Giant's candidacy. It was the best way, the eastern Republicans thought, to deal a blow to Buchanan. Some Republican leaders even hoped thereby to draw the Little Giant into the party.

Lincoln watched these moves anxiously. He wanted nothing to prejudice the Republican campaign in Illinois or to hurt his chances for the Senate, should he be selected as the party's candidate, as it seemed likely he would be. Besides, outside Republican support of Douglas might well destroy the party in Illinois. In a letter to Lyman Trumbull in November 1857, he wrote:

What think you of the probable "rumpus" among the Democracy over the Kansas Constitution? I think the Republicans should stand clear of it. In their view both the President and Douglas are wrong; and they should not espouse the cause of either, because they may consider the other a little the farther wrong of the two. From what I am told here, Douglas tried, before leaving, to draw off some

Republicans on this dodge, and even succeeded in making some impression on one or two.[58]

On December 28 he expressed alarm at the support being given to Douglas by Horace Greeley. Writing again to Trumbull, he said:

> What does the *New York Tribune* mean by its constant eulogising, and admiring, and magnifying Douglas? Does it, in this, speak the sentiments of the Republicans at Washington? Have they concluded that the Republican cause, generally, can be best promoted by sacrificing us here in Illinois? If so we would like to know it soon; it will save us a great deal of labor to surrender at once.
>
> As yet I have heard of no Republican here going over to Douglas; but if the *Tribune* continues to din his praises into the ears of its five or ten thousand Republican readers in Illinois, it is more than can be hoped that all will stand firm.[59]

But the Republicans of Illinois were not buying what the eastern Republicans were trying to sell. They refused to take their enemy to their bosoms. They felt they knew him better than their confreres back east. They did not trust the "Greek even when bearing gifts," as one stalwart wrote to Trumbull. "You cannot get the Republicans of Illinois to touch him with a 1,000-foot pole," wrote another to Trumbull.[60] The Chicago *Tribune* snorted: "There seems to be a considerable notion pervading the brains of the political wet nurses at the East, that the barbarians of Illinois cannot take care of themselves," while the Chicago *Journal* told easterners to keep hands off; the Illinoisans would know how to "deal with Senator Douglas in their own way."[61] State Auditor Jesse K. Dubois perhaps summed up the Republican views best, when he, too, wrote to Trumbull: "It is asking too much of human nature . . . to surrender to Judge Douglas . . . [and] let him step foremost in our ranks now and make us all take back seats."[62]

The Illinois Republicans were determined to run their own candidate. With one senatorship held by Trumbull, an ex-Democrat, it was only fair that the other should go to a former Whig, and Lincoln was recognized as the most deserving. If Douglas wanted to affiliate with the Republican Party openly, he might be given a place in the cabinet of the next President — but as for the senatorship, that clearly belonged to Lincoln. So spoke the Chicago *Tribune*.[63] As the time for the state convention at Springfield on June 16 drew near, numerous county conventions throughout the state declared for Lincoln as their choice for Senator. Thus the ground was cut from under other aspirants, such as "Long John" Wentworth, editor of the Chicago *Democrat*, and one of the ablest and most astute politicians in the party, who had recently been elected Mayor of Chicago.

In the meantime Lincoln was busy corresponding with key figures throughout the state. His purpose, besides furthering his own candidacy, was to clarify the essential issues between the Republicans and the Douglas Democrats, which had been muddied by the Little Giant's feud with Buchanan and the meddling of the eastern Republicans. In a letter to Jediah F. Alexander on May 15, he drew a most important distinction between the positions of the contending parties, which further exposed Douglas' inconsistency:

> As I understand, there remains all the difference there ever was between Judge Douglas and the Republicans — they insisting that Congress shall not keep slavery out of the territories before and up to the time they form State constitutions. No Republican has ever contended that, when a constitution is to be formed, any but the people of the territory shall form it. Republicans have never contended that Congress should dictate a constitution to any state or territory; but they have contended that the people should be perfectly free to form their constitution in their own way — as perfectly free from the presence of slavery amongst them, as from every other improper influence.
>
> In voting together in opposition to a constitution being forced upon the people of Kansas, neither Judge Douglas nor the Republicans, has conceded anything which was ever in dispute between them.[64]

This analysis revealed Lincoln's reasoning on Douglas' theory of unfavorable local law which supposedly could keep slavery out of a territory before a constitution was drafted and voted upon. This theory was based on Douglas' assumption that the door must be open to slavery in accordance with the Dred Scott decision, and that it then could be immediately shut in its face, in accordance with popular sovereignty. It chose to disregard two conclusions which seemed definitely to result from the Dred Scott decision. First, slavery was so sacred a property right that neither the people nor Congress could prevent its entering a territory, and second, once entered, it could not be cast out even by means of a constitution. In other words, the court said that slavery was untouchable, whether before or after a constitution.

Less than a week before the Republican convention was to meet, we find Lincoln attempting to explode a charge levelled by Douglas and his followers: the Republicans were uniting with the Buchanan Democrats, or the Danites, as Douglas was now calling them, in order to bring about the downfall of the Little Giant. Douglas was to repeat this charge over and over again in the course of the ensuing debates. In a letter to Samuel Wilkinson on June 10, Lincoln wrote what he thought of this charge:

> I know of no effort to unite the Republicans and Buchanan men, and believe there is none. Of course the Republicans do not try to keep the common enemy from dividing; but, so far as I know, or believe, they will not unite with either branch of the division. Indeed it is difficult for me to see, on what ground they could unite; . . . It is a trick of our enemies to try to excite all sorts of suspicions and jealousies amongst us.[65]

The stage was now set for the battle of the Illinois giants. In another few days the curtain would be lifted and the drama would unfold.

CHAPTER 4

Tall Sucker and Little Giant

The confrontation between Lincoln and Douglas is ample proof that truth is stranger than fiction. What contrived situation could bring two such fantastic opposites together on the same platform? The issues of the campaign were exciting of themselves, but the appearance and personalities of the contestants made them even more so. There promised to be such color and spice in this contest that it was certain to bring out the crowds.

Descriptions of Lincoln are many; those of Douglas, few. If their roles had been reversed, the opposite would be true. The myriad of tomes now in the libraries would have been written about Douglas, and Lincoln would have been remembered merely as the gifted eccentric who had opposed him. Though there are more contemporary eyewitness descriptions of Lincoln than of Douglas, this chapter will attempt to strike a balance in the comparison between them.

The nicknames of both men reflected their image before the public. Lincoln was "Abe," "Honest Abe" or "Old Abe" to his friends,[1] just as he was "Spot" or "Spotty" to his enemies. Jocularly, because of his size, he was sometimes called "Long Abe." The amusing title of "Tall Sucker" which identified him with Illinois, the Sucker State,[2] was usually applied to him by outsiders.

Douglas received the affectionate and admiring title of "Lit-

tle Giant" early in his career. Most sources indicate that it was
applied to him in 1834 when, in a debate on Jackson's policy
of refusing to recharter the United States Bank, Douglas
worsted the most prominent lawyer in Jacksonville, who was
notorious as "the greatest master of invective."[3] So sensational
was Douglas' performance and so high the excitement following his speech that some of the crowd rushed forward and
lifted him to their shoulders, shouting that he was their "little
gamecock" and "Little Giant," and proudly displaying him
to the onlookers.[4]

With the passage of time, however, the origin of the nickname seemed to have been lost, because during the debates
of 1858 the Peoria *Transcript* tried to satisfy the curiosity of
its readers with this story:

> It is not generally known how Stephen A. Douglas re-
> ceived the sobriquet of "Little Giant." He is indebted to Joe
> Smith, the Mormon Prophet, for first applying it to him. —
> It was elicited during an exciting discussion in the Illinois
> Legislature upon the Mormon difficulties, in which Douglas
> cut a conspicuous figure in the defense of the saints, when
> their great leader, in giving vent to his unbounded admira-
> tion for Douglas called him the "Little Giant."[5]

The first written mention of the nickname seems to have
appeared in the *Illinois State Register* on November 23, 1839
in reporting what was also probably the first debate between
Lincoln and Douglas. The occasion was a discussion preliminary to the presidential campaign of 1840, in which Lincoln
and one Cyrus Walker opposed Douglas. In reporting this
game of "two pluck one" as it was popularly called, the partisan *Register* said that "between two Whig Speakers our
Democratic 'little giant' . . . had a rough time of it," but in
spite of it all "literally swamped his adversaries."[6]

It is William Herndon, Lincoln's partner and biographer,
who has left us the most detailed descriptions of Lincoln. Billy
was the friend and associate who was closest to him over the
years. He was a careful observer and recorded meticulously
every nuance of his idol's physical makeup and character. It
was Herndon's purpose to present the truth about him, with
"nothing colored or suppressed" so that "the reader will see
and feel the presence of the living man."[7] He was not dis-

turbed that some of his frank observations might not, and in fact did not, sit well with a public that refused to believe its idols were human. He felt that Lincoln was great enough to withstand the harsh scrutiny of time. This is how he describes his physical appearance:

Mr. Lincoln was six feet four inches high. . . He was thin, wiry, sinewy, raw-boned; thin through the breast to the back, and narrow across the shoulders; . . . he . . . was stoop-shouldered, inclining to the consumptive by build. . . His structure was loose and leathery; his body was shrunk and shrivelled; he had dark skin, dark hair, and looked woe-struck. The whole man, body and mind, worked slowly, as if it needed oiling. Physically he was a very powerful man, lifting with ease four hundred, and in one case six hundred pounds. His mind was like his body, and worked slowly but strongly. . .

When he walked he moved cautiously but firmly; his long arms and giant hands swung down by his sides. . . He put the whole foot flat down on the ground at once, not landing on the heel; he lifted his foot all at once, not rising from the toe, and hence he had no spring in his walk. . . In sitting down on a common chair he was no taller than ordinary men. His legs and arms were abnormally, unnaturally long, and in undue proportion to the remainder of his body. It was only when he stood up that he loomed above other men.

Mr. Lincoln's head was long, and tall from the base of the brain and from the eyebrows. . . The size of his hat measured seven and one-eighth . . . his hair lay floating where his fingers or the winds left it, piled up at random. His nose was large, long, blunt and a little awry towards the right eye; his chin was sharp and upcurved; his eyebrows cropped out like a huge rock on the brow of a hill; his long, sallow face was wrinkled and dry, his ears were large, and ran out almost at right angles from his head, caused partly by heavy hats and partly by nature; his lower lip was thick, hanging, and undercurved, there was the one mole on the right cheek, and Adam's apple on his throat. . .

He was not a pretty man by any means, nor was he an ugly one; he was a homely man, careless of his looks, plain-looking and plain-acting.[8]

Donn Piatt, a young lawyer who canvassed southern Illinois for Lincoln during the presidential campaign of 1860, and subsequently served as a general during the Civil War, thought Lincoln the homeliest man he ever saw. "His body seemed a huge skeleton in clothes. Tall as he was, his hands and feet looked out of proportion, so long and clumsy were they."[9]

Did Abe Lincoln really appear ugly to all those who knew or met him? He himself thought that he was ugly and frequently told jokes on himself to illustrate this opinion. One of his favorites described how he met a stranger who thrust a gun in his face saying that he had sworn to shoot any man he found who was uglier than himself. Lincoln studied the fellow's face and then said: "If I am uglier than you are I don't want to live. Go ahead and shoot."[10]

A story is still current in Jonesboro of a young man who traveled many miles to this site of the second debate just to see if Lincoln was really as ugly as he was said to be.[11]

The impression Lincoln made on people depended, however, on the mood he was in. His face was very mobile and reflected sensitively the changing reactions of the moment. An excellent description of this is given by Nicolay:

> Lincoln's features were the despair of every artist who undertook his portrait. The writer saw nearly a dozen, one after another, soon after the first nomination to the presidency, attempt the task. They put into their pictures the large rugged features, and strong prominent lines; they made measurements to obtain exact proportions; they "petrified" some single look, but the picture remained hard and cold. Even before these paintings were finished it was plain to see that they were unsatisfactory to the artists themselves, and much more so to the intimate friends of the man; this was not he who smiled, spoke, laughed, charmed. . .
>
> Graphic art was powerless before a face that moved through a thousand delicate gradations of line and contour, light and shade, sparkle of the eye and curve of the lip, in the long gamut of expression from grave to gay, and back again from the rollicking jollity of laughter to that serious, far-away look. . . There are many pictures of Lincoln; there is no portrait of him.[12]

Walt Whitman, who had seen the President on several occasions, likewise thought that "none of the artists have caught the deep, though subtle and indirect expression of this man's face. They have only caught the surface."[13] Henry Villard, of

the *New York Herald*, was also of the opinion that he had
"never seen a picture of him that does anything like justice
to the original. He is a much better-looking man than any of
the pictures represent."[14] According to Donn Piatt, his face
in repose was "dull, heavy and repellent. It brightened like a
lit lantern when moved by some matter of human interest."[15]

The matters of human interest that could cause a change
in Lincoln's mood and in his countenance were explained
by Horace White:

> When [he was] taking part in a conversation, or addressing
> an audience, or telling a story, the dull, listless features
> dropped like a mask. The melancholy shadow disappeared
> in a twinkling. The eye began to sparkle, the mouth to smile,
> the whole countenance was wreathed with animation, so that
> a stranger would have said: "Why, this man, so angular and
> somber a moment ago, is really handsome."[16]

But what caused the melancholy that was remarked by most
observers and was relieved only when Lincoln was moved to
animation? Stuart, his former partner, attributed it to a slug-
gish liver and inactive bowels. He even gave him calomel pills
for this condition which Lincoln took for a time.[17] Judge David
Davis, before whom Lincoln practiced on the Eighth Judicial
Circuit, and who knew Lincoln well, thought domestic un-
happiness was responsible. And this is what Herndon had to
say:

> Lincoln's melancholy never failed to impress any man who
> ever saw or knew him. . . He was a sad-looking man, his
> melancholy dripped from him as he walked. . .
> Two things greatly intensified his characteristic sadness;
> one was the endless succession of troubles in his domestic life,
> which he had to bear in silence; and the other was unques-
> tionably the knowledge of his own obscure and lowly origin.
> The recollection of these things burned a deep impress on
> his sensitive soul.[18]

L. Pierce Clark, whose *Psycho-Biography* attempts a Freudian approach to the study of Lincoln, says that he "suffered
from neurotic depression rather than from melancholia, which
is a psychotic disorder, an actual mental aberration."[19] This
condition derived from "an excessive amount of narcissism
in relationship with a loved object," which involved a "need

to be loved" and "an inordinate desire for approbation." Lack of satisfaction in these respects would plunge a person of depressive temperament into "moods of deep gloom."[20]

However, a psychological study by Dr. Milton H. Shutes, who employs an eclectic rather than a Freudian approach, attributes the moods of depression chiefly to abnormality of the eyes and resulting eye strain. Some time between 1854 and 1856 Lincoln began to use glasses for reading. Oculists who have examined these glasses have found them excessively overcorrected, a fact indicating that Lincoln suffered from far-sightedness. "Far-sighted people," says Shutes, "are prone to frontal and basal headaches and other complaints. An uncorrected refractive error associated with eye-muscle imbalance is, with few exceptions, almost certain to cause, separately or together, headache, headspins, nervousness, irritability, fatigue, depression, nausea and other nervous symptoms."[21]

Whatever the explanation, the stump and the story served as Lincoln's release from habitual depression. Regarding Lincoln's penchant for story-telling, his friend, Joshua Speed, stated: "His world-wide reputation for telling anecdotes and telling them so well was in my judgment necessary to his very existence. Most men who have been great students, such as he was, in their hours of idleness have taken to the bottle, to cards, or dice. He had no fondness for any of these. Hence he sought relaxation in anecdotes."[22] Isaac Newton Arnold, another biographer, who was a Congressman during the Civil War, relates the following incident: After the crushing defeat at Fredericksburg, Arnold visited the President, who proceeded to read to him some passages from Artemus Ward, the humorist. Taken aback, Arnold asked how he could do such a thing while the Union forces were still in pell-mell retreat from the field of battle. Lincoln answered: "Mr. Arnold, if I could not get momentary respite from the crushing burden I am constantly carrying, my heart would break."[23]

Herndon describes how Lincoln's power as a raconteur and humorist drew people to him as honey draws ants. On the circuit when he relieved the tedium after court, all who were around including "the tavern loungers enjoyed it, and his melancholy, taking to itself wings, seemed to fly away."[24] Says Herndon:

In the role of a story-teller I am prone to regard Mr. Lincoln as without an equal. I have seen him surrounded by a crowd numbering as many as two and in some cases three hundred persons, all deeply interested in the outcome of a story which, when he had finished it, speedily found repetition in every grocery and lounging place within reach. His power of mimicry, and his manner of recital, were in many respects unique, if not remarkable. His countenance and all his features seemed to take part in the performance.

As he neared the pith or point of the joke or story every vestige of seriousness disappeared from his face. His little gray eyes sparkled; a smile seemed to gather up, curtain like, the corners of his mouth; his frame quivered with suppressed excitement; and when the point — or "nub" of the story, as he called it came, no one's laugh was heartier than his.[25]

Herndon's concluding observations are illuminating as to the effect of Lincoln's story-telling on his career: "Any lawyer, ambitious to gain prominence, would hardly dare thus to entertain a crowd, except at the risk of his reputation; but with Lincoln it gave him, in some mysterious way, a singularly firm hold on the people."[26]

Horace White, who accompanied Lincoln during the debates of 1858 as a reporter for the *Chicago Tribune*, describes how Lincoln filled in the time between speeches with stories:

From the beginning to the end of our travels the fund of anecdotes never failed, and, wherever we happened to be, all the people within ear shot would begin to work their way up to this inimitable story-teller. His stories were always "apropos" of something going on, and oftenest related to things that had happened in his own neighborhood. He was constantly being reminded of one, and, when he told it, his facial expression was so irresistibly comic that the bystanders generally exploded in laughter before he reached what he called the "nub" of it.[27]

During the course of the debates, the crowds looked with anticipation to a Lincoln story in illustration of some point, and on several occasions they were not disappointed.

Herndon's meticulous description of Lincoln is matched somewhat by that of a newspaper correspondent's impression of the Little Giant:

Mr. Douglas has a brow of unusual size, covered with heavy masses of dark-brown hair, now beginning to be sprinkled with silver. His forehead is high, open, and splendidly developed, based on dark, thick eyebrows of great width. His eyes, large and deeply set, are of the darkest and most brilliant hue. . . The chin is square and vigorous, and is full of eddying dimples — the muscles and nerves showing great mobility. . . Add now a rich, dark complexion; clear and healthy; smoothly-shaven cheeks and handsome throat; small, white ears; . . . small, white hands, small feet; a full chest and broad shoulders; and we have a picture of the Little Giant.[28]

Another reporter's description, however, differed in a few respects:

Perhaps you have never seen him — well, S. A. Douglas is a man standing five feet two or three, with a head big enough for six feet two, and a forehead prominent and intellectual enough for any man of any nation. His hair, which was once brown, is thin and gray; his eye cool and gray; his nose not prominent, but striking; his mouth large and firm. His whole face is round, and seems too large even for such broad shoulders as support it.[29]

The correspondent of the New York *Evening Post* wrote of his being "short, thick-set and burly" and having "a fierce, bull-dog look;"[30] while Carl Schurz, later to achieve fame as a cabinet officer and writer, described him standing beside Lincoln "like a dwarf . . . but . . . broad-chested, a massive head upon a strong neck — the very embodiment of force, combativeness, and staying power."[31]

The slender, frail youngster had filled out considerably as a man. Clark E. Carr, who in his youth had known the Little Giant, later wrote his biography, in which he notes that as a Senator "he had already become a little corpulent."[32] Nevertheless, despite his bulk, he was quick and animated in speech and manner — the opposite of Lincoln. Harriet Beecher Stowe, author of *Uncle Tom's Cabin*, who sat in the Senate gallery in 1856 and watched Douglas speak, thought that he was "the very ideal of vitality . . . short, broad, and thick-set, every inch of him has its own alertness and motion."[33]

Carl Schurz, who was at the Quincy debate, and wrote a penetrating account of it, contrasted the two chief actors, making mention of an unusual peculiarity of Douglas' facial features — "a deep horizontal wrinkle between his eyes, which was unusually dark and scowling."[34]

Photographs of Douglas show this marked peculiarity. Some also catch the strange power of his eyes. Douglas' eyes held Major George Murray McConnell under a spell, as they must have held many others of his followers. McConnell was the son of the man who befriended Douglas when he first came to Jacksonville and who lent him his law books. Many years later he recalled his vivid childhood memories of him:

> During the early years of my life, Mr. Douglas was often in my father's house. I remember most distinctly, perhaps, his eyes and his voice. The eyes were large, steady, and with a peculiar quality that impressed one as depth. . . . There is a portrait of Napoleon the eyes of which always produced the same effect on me, gave me the same creepy kind of thrill along the spinal column . . . a thrill as one looks down into limpid fathomless depths of water, or rather, when from the top of a tall tower, one lies flat and looks straight away from the earth into the infinite.[35]

McConnell lamented that Douglas was not taller.

> It has always seemed to me a misfortune for him that he was so short in stature. His walk in life forced him to "show himself" to his fellow men. . . He rose by sheer force of brain and will, above the disadvantage. . . I have always felt that if he had been given the imposing stature and presence of Webster, for example, he would have loomed larger in the history of his country.[36]

This regret seems without foundation, however. It was Douglas' size that undoubtedly helped endear him to people. It probably was also responsible in large measure for his developing compensatory traits strong and attractive enough to raise him high in the political councils of the nation. Carr describes one characteristic which drew people to him:

> [He was] what politicians would call a good mixer. There was no company in which he could not be a congenial companion. In company of the great at Washington and in the cabin of the frontier, with grave senators, with cabinet officials, and with the plain people — farmers and mechanics

and laboring men — he was equally at home. . . to such a
degree as to make them feel that he was one of them. . .

In all his public career he never forgot a friend, and never
failed to serve him in an emergency if within his power. His
friends realized this, and in turn gave him similar confidence
and support.[37]

Even more important was his "happy faculty of remembering names and faces." McConnell confirms this facet of Douglas'
personality:

> When he came to Jacksonville, he knew everybody. It was
> a wonderful power he had . . . of calling "Cap" and Dick and
> John and Patrick each by his proper name on the instant . . .
> never misplacing one of them. . . There is no more subtle or
> more powerful flattery possible to man. He gave to everyone
> of those humble and practically nameless followers the im-
> pression, the feeling, that he was the frank, personal friend
> of each one of them.[38]

A further insight into Douglas' character and his warm manner with people is afforded by a picture which Carr paints of
the "boy judge" — a picture as incredible as it is charming.
It is obviously one which was possible only in the days of the
unconventional frontier:

> When presiding as a judge on the bench he would frequent-
> ly, while the lawyers were addressing the jury, go down among
> the spectators and seat himself beside an old friend and visit
> with him, all the time keeping cognizance of what was
> going on, ready to respond when his attention to the case
> at bar was required, maintaining all the time the most per-
> fect order. He has been seen at Knoxville, when the court
> room was crowded, to seat himself upon the knee of old
> Governor McMurtry, and, with his arm upon his shoulder,
> talk with him for a considerable time, which, diminutive as
> was his stature, and great as was that of the Governor, did
> not seem incongruous.[39]

Unlike Lincoln, however, Douglas could not tell a story.
Carr says that "he would enjoy and laugh at stories, but there
is no record of his ever having told one."[40] It was just as well.
The perceptive Mrs. Stowe, prejudiced though she was, made
an observation which was an unintended tribute to Douglas'
personality:

It is a merciful providence that with all his alertness and adroitness, all his quick-sighted keenness, Douglas is not witty — that might have made him too irresistible a demagogue for the liberties of our laughter-loving people.[41]

THE HERITAGE OF THE AX

One of Lincoln's important physical assets was his great strength and unfailing good health. In spite of his thin, elongated frame and stooping shoulders, he had big powerful hands and arms. Mayor Henry Sanderson of Galesburg, at whose house Lincoln stopped to refresh himself with a warm bath before the fifth debate, saw Old Abe stripped and thought him "the strongest man I ever looked at."[42]

This heritage went back to his early boyhood when, according to his autobiography, his father "settled in an unbroken forest [in Indiana], and the clearing away of surplus wood was the great task ahead. Abraham, though very young, was large of his age, and had an ax put into his hands at once; and from that till within his twenty-third year he was almost constantly handling that most useful instrument."[43]

Those who knew him respected this great strength. Part of the Lincoln legend is the story of his wrestling match with Jack Armstrong, the leader of the tough "Clary's Grove Boys," when he first came to New Salem. His conquest of Armstrong established his reputation in that part of the country, and gave him acceptance by the respectable, as well as by the doubtful, elements of the pioneer community.

According to Nicolay and Hay, "he was often unfaithful to his Quaker traditions in those days of his youth," because he loved a little physical play and brawling occasionally.[44] Few there were who dared to enter into a contest with him. Thomas D. Jones, the Cincinnati sculptor who in December 1860 made a bust of Lincoln, recalls Lincoln saying: "All I had to do was to extend one hand to a man's shoulder, and with weight of body and strength of arms give him a trip that generally sent him sprawling on the ground, which would so astonish him as to give him a quietus."[45]

An incident is related of the campaign of 1838, when Lincoln came to the aid of his friend Edward D. Baker. In the course of a heated speech, Baker's antagonists threatened to

pull him down from the platform. Suddenly Lincoln appeared
as if from nowhere and came to his rescue, shouting above the
crowd that this was a land of free speech, and challenging anyone to take Baker from the rostrum while he was there. No
one saw fit to interfere, the crowd quieted down, and Baker
continued with his speech.[46]

The debate at Charleston was enlivened by an unexpected
exhibition of Lincoln's physical prowess. In the course of his
rebuttal Lincoln seized Orlando B. Ficklin, his old rival in
the Matson case and a former colleague in Congress, who
was seated on the platform as a prominent supporter of Douglas, and thrust him before the crowd to testify to his (Lincoln's)
record in the voting of supplies in the Mexican War. Poor
Ficklin could offer little resistance while he was in the powerful
grip of Lincoln's big hand, and he must have felt just as sheep-
ish as he was embarrassed.

It is understandable that Lincoln's strong physique enabled
him to hold up against the rigors of a speaking campaign with
little adverse effect. In fact, as the campaign of 1858 proceeded,
it was noted that Lincoln seemed to thrive on the experience
and to appear fresher at the end than when he started.

The same was not true of Douglas. We have already seen
how he had a breakdown in health when he was a boy, and
how he became seriously ill of fever on his way to the West.
He displayed an unaccountable robustness in the gruelling
five-month congressional canvas which he conducted against
John T. Stuart in 1838. However, the spring of 1843 again
found his health impaired to such an extent that he contemplated resigning his judgeship. When his party needed him to
contest the congressional seat of his district against Orville H.
Browning, he resigned his office to make the race.

As was the case five years before, the candidates traveled
the district together, engaging in joint discussion. Unlike the
first canvass, this was only a three-month affair. Douglas
emerged the winner this time, but according to James W.
Sheahan, Douglas' biographer, "so great had been the exertions
and labors of the candidates, that on election-day both were
prostrated with illness from which neither recovered for nearly
two months."[47]

In 1848 Douglas suffered another attack of fever, followed
the next year by a siege of cholera and diarrhea, which left

permanent scars on his health. He was not the type to spare himself, however, and his strenuous activity and apparently enormous energy belied the inroads on his constitution. During the Lecompton debate, he was under such severe strain that Republican Senator James Dixon, won to admiration of the Little Giant for his courageous battle, wrote:

> Douglas is quite unwell. He came into our night session about midnight on Monday, but we sent him home. He was not fit to be there. He is very nervous, though he does not show it at all in his looks or appearance. . . For ten days and nights he did not sleep at all, and for four days last week he was confined to his bed.[48]

Douglas also had trouble with his throat, the result undoubtedly of his constant debating and campaigning. It seemed to require treatment every year, and in 1855 it became ulcerated, necessitating an operation. As a result of these experiences, toward the end of the 1858 campaign against Lincoln, the strain began to show on the Little Giant. Both his appearance and his voice suffered. The difference between him and Lincoln in this regard was noted by several newspaper correspondents.[49]

"THE GLASS OF FASHION"

The contrast between the two opponents was just as vivid in the matter of dress. Herndon himself pointed it up: "He was careless of his dress, and his clothes, instead of fitting neatly as did the garments of Douglas on the latter's well-rounded form, hung loosely on his giant frame."[50] Elihu B. Washburne, a staunch Lincoln admirer, described Old Abe as he appeared when they were at a River and Harbor Convention at Chicago in 1847: "No one who saw him can forget his personal appearance at that time. . . He had on a short-waisted, thin swallow-tail coat, a short vest of the same material, thin pantaloons, scarcely coming down to his ankles, a straw hat and a pair of brogans with woolen socks."[51]

According to Herndon:

> His hat was brown, faded, and the nap usually worn or rubbed off. He wore a short cloak and sometimes a shawl. . . On the circuit he carried in one hand a faded green umbrella,

with "A. Lincoln" in large white cotton or muslin letters
sewed on the inside. The knob was gone from the handle, and
when closed a piece of cord was usually tied around it in the
middle to keep it from flying open. In the other hand he
carried a literal carpet-bag, in which were stored a few papers
to be used in court, and underclothing enough to last until
his return to Springfield.[52]

While Lincoln undoubtedly was not a model of fashion,
his later photographs show him to be dressed in good taste.
As a prominent citizen he probably was not without awareness
of the necessity of making a presentable appearance. It is also
hardly likely that a "lady of quality" like Mary Todd would
allow her husband, for all his carelessness, to appear in public
in such a way as to reflect on the family. Lincoln's clothes might
have been too short or too baggy for his tall spare frame and
they might have been unbrushed, and the pioneer customs of
Springfield might have been tolerant of a lack of fastidiousness
in dress, but Lincoln at the time of the debates had improved
considerably since his early days. That this was true is revealed
in a story recounted by Herndon of Lincoln's trip to New
York in February 1860 to make his memorable speech at
Cooper Union:

> On his return home Lincoln told me that for once in his
> life he was greatly abashed over his personal appearance. The
> new suit of clothes which he donned on his arrival in New
> York were ill-fitting garments, and showed the creases made
> while packed in the valise; and for a long time after he began
> his speech and before he became "warmed up" he imagined
> that the audience noticed the contrast between his Western
> clothes and the neat-fitting suits of Mr. William Cullen Bryant
> and others who sat on the platform. The collar of his coat on
> the right side had an unpleasant way of flying up whenever
> he raised his arm to gesticulate. He imagined the audience
> noticed that also.[53]

It was on this occasion that Lincoln had his picture taken
for the first time by the famous photographer Mathew Brady.
It is a good photograph in spite of the "store clothes," and one
can understand why Lincoln is reported to have said that it
helped to make him President.

Douglas, on the other hand, advanced beyond the simple
requirements of Springfield. Long years in Washington as a

figure of national prominence had invested him with a courtliness and polish which were reflected in his clothes, as well as in his manners. Unlike Lincoln, who was practically indifferent to the acquisition of money, Douglas had accumulated a sizable fortune, particularly through shrewd investments in Chicago real estate, and he was able to live in the style expected of one of the foremost statesmen of the time. Clark E. Carr states that after he attained high position he was almost "the glass of fashion."[54] During the great debates, reporters frequently commented on his appearance, one of them recording that Douglas wore a white hat and coat.[55] Carl Schurz, who was at the sixth debate said: "On the stage at Quincy he looked rather natty and well-groomed, being clothed in excellently fitting broadcloth and shining linen."[56]

The Little Giant was as generous in his use of money as he was competent in its acquisition. In 1856 he sold one hundred acres of land for $100,000 in order to aid the Buchanan campaign. In the same year he deeded ten acres of valuable land, estimated to be worth $6000 an acre, to help found the University of Chicago.

In other personal habits the opponents were also unlike. We have already learned from Herndon that Lincoln did not drink. In fact, he was one of the leading temperance advocates in Springfield, and at one time was the orator of the day at a great temperance gathering. He also did not smoke. Douglas, on the other hand, both drank and smoked.[57]

Horace White, discussing Douglas' charge at the first debate that Lincoln as a young man "could ruin more liquor than all of the boys in town together," states: "Everybody who knew Lincoln knew that he never used liquor or tobacco at all. . . . Not only was Douglas' statement essentially false as to Lincoln, but it would have been a true description of himself at the time of the Ottawa debate. The fact was that Douglas at that time was drinking himself to death — an end which he reached three years later."[58] Carl Schurz, describing Douglas at Quincy, says that "his face seemed a little puffy, and it was said that he had been drinking hard with some boon companions either on his journey or since his arrival."[59]

In the course of his many speeches during the campaign, Douglas made a number of reckless and abusive statements, which were attributed to the fact that he had been drinking.

Lincoln generally responded to these attacks with a humorous rejoinder. On one occasion when Douglas referred to the fact that Lincoln had run a grocery store and sold liquor, he said: "The difference between Judge Douglas and myself on the grocery question is, that while I have stood on one side of the counter, he has been equally attentive on the other."[60] However, at the time of the Charleston debate, when he was apparently nettled by Douglas' behavior, he is said to have remarked: "I flatter myself that thus far my wife has not found it necessary to follow me around from place to place to keep me from getting drunk."[61]

As against such statements damaging to Douglas we have the statement of his biographer, Clark Carr, who writes:

> In the bitterness of political acrimony it was frequently stated that the Senator was too much addicted to drink. It cannot be denied that, at a time when excessive conviviality among politicians was the rule rather than the exception, he joined in the conviviality of his friends; but there is no authenticated instance of his having drunk to such excess as to warrant such an accusation. The writer saw him many times on public occasions when he spoke, and at social gatherings, and never saw any reason for such an accusation.[62]

How did the rivals compare in their platform style when addressing an audience? Herndon gives his usual meticulous description of Lincoln:

> When he arose to address courts, juries, or crowds of people, . . . at first he was very awkward, and it seemed a real labor to adjust himself to his surroundings. . . When he began speaking, his voice was shrill, piping, and unpleasant. . .
> He generally placed his hands behind him, the back of his left hand in the palm of his right, the thumb and fingers of his right hand clasped around the left arm at the wrist. . . As he proceeded he became somewhat animated, and to keep in harmony with his growing warmth his hands relaxed their grasp and fell to his side. Presently he clasped them in front of him, interlocking his fingers, one thumb meanwhile chasing another. His speech now requiring more emphatic utterance, his fingers unlocked and his hands fell apart. His left arm was thrown behind, the back of his hand resting against his body, his right hand seeking his side.

By this time he had gained sufficient composure, and his real speech began. He did not gesticulate as much with his hands as with his head. He used the latter frequently, throwing it with vim this way and that. . . It sometimes came with a quick jerk. . . He never sawed the air nor rent space into tatters and rags as some orators do. . .

As he moved along in his speech he became freer and less uneasy in his movements. . . There was a world of meaning and emphasis in the long, bony finger of his right hand as he dotted the ideas on the minds of his hearers. Sometimes, to express joy or pleasure, he would raise both hands at an angle of about fifty degrees, the palms upward. If the sentiment was one of detestation — denunciation of slavery, for example — both arms, thrown upward and fists clenched, swept through the air. This was one of his most effective gestures, and signified most vividly a fixed determination to drag down the object of his hatred and trample it in the dust.

He always stood squarely on his feet . . . He never . . . walked backward and forward on the platform. To ease his arms he frequently caught hold, with his left hand, of the lapel of his coat, keeping his thumb upright and leaving his right hand free to gesticulate. . .

As he proceeded with his speech the exercise of his vocal organs altered somewhat the tone of his voice. It lost in a measure its former acute and shrilling pitch, and mellowed into a more harmonious and pleasant sound.[63]

The first known description of Lincoln as a speaker appeared in the November 23, 1839 issue of the *Illinois State Register,* the Democratic paper which published what has previously been mentioned as the first Lincoln-Douglas debate on record:

He has . . . a sort of assumed clownishness in his manner which does not become him, and which does not truly belong to him. It is . . . assumed for effect. Mr. Lincoln will sometimes make his language correspond with this clownish manner, and he can thus frequently raise a loud laugh among his Whig hearers, but this entire game of buffoonery convinces the mind of no man, and is utterly lost on the majority of his audience.

We seriously advise Mr. Lincoln to correct this clownish fault, before it grows upon him.[64]

In later years Judge Logan recalled his impression of his future partner when he saw him canvassing for election in the summer of 1832:

> He was a very gawky and rough-looking fellow then; his pantaloons didn't meet his shoes by six inches. But after he began speaking I became very much interested in him. He made a very sensible speech. His manner was very much of the same as in after life; that is, the same peculiar characteristics were apparent then, though of course in after years he evinced more knowledge and experience. But he had then the same novelty and the same peculiarity in presenting his ideas. He had the same individuality that he kept all through his life.[65]

When Horace White heard him speak on the Kansas-Nebraska Act at Springfield in October 1854, it was a warm day and Mr. Lincoln was in his shirtsleeves when he stepped on the platform. White noted his "thin, high-pitched falsetto voice," but it had such "varying power" that it "could be heard at a long distance in spite of the bustling tumult of the crowd."[66]

Old Abe also had the accent and pronunciation peculiar to his native state, Kentucky. This was natural. The manner of speech and the picturesque twang of the Kentucky immigrants was characteristic of the southern part of Illinois where large numbers of them had settled. Lincoln pronounced "such" as "sich," and "Mr. Chairman" as "Mr. Cheerman." He frequently substituted "ain't" for "isn't" and "don't" for "doesn't." In spite of the care which he exercised during the debates, these solecisms occasionally crept into his speeches.

To White the most vivid remembrance of Lincoln as a speaker was "the tall, angular form with the long, angular arms, at times bent nearly double with excitement . . . the mobile face wet with perspiration which he discharged in drops as he threw his head this way and that like a projectile."[67]

Carl Schurz added to this picture in his recollections of the Quincy debate:

> He swung his long arms sometimes in a very ungraceful manner. Now and then, to give particular emphasis to a point, he would bend his knees and body with a sudden downward jerk and then shoot up again with a vehemence

that raised him to his tiptoes and made him look much taller
than he really was.[68]

When Lincoln was stumping New England for the Whig
ticket in September 1848, he struck George H. Monroe, a
young Whig, with his "familiar and off-hand style." He turned
up the sleeves of his black alpaca coat and then the cuffs of his
shirt. "Next he loosened his necktie, and soon after he took
it off altogether."[69]

While Lincoln, as Judge Logan pointed out, may have retained many of his individual peculiarities on the stump, it is
also true that over the years he discarded the earlier crudities
which annoyed the *Illinois State Register*. Off the stump, he
could make a speech without these peculiar mannerisms and
still impress an audience.

Major George Haven Putnam, who was present when Lincoln made his momentous speech at Cooper Union in 1860,
later described his reaction. The cultivated New Yorkers expected "a wild and woolly talk, illuminated by more or less
incongruous anecdotes," but, wrote Putnam:

> The first impression of the man from the West did nothing
> to contradict the expectation of something weird, rough and
> uncultivated. The long, ungainly figure upon which hung
> clothes that, while new for this trip, were evidently the work
> of an unskilful tailor; the large feet, and clumsy hands of
> which, at the outset, at least, the orator seemed to be unduly
> conscious; the long, gaunt head, capped by a shock of hair
> that seemed not to have been thoroughly brushed out, made
> a picture which did not fit in with New York's conception
> of a finished statesman. The first utterance of the voice was
> not pleasant to the ear, the tone being harsh and the key
> too high.
>
> As the speech progressed, however, the speaker seemed to
> get into control of himself, the voice gained a natural and
> impressive modulation, the gestures were dignified and ap-
> propriate, and the hearers came under the influence of the
> earnest look from the deeply-set eyes.[70]

A young contemporary of Douglas who heard him speak in
his home town of Jacksonville in 1838 recalled that he was
"surrounded by a motley crowd of backwoods farmers and
hunters, dressed in homespun or deerskin, [and that] he even

then showed signs of that dexterity in debate, and vehement, impressive declamation of which he became such a master."[71]

The Little Giant brought the rough style of oratory and debate characteristic of the pioneer West with him to Congress. The impression it left on John Quincy Adams was recorded in his diary in February 1844, more than a year before their memorable clash on the Mexican War, in which Douglas discomfited "Old Man Eloquent":

> Stephen A. Douglas, of Illinois, had taken the floor last evening, and now raved out his hour in abusive invectives . . . upon the Whig party. His face was convulsed, his gesticulation frantic, and he lashed himself into such a heat that if his body had been made of combustible matter it would have burnt out. In the midst of his roaring, to save himself from choking, he stripped off and cast away his cravat, unbuttoned his waistcoat, and had the air and aspect of a half-naked pugilist. And this man comes from a judicial bench, and passes for an eloquent orator![72]

Douglas, of course, changed with the years. With his acquired urbanity he discarded, like Lincoln, the cruder aspects of his platform manner, while retaining the force and vigor of his unique and powerful style.

When he was back campaigning in the West, however, Douglas often reverted to his old stump style, especially when hard pressed, as he was during the debates with Lincoln. To Carl Schurz at Quincy:

> He was, from the start, angry, dictatorial, and insolent in the extreme . . . and he went on in that style with a wrathful frown upon his brow, defiantly shaking his head, clenching his fists, and stamping his feet.[73]

Schurz, who confessed that he detested Douglas deeply, nevertheless went on to say that "his sentences were well put together, his points strongly accentuated, his argumentation seemingly clear and plausible."[74]

Probably the outstanding attribute of Douglas as a speaker was his voice. Its enchanting effect upon the ear must have heightened the appeal of his words and arguments. In this respect he had the advantage of Lincoln, the logic of whose sentences had to overcome the first unfavorable impressions caused by his voice.

A newspaper account described Douglas' voice as a "rich, musical baritone."[75] Clark Carr thought it "deep and strong,"[76] while Harriet Beecher Stowe wrote: "He has two requisites of a debater — a melodious voice and a clear, sharply defined enunciation."[77]

George Murray McConnell, continuing his description of the spell of Douglas' personality upon him, said:

> In ordinary intercourse he was not what could be fairly called a "loud talker." The vocal strength used was always adapted to the circumstances. But there was a certain quality of broad, deep, vibrant energy in the tone that was strangely enthralling alike to one or two, or to a throng of many thousands. His voice rose and fell, round, deep, sonorous, with the effortless volume of a great organ tone.[78]

The minds of the two opponents, which lay behind their platform manner, were also unlike. Douglas' was quick and incisive. His memory for political facts, dates and details was encyclopedic, and he used it with devastating effect on many occasions. He was an improviser, alert to the immediate implications of any situation and ready to take practical advantage of it.

Lincoln's mind, on the other hand, was slow and deliberative, but the effect of its conclusions deeper and longer-lasting.

To Herndon, who used to prod him to "speak with more vim, and arouse the jury," he once replied that the "long, labored movements" of his mind were rather like the large blade of a jackknife than the small blade of a penknife:

> I may not emit ideas as rapidly as others, because I am compelled by nature to speak slowly, but when I do throw off a thought it seems to me, though it comes with some effort, it has force enough to cut its own way and travel a greater distance.[79]

Lincoln also characterized his mind as "slow to learn and slow to forget," and like a "piece of steel — very hard to scratch anything on it, and almost impossible after you get it there to rub it out."[80]

Herndon wrote that Lincoln was "remorseless in his analysis of facts and processes." Only after he had gone through an exhaustive process could he form an idea and express it:

Everything had to run through the crucible of his mind; and when at last he did speak, his utterances rang out with the clear and keen ring of gold upon the counters of the understanding.[81]

His eloquence lay in the strength of his logical faculty, his supreme power of reasoning; in his clear and accurate vision; in his cool and masterly statement of principles around which the issues gather; and in the grouping of the facts that are to carry conviction to the minds of men of every grade of intelligence. He was so clear that he could not be misunderstood or long misrepresented.[82]

Leonard Swett, a young lawyer who practiced with Lincoln on the circuit, had much the same to say as Herndon:

The force of his logic was in conveying to the minds of others the same clear and thorough analysis he had in his own, and if his own mind failed to be satisfied, he had little power to satisfy anybody else. He never made a sophistical argument in his life, and never could make one. I think he was of less real aid in trying a thoroughly bad case than any man I was ever associated with. If he could not grasp the whole case and believe in it, he was never inclined to touch it.[83]

Long Abe was highly regarded by members of the bar because "he never intentionally misrepresented the evidence of a witness nor the argument of an opponent."[84] He adhered to the same standards in politics. In this respect he differed from Douglas, and fully deserved his nickname of "Honest Abe."

There is one characteristic of Lincoln as a stump speaker, however, for which no commentator seems to have given him credit and which the debates illustrate. Though he might have been slow in coming to conclusions, once having reached them, he was as quick and agile in the repartee of rough-and-tumble, extemporaneous disputation as was Douglas.

It must not be thought, that all who knew Lincoln had the same reaction to him or thought as highly of him. Herndon speaks of the "envy of his rivals at the bar, and the jealousy of his political contemporaries," though he mentions "it made no difference in Lincoln's treatment of them."[85] It is reasonable to suppose that, even though not motivated by envy or jealousy, there were many who could not recognize any extraordinary qualities in Lincoln, and in fact regarded him as less than mediocre. One such person was Herndon's younger brother, Elliot, a prominent lawyer in Springfield, who, though a "good friend," was nevertheless a political opponent of Lincoln. At the request of Billy, who was gathering material on Lincoln, Elliot wrote out his opinion of "the mind of the late President":

> The opinion I have was formed by a personal and professional acquaintance of over ten years, and has not been altered or influenced by any of his promotions in public life. The adulation by base multitudes of a living, and the pageantry surrounding a dead, President do not shake my well-settled convictions of the man's mental calibre.
>
> Physiologically and phrenologically the man was a sort of monstrosity. . . I believe it to be inconsistent with the laws of human organization for any such creature to possess a mind capable of anything called great. The man's mind partook of the incongruities of his body. He had no mind not possessed by the most ordinary of men. It was simply the peculiarity of his mental and the oddity of his physical structure, as well as the qualities of his heart that singled him out from the mass of men. His native love of justice, truth, and humanity led his mind a great way in the accomplishment of his objects in life. That passion or sentiment steadied and determined an otherwise indecisive mind.[86]

PERSONAL MAGNETISM

What impression did his contemporaries have of Douglas' powers of debate? Even his political opponents conceded his brilliance, while at the same time they condemned his methods and his motives.

Billy Herndon had this to say:

> He had had extensive experience in debate, and had been trained by contact for years with the great minds and orators in Congress. He was full of political history, well informed on general topics, eloquent almost to the point of brilliancy, self-confident to the point of arrogance, and a dangerous competitor in every respect. What he lacked in ingenuity he made up in strategy, and if in debate he could not tear down the structure of his opponent's argument by a direct and violent attack, he was by no means reluctant to resort to a strained restatement of the latter's position or to the extravagance of ridicule.[87]

However, the perceptive Herndon was essentially fair in his estimate. He drew a distinction between Douglas the man and Douglas the politician:

> I always found Douglas at the bar to be a broad, fair, and liberal-minded man. Although not a thorough student of the law his large fund of good common-sense kept him in the front rank. He was equally generous and courteous, and he never stooped to gain a case. I know that Lincoln entertained the same view of him. It was only in politics that Douglas demonstrated any want of inflexibility and rectitude, and then only did Lincoln manifest a lack of faith in his morals.[88]

Harriet Beecher Stowe was harsher on Douglas, though in her appraisal she could not help acknowledging his skill:

> His forte in debating is his power of mystifying the point. With the most off-hand assured airs in the world, and a certain appearance of honest superiority, like one who has a regard for you and wishes to set you right on one or two little matters, he proceeds to set up some point which is not that in question, but only a family connection of it, and this point he attacks with the very best of logic and language.[89]

Even the intolerant Horace White, who regarded Douglas as "the most dangerous enemy of liberty," grudgingly admitted his admiration:

> He could make more out of a bad case, I think, than any other man this country had ever produced, and I hope the country will never produce his like again in this particular. If his fate had been cast in the French Revolution, he would have out-demagogued the whole lot of them. . . But mere dexterity would not alone have borne him along his pathway in life. He had dauntless courage, unwearied energy, engaging manners, boundless ambition, unsurpassed powers of debate, and strong personal magnetism.[90]

We have already become familiar with Douglas' courage in a previous chapter. This quality also wrung admiration from famed political opponents. The outspoken Greeley said: "I detest his doctrines, but I like his pluck."[91] Defending himself against the charges of Chase and the abolitionists when the Kansas-Nebraska Bill was being debated, Douglas was so brilliant in meeting the attacks of all opponents on the floor of the Senate that Seward was moved to say in tribute: "I have never had so much respect for the Senator as I have tonight."[92]

But there was another side to the picture. At times in the heat of debate, Douglas' combative nature led him to indulge in vituperation. This pugnacity traced back to the early Illinois days when it expressed itself not merely in words but also in physical assault.

No psychological study has been made of Douglas, but it would seem reasonable to assume that he was sensitive of his size and physical frailty, and that he was determined to compensate for it by aggressiveness and the superiority of his intellectual powers. In a frontier community which respected fearlessness, Douglas resolved to excel.

We have seen how he was called "Little Gamecock," as well as "Little Giant." It might seem that the little gamecock would be content to limit his combativeness to the speaker's platform, but he did not shy away from a physical encounter, even though his opponent was bigger and stronger than himself. Thus, when he and his opponent, John T. Stuart, were canvassing the district together for Congress in 1838, the rivals ended up in a brawl. Stuart was six feet tall and heavily built, but, according to several versions, the little gamecock gave as good as he received. Douglas at this time weighed only about a hundred pounds.

Another incident, less than two years later, involved an attack on Simeon Francis, the editor of the *Sangamo Journal*. Lincoln wrote a letter to his partner Stuart in Washington describing it:

> Yesterday Douglas, having chosen to consider himself insulted by something in the *Journal,* undertook to cane Francis in the street. Francis caught him by the hair and jammed him back against a market-cart, where the matter ended by Francis being pulled away from him. The whole affair was so ludicrous that Francis and everybody else, Douglas excepted, have been laughing about it ever since.[93]

Douglas' willingness to engage in physical combat with anyone regardless of size undoubtedly endeared him to the frontier folk just as much as did his forensic powers. Accordingly, he stamped himself as a formidable opponent, with whom it was dangerous to tangle. He was a scrapper, and though in

later life he generally managed to keep his temper within the
bounds of civility, his restraints were sometimes lowered and
he would revert to the habits of the brawling frontier. Thus
we shall find him in bellicose mood in the course of the 1858
campaign, when he not only breaks out into abuse and invective, but also threatens to fight Lincoln himself. We shall also
witness the delightful manner in which Lincoln disposes of
the threat.

The Little Giant never nursed grudges, however, nor did
he maintain his belligerent attitude long. In this respect he
was like Lincoln who never bore personal animosities, being
opposed to the cause rather than to the man. On one occasion
when Horace Greeley attacked him in the *New York Tribune,*
a mutual acquaintance asked whether he had any objection
to meeting his assailant. "Not at all," Douglas replied. "I
always pay political debts as I go along. I don't let them interfere with social intercourse."[94]

What did the rivals think of each other? Douglas, as we
have seen, had broken lances with Lincoln on enough occasions to have respect for him, which his generous, impetuous
nature moved him to express frankly. When he learned that
Lincoln had been designated to oppose him for the senatorship,
he said to one of his supporters: "I shall have my hands full.
He is the strong man of his party — full of wit, facts, dates —
and the best stump speaker, with his droll ways and dry jokes,
in the West. He is as honest as he is shrewd; and if I beat him
my victory will be hardly won."[95] At another time he stated:
"Of all the damned Whig rascals about Springfield, Abe Lincoln is the ablest and the most honest."[96]

Lincoln's opinion of Douglas was less complimentary. The
first time he saw Douglas was in 1834 when the latter came to
Vandalia, the state capital, to win the appointment as State's
Attorney away from John J. Hardin. Lincoln was not impressed
with the stripling, and characterized him as "the least man he
had ever seen."[97] As Douglas swiftly mounted the ladder of
preferment over the years, Lincoln grew to share Herndon's
opinion that while Douglas' rectitude as a lawyer was unim-
peachable, his motives and tactics in the political field were
open to question.[98]

Jesse W. Weik, in his study of Lincoln, relates an incident
illuminative of this opinion. Clifton H. Moore, of the town

of Clinton, who was an associate of Lincoln and rode the circuit with him, told Weik:

> On the day Mr. Lincoln delivered his speech at Clinton during the campaign of 1858 he was in my office; and I shall always remember with regret one thing he said about Douglas, which was this: "Douglas will tell a lie to ten thousand people one day, even though he knows he may have to deny it to five thousand the next."[99]

William Gardner, a Douglas biographer, states that Lincoln was jealous of Douglas. Strong substantiation of this is provided by a fragment written by Lincoln about 1856:

> Twenty-two years ago Judge Douglas and I first became acquainted. We were both young then; he a trifle younger than I. Even then, we were both ambitious; I, perhaps, quite as much so as he. With me, the race of ambition has been a failure — a flat failure; with him it has been one of splendid success. His name fills the nation; and is not unknown, even, in foreign lands. I affect no contempt for the high eminence he has reached. So reached, that the oppressed of my species might have shared with me in the elevation, I would rather stand on that eminence, than wear the richest crown that ever pressed a monarch's brow.[100]

It is interesting that two poets, Carl Sandburg and Edgar Lee Masters, who wrote biographies of Lincoln, share Gardner's opinion. Masters is in general vitriolic in his appraisal of Lincoln,[101] while Sandburg notes a "streak of jealousy"[102] in him. Such as it was, however, it was a jealousy unmarred by animosity. Lincoln's relations with Douglas were generally friendly and correct. He never became bellicose and abusive on the stump toward Douglas as Douglas sometimes was toward him.

A PSYCHOLOGICAL PERSPECTIVE

The psychoanalytical overtones in L. Pierce Clark's biography, and more especially the psychological study by Dr. Milton H. Shutes, provide significant insights into Lincoln's mind, character and actions, though this subject is inexhaustible and further investigations would be revealing. A psychological study of Douglas is also needed.

The physical appearance alone of the two men provides material for a fascinating work. The psychologist, G. Stanley Hall, who attached great importance to physical traits, wrote:

> Lincoln's height, long limbs, rough exterior and frequent feeling of awkwardness, must have made him realize very early that to succeed in life he must cultivate intrinsic mental or moral traits. . . The mere factor of height and physical strength gives a man, even in civilized life, a certain superiority of which he and others are conscious. If Lincoln had been a little man, he would have been a very different one.[103]

It is not the purpose of this book to make a psychological study of the two opponents, but it seems logical to assume that both suffered originally from an inferiority complex because of their physical appearance. Superior mental endowment enabled both to pursue a common ambition: the desire to excel in spite of physical and environmental handicaps, with each expressing his drive in a different way, because of the difference in his makeup. Douglas compensated for his small size by aggressiveness, while Lincoln, secure in his physical strength, made up for his unattractiveness and ungainliness by wit and humor, and by stern discipline of his intellectual powers.

Modern psychology views superiority and inferiority complexes as opposite sides of the same coin. The early feeling of inferiority on the part of both men was undoubtedly replaced by one of superiority. Each had tested himself against other men on the stump, in the courts, and in the political arena, and had not found himself wanting. Douglas, however, had reaped the largest rewards of recognition, while Lincoln, measuring himself against the Little Giant, and acknowledging himself in his own mind to be the superior, could not help but feel disturbed by the disparity in their fortunes. Perhaps that is also why Lincoln felt so downcast by his defeats.

Lincoln's view of Douglas undoubtedly changed after his election to the presidency and the secession of the South. The Little Giant went to heroic lengths to help preserve the Union, both before and after the presidential election of 1860. His efforts were of the greatest consequence to Lincoln and the North. Only his early death removed him from the role which might possibly have won for him at last the prize for which he had striven so mightily — the presidency.

As the Little Giant and Long Abe stood on the platform together facing the huge crowds gathered in front of them, what impression did they make on the onlooker? The one who had the greater eye and ear appeal was undoubtedly Douglas. His bulldog face and figure, his fine clothes, his confident manner and graceful gestures, and his deep melodious voice, exercised an immense and irresistible fascination. His small size was also an advantage. The American people have always liked the little fellow, especially when he is top dog, as was Douglas, who enjoyed official position and national prestige.

On the other hand, Lincoln's tall ungainliness, careless dress, awkward gestures, high-pitched voice, and apparent hesitance resulting from his slowness to warm up to his task, were not the kind of weapons with which to capture an audience. It remained for his appeal to the mind, rather than to the eyes and ears, to erase the first unfavorable impression.

PART III

The Debates

Political campaigns were among the most exciting events in the early mid-West. To the pioneering folk they were even more exciting than the quilting bees, corn huskings, house raisings, wrestling matches, horse races, dances and fairs, which provided amusement and interest in those days.

For a period of several weeks the stirring pageantry of parades, fireworks, bands, cannon, colorful banners, transparencies and floats, kept excitement at a high pitch. But these were merely the handmaidens to the speechmaking.

The stump speakers were the heroes of the day. It was no hardship, but the keenest of pleasures for a crowd to stand for two to three hours, sometimes in drenching rain and cold and listen to a rousing political speech.

This was democracy in action. Every citizen, by his attendance and interest, was an active participant.

A campaign might be a grim battle for high stakes to the contestants, but it was a thrill and the greatest of spectacles to the voters.

CHAPTER 5

Living Dog and Dead Lion

It was Lincoln who fired the first shot of the campaign. On the evening of June 16 before the Republican State Convention at Springfield he made what became known as his "house divided" speech. It proved to be sensational and sent the campaign off to an explosive start.

The convention had adopted without a dissenting vote a resolution declaring that "Abraham Lincoln is the first and only choice of the Republicans of Illinois for the United States Senate, as the successor of Stephen A. Douglas." This was designed to serve as an instruction to the Republican candidates for the legislature, for prior to the passage of the Seventeeth Amendment providing for direct popular election, it was the state legislatures that elected the Senators who served in Washington. The contest between Lincoln and Douglas, therefore, was for the election of candidates on the party slate who would be committed to vote for them.

Lincoln had known that the convention would take this step as a result of the endorsements of preliminary Republican meetings throughout the state. In anticipation, he had for days carefully prepared his speech, scribbling down his thoughts as they came to him on scraps of paper and filing them away in his old top hat.

He was concerned, however, about the advisability of saying the things that he felt should be said. As he saw the political situation, the Union was a "house divided," with slavery the cause of dissension. The nation could not continue forever that way. It would eventually have to be all free or all slave. These were the alternatives that faced the American public.

But was it wise for him to say so, especially now that he was striving for his biggest prize? His meaning could be easily misconstrued as openly inviting war between the North and the South. Knowing Douglas as he did, he could be certain that the Little Giant would place that interpretation on his words, and thus put him in a difficult position from which no amount of explanation might extricate him.

In his slow and cautious way he had turned the matter in his mind for a long time. He had expressed the thought of a "house divided" in the letter to Judge Robertson of Kentucky three years before, but it was one thing to write it in private correspondence and another to say it publicly in a featured speech.[1] The same thought had been expressed by Birney in the old Liberty Party days, and similar ideas had been voiced by abolitionists like Henry Ward Beecher and Theodore Parker. But it was dangerous for a politician who wished to woo conservative votes to come out with such a statement.

He therefore called a caucus of his friends and read the speech to them. All advised against the "house divided" paragraph. It was too radical, they thought, and might alienate the anti-Lecompton Democrats and the Old Line Whigs. Besides, there was no question that it would give the wily Douglas all the ammunition he needed. Herndon was the lone dissenter, writing later that he had exclaimed: "Lincoln, deliver that speech as read, and it will make you President."[2] But Lincoln had already decided not to make any changes. He felt that the time had come to speak out, and he told his friends: "If it is decreed that I should go down because of this speech, then let me go down linked to the truth."[3]

His opening words, therefore, went directly to the point:

> If we could first know where we are, and whither we are tending, we could then better judge what to do, and how to do it. We are now far into the fifth year, since a policy was initiated, with the avowed object, and confident promise, of putting an end to slavery agitation. Under the operation of that policy, that agitation has not only, not ceased, but has constantly augmented. In my opinion, it will not cease, until a crisis shall have been reached, and passed.

> "A house divided against itself cannot stand." I believe
> this government cannot endure, permanently half slave and
> half free. I do not expect the Union to be dissolved — I do
> not expect the house to fall — but I do expect it will cease
> to be divided. It will become all one thing, or all the other.
> Either the opponents of slavery, will arrest the further spread
> of it, and place it where the public mind shall rest in the
> belief that it is in course of ultimate extinction; or its advo-
> cates will push it forward, till it shall become alike lawful in
> all the states, old as well as new — North as well as South.[4]

Lincoln had also become convinced, like Seward and other
Republicans, that there was a tacit understanding, if not a conspiracy, among those in power and their henchmen to foist
slavery upon the entire country, and that they were pursuing
a careful plan toward this end, the outlines of which were
clear to anyone who would take the trouble to look. He ap-
praised the southern Ultras as an unscrupulous group who
would be satisfied with nothing less than the vindication and
triumph of their "peculiar institution." The repeal of the
Missouri Compromise, the Kansas-Nebraska Act, and the Dred
Scott decision were the obvious steps toward this ultimate goal.
Through their tools, both witting and unwitting, the entrenched Ultras were manipulating Congress, the presidency
and the Supreme Court toward its accomplishment.

Like a good lawyer, Lincoln was too shrewd to make an outright charge which he was unable to prove by specific and con-
crete evidence. He could, however, draw the necessary infer-
ences, and this he was determined to do. In careful language,
using only the first names of Douglas, Pierce, Taney and Buchanan, he drew a colorful metaphor of how the three branches
of government were operating in concert to make slavery universal. Thus, while he might be put on the defensive with
regard to the "house divided" portion of his speech, Douglas
would in turn be put on the defensive in refuting the accusation that he was plotting with the pro-slavery forces. We shall
see Douglas ignore this charge for a time, but finally respond
to Lincoln's goading and defend against it. Lincoln said:

> When we see a lot of framed timbers, different portions
> of which we know have been gotten out at different times
> and places and by different workmen — Stephen, Franklin,
> Roger and James, for instance — and when we see these

timbers joined together, and see they exactly make the frame
of a house or a mill, all the tenons and mortices exactly fitting, and all the lengths and proportions of the different
pieces exactly adapted to their respective places, and not a
piece too many or too few — not omitting even scaffolding —
or, if a single piece be lacking, we can see the place in the
frame exactly fitted and prepared to yet bring such piece
in — in such a case, we find it impossible to not believe that
Stephen and Franklin and Roger and James all understood
one another from the beginning, and all worked upon a
common plan or draft drawn up before the first lick was
struck.[5]

The final step in the plan, the "single piece lacking," would
be a decision by the Supreme Court that "the Constitution of
the United States does not permit a state to exclude slavery,"
was Lincoln's contention. "Welcome or unwelcome such decision is probably coming, and will soon be upon us, unless
the power of the present political dynasty shall be met and
overthrown."[6]

Lincoln spoke the last clause with a definite purpose. At the
outset of the campaign he wished to scotch once and for all
the possibility of Republicans supporting Douglas because of
his falling out with Buchanan over the Lecompton Constitution. For how could Douglas be depended upon to overthrow
the dynasty? . . . :

There are those who . . . whisper us softly, that Senator
Douglas is the aptest instrument there is, with which to effect
that object. They do not tell us, nor has he told us, that he
wishes any such object to be effected. . .
They remind us that he is a very great man, and that the
largest of us are very small ones. Let this be granted. But "a
living dog is better than a dead lion." Judge Douglas, if not
a dead lion for this work, is at least a caged and toothless one.
How can he oppose the advances of slavery? He don't care
anything about it. . . Our cause . . . must be intrusted to,
and conducted by its own undoubted friends . . . who do care
for the result. Two years ago the Republicans . . . of strange,
discordant, and even, hostile elements, . . gathered from the
four winds, and formed and fought the battle through. . .
Did we brave all then, to falter now? . . . when that same
enemy is wavering, dissevered and belligerent? The result is
not doubtful. . . if we stand firm, we shall not fail.[7]

Lincoln was proud of his speech. When he had finished delivering it, he went to the office of the *Illinois State Journal,* proofread the galleys, and himself marked the words and phrases to be italicized.

The Republican press throughout the state hailed the speech. Greeley's *New York Tribune* reproduced it in full with a brief editorial in praise. But privately the Republican leaders in Illinois had misgivings. Some of Lincoln's friends wrote him censorious letters, and Leonard Swett predicted his defeat because of the opening lines of his speech.[8]

But Lincoln was unconcerned. To one insistent complainant who followed him into his office, he said, "If I had to draw a pen across my record, and erase my whole life from sight, and I had one poor gift or choice left as to what I should save from the wreck, I should choose that speech and leave it to the world unerased."[9]

Billy Herndon was so proud of his partner's speech that he sent a copy of it to Theodore Parker with whom he corresponded regularly. Parker wrote back: "Many thanks for your letter and for the admirable speech of Mr. Lincoln. I think I shall congratulate you on his Senatorial dignity next winter."[10]

The danger of misconstructions being placed on his speech, however, was reflected in a letter Lincoln wrote to John L. Scripps:

I am much flattered by the estimate you place on my late specch; and yet I am much mortified that any part of it should be construed so differently from any thing intended by me. The language, "place it where the public mind shall rest in the belief that it is in course of ultimate extinction," I used deliberately, not dreaming then, nor believing now, that it asserts or intimates any power or purpose, to interfere with slavery in the states where it exists. . . I have declared a thousand times, and now repeat that, in my opinion, neither the General Government, nor any other power outside of the slave states, can constitutionally or rightfully interfere with slaves or slavery where it already exists. I believe that whenever the effort to spread slavery into the new territories, by whatever means, and into the free states themselves, by Supreme Court decisions, shall be fairly headed off, the institution will then be in course of ultimate extinction; and by the language used I meant only this.[11]

Scripps was the editor of the Chicago *Daily Democratic Press,* a Republican paper which a few days later merged with the *Chicago Tribune.* He was also to write the first campaign biography of Lincoln in 1860. If people like Scripps could raise doubts about the construction of the speech, it was easy to see what Douglas would do with it.

To add to the difficulties that loomed, rumors began circulating that Senator Crittenden had let it be known that he favored Douglas. If true, this would be a blow as severe to Lincoln's chances as the attitude and actions of Greeley. To the Old Line Whigs, the Kentucky Senator was the inheritor of Clay's mantle. Though an outsider, his influence would be hard to counteract. Lincoln determined to find out for himself whether the rumors were true. On July 7, therefore, he wrote to Crittenden:

> I beg you will pardon me for the liberty in addressing you upon only so limited an acquaintance, and that acquaintance so long past. I am prompted to do so by a story being whispered about here that you are anxious for the re-election of Mr. Douglas to the United States Senate . . . and that you are pledged to write letters to that effect to your friends here in Illinois, if requested. I do not believe the story, but still it gives me some uneasiness. If such was your inclination, I do not believe you would so express yourself. It is not in character with you as I have always estimated you.
>
> You have no warmer friends than here in Illinois, and I assure you nine-tenths — I believe ninety-nine hundredths — of them would be mortified exceedingly by anything of the sort from you. When I tell you this, make such allowance as you think just for my position, which, I doubt not, you understand. Nor am I fishing for a letter on the other side. Even if such could be had, my judgment is that you would be better hands off!
>
> Please drop me a line; and if your purposes are as I hope they are not, please let me know. The confirmation would pain me much, but I should still continue your friend and admirer.[12]

Crittenden's reply was slow in coming. In the meantime the situation remained cloudy.

The Democratic press took up Lincoln's metaphor of the living dog and the dead lion. Another battle — that of the rival newspapers — began to sputter in anticipation of the main conflict. It would not be long before the headlines of both sides would be screaming with the gusto which characterized a western political campaign. "Douglas Skins the Living Dog" and "The Dead Lion Frightens the Canine,"[13] would be typical. In a few weeks, as both candidates started on their stumping tours, an article would state:

> Abe Lincoln who compared himself to a "living dog" and Douglas to a "dead lion" will rapidly discover that instead of "living" he is one of the smallest of defunct puppies.... His comparison in some degree was true — it is very much like a puppy-dog fighting a lion.[14]

Douglas replied to Lincoln's speech on July 9th. Accompanied by his lovely wife Adele, he entered Chicago to a reception of triumphal proportions. Bands, flags, fireworks, and booming guns accorded him a mighty welcome in this Republican stronghold. It was the complete reverse of the funereal greeting of four years before when he had tried to defend his Nebraska Act. At night from the balcony of the famous Tremont House he spoke to a huge crowd in the square below.

Douglas had no illusions as to the significance of the demonstration. He knew that he had a tough fight on his hands. At the state convention the previous April, the Buchaneers or administration men had tried to wrest control of the Democratic organization from him. They had failed, and in June had held their own convention, calling themselves the National Democratic Party. They decided to run a candidate in every county and district in opposition to the Douglas men, even if it resulted in the victory of the Republican candidates. They were determined to defeat Douglas at any cost. They called upon the willing President to help with the power of his patronage. Several editors of influential newspapers were lured from the Douglas banner by the bestowal of postmasterships. Marshalships and other federal plums were distributed where they would do the most harm to the Little Giant.

This zeal to destroy him had led Douglas to charge in a Senate speech that administration Democrats and Republicans were engaged in a plot against him. It was a good point to enshrine him in the role of popular champion who was being persecuted by a wicked administration, and thus to attract the

votes of rank and file Republicans. It also gave Douglas a conspiracy charge of his own to level against Lincoln. There is
some evidence to show that the Danite leaders, Douglas' term
of opprobrium for the Buchaneers, had been working with the
Republican campaign managers but, if so, it was clear that
Lincoln was ignorant of it, and could truthfully deny the
charge.[15]

As Douglas stood before the assembled throng he appeared
tired. It had been a difficult term for him in the Senate, bristling with the tensions of the fight over Lecompton and of his
break with the administration, and the strain had made him
ill. The trip from Washington via New York where he had
stopped briefly to visit his mother had been filled with the busy
routine of political fetes and meetings. He had had little chance
to rest. But this was the opening of the campaign, and the
occasion was most auspicious. Inspired by the crowd, he began
to speak.

Seated near him in a recess of the balcony window was Abraham Lincoln. Douglas had learned that he was present and
had offered him a chair. Also present were three young men
who were to prove of great importance in the campaign. They
were experts in shorthand or "phonographic" reporting, as it
was then called. One, Robert R. Hitt, was engaged by the Republican *Chicago Press and Tribune,* on whose staff Horace
White was serving as a political correspondent. The other two,
James B. Sheridan and Henry Binmore, reported for the Democratic *Chicago Times.* This was to be the first time in Illinois
history that a verbatim report of a campaign speech was to be
made. Thereafter the phonographic reporters were to cover the
seven formal debates.

Flushed with the adulation of the crowd accorded him because of his Lecompton fight, Douglas sought to use the occasion to win the Republicans to him by interpreting their opposition to the Lecompton Constitution as support for his Kansas
doctrine. "I was rejoiced," he said, "when I found in this great
contest the Republican party coming up manfully and sustaining the principle that the people of each territory, when
coming into the Union, have the right to decide for themselves
whether slavery shall or shall not exist within their limits . . .
to have slavery or freedom . . . as they deemed best."[16]

As he went along, he grew expansive, and patronizingly paid

his respects to Lincoln as his rival. "I take great pleasure in saying," he remarked, "that I have known, personally and intimately, for about a quarter of a century, the worthy gentleman who has been nominated for my place, and I will say that I regard him as a kind, amiable, and intelligent gentleman, a good citizen and an honorable opponent; and whatever issue I may have with him will be of principle, and not involving personalities."[17]

Pointing out that he had vindicated the Compromise of 1850 before the people of Chicago who had then passed resolutions in its favor, he asked: "What was my duty in 1854, when it became necessary to bring forward a bill for the organization of the territories of Kansas and Nebraska? Was it not my duty, in obedience to your standing instructions to your Senators . . . to incorporate in that bill the great principle of self-government?"[18]

His opposition to Lecompton was "that it undertook to put a constitution on the people of Kansas against their will . . . and thus violated the great principle upon which all our institutions rest."

It was this principle, "the right of every community to judge and decide for itself, whether a thing is right or wrong, whether it would be good or evil . . . the right of free action, the right of free thought," which was "dearer to every true American than any other under a free government."[19]

"It is no answer to this argument," he asserted, "to say that slavery is an evil and hence should not be tolerated. You must allow the people to decide for themselves whether it is a good or an evil. . . Whenever you put a limitation upon the right of any people to decide what laws they want, you have destroyed the fundamental principle of self-government."[20]

After thus laying his groundwork, he went to the attack. As expected, his target was the "house divided" thesis. Lincoln's speech was "evidently well prepared and carefully written" and contained "two distinct propositions." "His first and main proposition," he said, "I will give in his own language, scripture quotations, and all." Then to the laughter of the audience he quoted the "house divided" passage. When finished, he analyzed it:

In other words, Mr. Lincoln asserts as a fundamental

principle of this government, that there must be uniformity in the local laws and domestic institutions of each and all the states of the Union; and he therefore invites all the non-slaveholding states to band together, organize as one body, and make war upon slavery in Kentucky, upon slavery in Virginia, upon the Carolinas, upon slavery in all of the slave-holding states in the Union, and to persevere in that war until it shall be exterminated. He then notifies the slave-holding states to stand togeher as a unit and make an aggressive war upon the free states of this Union with a view of establishing slavery in them all; of forcing it upon Illinois, of forcing it upon New York, upon New England, and upon every other free state, and that they shall keep up the warfare until it has been formally established in them all.

In other words, Mr. Lincoln advocates boldly and clearly a war of sections, a war of the North against the South, of the free states against the slave states — a war of extermination — to be continued relentlessly until the one or the other shall be subdued and all the states shall either become free or become slave.[21]

He was opposed to "uniformity in the local institutions and domestic regulations of the different states of the Union."

The fathers of the Revolution, and the sages who made the Constitution well understood that the laws and domestic institutions which would suit the granite hills of New Hampshire would be totally unfit for the rice plantations of South Carolina; they well understood that the laws which would suit the agricultural districts of Pennsylvania and New York would be totally unfit for the large mining regions of the Pacific, or the lumber regions of Maine. They well understood that the great varieties of soil, of production and of interests, in a republic as large as this required different local and domestic regulations in each locality, adapted to the wants and interests of each separate state. . .

Uniformity in local and domestic affairs would be destructive of state rights, of state sovereignty, of personal liberty and personal freedom. Uniformity is the parent of despotism the world over. . .[22]

Douglas then assailed Lincoln's "other proposition . . . a crusade against the Supreme Court of the United States on account of the Dred Scott decision." "What security have you for your property," he asked, "for your reputation, and for your personal rights, if the courts are not upheld? . . . The decision of the highest tribunal known to the Constitution of the country must be final till it has been reversed by an equally high authority."[23]

The Little Giant then went on to expand his thesis repeating that "this government of ours is founded on the white basis," and that he was "in favor of preserving not only the purity of the blood, but the purity of the government from any mixture or amalgamation with inferior races."[24]

"Fellow-citizens," he said, "you now have before you the outlines of the propositions which I intend to discuss . . . during the pending campaign." And then he closed by taking the role of martyr:

> I have made up my mind to appeal to the people against the combination which has been made against me. The Republican leaders have formed an alliance, an unholy, unnatural alliance with a portion of the unscrupulous federal office-holders. I intend to fight that allied army wherever I meet them. I know they deny the alliance while avowing the common purpose, yet these men are trying to divide the Democratic party for the purpose of electing a Republican Senator in my place. . .
>
> I shall deal with these allied forces just as the Russians dealt with the allies at Sebastopol. The Russians when they fired a broadside at the common enemy did not stop to inquire whether it hit a Frenchman, an Englishman or a Turk, nor will I stop to inquire, nor shall I hesitate, whether my blows hit the Republican leaders or their allies, who are holding the federal offices and yet acting in concert with the Republicans to defeat the Democratic party and its nominees.[25]

By this time the Little Giant, by his own admission, was exhausted. "It is now two nights since I have been in bed, and I think I have a right to a little sleep,"[26] he said. He bade a gracious farewell to the crowd and promised to speak to them on other occasions before the November election.

Lincoln was quick to return to the attack. A notice in the papers the next morning and the distribution of handbills throughout the day announced that Lincoln would reply to Douglas at the same place that very night. Considering the short notice and the absence of fanfare, the crowd that showed up was fairly large. Democratic authorities had estimated the number that had listened to Douglas at 30,000; Republicans had thought it was 12,000. Whatever the number, Lincoln's crowd was smaller, but according to one Republican account, it was "in point of enthusiasm about four times as great."[27] Lincoln was extremely pleased with the gathering and wrote to that effect to one of his friends. There was no discounting the fact, however, that Douglas had displayed tremendous drawing power in an admittedly Republican area.

Old Abe was anxious to get back at Douglas. He had sat and listened to the Little Giant's distortion of the "house divided" thesis in enforced silence. Douglas had twisted Lincoln's words beyond any resemblance of their intended meaning. Unless corrected immediately his misconstructions would work havoc with the Republican campaign. As for the conspiracy charge leveled against him, he had ignored it completely.

Lincoln was clearly on the defensive now. He had to carry the battle to the foe. Taking out a small pile of papers, he said: "I do not intend to indulge in that inconvenient mode, sometimes adopted in public speaking, of reading from documents; but I shall depart from that rule so far as to read a little scrap from his speech . . . provided I can find it in the paper." As he fumbled through the *Chicago Press and Tribune,* someone in the crowd yelled: "Get out your specs."[28]

Lincoln finally found what he wanted and read Douglas' diatribe comparing the alliance against him with allied forces against the Russians at Sebastopol. "Well, now, gentlemen," he said, "is not that very alarming?" Then to the accompaniment of laughter and applause, he continued:

> Just to think of it! right at the outset of this canvass, I, a poor, kind, amiable, intelligent (Laughter) gentleman, (Laughter and renewed cheers) I am to be slain in this way. Why, my friend, the Judge, is not only, as it turns out, not a dead lion, nor even a living one — he is the rugged Russian Bear! (Roars of laughter and loud applause.)
>
> But if they will have it — for he says that we deny it — that there is any such alliance, as he says there is . . . that the administration men and we are allied, and we stand in the attitude of English, French and Turk, he occupying the position of the Russian, in that case, I beg that he will indulge us while we barely suggest to him, that these allies took Sebastopol. (Long and tremendous applause.) . . .

If for the Republican party to see the other great party to which they are opposed divided among themselves, and not try to stop the division and rather be glad of it — if that is an alliance I confess I am in; but if it is meant to be said that the Republicans had formed an alliance going beyond that, by which there is contribution of money or sacrifice of principle on the one side or the other, so far as the Republican party is concerned, if there be any such thing, I protest that I neither know anything of it, nor do I believe it. . .[29]

Lincoln now turned to Douglas' part in the defeat of the Lecompton Constitution. "Who defeated it?" he asked. "Judge Douglas," a voice called out, and Lincoln suddenly found himself being heckled:

Mr. Lincoln — Yes, he furnished himself, and if you suppose he controlled the other Democrats that went with him, he furnished three votes, while the Republicans furnished twenty. (Applause.)

That is what he did to defeat it. In the House of Representatives he and his friends furnished some twenty votes, and the Republicans furnished ninety odd. (Loud applause.) Now who was it that did the work?

A Voice — Douglas.

Mr. Lincoln — Why, yes, Douglas did it! To be sure he did. Let us, however, put that proposition another way. The Republicans could not have done it without Judge Douglas. Could he have done it without them? (Applause) Which could have come the nearest to doing it without the other? (Renewed applause. "That's it," "that's it," "good," "good.")

A Voice — Who killed the bill?

Another Voice — Douglas.

Mr. Lincoln — Ground was taken against it by the Republicans long before Douglas did it. The proportion of opposition to that measure is about five to one.

A Voice — Why don't they come out on it?

Mr. Lincoln — You don't know what you are talking about, my friend. I am quite willing to answer any gentleman in the crowd who asks an *intelligent* question. (Great applause.)[30]

Senator Trumbull, Lincoln went on, who had opposed the Lecompton Constitution long before Douglas, was receiving no credit for it. "I defy you to show a printed resolution passed in a Democratic meeting . . . in favor of Trumbull or any of the five to one Republicans who beat that bill. Everything must be for the Democrats! They did everything. . . ."[31]

From this Lincoln went to the main point — his defense of the "house divided" thesis and the untwisting of Douglas' distortions. He, too, quoted the vital paragraph:

> He says I am in favor of making all the states of this Union uniform in all their internal regulations. He says that I am in favor of making war by the North upon the South for the extinction of slavery; that I am also in favor of inviting . . . the South to a war upon the North, for the purpose of nationalizing slavery.
>
> Now, it is singular enough, if you will carefully read that passage over, that I did not say that I was in favor of anything in it. I only said what I expected would take place. I made a prediction only — it may have been a foolish one perhaps. I did not even say that I desired that slavery should be put in course of ultimate extinction. I do say so now, however, (Great applause.) so there need be no longer any difficulty about that. It may be written down in the great speech. (Applause and laughter.)
>
> Gentlemen, Judge Douglas informed you that this speech of mine was probably carefully prepared. I admit that it was. I am not master of language; I have not a fine education; I am not capable of entering into a disquisition upon dialectics, as I believe you call it; but I do not believe the language I employed bears any such construction as Judge Douglas put upon it. But I don't care about a quibble in regard to words. I know what I meant, and I will not leave this crowd in doubt, if I can explain it to them, what I really meant in the use of that paragraph. . .
>
> This government has endured eighty-two years, half slave and half free . . . because, during all that time, until the introduction of the Nebraska Bill, the public mind did rest, all the time, in the belief that slavery was in course of ultimate extinction. . .
>
> I have always hated slavery, I think as much as any Abolitionist. (Applause.) I have been an Old Line Whig. I have always hated it, but I have always been quiet about it until this new era of the introduction of the Nebraska Bill began. I always believed that everybody was against it, and that it was in course of ultimate extinction. . .

Such was the belief of the framers of the Constitution itself. Why did those old men, about the time of the adoption
of the Constitution, decree that slavery should not go into
the new territory, where it had not already gone? Why
declare that within twenty years the African slave trade,
by which slaves are supplied, might be cut off by Congress?
Why were all these acts? . . . What were they but a clear
indication that the framers of the Constitution intended and
expected the ultimate extinction of that institution? (Cheers.)
. . . When I say that I think the opponents of slavery will
resist the farther spread of it, and place it where the public
mind shall rest with the belief that it is in course of ultimate
extinction, I only mean to say, that they will place it where
the founders of this government originally placed it. . .[32]

I do not believe in the right of Illinois to interfere with
the cranberry laws of Indiana, the oyster laws of Virginia,
or the liquor laws of Maine. I have said these things over
and over again. How is it, then, that Judge Douglas infers
. . . that I am in favor of Illinois going over and interfering
with the cranberry laws of Indiana? . . .

Because he looks upon all this matter of slavery as an exceedingly little thing — only equal to the question of the
cranberry laws of Indiana — as something having no moral
question to it. . . so small a thing, that he concludes, if I
could desire that anything should be done to bring about
the ultimate extinction of that little thing, I must be in favor
of bringing about an amalgamation of all the other little
things in the Union. . .

It so happens that there is a vast portion of the American
people that do not look upon that matter as being this very
little thing. They look upon it as a vast moral evil; they can
prove it is such by the writings of those who gave us the
blessings of liberty which we enjoy — while we agree that, by
the Constitution we assented to, in the states where it exists
we have no right to interfere with it because it is in the
Constitution and we are by both duty and inclination to
stick by that Constitution in all its letter and spirit from
beginning to end. . .

So much then as to my wish to have uniformity . . . by
which I suppose it is meant if we raise corn here, we must
make sugar cane grow here too, and we must make those
which grow North, grow in the South. . . . So much for all
this nonsense — for I must call it so.[33]

Turning now to the Dred Scott decision, Lincoln said that he did not resist it, because it was obviously impossible to take Dred Scott from his master:

> All I am doing is refusing to obey it as a political rule. If I were in Congress, and a vote should come up on a question whether slavery should be prohibited in a new territory, in spite of that Dred Scott decision, I would vote that it should. . . Judge Douglas said last night that . . . he would abide by it until it was reversed. Just so! . . . We will try to reverse that decision . . . and we mean to do it peaceably.[34]

After disposing of the Dred Scott issue, as he thought, Lincoln returned to Douglas' charge of an unholy alliance by means of which he intended to win away Republican voters:

> He is cautious to say that that warfare of his is to fall upon the leaders of the Republican party. . . He wants it understood that the mass of the Republican party are really his friends. . . . I want to ask . . . where you, as the Republican party, would be placed if you sustained Judge Douglas in his present position by a reelection? I do not claim, gentlemen, to be unselfish, I do not pretend that I would not like to go to the United States Senate, (Laughter), I make no such hypocritical pretense. . .
> But where will you be placed if you re-endorse Judge Douglas? Don't you know how apt he is — how exceedingly anxious he is at all times to seize upon anything and everything to persuade you that something he has done you did yourselves? Why he tried to persuade you last night that our Illinois legislature instructed him to introduce the Nebraska Bill. There was nobody in that legislature ever thought of such a thing; and when he first introduced the bill, he never thought of it; but still he fights furiously for the proposition, and that he did it because there was a standing instruction to our Senators to be always introducing Nebraska bills. (Laughter and applause.) . . .
> If you endorse him you tell him you do not care whether slavery be voted up or down, and he will close, or try to close your mouths with his declaration repeated by the day, the week, the month and the year. Is that what you mean? (Cries of "no," one voice "yes.") . . . Now I could ask the Republican party after all the hard names that Judge Douglas has called them by — all his repeated charges of their inclination to marry with and hug negroes — all his declarations of Black

> Republicanism . . . if he be endorsed by Republican votes
> where do you stand? Plainly you stand ready saddled, bridled
> and harnessed and waiting to be driven over to the slavery
> extension camp of the nation (A voice "we will hang our-
> selves first.") — just ready to be driven over tied together in
> a lot — to be driven over, every man with a rope around his
> neck, that halter being held by Judge Douglas.[35]

Lincoln next took up Douglas' interpretation of the Declaration of Independence, pointing out again that settlers from
Europe — the Germans, Irish, French and Scandinavians —
would be excluded from its benefits. "If one man says it does
not mean a negro," he asserted, "why not another say it does
not mean some other man?" Dramatically he queried the
crowd: "If that Declaration is not the truth, let me get the
statute book, in which we find it and tear it out! Who is so
bold as to do it! (Voices — "me" "no one," etc.) If it is not true
let us tear it out! (Cries of "no, no,") let us stick to it then,
(Cheers.) let us stand firmly by it then."[36] In conclusion, he
went once more to the Bible:

> My friend has said to me that I am a poor hand to quote
> Scripture. I will try it again, however. It is said in one of the
> admonitions of the Lord, "As your Father in Heaven is per-
> fect, be ye also perfect." The Savior, I suppose, did not
> expect that any human creature could be perfect as the
> Father in Heaven; but He said, "As your Father in Heaven
> is perfect, be ye also perfect." He set that up as a stand-
> ard   So I say in relation to the principle that all men
> are created equal, let it be as nearly reached as we can. If
> we cannot give freedom to every creature, let us do nothing
> that will impose slavery upon any other creature. (Ap-
> plause.) . . .
> Let us discard all this quibbling about this man and the
> other man — this race and that race and the other race being
> inferior, and therefore they must be placed in an inferior
> position — discarding our standard that we have left us. Let
> us discard all these things, and unite as one people through-
> out this land, until we shall once more stand up declaring
> that all men are created equal.[37]

The following week the two contestants remained in Chicago laying plans and discussing strategy with their party
managers. Douglas was due at Springfield for a speech on

Saturday, July 17, with a stop the day before at Bloomington. Republican strategy called for Lincoln to stick close to him and follow him around.

So when Douglas left Chicago, Lincoln was on the same train. The Little Giant was ensconced in a private car while Old Abe rode in the coach. Charges were later made that the Illinois Central Railroad favored Douglas and had provided him with the conveyance free of charge, but in the absence of substantiating evidence to the contrary, it would seem that the Little Giant paid for it out of his own funds. Envisioning a strenuous campaign which would carry him without letup to all parts of the state, his provision for a private car made sense. Not only would it spare his health and strength, but it would also provide necessary conveniences for his wife.

The car was gaily decorated with flags, mottoes and bunting. When it reached Joliet, a few miles out of Chicago, a flatcar was added, on which was mounted a small cannon attended by two young men in semi-military uniform. At every stop the cannon was fired to herald the arrival of the Little Giant. Thereafter "Popular Sovereignty," as the cannon was called, traveled with Douglas around the state adding picturesqueness to an already colorful campaign.

Bloomington, where Douglas was scheduled to speak, was the scene of Lincoln's famous "lost speech" of 1856. Formerly Whig territory, it now was a town of strong Republican sympathies. It was certain that Douglas would not neglect to pitch some part of his speech in the direction of conservative Old Line Whigs, like John T. Stuart. Lincoln's former law partner could not stomach the Republican Party's position on slavery. Others, like Judge T. Lyle Dickey, who was one of Lincoln's good friends, thought that Greeley was right, and that Douglas deserved the support of all who were opposed to Buchanan and the administration Ultras. It was Dickey, in fact, who was the source of the rumors that Crittenden favored Douglas. Crittenden had told Dickey in Washington how he felt about the Illinois senatorial campaign, and Dickey was desirous now of getting the old Kentucky stalwart to express these sentiments in writing.

Douglas also cocked an eye toward the votes of the Native-American Know-Nothings who were opposed to him for previous attacks upon them and for the fact that his wife was a

Catholic. He would be sure to make the most of the rumors that were circulating because Senator Crittenden was just as much of an oracle to the Native-Americans as he was to the Whigs.

IN THE WHIG STRONGHOLD

Good as Douglas' Chicago speech was, the one at Bloomington was better. Comparatively well rested over the previous week, he spoke in his most vigorous and slashing style. Though he covered essentially the same points as he did at Chicago, this speech was considered so effective that arrangements were made to distribute 80,000 copies of it throughout the state.

At the outset of the speech the Little Giant made a bow in Crittenden's direction. At the same time he tried to correct the weakness by means of which Lincoln had discounted his part in the Lecompton fight:

> I only did what it was in the power of any one man to do. There were others, men of eminent ability, men of wide reputation, renowned all over America, who led the van and are entitled to the greatest share of the credit.
>
> Foremost among them all, as he was head and shoulders above them all, was Kentucky's great and gallant statesman, John J. Crittenden. ("Good, good," and cheers.) By his course upon this question he has shown himself a worthy successor of the immortal Clay, and well may Kentucky be proud of him. (Applause.)
>
> I will not withhold, either, the need of praise due the Republican party in Congress for the course which they pursued. In the language of the *New York Tribune* they came to the Douglas platform, abandoning their own, (Cheers,) believing that under the peculiar circumstances they would in that mode best subserve the interests of the country. ("Good, good," and applause.) My friends, when I am battling for a great principle I want aid and support from whatever quarter I can get it in order to carry out that principle. ("That's right.") [38]
>
> Nor is it for me to inquire into the motives which animated the Republican members of Congress. It is enough that they came square up and endorsed the great principle of the Kansas-Nebraska Bill. . .
>
> I was the more rejoiced at the action of the Republicans

on that occasion for another reason. I could not forget, you will not soon forget, how unanimous that party was in 1854 in declaring that never should another slave State be admitted to the Union under any circumstances whatever, and yet we find that during this last winter they came up and voted to a man declaring that Kansas should come in as a State with slavery under the Lecompton Constitution, if her people desired it, and that if they did not that they might form a new constitution with slavery or without, just as they pleased.

I do not question the motive when men do a good act; I give them credit for the act; and if they stand by that principle in the future, and abandon their heresy of "no more slave States even if the people want them," I will then give them still more credit. I am afraid though that they will not stand by it in the future. (Laughter.) If they do, I will freely forgive them all the abuse they heaped upon me in 1854, for having advocated and carried out that same principle in the Kansas-Nebraska bill.[39]

Taking up the question of Negro equality, Douglas answered Lincoln's scriptural quotation with one of his own:

He quotes Scripture again and says: "As your father in Heaven is perfect, be ye also perfect." . . . He is willing to give the negro an equality under the law in order that he may approach as near perfection or an equality with the white man as possible. To the same end he quotes the Declaration of Independence . . . that the right of the negro is a divine right . . . and rendered inalienable. . .

I do not believe that the signers of the Declaration . . . had any reference to negroes . . . or to the Chinese or Coolies, the Indians, the Japanese, or any other inferior race. They were speaking of the white race, the European race. . . In Kentucky they will not give a negro any political or civil rights. I shall not argue the question whether Kentucky in so doing has decided right or wrong. . . I believe the Kentuckians have consciences as well as ourselves; they have as keen a perception of their religious, moral and social duties as we have, and I am willing that they shall decide this slavery question for themselves, and be accountable to their God for their action. . . I will not judge them lest I shall be judged.[40]

He also matched Lincoln's "house divided" statement with a

second scriptural quotation. Repeating that Lincoln advocated forcing either the North or South to submission, he said: "I would apply the same Christian rule to the States of the Union that we are taught apply to individuals, 'do unto others as you would have others do unto you,' and this would secure peace."[41]

At the conclusion of his speech, the Little Giant invoked the shades of Clay and Webster:

> These are my views and these are the principles to which I have devoted all my energies since 1850, when I acted side by side with the immortal Clay and the God-like Webster in that memorable struggle in which Whigs and Democrats united upon a common platform of patriotism and the Constitution, throwing aside partisan feelings in order to restore peace and harmony to a distracted country.
>
> And when I stood beside the death bed of Mr. Clay, and heard him refer with feelings and emotions of the deepest solicitude to the welfare of the country, and saw that he looked upon the principle embodied in the great Compromise measures of 1850, the principle of the Nebraska bill, the doctrine of leaving each State and Territory free to decide its institutions for itself, as the only means by which the peace of the country could be preserved and the Union perpetuated, — I pledged him, on that death bed of his, that so long as I lived my energies should be devoted to the vindication of that principle, and of his fame as connected with it.
>
> I gave the same pledge to the great expounder of the Constitution, he who has been called the "God-like Webster." I looked up to Clay and him as a son would to a father, and I call upon the people of Illinois, and the people of the whole Union to bear testimony that never since the sod has been laid upon the graves of these eminent statesmen have I failed on any occasion to vindicate the principle with which the last great, crowning acts of their lives were identified, or to vindicate their names whenever they have been assailed; and now my life and energy are devoted to this great work as the means of preserving this Union.[42]

He took leave of the audience with the words: "I have a heavy day's work before me tomorrow. I have several speeches to make. My friends, in whose hands I am, are taxing me beyond human endurance, but I shall take the helm and control them hereafter."[43]

Lincoln was seated on the platform throughout the speech.

When it was over, the crowd called loudly for him. He finally
came forward to the cheers of his many partisans, but only to
say that "this meeting was called by the friends of Judge Douglas and it would be improper for me to address it."[44] He promised to return and make a speech soon.

The next afternoon, Saturday the 17th, Douglas spoke at
Springfield in an open grove. Though there had been a heavy
downpour which left the ground soggy and the trees dripping,
a vast crowd was on hand to give the Little Giant a tremendous
reception, "impossible to describe." What made matters particularly gloomy for the Republican managers was the fact that
Douglas was introduced by Benjamin S. Edwards, an Old Line
Whig.

The Senator repeated essentially what he had said at Chicago
and Bloomington, but seasoned campaigner that he was, he
made his points with greater clarity and polish.

Speaking of the Dred Scott decision, he found the vulnerable
point in Lincoln's position:

> He says he is going to reverse it. How? He is going to take
> an appeal. To whom is he going to appeal? (Laughter.) The
> Constitution of the United States provides that the Supreme
> Court is the ultimate tribunal, the highest judicial tribunal
> on earth, and Mr. Lincoln is going to appeal from that. To
> whom? I know he appealed to the Republican State Conven-
> tion of Illinois, (Laughter,) and I believe that convention
> reversed the decision, but I am not aware that they have yet
> carried it into effect. (Renewed laughter.)
>
> How are they going to make that reversal effectual? Why,
> Mr. Lincoln tells us in his late Chicago speech. He explains
> it as clear as light. He says to the people of Illinois that if
> you elect him to the Senate he will introduce a bill to re-
> enact the law which the court pronounced unconstitutional.
> (Shouts of laughter, and voices, "spot the law.") Yes, he is
> going to spot the law. The court pronounces that law, pro-
> hibiting slavery, unconstitutional and void, and Mr. Lincoln
> is going to pass an act reversing that decision and making it
> valid. I never heard before of an appeal being taken from the
> Supreme Court to the Congress of the United States to re-
> verse its decision. . .
>
> But Mr. Lincoln intimates that there is another mode by
> which he can reverse the Dred Scott decision. How is that?
> Why, he is going to appeal to the people to elect a President

who will appoint judges who will reverse the Dred Scott decision. . . ("He never will, sir," and great cheering.) I do not believe he ever will. ("Bravo," and applause.) But suppose he should; when that Republican President shall have taken his seat — Mr. Seward, for instance — will he then proceed to appoint judges? No! he will have to wait until the present judges die before he can do that, and perhaps his four years would be out before a majority of these judges found it agreeable to die; (Laughter and cheers,) and it is very possible, too, that Mr. Lincoln's senatorial term would expire before these judges would be accommodating enough to die. ("That's right.") If it should so happen I do not see a very great prospect for Mr. Lincoln to reverse the Dred Scott decision.

But suppose they should die, then how are the new judges to be appointed? Why, the Republican President is to call up the candidates and catechise them, and ask them, "How will you decide this case if I appoint you judge?" (Shouts of laughter.) Suppose, for instance, Mr. Lincoln to be a candidate for a vacancy on the supreme bench to fill Chief Justice Taney's place, (Renewed laughter) and when he applied to Seward, the latter would say, "Mr. Lincoln, I cannot appoint you until I know how you will decide the Dred Scott case." Mr. Lincoln tells him, and then (Seward) asks him how he will decide Tom Jones' case, and Bill Wilson's case, and thus catechises the judge as to how he will decide any case which may arise before him. Suppose you get a Supreme Court composed of such judges, who have been appointed by a partisan President upon their giving pledges how they would decide a case before it arise, what confidence would you have in such a court? ("None, none.")

It is a proposition to make that court the corrupt, unscrupulous tool of a political party. But Mr. Lincoln cannot conscientiously submit, he thinks, to the decision of a court composed of a majority of Democrats. If he cannot, how can he expect us to have confidence in a court composed of a majority of Republicans, selected for the purpose of deciding against the Democracy, and in favor of the Republicans? (Cheers.) The very proposition carries with it the demoralization and degradation destructive of the judicial department of the federal government.[45]

Despite the aggressive character of his speech, Douglas took to the defensive in two respects. To Lincoln's claim that the

Dred Scott decision destroyed popular sovereignty because neither Congress nor the territorial legislatures could prohibit slavery there, he answered: "I will not stop to inquire whether the court will carry the decision that far or not. It would be interesting as a matter of theory, but of no importance in practice." His view was, that if the "majority of the people were opposed to slavery, it would soon be abolished."[46]

This time, though, he took notice of Lincoln's charge of conspiracy, but dismissed it with the brief remark: "If Mr. Lincoln deems *me* a conspirator of that kind, all I have to say is that *I* do not think so badly of the President of the United States and the Supreme Court of the United States . . . as to believe that they were capable . . . of entering into political intrigues for partisan purposes."[47]

Lincoln was not present on this occasion. He was busy preparing for his own speech to be given that same night at the Republican counter-rally in the Hall of Representatives. Besides, he had already sized up Douglas' arguments and strategy. He knew that the arguments would be the same, and the strategy would be to repeat them with little variation. He therefore did not need to hear Douglas again in order to prepare his reply.

Responding to the urgings of his supporters who thought that Douglas was getting the better of the exchanges, Lincoln determined to be more aggressive. In addition to answering Douglas' points, he thought he would try a different line. There were two disadvantages that he and the Republican Party were laboring under — the superiority of Douglas' position as a candidate, and the unfair apportionment of the state in favor of the Democrats. He hoped, by stressing his own unfavorable situation in these two respects, to counteract the sympathy which Douglas was conjuring up as a persecuted champion and to attach it to himself.

As it was later to turn out, the distorted apportionment did give the election to Douglas. Swift changes in population had not brought accompanying revisions in the apportionment of representatives to the legislature. The southern third of the state had been the first to be settled. Families, like Lincoln's, had emigrated from nearby Kentucky and the border states whose political tradition was Democratic and whose sympathies were pro-slavery. Later the northern third of the state had been settled by emigrants from the free states of the east. Anti-slavery in outlook, they formed the backbone of the Republican party. Although continued heavy immigration had subsequently rendered this area more populous than the southern part, its strength was not reflected politically, because the apportionment of earlier times remained essentially unchanged. The two elements met in the central third of the state, thus turning it into the battleground of the campaign.

When Lincoln arose to speak, an "immense audience" was on hand to hear his reply to Douglas. After dealing with the antiquated apportionment of the state's election districts, he said:

> There is still another disadvantage under which we labor, and to which I will ask your attention. It arises out of the relative positions of the two persons who stand before the state as candidates for the Senate. Senator Douglas is of world wide renown. All the anxious politicians of his party, or who have been of his party for years past, have been looking upon him as certainly, at no distant day, to be the President of the United States.
>
> They have seen in his round, jolly, fruitful face, post-offices, landoffices, marshalships, and cabinet appointments, chargeships and foreign missions, bursting and sprouting out in wonderful exuberance ready to be laid hold of by their greedy hands. (Great laughter.) And as they have been gazing upon this attractive picture so long, they cannot, in the little distraction that has taken place in the party, bring themselves to give up the charming hope; but with greedier anxiety they rush about him, sustain him, and give him marches, triumphal entries, and receptions beyond what even in the days of his highest prosperity they could have brought about in his favor.
>
> On the contrary nobody has ever expected me to be President. In my poor, lean, lank, face, nobody has ever seen that any cabbages were sprouting out. (Tremendous cheering and laughter.) These are disadvantages all, taken together, that the Republicans labor under. We have to fight this battle upon principle, and upon principle alone. . . we have to fight this battle without many — perhaps without any — of the external aids which are brought to bear against us.[48]

Lincoln then attacked Douglas' doctrine of popular sovereignty. "It is to be labelled upon the cars in which he travels;

put upon the hacks he rides in; to be flaunted upon the arches he passes under, and the banners which wave over him," he said. "It is to be dished up in as many varieties as a French cook can produce soups from potatoes."[49]

No one was opposed to the people of a state making their own constitution, he continued. "This being so, what is Judge Douglas going to spend his life for? . . . Does he expect to stand up in majestic dignity, and go through his apotheosis and become a god, in the maintaining of a principle which neither a man nor a mouse in all God's creation is opposing? (Tremendous cheering.)"[50]

Turning to the Lecompton Constitution and the credit Douglas was taking for his fight upon it, he said: "I wish to know what there is in the opposition of Judge Douglas . . . that entitles him to be considered the only opponent to it — as being par excellence the very quintessence of that opposition."[51] Pointing out that the Douglas faction had supplied only twenty of the hundred and twenty votes that defeated the measure in the House of Representatives, he asked:

> If, as Judge Douglas says, the honor is to be divided and due credit is to be given to other parties, why is just so much given as is consonant with the wishes, the interests and advancement of the twenty? My understanding is, when a common job is done, or a common enterprise prosecuted, if I put in five dollars to your one, I have a right to take out five dollars to your one. But he does not so understand it.
>
> Does he place his superior claim to credit, on the ground that he performed a good act which was never expected of him? He says I have a proneness for quoting scriptures. If I should do so now, it occurs that perhaps he places himself somewhat upon the ground of the parable of the lost sheep which went astray upon the mountains, and when the owner of the hundred sheep found the one that was lost, and threw it upon his shoulders, and came home rejoicing, it was said that there was more rejoicing over the one sheep that was lost and had been found, than over the ninety and nine in the fold. (Great cheering, renewed cheering.) The application is made by the Savior in this parable, thus, "Verily, I say unto you, there is more rejoicing in heaven over one sinner that repenteth, than over ninety and nine just persons that need no repentance." (Cheering.)

And now, if the Judge claims the benefit of this parable,

let him repent. (Vociferous applause.) Let him not come up here and say: I am the only just person; and you are the ninety-nine sinners! Repentance, before forgiveness is a provision of the Christian system, and on that condition alone will the Republicans grant his forgiveness. (Laughter and cheers.)[52]

Expressing annoyance with Douglas' misrepresentation of his "house divided" statement, Lincoln asserted that he would once more, for the last time, he hoped, explain it. Then, if Douglas repeated his misrepresentation, it would be clear that he did so willfully. He said:

> I set out in this campaign with the intention of conducting it strictly as a gentleman, in substance at least, if not in the outside polish. The latter I shall never be, but that which constitutes the inside of a gentleman I hope I understand, and am not less inclined to practice than others. (Cheers.) It was my purpose and expectation that this canvass would be conducted upon principle, and with fairness on both sides; and it shall not be my fault, if this purpose and expectation shall be given up.[53]

Douglas had charged that in the "house divided" statement Lincoln wished to make the country either all free or all slave. He quoted the passage. "Now," Lincoln said, "you all see, from that quotation, I did not express my wish on anything. In that passage I indicated no wish or purpose of my own; I simply expressed my expectation. Cannot the Judge perceive the distinction between a purpose and an expectation? I have often expressed an expectation to die, but I have never expressed a wish to die."[54]

Lincoln then took up the question of opposition to the Dred Scott decision. Political resistance to a decision was permissible, he said. He cited the opposition of the Democratic Party to a national bank since the time of Jackson, even though the Supreme Court had declared the bank constitutional. He had pointed this out to Douglas before, but Douglas chose to ignore it. "I do not expect to convince the Judge," he said. "It is part of the plan of his campaign, and he will cling to it with a desperate grip. Even, turn it upon him — turn the sharp point against him, and gaff him through — he will still cling to it till he can invent some new dodge to take the place of it.

The plain truth is simply this: Judge Douglas is for Supreme
Court decisions when he likes and against them when he does
not like them." Did Douglas wish to know what he was going
to do with the Dred Scott decision? "Well, Judge, will you
please tell me what you did about the bank decision? Will
you not graciously allow us to do with the Dred Scott decision
precisely as you did with the bank decision?"[55]

Lincoln now addressed himself to Douglas' attempt to woo
the Whigs and Native-Americans:

> Judge Douglas has a very affectionate leaning towards the
> Americans and Old Whigs. Last evening, in a sort of weeping
> tone, he described to us a death-bed scene. . . the Judge has
> evidently promised himself that tears shall be drawn down
> the cheeks of all Old Whigs, as large as half grown apples.
>
> Mr. Webster, too, was mentioned; but it did not quite
> come to a death-bed scene, as to him. It would be amusing,
> if it were not disgusting, to see how quick these compromise-
> breakers administer on the political effects of their dead
> adversaries, trumping up claims never before heard of, and
> dividing the assets among themselves.[56]

Old Abe next picked up the change in interpretation of the
Declaration of Independence which Douglas had introduced
in his Bloomington speech and repeated in the Springfield
speech that afternoon:

> In his construction of the Declaration last year he said it
> only meant that Americans in America were equal to Eng-
> lishmen in England. Then, when I pointed out to him that
> by that rule he excludes the Germans, the Irish, the Portu-
> guese, and all the other people who have come amongst us
> since the Revolution, he reconstructs his construction. In his
> last speech he tells us it meant Europeans.
>
> I press him a little further, and ask if it meant to include
> the Russians in Asia? or does he mean to exclude that vast
> population from the principles of our Declaration of Inde-
> pendence? I expect ere long he will introduce another amend-
> ment to his definition. He is not at all particular. He is sat-
> isfied with anything which does not endanger the nationaliz-
> ing of negro slavery. It may draw white men down, but it
> must not lift negroes up.
>
> Certainly the negro is not our equal in color — perhaps
> not in many other respects. . . In pointing out that more

has been given you, you can not be justified in taking away the little which has been given him. All I ask for the negro is that if you do not like him, let him alone. If God gave him but little, that little let him enjoy.[57]

Lincoln concluded by again charging Douglas with conspiracy to nationalize slavery. Douglas, he said, had not contradicted the charge thus far. Not having been present when Douglas spoke in the afternoon, Lincoln did not know that the Little Giant had at last taken cognizance of the charge but had dismissed it cavalierly with a brief denial. Nevertheless it served to put Douglas on the defensive.

Lincoln was well satisfied with himself. To Jonathan Mathers, one of his supporters, who had written him advice, he answered:

Your suggestions as to placing one's self on the offensive, rather than the *defensive,* are certainly correct. That is a point which I shall not disregard. I spoke here on Saturday-night. . . You, doubtless, will see it [the speech]; and I hope you will perceive in it, that I am already improving.[58]

The Republican campaign managers, however, were not as satisfied as Lincoln. They were disconcerted and uneasy because of the strong impression that Douglas was creating, the huge crowds that he was drawing and the support that he was attracting. There was no doubt also that the rumors about Crittenden and the actions of Greeley were having a harmful effect. Greeley had ceased urging Illinois Republicans to support Douglas when it became apparent that Lincoln was to be their candidate, and he subsequently wrote to Herndon that he would do "all I reasonably can to elect Lincoln."[59] He could not, however, undo the damage that had already been done.

The Republican leaders decided to call for help. The man to whom they turned was Senator Trumbull. He was a powerful and aggressive speaker, and was already being mentioned as a candidate for the Republican presidential nomination in 1860. Hurry out to Illinois, wrote Norman B. Judd, the Republican State Chairman. "Lincoln has commenced it [the fight] gallantly. The only trouble will be that he will allow Douglas to put him on the defensive."[60] State Auditor Jesse K. Dubois also wrote to Trumbull to hurry out and take charge.[61]

He felt that former Democrats like him were necessary to off-set the influence of such Whigs and Republicans as Crittenden and Greeley.

Herndon, on the other hand, was pleased with the way his partner was conducting the campaign. He appreciated the difficulties Lincoln had to face in an opponent like Douglas. When Theodore Parker sent him a copy of his Fourth of July oration, Herndon thanked him and wrote: "We are approaching a very animated, warm, energetic canvass; and if it does not get into personalities it will be a great . . . canvass. I fear, however, that personalities will creep into the debates. . . We Republicans have a clever villain to combat. Mr. Douglas is an ambitious and an unscrupulous man; he is the greatest liar in all America; he misrepresents Lincoln throughout, and our people generally are not logical enough to see the precise manner, point and issue of the deception. He holds up in glowing letters "squatter sovereignty," which he knows is dead and buried under the Dred Scott case."[62]

CHAPTER 6

Canvass Western-Style

As he had promised in his Bloomington speech, Douglas now took charge of his campaign. Together with the Democratic State Committee, he drew up a list of speaking engagements, extending at first through the 21st of August at Ottawa, and later through the month of October. In the meantime, Lincoln left for Chicago where he conferred with Norman Judd and the Republican State Committee. Their answer to the Douglas list was to publish a list of their own, according to which Lincoln was scheduled to appear at many of the same places either on the same day as Douglas or a day later.

This brought a howl of rage from the Douglas papers. Lincoln was trailing Douglas, they said. He could not get crowds of his own, so he had to take advantage of those who came to hear the Little Giant. Together with the fact that Lincoln had followed Douglas ever since the latter had returned to Illinois, it made a sensitive point to which the Republican press reacted sharply. The *Illinois State Journal* berated the *Chicago Times* for its "personal attack upon Mr. Lincoln for presuming to be present when Mr. Douglas speaks. One would think from this that Mr. Douglas has a patent right to audiences in Illinois. We hope that Mr. Lincoln will continue to follow up Senator Douglas with a sharp stick. . ."[1]

The *Chicago Times* retorted: "We have a suggestion to make. . . There are two very good circuses and menageries traveling through the State; these exhibitions always draw good crowds at country towns. Mr. Judd, in behalf of his candidate, at a reasonable expense, might make arrangements with the managers of these exhibitions to include a speech from Lincoln in their performances."[2]

That Lincoln thought well of the Republican tactics, however, is evident from a letter he wrote on September 3: "My recent experience shows that speaking at the same place the next day after Douglas is the very thing — it is, in fact, a concluding speech on him."[3] In spite of this, the Republican managers were insistent that Lincoln be more aggressive. They decided that he should issue a challenge for a series of joint debates.

Pressure for a challenge had come originally from the Republican press. Greeley had suggested it as early as July 12 in the *New York Tribune* saying that he hoped "Messrs. Lincoln and Douglas will speak together at some fifteen or twenty . . . points throughout the state."[4] The *Chicago Press and Tribune* called for the candidates "to canvass the State together in the usual western style,"[5] by which was meant the way Douglas and John T. Stuart conducted their famous battle for Congress twenty years before.

Accordingly, on July 24 Lincoln sent the following letter to Douglas:

> Will it be agreeable to you to make an arrangement for you and myself to divide time, and address the same audiences during the present canvass? Mr. Judd, who will hand you this, is authorized to receive your answer; and, if agreeable to you, to enter into the terms of such arrangement.[6]

Douglas was unhappy to receive the challenge. "Between you and me," he told his aides on receipt of the letter, "I do not feel that I want to go into this debate. The whole country knows me and has measured me. Lincoln, as regards myself, is comparatively unknown, and if he gets the best of this debate — and I want to say he is the ablest man the Republicans have got — I shall lose everything. Should I win, I shall gain but little."[7]

Nevertheless, Douglas answered the challenge immediately.

The lengthy correspondence that ensued back and forth is interesting because it reveals the candidates quibbling like a couple of schoolboys over petty details and minor advantages:

July 24, 1858

Your note of this date, in which you inquire if it would be agreeable to me to make an arrangement to divide the time and address the same audiences during the present canvass, was handed me by Mr. Judd. . .

I . . . made a list of appointments covering the entire period until late in October. . . These appointments have all been made for Democratic meetings, and arrangements have been made by which the Democratic candidates for Congress, for the Legislature and other offices will be present and address the people. It is evident, therefore, that these various candidates, in connection with myself, will occupy the whole time of the day and evening, and leave no opportunity for other speeches. . .

I cannot refrain from expressing my surprise, if it was your original intention to invite such an arrangement, that you should have waited until after I had made my appointments, inasmuch as we were both here in Chicago together for several days after my arrival. . .

I will, in order to accommodate you as far as it is in my power to do so, take the responsibility of making an arrangement with you for a discussion between us at one prominent point in each congressional district in the state, except the second and sixth districts, where we have both spoken, and in each of which cases you had the concluding speech.

If agreeable to you, I will indicate the following places as those most suitable in the several congressional districts at which we should speak, to wit: Freeport, Ottawa, Galesburg, Quincy, Alton, Jonesboro and Charleston. I will confer with you at the earliest convenient opportunity in regard to the mode of conducting the debate, the times of meeting at the several places, subject to the condition, that where appointments have already been made by the Democratic State Central Committee at any of those places, I must insist upon you meeting me at the times specified.[8]

In referring to the Congressional districts where both had already spoken, Douglas had in mind Chicago in the second district and Springfield in the sixth.

CAMPAIGN JOURNALISM

With the publication of the correspondence, the partisan press could no longer restrain itself. Up to this point, both sides had been fairly temperate, but now they let go with the extreme recklessness which reflected the party zeal of the time.

A partial explanation for this is the fact that the editors of the influential papers were often personal friends and close associates of the candidates. This was particularly true in the case of Charles H. Lanphier, of the *Illinois State Register,* and James W. Sheahan of the *Chicago Times,* a paper which was founded with Douglas' financial help. Sheahan later wrote a campaign biography of the Little Giant. Simeon Francis, co-owner and editor of the *Illinois State Journal,* formerly the *Sangamo Journal,* was a close friend of Lincoln, and even after he had sold his interest in 1855, that paper continued to support Lincoln and the Republican side.

Thus it was that with partisan vindictiveness the Republican *Chicago Press and Tribune* termed Douglas' reply "long-winded" and "pettifogging," and exclaimed: "The little dodger shirks, and backs out, except at half a dozen places which he himself selects. . . He would rather go about the country like a strolling mountebank, with his cannon, todies and puffers, to shoot, cheer and blow for him, than to stand up to the work with a full grown man to confront him."[9]

The *Chicago Journal* snapped: "He . . . shows the white feather, and . . . skulks behind the appointments of the emasculated Democratic State Committee."[10]

The heat of the conflict sometimes affected the quality of the English employed in the tirades, as this bon mot from the *Chicago Times* attests: "Mr. Lincoln . . . dreaded personally the consequence of a joint discussion . . . and at last, believing that Douglas, having announced his meetings would not change his program, has allowed his friends to persuade him to make a challenge. . . We doubt very much if Mr. Lincoln's friends can screw his courage up sufficiently to enable him to accept this offer, whether he will even go through with the seven appointments."[11]

The eastern press, removed from the scene, viewed the developments in Illinois rather calmly, but the neighboring western papers got into the argument as though it were theirs. In Burlington, Iowa, the *Hawkeye* wrote: "Lincoln has challenged Douglas to canvass Illinois together, addressing the people from the same stump. Judge Douglas dodges." To which the *Gazette* countered: "Judge Douglas dodges, eh? . . . Douglas will meet Lincoln if Lincoln *dare* to meet Douglas; and the only dodging there will be on the part of the 'Little Giant' will take place when the people of Illinois, through their representatives elect, *dodge him* into the Senatorship again, as they most assuredly will."[12]

For the remainder of the campaign, the press of Illinois gave "little or no aid to the searcher after truth."[13] Opposite reports appeared in the partisan papers on everything, except perhaps the weather. Whatever Lincoln or Douglas said or did, or whatever happened to either was magnified with extravagance or belittled with contempt depending on which side published it.

A few days later, Lincoln personally handed Douglas his reply. It was no coincidence that they met on the road. As a result of their previously arranged speaking schedules, the rivals were constantly running across each other. On July 28, for instance, they even had dinner together in Decatur as guests of the proprietor of Oglesby House.

This time, Douglas was returning to Bement from Monticello where he had just spoken. About two miles out of town he met Lincoln who was on his way to Monticello to speak. They stopped their carriages, and Lincoln jumped out to inform Douglas that he had his reply with him. He had not, however, compared the original with the copy, he said, and would the Judge care to compare the two now? No, he would not, answered the Judge; Lincoln could compare them at Monticello and then send the reply to the Bryant House at Bement where he was staying. In the course of the conversation, according to the reporter of the *Chicago Times,* Douglas with tongue in cheek urged Lincoln to return with him to Bement, promising him a larger crowd there than he would get at Monticello.[14] Lincoln, of course, declined this invitation.

After speaking at Monticello, Lincoln went to Bement to deliver his reply. There is a tradition that both men stayed up into the small hours of the night at the Bryant House to arrange the details of their joint meetings:[15]

July 29, 1858

Yours of the 24th. in relation to an arrangement to divide
time and address the same audiences, is received; and, in
apology for not sooner replying, allow me to say that when
I sat by you at dinner yesterday I was not aware that you had
answered my note. . . Protesting that your insinuations of
attempted unfairness on my part are unjust, and with the
hope that you did not very considerately make them, I proceed to reply. . .

As to your surprise that I did not sooner make the proposals to divide time with you, I can only say I made it as
soon as I resolved to make it. I did not know but that such
proposal would come from you; I waited respectfully to see.
. . . When your appointments were announced in the papers,
extending only to the 21st. of August, I, for the first time, considered it certain that you would make no proposal to me;
and then resolved . . . I would make one to you. . .

For you to say that we have already spoken at Chicago and
Springfield, and that on both occasions I had the concluding
speech, is hardly a fair statement. The truth rather is this.
At Chicago, July 9th, you made a carefully prepared conclusion on my speech of June 16th.; twenty-four hours after I
made a hasty conclusion on yours of the 9th; you had six
days to prepare, and concluded on me again at Bloomington
on the 16th.; . . . The dates of making all these speeches, will
show, I think, that in the matter of time for preparation, the
advantage has all been on your side; . . .

I agree to an arrangement for us to speak at the seven
places you have named, and at your own times, provided you
name the times at once, so that I, as well as you, can have to
myself the time not covered by the arrangement. As to other
details, I wish perfect reciprocity, and no more. I wish as
much time as you, and that conclusions shall alternate.
That is all.

P.S. As matters now stand, I shall be at no more of your
exclusive meetings. . .[16]

To this missive, Douglas replied:

. . . The times and places designated, are as follows:

Ottawa, La Salle County	August	21st,	1858
Freeport, Stephenson County	do	27th,	do
Jonesboro, Union County	September	15th,	do
Charleston, Coles County	do	18th,	do
Galesburg, Knox County	October	7th,	do

    Quincy, Adams County   do   13th, do
    Alton, Madison County   do   15th, do
  I agree to your suggestion that we shall alternately open and close the discussion. I will speak at Ottawa one hour, you can reply, occupying an hour and a half, and I will then follow for half an hour. We will alternate in like manner in each successive place.[17]

The next day Lincoln sent the following letter, thereby closing the correspondence on the debates:

                                     July 31, 1858
  Yours of yesterday, naming places, times, and terms, for joint discussions between us, was received this morning. Although, by the terms, as you propose, you take *four* openings and closes to my *three,* I accede, and thus close the arrangement. . .[18]

The press had its usual rabid comments on the proceedings. The *Chicago Times* wrote: "We are not disposed to criticize too harshly the style of Mr. Lincoln's letter. . . But the public will have their opinion of it, and it can be none other than it is as badly conceived as bunglingly expressed. We hope, however, that we have seen the '*conclusion*' of the correspondence, and do not question that by the time Mr. Lincoln has '*concluded*' on Senator Douglas . . . and permitted Senator Douglas to '*conclude*' on him . . . he will '*conclude*' that he better haul off and lay by for repairs."[19]
  The *Chicago Daily Journal* struck back: "The *Times* finds fault with Mr. Lincoln's letter . . . because it is 'bunglingly expressed.' Our neighbor should recollect that he has not the advantage of having the Douglas candidate for Superintendent of Public Instruction *to correct it for him!*"[20] And the *Illinois State Journal* wrote: "Mr. Douglas reluctantly consents to allow himself to be used up by Mr. Lincoln at seven different places. It is clear that Mr. Douglas is not fond of Mr. Lincoln's rough handling and is anxious to get out of an ugly scrape on any terms."[21]
  While Lincoln and the Republican campaign committee could congratulate themselves on getting their "artful dodger" to share the stump, serious trouble was brewing from another direction. On July 29, Crittenden wrote in answer to Lincoln's letter. He had frequently mentioned his sentiments about

Douglas in Washington and elsewhere, he said. There was no secret about it. However, he had not written to anyone in Illinois since Congress adjourned, but he now had several letters to which he felt he must respond. One of them, from Judge Dickey on July 19, asked whether he had not had a certain conversation with the writer in Washington concerning Douglas. His answer would, of course, be "yes."

Crittenden followed his letter to Lincoln by replying to Dickey on August 1. He had no objection, he said, to Dickey's repeating the conversation because he himself had done so frequently, though he did not wish to be an intermeddler in another state's elections. "I did in that conversation speak of Senator Douglas in high and warm terms," he wrote. Douglas had "the courage and patriotism to take an elevated, just, and independent position on the Lecompton question at the sacrifice of old party ties and in defiance of the power of an angry administration." He admired Douglas' "noble conduct."[22]

Though the publication of the letter would do Lincoln's cause great harm, Dickey refrained from giving it immediately to the press. He thought that once Crittenden's position was public and open, some way might be found to counteract its effectiveness. Perhaps Lincoln or other Whigs could get the Kentucky Senator to soften his stand by writing a complimentary letter on behalf of Lincoln. Besides, with the trend of the campaign seeming to favor Douglas, the rumors alone about the letter were proving damaging enough. It would be time to release it if matters should take a turn for the worse. Dickey therefore withheld it until a few days before the end of the campaign, when the balance seemed to swing against Douglas and it was virtually impossible, because of the shortness of time, for the Republicans to take countermeasures.[23]

With three weeks to go before the first formal debate at Ottawa on August 21, Douglas continued vigorously on his stumping tour which he had started on July 27 through the central part of the state.

Lincoln, according to his original itinerary, had stuck close to the Little Giant's coattails. Thus, at Clinton on the 27th, he was in the crowd when Douglas spoke in the afternoon, and he himself took the platform thereafter in the evening. The next day the rivals even dined together at Decatur as Lincoln mentioned in the opening sentence of his letter of July 29.

However, as he had promised in the postscript of that letter, he now refrained from being at any more of Douglas' "exclusive meetings." He had been scheduled to speak as Douglas was at Hillsboro on August 2, Greenville on the 4th, and Edwardsville on the 6th, but he wrote to friends in these towns cancelling his appearance because "Judge Douglas strongly intimated in his published letter (July 24) that my presence would be an intrusion."[24] But in those places where he was to follow Douglas the next day, the schedule remained unmodified. Throughout the rest of the campaign the paths of the two would not cross, except in one instance, which is described in a later chapter, when a dramatic clash resulted.

After going east, Douglas turned westward in the central portion of the state. The tour he had set for himself was a punishing one, requiring him to speak every day or every other day. To reach many of his destinations which were at a distance from the railroads, he had to travel by stage and carriage along abominable roads. Sometimes he was able to take the river packet, as he did to Beardstown on the Illinois River. Whatever the mode of conveyance, he was on the move at all hours of the day and night. At Mattoon he waited for the 10:40 P.M. train until 3:30 A.M., arriving at Paris, his next destination, at 6:00 A.M. The strenuous character of his itinerary moved the *Chicago Times* to comment: "Senator Douglas is taxing his strength severely, but it does not seem to impair his health."[25]

Everywhere he was greeted by large and enthusiastic crowds. Saluting batteries, marching bands, flags and streamers attested to the popularity of the Little Giant. At Winchester, where he got his start as a schoolteacher twenty-five years before, some of his old pupils and their children were in the crowd. In speaking to them he said with some exaggeration, "Here I made the first six dollars I ever earned in my life. My first election to public office by the people was conferred upon me by those whom I am now addressing and their fathers."[26]

Lincoln, in the meantime, remained in Springfield. He was busy writing letters of advice and encouragement to lieutenants in various parts of the state, preparing campaign material, and doing a lot of thinking. A fragment which he jotted down, attributed to this time, reads: "As I would not be a *slave*, so I would not be a *master*. This expresses my idea of democracy.

Whatever differs from this, to the extent of the difference, is
no democracy."[27]

It was at this time, too, that he received a letter from Henry
Asbury, a Quincy lawyer, urging him to press upon Douglas the
question which subsequently became the famous second question of the Freeport debate: Could slavery be lawfully excluded from the territories? In reply to the suggestion he wrote:

> You shall have hard work to get him directly to the point,
> whether a territorial Legislature has or has not the power
> to exclude slavery. But if you succeed in bringing him to it,
> though he will be compelled to say it possesses no such
> power; he will instantly take ground that slavery can not
> actually exist in the territories, unless the people desire it,
> and so give it protective territorial legislation. If this offends
> the South he will let it offend them; as at all events he means
> to hold on to his chances in Illinois. . . . He cares nothing for
> the South — he knows he is already dead there.[28]

This reaction throws light on Lincoln's motives in forcing
Douglas' avowal of the "Freeport Doctrine," or "Freeport
Heresy" as the South viewed it. In spite of his answer to Asbury,
it is clear that he gave much thought to the problem of whether
to pose the question, knowing full well what Douglas' answer
would be.

ENTER TRUMBULL

Even though Lincoln was biding his time in Springfield
until his scheduled appearance at Beardstown on August 12,
the campaign began to warm up with the arrival of Trumbull
in Illinois. If the Republicans wished to put the Little Giant
on the defensive, Trumbull was the man to do it. At Chicago
on August 7, he made a "ferocious" speech against Douglas.
He raked up the fires of the Toombs Bill which had been so
bitterly debated in the Senate the previous December. With
burning tongue he charged Douglas, as chairman of the Committee on Territories, with responsibility for the omission of
the original clause in the bill which provided for submission
of a state constitution to the vote of the people of Kansas:

> I make the distinct charge that there was a preconcerted
> arrangement and plot entered into by the very men who now
> claim credit for opposing a constitution not submitted to

the people, to have a constitution formed and put in force
without giving the people an opportunity to pass upon it.
This, my friends, is a serious charge, but I charge it tonight
that the very men who traverse the country under banners
proclaiming popular sovereignty, by design concocted a bill
to force a constitution upon that people. . .

And you want to satisfy yourself that he was in the plot
to force a constitution upon that people? I will satisfy you.
I will cram the truth down any honest man's throat until he
cannot deny it, and to the man who does deny it I will cram
the lie down his throat until he shall cry, "Enough!" . . . It
is the most damnable effrontery that man ever put on to con-
ceal a scheme to defraud and cheat the people out of their
rights, and then claim credit for it.[29]

Trumbull's speech had the desired effect. Douglas was so
enraged by the charges that he lost his temper. At Beardstown
on August 11 he flamed back. Having hitherto virtually ignored Lincoln's conspiracy charges, he now termed them "an
infamous lie." And against Trumbull he employed the following choice invective:

> When this charge was once made in a much milder form,
> in the Senate of the United States, I did brand it as a lie in
> the presence of Mr. Trumbull, and Mr. Trumbull sat and
> heard it thus branded, without daring to say it was true. I
> tell you he knew it to be false when he uttered it at Chi-
> cago. . .
> The miserable, craven-hearted wretch! he would rather
> have both ears cut off than to use that language in my pres-
> ence, where I could call him to account. I see the object is
> to draw me into a personal controversy, with the hope thereby
> of concealing from the public the enormity of the principles
> to be occupied by these personal assaults. I have none to
> make on Mr. Lincoln; I have none to make on Mr. Trum-
> bull; I have none to make on any other political opponent.
> If I cannot stand on my own public record, on my own pri-
> vate and public character . . . I will not attempt to rise by
> traducing the character of other men. I will not make a
> blackguard of myself by imitating the course they have pur-
> sued against me. I have no charges to make against them.[30]

The Little Giant was now fighting on his opponents' ground
and Old Abe knew how to take advantage of it. Following

Douglas next day at Beardstown, he again hit home with the charge of conspiracy:

> It was not until he went into a small town, [Clinton] in DeWitt County, where he delivered his fourth or fifth regular speech, that he found it convenient to notice this matter at all. At that place (I was standing in the crowd when he made his speech.) he bethought himself that he was charged with something; and his reply was that "his self-respect alone" prevented his calling it a falsehood. Well, my friends, perhaps he so far lost his self-respect in Beardstown as to actually call it a falsehood! . . .
>
> I say to you, gentlemen, that it would be more to the purpose for Judge Douglas to say that he did *not* repeal the Missouri Compromise; that he did *not* make slavery possible where it was impossible before; . . . that he did *not* make a hasty indorsement of the Dred Scott decision, over at Springfield; . . . that that decision does *not* take away from the Territorial Legislature the power to exclude slavery, and that he did *not* in the original Nebraska bill so couple the words *State* and *Territory* together, that what the Supreme Court has done in forcing open all the Territories for slavery, it may yet do in forcing open all the States — I say it would be vastly more to the point for Judge Douglas to say he did *not* do some of these things, did *not* forge some of these links of overwhelming testimony, than to go vociferating about the country that possibly he may hint that somebody is a liar!
>
> I repeat and renew, and shall continue to repeat and renew this "charge" until he denies the evidence, and then I shall so fasten it upon him that it will cling to him as long as he lives.[31]

Douglas had not cooled off by the time he reached Havana further up the Illinois River two days later. Lincoln's boat docked at the same destination while Douglas was speaking. When someone suggested that he go to hear Douglas, he declined. "The Judge was so put out by my listening to him at Bloomington and Clinton," he said, "that I promised to leave him alone at his own meetings for the rest of the campaign. I understand that he is calling Trumbull and myself liars, and if he should see me in the crowd he might be so ashamed of himself as to omit the most telling part of his argument."[32]

That Douglas must have poured out heavy quantities of abuse is attested to by a friend of Horace White who had been in the crowd. This friend told White that he had heard Douglas call Lincoln "a liar, a coward, a wretch and a sneak" and he therefore concluded that the Little Giant had been drinking.[33] Other exciting scenes must also have taken place, as we deduce from Lincoln' reply the next day:

> I am informed, that my distinguished friend yesterday became a little excited, nervous, perhaps, (laughter) and he said something about *fighting* as though referring to a pugilistic encounter between him and myself. Did anybody in this audience hear him use such language? (Cries of "yes.")
>
> I am informed, further, that somebody in *his* audience, rather more excited, or nervous, than himself, took off his coat, and offered to take the job off Judge Douglas' hands, and fight Lincoln himself. Did anybody here witness that warlike proceeding? (Laughter and cries of "yes.") Well, I merely desire to say that I shall fight neither Judge Douglas nor his second. (Great laughter.)
>
> I shall not do this for two reasons, which I shall now explain. In the first place, a fight would *prove* nothing which is in issue in this contest. It might establish that Judge Douglas is a more muscular man than myself, or it might demonstrate that I am a more muscular man than Judge Douglas. But this question is not referred to in the Cincinnati platform, nor in either of the Springfield platforms. (Great laughter.) Neither result would prove him right or me wrong. And so of the gentleman who volunteered to do his fighting for him. If my fighting Judge Douglas would not prove anything it would certainly prove nothing to fight his bottleholder. (Continued laughter.)
>
> My second reason for not having a personal encounter with the Judge is, that I don't believe he wants it himself. (Laughter.) He and I are about the best friends in the world, and when we get together he would no more think of fighting me than of fighting his wife. Therefore, ladies and gentlemen, when the Judge talked about fighting, he was not giving vent to any ill-feeling of his own, but merely trying to excite — well, *enthusiasm* against me on the part of his audience. And as I find he was tolerably successful, we will call it quits. (Cheers and laughter.)[34]

How much Lincoln enjoyed this fun at Douglas' expense is seen from this additional sally:

> One other matter of trifling consequence, and I will pro-

ceed. I understand that Judge Douglas yesterday referred to
the fact that both Judge Trumbull and myself are making
speeches throughout the State to beat him for the Senate,
and that he tried to create a sympathy by the suggestion that
this was playing *two upon one* against him. It is true that
Judge Trumbull has made a speech in Chicago, and I believe
he intends to co-operate with the Republican Central Committee in their arrangements for the campaign to the extent
of making other speeches in different parts of the State.
Judge Trumbull is a Republican, like myself, and he naturally feels a lively interest in the success of his party. Is there
anything wrong about that?

But I will show you how little Judge Douglas's appeal to
your sympathies amounts to. At the next general election,
two years from now, a Legislature will be elected which will
have to choose a successor to Judge Trumbull. Of course
there will be an effort to fill his place with a Democrat. This
person, whoever he may be, is probably out making stump-
speeches against me, just as Judge Douglas is. It may be one
of the present Democratic members of the lower house of
Congress — but who ever he is, I can tell you he has got to
make some stump speeches now, or his party will not nominate him for the seat occupied by Judge Trumbull.

Well, are not Judge Douglas and this man playing *two*
upon one against me, just as much as Judge Trumbull and
I are playing *two upon one* against Judge Douglas? (Laughter.) And if it happens that there are two Democratic aspirants for Judge Trumbull's place, are they not playing three
upon one against me, just as we are playing *two upon one*
against Judge Douglas? (Renewed laughter.)[35]

The repercussions over Trumbull's role in the campaign
did not subside, however, with the outbursts at Beardstown
and Havana. They were to crop up again, especially at Charleston when Douglas' irritation over the charges in connection
with the Toombs Bill would become the chief topic of the
fourth debate.

BEACON FOR POSTERITY

With one week remaining before the first formal debate at
Ottawa on the 21st, both candidates proceeded north up the
Illinois River to their destination, stopping to speak at Lewis-
town, Peoria and smaller towns close by. At Lewistown, Doug-

las' voice betrayed the first signs of strain. After speaking for an hour he had to stop and someone else had to take over for him.

From Lewistown also the *Chicago Press and Tribune* printed an extract of Lincoln's speech which Horace White later claimed had been delivered at Beardstown Regardless of the place of delivery, it was revelatory of the deepening growth of Lincoln's thought on the moral issues of the slavery question and of his ability to give new and stirring expression to it.

The shorthand reporters had evidently not been present to transcribe the words, but White was so moved by them that he reconstructed them the next day and showed them to Lincoln. Lincoln's comment was: "Well, those are my views, and if I said anything on the subject, I must have said substantially that, but not nearly so well as that is said."[36] The words comprised his concluding remarks on the Declaration of Independence:

> If slavery had been a good thing, would the Fathers of the Republic have taken a step calculated to diminish its beneficent influences among themselves, and snatch the boon wholly from their posterity? . . . In their enlightened belief, nothing stamped with the divine image and likeness was sent into the world to be trodden on, and degraded, and imbruted by its fellows. They grasped not only the whole race of man then living, but they reached forward and seized upon the farthest posterity. They erected a beacon to guide their children and their children's children, and the countless myriads who should inhabit the earth in other ages.
>
> Wise statesmen as they were, they knew the tendency of prosperity to breed tyrants, and so they established these great self-evident truths, that when in the distant future some man, some faction, some interest, should set up the doctrine that none but rich men, or none but white men, were entitled to life, liberty and the pursuit of happiness, their posterity might look up again to the Declaration of Independence and take courage to renew the battle which their fathers began — so that truth, and justice, and mercy, and all the humane and Christian virtues might not be extinguished from the land; so that no man would hereafter dare to limit and circumscribe the great principles on which the temple of liberty was being built.[37]

In the meantime Douglas had prepared a plan to regain the offensive. He aimed to prove that the Republican Party stood convicted as traitorous out of its own mouth. How did he expect to do this? To understand it, we must go back four years.

When the anti-Nebraska elements, dominated by the abolitionists, were organizing into the Republican Party in 1854, meetings and conventions throughout the state drew up resolutions which were radical in nature. These contained the usual demands for which there was some constitutional sanction: abolition of slavery wherever Congress had jurisdiction (meaning the territories and the District of Columbia) and limitation of slavery to those states where it already existed. But the resolutions also called for action repugnant to the Constitution, such as the repeal of the Fugitive Slave Law, and the non-admission of new slave states into the Union. Aside from minor variations, the wording of most of these platforms was the same; one convention copying from another.

Douglas' plan was to quote from these resolutions and thus show that the Republican Party — and Lincoln — were not only radicals, but subverters of the Constitution. He remembered the occasion of the State Fair at Springfield in 1854 when he and Lincoln had clashed on the Kansas-Nebraska Act and public announcement had been made of a Republican organization meeting to follow. Surely, he thought, Lincoln must have been there. Had he not been listed as a member of the Republican State Central Committee? He therefore must have approved the seditious Springfield resolutions concocted by that fanatical abolitionist, Codding.

What Douglas did not know was that Lincoln, on the shrewd advice of Herndon, had avoided that meeting by suddenly finding "court business" in Tazewell County, and that he had subsequently written to Codding protesting against his being made a member of the Republican State Central Committee without his knowledge or consent. Nor did Douglas know, or if he knew, did he care to take cognizance of the fact, that Lincoln had not affiliated with the Republican Party until 1856 and that, as a result of his influence, the state platform drawn up at Bloomington in that year had been purged of those recommendations which were of doubtful constitutional validity.

Having the opening speech at Ottawa, Douglas intended to take Lincoln by surprise with his maneuver. He reasoned that

Old Abe would undoubtedly expect him to rehearse the usual arguments and to defend himself against his and Trumbull's odious charges. Lincoln, therefore, would have his own reply more or less set — improved, no doubt, over his previous efforts, but varying little from what he had said in their former exchanges. Well, he would throw Old Abe off balance with such embarrassing charges, that it would be he who would once again be put on the defensive, and his well-prepared speech rendered useless.

Accordingly, Douglas began checking into the matter of the Republican platforms. An issue of the *Illinois State Register* of August 1856 had printed a speech delivered in Congress by Douglas' devoted follower and colleague, Representative Thomas L. Harris, wherein he denounced the Republican Party by quoting from resolutions supposedly adopted at Springfield in 1854. Douglas asked Editor Lanphier to corroborate this information by checking with Harris and going through the paper's files of 1854. Even though time was short, he wanted the information before "next Saturday," the day of the debate. Lanphier did as he was requested and dutifully brought the material to Ottawa.[38]

Armed with this ammunition, the Little Giant was confident of dealing his rival a devastating blow.

CHAPTER 7

"I Will Bring Him to His Milk":
The Ottawa Debate

Saturday, August 21, dawned hot and dusty on Ottawa. Excitement was in the air. The town's population of somewhat over 7,000 had doubled overnight. Accommodations were at a premium. Chester P. Dewey, reporter for the *New York Evening Post,* who had come to join Horace White and Robert Hitt for the campaign, had to sleep on a sofa at the hotel. "By wagon, by rail, by canal, the people poured in," he wrote to his paper:

> Men, women, and children, old and young, the dwellers on the broad prairies, had turned their backs upon the plough. Military companies were out; martial music sounded, and salutes of artillery thundered in the air. Eager marshals in partisan sashes rode furiously about the streets. Peddlers were crying their wares at the corners, and excited groups of politicians were canvassing and quarrelling everywhere. And still they came, the crowd . . . growing more eager and hungry, perhaps more thirsty, though every precaution was taken against this latter evil. About noon the rival processions were formed, and paraded the streets amid the cheers of the people.[1]

The candidates approached the town from different directions. Lincoln had gone from Peoria to Morris, which was twenty miles east of Ottawa, whence he was brought by a special train on seventeen cars filled with Republican partisans from Chicago and Joliet. In the entourage was a contingent of abolitionists, including Owen Lovejoy. The powerful Negro orator and former slave, Fred Douglass, was also due in Illinois though, as it turned out, he would not actively enter the campaign until later. At the station, Lincoln was greeted by an "immense" crowd and welcomed by Joseph O. Glover, mayor of this Republican town, whose weekend guest he was to be.

Douglas arrived from Peru, situated sixteen miles to the west of Ottawa. He came in an "elegant carriage drawn by four splendid horses." Four miles out of Ottawa he was met by a "delegation composed of several hundreds, bearing flags and banners, and escorted into the city amid the booming of cannon . . ." to the Geiger House.[2]

The debate had been scheduled to start at two o'clock, but by one o'clock the crowd had filled the public square. They had even taken possession of the crude speaker's platform so that the officials and the reporters found difficulty in getting to their places. Some adventurous spirits had gone so far as to climb on the wooden awning overhead, which eventually gave way and tumbled its load of men and boys on the heads of the reception committee below. Fortunately no one was hurt. The crowd which had gathered was estimated at from 10,000 to 20,000 depending on the bias of the estimator.

It took a half hour to restore order out of the chaos and the excitement. At 2:30 P.M. Douglas began speaking and the battle was on!

The Little Giant was in fine form. He displayed fully the art which marked him as the master stump-speaker of his day. With biting sarcasm he gibed at Lincoln's background and political tenets:

> I have known him for nearly twenty-five years. There were many points of sympathy between us when we first got acquainted. We were both comparatively boys, and both struggling with poverty in a strange land. I was a school-teacher in the town of Winchester, and he a flourishing grocery-keeper in the town of Salem. . . I made as good a school-teacher as I could and when a cabinetmaker I made a good bedstead and tables, although my old boss said I succeeded better with bureaus and secretaries than anything else; but I believe that Lincoln was always more successful in business

than I, for his business enabled him to get into the legislature.

I met him there, however, and had a sympathy with him,
because of the uphill struggle we both had in life. He was
then just as good at telling an anecdote as now. He could
beat any of the boys wrestling, or running a foot race, in
pitching quoits or tossing a copper, could ruin more liquor
than all the boys of the town together, and the dignity and
impartiality with which he presided at a horse race or fist
fight, excited the admiration and won the praise of everybody
that was present and participated. . .

In 1846, when Wilmot introduced his celebrated proviso,
and the abolition tornado swept over the country, Lincoln
turned up as a member of Congress from Sangamon district.
I was then in the Senate of the United States, and was glad
to welcome my old friend and companion. Whilst in Congress, he distinguished himself by his opposition to the Mexican war, taking the side of the common enemy against his
own country; and when he returned home he found that the
indignation of the people followed him everywhere, and he
was . . . submerged or obliged to retire into private life, forgotten by his former friends.[3]

He also rehearsed the familiar arguments about Negro inferiority, and the social, as well as political, dangers from the
free Negro. He touched on the Dred Scott decision and its
relation to his favorite doctrine of popular sovereignty. He
blasted at the "house divided" theory, and pointed to the acts
of the founding fathers for proof that it was not only possible,
but intended for the union to exist half-slave and half-free.

But the highlight of his speech was the bombshell he threw
at Lincoln in the form of the "Springfield Resolutions" of
1854. He quoted the radical "Codding" resolutions in full,
and declared that Lincoln, in association with the abolitionists
Giddings, Chase, Fred Douglass and "Parson" Lovejoy had
constructed this platform for the new Black Republican Party
of Illinois. His rich voice thundered out the challenge:

> I desire to know whether Mr. Lincoln to-day stands as he
> did in 1854 in favor of the unconditional repeal of the Fugi-
> tive Slave Law. I desire him to answer whether he stands
> pledged to-day, as he did in 1854, against the admission of
> any more slave states into the Union, even if the people want
> them. I want to know whether he stands pledged against the

admission of a new state into the Union with such a constitution as the people of the state may see fit to make. I
want to know whether he stands to-day pledged to the abolition of slavery in the District of Columbia. I desire him
to answer whether he stands pledged to the prohibition of
the slave trade between the different states. I desire to know
whether he stands pledged to prohibit slavery in all the territories of the United States, north as well as south of the
Missouri Compromise line. I desire him to answer whether
he is opposed to the acquisition of any more territory unless
slavery is first prohibited therein. . . I ask Abraham Lincoln
to answer these questions, in order that when I trot him
down to lower Egypt I may put the same questions to him.[4]

The bombshell seemed to explode in all directions at once.
As the Little Giant continued, he got so wrapped up in his
subject that he had to be told that his time was out.

PUBLIC CATECHISM

When Lincoln began his reply he had no choice but to defend against Douglas' charges. He dealt first with the resolutions:

As to those resolutions that he took such a length of time
to read, as being the platform of the Republican party in
1854, I say I never had anything to do with them. . . I believe *this* is true: . . . there was a call for a convention to
form a Republican party at Springfield, and I think that my
friend Mr. Lovejoy, who is here upon this stand, had a hand
in it. I think . . . he will be able to recollect that he tried to
get me into it, and I would not go in.
    I believe it is also true, that I went away from Springfield
when the convention was in session, to attend court in Tazewell County. It is true they did place my name, though
without my authority, upon the committee, and afterwards
wrote me to attend the meeting of the committee, but I
refused to do so, and I never had anything to do with that
organization. This is the plain truth about all that matter
of the resolutions.[5]

Desiring, nevertheless, to illustrate his position on the Fugitive Slave Law, he said he would read from his Peoria speech of
1854. As he searched through his papers, a voice called out:
"Put on your specs." To the laughter of the crowd, he replied:

"Yes, sir, I am obliged to do so. I am no longer a young man."[6]
He pointed out that he had said:

> When they [the South] remind us of their constitutional
> rights, I acknowledge them, not grudgingly, but fully, and
> fairly, and I would give them any legislation for the re-
> claiming of their fugitives which should not, in its strin-
> gency, be more likely to carry a free man into slavery, than
> our ordinary criminal laws are to hang an innocent one.[7]

He then went on to declare:

> I have reason to know that Judge Douglas *knows* that I
> said this. I think he has the answer here to one of the ques-
> tions he put to me. I do not mean to allow him to catechise
> me unless he pays back for it in kind. I will not answer
> questions one after another unless he reciprocates, but as he
> made this inquiry and I have answered it before, he has got
> it without my getting anything in return. He has got my
> answer on the Fugitive Slave Law.[8]

Next he took up the Mexican War charge introducing it
with a humorous reference to Douglas' insinuations about his
early life:

> The Judge is woefully at fault about his early friend Lin-
> coln being a "grocery keeper." I don't know as it would
> be a great sin, if I had been, but he is mistaken. Lincoln
> never kept a grocery anywhere in the world. It is true that
> Lincoln did work the latter part of one winter in a small
> still house, up at the head of the hollow.
> And so I think my friend, the Judge, is equally at fault
> when he charges me at the time when I was in Congress of
> having opposed our soldiers who were fighting in the Mexi-
> can war. The Judge did not make his charge very distinctly
> but I can tell you what he can prove by referring to the
> record. You remember I was an Old Whig, and whenever
> the Democratic party tried to get me to vote that the war
> had been righteously begun by the President, I would not
> do it. But whenever they asked for any money, or land
> warrants, or anything to pay the soldiers there, during all
> that time, I gave the same votes that Judge Douglas did.
> When he, by a general charge, conveys the idea that I
> withheld supplies from the soldiers who were fighting in the
> Mexican War, or did anything else to hinder the soldiers,

he is, to say the least, grossly and altogether mistaken, as a consultation of the records will prove to him.[9]

As Lincoln warmed to his arguments, he displayed the ability as a rough-and-tumble debater which had caused Douglas to say that he would have his hands full with Old Abe. Referring again to the Peoria speech, he refuted Douglas' accusation that he favored social and political equality with the Negro:

> Anything that argues me into his idea of perfect social and political equality with the negro, is but a specious and fantastic arrangement of words, by which a man can prove a horse chestnut to be a chestnut horse. . . I have no purpose to introduce political and social equality between the white and the black races. There is a physical difference between the two, which in my judgment will probably forever forbid their living together upon the footing of perfect equality, and inasmuch as it becomes a necessity that there must be a difference, I, as well as Judge Douglas, am in favor of the race to which I belong, having the superior position.
>
> I have never said anything to the contrary, but I hold that notwithstanding all this, there is no reason in the world why the negro is not entitled to all the natural rights enumerated in the Declaration of Independence, the right to life, liberty and the pursuit of happiness.[10]

He twitted Douglas with having called him a liar at Clinton in answer to the charge that he was engaged in a conspiracy to nationalize slavery. He renewed the charge by referring to the language of the Nebraska Bill which spoke about not legislating slavery "into any territory or state":

> I have always been puzzled to know what business the word "state" had in that connection. Judge Douglas knows. He put it there. . . The law they were passing was not about states, and was not making provisions for states. . .
>
> After seeing the Dred Scott decision, which holds that the people cannot exclude slavery from a *territory,* if another Dred Scott decision shall come, holding that they cannot exclude it from a state, we shall discover that when the word was originally put there, it was in view of something which was to come . . . it was the *other half* of something. . . If there is any different reason for putting it there, Judge Douglas, in a good-humored way, without calling anybody a liar, *can tell what the reason was.*[11]

He accused Douglas of making a similar charge himself in a speech in the Senate when he assailed the *Washington Union,* acknowledged as the voice of the Administration, for stating in an article that it was unconstitutional for any state to prohibit the citizens of another state from settling with their slaves within its borders, and for advocating other extreme pro-slavery concepts which subsequently were incorporated into the Lecompton Constitution. Douglas had charged that the action of the *Washington Union,* was a "fatal blow being struck at the sovereignty of the states of this Union":

> Whom does he make that charge against? Does he make it against that newspaper editor merely? No; he says it is identical in spirit with the Lecompton Constitution, and so the framers of that constitution are brought in with the editor of the newspaper in that "fatal blow being struck." He did not call it a "conspiracy." In his language it is a "fatal blow being struck." And if the words carry the meaning better when changed from a "conspiracy" into a "fatal blow being struck," I will change my expression and call it "fatal blow being struck."
>
> We see the charge made not merely against the editor of the *Union* but all the framers of the Lecompton Constitution; and not only so, but the article was an *authoritative* article. By whose authority? Is there any question but he means it was by the authority of the President, and his Cabinet — the administration?[12]

He followed this up by showing how Douglas and men like him were preparing the public mind for the next and final step in fastening slavery upon the whole country:

> What is necessary for the nationalization of slavery? It is simply the next Dred Scott decision. It is merely for the Supreme Court to decide that no state under the Constitution can exclude it, just as they have already decided that under the Constitution neither Congress nor the territorial legislature can do it. When that is decided and acquiesced in, the whole thing is done. . .
>
> Let us consider what Judge Douglas is doing every day to that end. . . what influence he is exerting on public sentiment. In this and like communities, public sentiment is everything. With public sentiment, nothing can fail; without it nothing can succeed. Consequently he who moulds public

sentiment, goes deeper than he who enacts statutes or pro-
nounces decisions. . . Judge Douglas is a man of vast influence, so great that it is enough for many men to profess to
believe anything, when they once find out that Judge Douglas
professes to believe it.

This man sticks to a decision which forbids the people of a
territory from excluding slavery, and he does so not because
he says it is right in itself — he does not give any opinion on
that . . . but because a decision of the Court is to him a
"Thus saith the Lord." He places it on that ground alone,
and you will bear in mind that thus committing himself
unreservedly to this decision, *commits* him to the next one
just as firmly as to this.[13]

Lincoln clinched the point by striking at Douglas' sensitive
past history as a judge:

There is nothing that can divert or turn him away from
this decision. I remind him of a time when the large party
to which Judge Douglas belonged, were displeased with a
decision of the Supreme Court of Illinois, because they had
decided that a Governor could not remove a Secretary of
State.

Judge Douglas will not deny that he was then in favor of
overslaughing that decision by the mode of adding five new
judges, so as to vote down the four old ones. Not only so, but
it ended in *the Judge's sitting down on that very bench as
one of the five new Judges to break down the four old ones.*
It was in this way precisely that he got his title of Judge. . .
When he says a court of this kind will lose the confidence of
all men, will be prostituted and disgraced by such a proceeding, I say, "You know best, Judge; you have been through
the mill."

But I cannot shake Judge Douglas' teeth loose from the
Dred Scott decision. . . I may point out to the Judge, and
say that he is bespattered all over, from the beginning of his
political life to the present time, with attacks upon judicial
decisions — I may cut off limb after limb of his public record,
and strive to wrench him from a single dictum of the Court —
yet, I cannot divert him from it. He hangs to the last, to the
Dred Scott decision. These things show there is a purpose
strong as death and eternity for which he adheres to this
decision, and for which he will adhere to *all other decisions*
of the same Court.[14]

As his hour and a half of speaking drew to a close, Lincoln tied all his arguments into a peroration which appealed to the moral sense, as well as to the patriotism, of his auditors:

> Henry Clay once said of a class of men who would repress all tendencies to liberty and ultimate emancipation, that they must, if they would do this, go back to the era of our independence, and muzzle the cannon which thunders its annual joyous return; they must blow out the moral lights around us; they must penetrate the human soul, and eradicate there the love of liberty...
>
> To my thinking, Judge Douglas is, by his example and vast influence, doing that very thing in this community. . . When he invites any people willing to have slavery, to establish it, he is blowing out the moral lights around us. When he says he "cares not whether slavery is voted down or voted up," — that it is a sacred right of self-government — he is in my judgment penetrating the human soul and eradicating the light of reason and the love of liberty in this American people.
>
> And now I will only say that when, by all these means and appliances, Judge Douglas shall succeed in bringing public sentiment to an exact accordance with his own views — when these vast assemblages shall echo back all these sentiments — when they shall come to repeat his views and to avow his principles, and to say all that he says on these mighty questions — then it needs only the formality of the second Dred Scott decision, which he endorses in advance, to make slavery alike lawful in all the states — old as well as new, North as well as South.[15]

Lincoln finished well within his time. He relinquished the platform with several minutes remaining. Of even this innocuous fact, the shrewd Douglas determined to take advantage.

The Little Giant was quick to spring to the attack once more. All of his fighting qualities were aroused. He took up again the issue of the seeming contradictions between the Black Republican Party and its candidate. He charged that it was not denied that the resolutions were the platform of the Republican Party, "but Mr. Lincoln now says," he gibed, "that he does not think he was there, but thinks he was in Tazewell, holding court. . . . Now I want to remind Mr. Lincoln that he was at Springfield when that convention was held and those resolutions adopted."[16]

Douglas' bellicose manner brought shouts and interruptions from the Lincoln partisans, and the chairman of the Republican Committee had to call for order.

"He spoke in the hall of the House," Douglas continued, "and when he got through his speech — my recollection is distinct, and I shall never forget it — Mr. Codding walked in as I took the stand to reply, and gave notice that the Republican State Convention would meet instantly in the Senate chamber, and called upon the Republicans to retire there and go into this very convention, instead of remaining and listening to me."

Lincoln interrupted: "Let the Judge add that Lincoln went along with them."

"I will not add that for I do not know it," retorted Douglas.

"I do know it," said Lincoln.

"But whether he knows or not my point is this, and I will yet bring him to his milk on this point,"[17] said Douglas, and he continued:

> This denial of his that he did not act on the committee is a miserable quibble to avoid the main issue, which is that this Republican platform declares in favor of the unconditional repeal of the Fugitive Slave Law. Has Lincoln answered whether he endorsed that or not? I called his attention to it when I first addressed you and asked him for an answer and I then predicted that he would not answer. How does he answer? Why that he was not on the committee that wrote the resolutions. I then repeated the next proposition contained in the resolution, which was to restrict slavery in those states in which it exists and asked him whether he endorsed it. Does he answer yes, or no? He says in reply, "I was not on the committee at the time: I was up in Tazewell."
>
> The next question I put to him was, whether he was in favor of prohibiting the admission of any more slave states into the Union. I put the question to him distinctly, whether, if the people of the territory, when they had sufficient population to make a state, should form their constitution recognizing slavery, he would vote for or against its admission. He is a candidate for the United States Senate, and it is possible, if he should be elected, that he would have to vote directly on that question. I asked him to answer me and you whether he would vote to admit a state into the Union, with slavery or without it, as its own people might choose. He did not

answer that question. He dodges that question also, under the cover that he was not on the committee at the time, that he was not present when the platform was made. . .

Then again, this platform which was made at Springfield by his own party, when he was its acknowledged head, provides that Republicans will insist on the abolition of slavery in the District of Columbia, and I asked Lincoln specifically whether he agreed with them in that? Did you get an answer? He is afraid to answer it.

He knows I will trot him down to Egypt. I intend to make him answer there, or I will show the people of Illinois that he does not intend to answer these questions. . . Each of the questions I have put to him are practical questions, questions based upon the fundamental principles of the Black Republican party, and I want to know whether he is the first, last and only choice of a party with whom he does not agree in principle. . . I want to know whether that party is unanimously in favor of a man who does not adopt the creed and agree with them in their principles.[18]

He finished this attack with a barb:

The Black Republican party stands pledged . . . but he cannot devise his answer; he has not made up his mind, whether he will or not. He talked about everything else he could think of to occupy his hour and a half, and when he could not think of anything more to say, without an excuse for refusing to answer these questions, he sat down long before his time was out.[19]

Douglas next addressed himself to the conspiracy charge, which he brushed off with heavy ridicule:

He says he will repeat it [the charge] until I answer his folly and nonsense about Stephen, and Franklin, and Roger, and Bob, and James.

He studied that out, prepared that one sentence with the greatest care, committed it to memory, and put it in his first Springfield speech, and now he carries that speech around and reads that sentence to show how pretty it is. His vanity is wounded because I will not go into that beautiful figure of his about the building of a house. All I have to say is, that I am not green enough to let him make a charge which he acknowledges he does not know to be true, and then take up my time in answering it, when I know it to be false and nobody else knows it to be true.

I have lived twenty-five years in Illinois. I have served you with all the fidelity and ability which I possess, and Mr. Lincoln is at liberty to attack my public action, my votes, and my conduct; but when he dares to attack my moral integrity, by a charge of conspiracy between myself, Chief Justice Taney, and the Supreme Court and two Presidents of the United States, I will repel it.

Mr. Lincoln has not character enough for integrity and truth merely on his own *ipse dixit* to arraign President Buchanan, President Pierce, and nine judges of the Supreme Court, not one of whom would be complimented by being put on an equality with him. There is an unpardonable presumption in a man putting himself up before thousands of people, and pretending that his *ipse dixit*, without proof, without fact and without truth, is enough to bring down and destroy the purest and best of living men.[20]

The Little Giant now devoted a few minutes to the wording of the Nebraska Bill:

Mr. Lincoln wants to know why the word "state" as well as "territory" was put into the Nebraska Bill! I will tell him. It was put there to meet just such false arguments as he has been adducing. That first, not only the people of the territories should do as they pleased, but that when they come to be admitted as states, they should come into the Union with or without slavery, as the people determined. I meant to knock in the head this abolition doctrine of Mr. Lincoln's, that there shall be no more slave states, even if the people want them. . .

What was the origin of the Missouri difficulty and the Missouri Compromise? The people of Missouri formed a constitution as a slave state, and asked admission into the Union, but the Free Soil party of the North being in a majority, refused to admit her because she had slavery as one of her institutions. Hence this first slavery agitation arose upon a state and not upon a territory, and yet Mr. Lincoln does not know why the word state was placed in the Kansas-Nebraska Bill.[21]

Time was running out. The orator drew his rebuttal to a close:

He does not want to avow his principles. I do want to avow mine, as clear as sunlight in mid-day. Democracy is founded upon the eternal principle of right. The plainer these principles are avowed before the people, the stronger will be the support which they will receive. I only wish I had the power to make them so clear that they would shine in the heavens for every man, woman, and child to read.[22]

He talked on for another few sentences, caught the signal that his time was out and sat down. The first debate was over.

THE PRESS IN FULL CRY

The crowd broke loose. A great throng followed after Douglas as he made his way from the stand, swinging his big hat from right to left in acknowledgement of the cheers. The Republicans were equally enthusiastic. Half a dozen brawny men seized Lincoln, and hoisting him upon their shoulders, carried him through the streets, accompanied by "five thousand" singing the "Star-Spangled Banner" and "Hail Columbia." Lincoln later told Horace White that the experience was "extremely mortifying" to him.[23]

The newspapers reported the day's events with customary recklessness. The correspondent of the *Philadelphia Press*, a Democratic paper, wrote that "Lincoln is the worst used-up man in the United States," and that "he is driven almost to desperation. You will find that before he passes through this discussion, there will scarcely be anything left of him. He now exhibits the appearance of great mental and bodily suffering. He has six appointments to meet Judge Douglas yet. *I don't believe that he will fill them all.*"[24]

Another Democratic paper, the St. Louis *Morning Herald*, reported that "hundreds of those who had been applauding Lincoln all along, now turned and applauded Douglas." It then concluded that "if Douglas commences by triumphing in a Republican district, Lincoln may as well hang up his hat, take a back seat, and wait until 1860, as Douglas will then be President; and then Mr. Lincoln may make another effort for an election to the United States Senate, without having a Douglas to contend with."[25]

Lincoln was also described as getting "very blue about his chops" in the course of Douglas' rejoinder, and as "withering" and "writhing" before the Little Giant's "bold, lucid and eloquent argumentation."

In referring to the incident of Lincoln's being carried off

the platform, the opposition went to ludicrous extremes. Lincoln's arch-enemy, the *Illinois State Register,* described the scene as follows:

> This funereal escort passed through the crowd and bore Mr. L., to his quarters ... with his long arms about his carriers' shoulders, his long legs dangling nearly to the ground, while his long face was an incessant contortion to wear a winning smile that succeeded in being a ghastly one. . . . It was really not a pretty picture, though hugely an amusing one. . . We suppose that this farce was deemed necessary as an after piece to the three act tragedy on the stand: "The impalement of Hon. Abraham Lincoln." — It was in full keeping with that gentleman's tailing tactics since the commencement of the canvass.[26]

The low point, however, was touched by the *Chicago Times* which wrote:

> When Douglas and the Democrats had left the square, Lincoln essayed to descend from the stage, but his limbs refused to do their office. During Douglas' last speech Lincoln had suffered severely; alternately burning with fever, and then suddenly chilled with shame, his respiratory organs had become obstructed, his limbs got cold, and he was unable to walk.
> In this extremity, the Republican Marshall called half a dozen men, who, lifting Lincoln in their arms, carried him along. By some mismanagement the men selected for this office happened to be very short in stature, and the consequence was, that while Lincoln's head and shoulders towered above theirs, his feet dragged on the ground. Such an exhibition as the "toting" of Lincoln from the square to his lodgings was never seen at Ottawa before.[27]

The *Louisville Journal* applied the coup de grace: "If they had foreseen how he would come out in the debate, they would have borne him off before it commenced."[28]

The Republican papers matched their opponents stroke for stroke. The *Chicago Press and Tribune* said that when Douglas sprang to his feet to reply to Lincoln, "his face was livid with passion. . . We have never seen a face so distorted with rage. . . . He resembled a wild beast in looks and gesture, and a maniac in language and argument."[29] It then concluded that "it was the opinion of every unprejudiced listener, that Douglas would give a year off the end of his life if he could escape meeting Lincoln at the six discussions through which he must pass."

The Peoria *Transcript* thought that Douglas' speech was delivered "in a coarse, vulgar, boisterous style,"[30] and later commented: "The complete manner in which Lincoln used up Douglas . . . is evinced by the desperation of the latter's newspaper organs."[31] The *Chicago Journal* presented this tidbit: "The late Mr. Douglas. — Since the flailing Senator Douglas received at Ottawa on Saturday, we suggest that his friends hereafter address him as the late Mr. Douglas."[32]

But just as the Democratic press had its "toting-off-Lincoln" incident, the Republican papers had their "milk" incident. The Quincy *Whig* quoted Douglas' phraseology — "bring him to his milk" and "trot him down to Egypt" — and commented: "Isn't this beautiful language to come from a United States Senator? Mr. Douglas is as much a blackguard as he is a demagogue."[33]

The *Illinois State Journal* printed a letter from a "reader":

> I have a cow which won't give milk; in short, she has "dried up." I wonder if Mr. Douglas would undertake to "trot her out" and "bring her to her milk." I understand he thinks himself peculiarly gifted in that line.[34]

Other papers also suddenly reported farmers who had several cows which had "gone dry" and hoped Douglas would respond to the call to bring them to their milk.

The sarcasm and jest to which the milk incident lent itself were so appealing to the Republicans that they rode it without ceasing throughout the entire campaign. A later twist appeared in the Peoria *Transcript*:

> Mr. Editor: — While Mr. Douglas was speaking at the court house on Monday last a peculiar white substance was observed at each corner of his mouth. I have heard various conjectures as to the cause. Can you throw any light upon the subject?

To which the answer given was:

> While the Little Giant was in full blast at Galesburg and frothing at both sides of his mouth, two ladies standing side by side were overheard questioning and answering one another thus: "What is that on each side of Mr. Douglas'

mouth?" Said the other, "Oh, he has been taking some of Lincoln's milk and it has soured on his stomach!"[35]

But it was against the so-called Codding resolutions of Springfield that the Republicans struck their heaviest blows. Douglas' thrust had touched a sensitive point. The *Chicago Press and Tribune* immediately investigated and discovered that the resolutions had not been adopted at Springfield. "Forgery!" shouted the Republican press. "Forgery!" thundered the Republican campaign speakers. Douglas, Lanphier and Harris knew the resolutions were fraudulent, they said. Here was a clear case of conspiracy and downright dishonesty.

Subsequent investigation by Douglas revealed that the resolutions as worded and reported by Lanphier had actually been adopted by a local convention at Aurora in Kane County. He had thus fallen into a blunder. But the Little Giant had his own way of handling a bad situation. He had made a mistake, he would tell future audiences, but only as to the "spot" of the resolutions. Weren't all the platforms adopted in 1854 practically the same except as to minor wording? They represented the true goals and objectives of the revolutionary, dangerous Republican Party.

Douglas' argument was a shrewd one. Conservatives, who opposed slavery but feared radical measures, would be inclined to look beyond a mere error in time or place to what they considered the essence of Republican principle. A great deal of uneasiness would likewise be engendered in impatient radical circles. This group would have doubts as to the calibre of the conservative Lincoln who was supposed to be the standard-bearer of freedom. Such doubts were reflected in a letter by the outspoken Parker to Billy Herndon. About the candidate whose "house divided" speech had earlier so impressed him, he now had this to say:

> I thought Douglas had the best of it. He questioned Mr. Lincoln on the great matters of Slavery, and put the most radical questions, which go to the heart of the question, before the people. Mr. Lincoln did not meet the issue. He made a technical evasion; "he had nothing to do with the resolutions in question." Suppose he had not, admit they were forged. Still they were the vital questions, pertinent to the issue, and Lincoln dodged them. That is not the way to fight the battle of freedom.[36]

CHAPTER 8

A Heresy Is Broadcast: The Freeport Debate

Lincoln's reactions to the Ottawa debate were reflected in a letter to J. C. Cunningham of Urbana the next day. "Douglas and I, first time this Canvass, crossed swords here yesterday;" he wrote, "the fire flew some and I am glad to know that I am alive."[1] Douglas' attack had succeeded in taking him by surprise. He had countered as cautiously as he could, just as one would in a courtroom, but it was not enough merely to come off alive. Douglas had left the impression that Lincoln had evaded his questions. This situation had to be remedied, and the battle carried to the Little Giant.

Lincoln, therefore, pondered a counterattack. Not only would he answer his opponent's interrogatories in detail, but he would ask some questions of his own. One of the questions that would be appropriate was the one suggested by Henry Asbury a month before: Was there any lawful way in the face of the Dred Scott decision to exclude slavery from the territories? He knew very well what the answer would be, as he had told Asbury. Douglas had stated his position not only in his early campaign speeches, but even as far back as June of the previous year when he had defended the Dred Scott decision in Springfield, and tried to reconcile it with his theory of unfriendly legislation.

Forcing a repetition of this stand, however, was good campaign strategy. It would help to widen the cleavage within the

Democratic Party. Besides, Douglas' previous statements had been before local audiences and therefore for local consumption. Now, with the whole country following the debates, it was certain to focus the attention of the South on his straddle and would further injure his candidacy for the presidential nomination in 1860.

Accordingly, in the six-day interval before their next meeting at Freeport on August 27, Lincoln carefully worked out his answers to Douglas' interrogatories and framed four questions of his own, all of them designed to emphasize the differences between the Little Giant and the Danites. Asbury's question, which was subsequently to receive so much attention and to be the subject of so much controversy, was the second of the four.

Meantime, Lincoln was on the move. His itinerary took him southwest to Augusta in the extreme west-central part of the state, where he addressed a Republican Congressional convention. He then doubled back to Freeport which was in the extreme north. On the way he stopped for speeches at Galesburg and at the little towns of Henry, Macomb and Amboy where he spent the night of the 26.

While Lincoln was thus busy traveling from one part of the state to another, Douglas proceeded directly toward Freeport. On the 25 he spoke at Galena in the northwestern tip. He was again having trouble with his voice. "Senator Douglas spoke for two hours and a quarter with great apparent ease," the *Chicago Times* reported, "although for the past few days he has been suffering from a severe bronchial affection from which he has not yet entirely recovered."[2]

The rivals entered Freeport to triumphal receptions. Douglas arrived from Galena on Thursday evening, August 26. As he stepped from the train, he was greeted by a shouting and cheering throng carrying torches. A salute was fired, and then to music and the booming of cannon, the Little Giant was escorted by torchlight procession to the town's newest and finest hotel, the Brewster House. There Colonel James Mitchell, the town's leading Democrat, made a reception speech. Later, he was called to the balcony and acknowledged the crowd's welcome with a brief address.

Lincoln arrived at ten o'clock the next morning. The tremendous reception accorded him demonstrated the strong Re-

publican character of the town and of its adjoining areas.
Special low-rate excursion trips had brought supporters from
nearby towns. An excursion from Chicago cost only $4.35, in-
stead of the usual $7.20. "By starting on the 9½ train tomorrow
morning, you reach Freeport at 3 P.M., an hour after the
speaking commences," an article in the *Chicago Press and
Tribune* said.[3]

Freeport was only 120 miles from Chicago, but train travel
was slow in those days. "All should therefore, leave by tonight's
train . . . at 45 minutes after 10 o'clock," the article went on
to advise. "Comfortable sleeping cars will be put on, and all
can reach Freeport in season for the whole fun, without losing
any time."[4] In another article the paper told its readers: "It is
expected that Douglas will try to 'bring Mr. Lincoln to his
milk' and all who are curious to know what the process used
will be, and what will result therefrom, will not fail to be on
hand."[5]

Freeport was approximately the size of Ottawa, but the crowd
that augmented its population of 7,000 was estimated to exceed by one-third the swollen gathering of the previous week,
with Republicans outnumbering Douglasites four to one. The
New York Post reporter described the streets as "fairly black
with people" and the day as "abundantly refreshing to hotel
and saloon keepers, who stand aghast at the multitudes to
be fed."[6]

The Republicans, anxious to outdo the reception given
Douglas, gathered at the station 2,000 strong, according to
the *Chicago Press and Tribune* — it was 5,000, said the
Illinois State Journal — to greet their champion when he
arrived from Amboy. Delegations proudly displayed their
banners: CARROLL COUNTY for ABRAHAM LINCOLN,
THE GALENA LINCOLN CLUB, WINNEBAGO COUN-
TY FOR "OLD ABE." To the boom of cannon and the shouts
of the multitude, Lincoln proceeded to the Brewster House,
where Thomas J. Turner, mayor of the town, made the reception speech. Later, Lincoln, in his turn, made a brief speech
from the balcony. But the crowd was too enthusiastic to be
satisfied. As the various delegations paraded by, he was constantly recalled to the balcony. On one occasion, Douglas and
he appeared together, thus affording a vivid preliminary

glimpse of the disparity in the appearance and dress of the two men.

Unfavorable weather did not discourage the ardor of the throngs. The day had broken chilly and cloudy. Gusts of wind and bursts of sunshine alternated during the forenoon, but by twelve o'clock the weather settled cold, damp, and misty, heavy with the threat of rain. Long before the debate was scheduled to begin, the excited mob had pushed its way to the grove near the hotel where the speakers' platform and seats for listeners had been set up. Here, as in Ottawa, all was confusion and disorder. The *New York Post* described the scene:

> They have a wretched way in Illinois of leaving the platform unguarded and exposed to the forcible entry of the mob, who seize upon it an hour or so before the notabilities arrive, and turn a deaf ear to all urgent appeals to evacuation. Hence orators, committee of reception, invited guests, and last, but not least, the newspaper gentry, have to fight a hand-to-hand conflict for even the meagerest chance for standing room. This consumes half an hour or so, during which the crowd, taking their cue from those of high places, improvise a few scuffles for position among themselves.[7]

By two o'clock 15,000 people were jammed around the platform. A little while before, Lincoln in company with a dozen raw-boned farmers, had driven the short distance from the hotel in a Conestoga wagon drawn by six enormous horses. His friends had heard that Douglas was to ride in a splendid carriage drawn by white horses, and they had decided on this burlesque to point up the contrast between them. When Douglas saw what was happening, he refused to ride, and instead walked to the grove accompanied by Colonel Mitchell and a group of cheering supporters.

THE SEVEN INTERROGATORIES

In accordance with his agreement with Douglas, it was Lincoln's turn to speak first. He was introduced by Tom Turner, and as he stepped to the front of the platform, a curious incident occurred. It was discovered that Hitt, the shorthand reporter for the *Chicago Press and Tribune,* was not present. William Bross, one of the owners of the paper, called out:

"Hold on, Lincoln. You can't speak yet. Hitt ain't here, and there is no use of your speaking unless the *Press and Tribune* has a report."

"Ain't Hitt here?" asked Lincoln. "Where is he?"

Hitt was caught in the crowd. It was a few minutes before he was able to fight his way to the platform. But Lincoln had already started speaking and Hitt had to get his opening remarks from someone else — according to the *Chicago Times,* it was Bross himself.[8]

Lincoln lost no time in taking up Douglas' interrogatories. He prefaced his answers by clarifying his connection with the Republican movement in these words: "I have supposed myself, since the organization of the Republican Party at Bloomington, in May 1856, bound as a party man by the platforms of the party, then and since. If in any interrogatories which I shall answer I go beyond the scope of what is within these platforms it will be perceived that no one is responsible but myself." He then continued:

> I will take up the Judge's interrogatories as I find them printed in the Chicago *Times,* and answer them *seriatim.* . .
>
> Question 1. "I desire to know whether Lincoln to-day stands, as he did in 1854, in favor of the unconditional repeal of the Fugitive Slave Law?"
>
> Answer. I do not now, nor ever did, stand in favor of the unconditional repeal of the fugitive slave law.
>
> Q. 2. "I desire him to answer whether he stands pledged to-day, as he did in 1854, against the admission of any more slave states into the Union, even if the people want them?"
>
> A. I do not now, nor ever did, stand pledged against the admission of any more slave states into the Union.
>
> Q. 3. "I want to know whether he stands pledged against the admission of a new state into the Union with such a constitution as the people of that state may see fit to make."
>
> A. I do not stand pledged against the admission of a new state into the Union, with such a constitution as the people of that state may see fit to make.
>
> Q. 4. "I want to know whether he stands to-day pledged to the abolition of slavery in the District of Columbia?"
>
> A. I do not stand to-day pledged to the abolition of slavery in the District of Columbia.
>
> Q. 5. "I desire him to answer whether he stands pledged to the prohibition of the slave trade between the different states?"

A. I do not stand pledged to the prohibition of the slave trade between the different states.

Q. 6. "I desire to know whether he stands pledged to prohibit slavery in all the territories of the United States, north as well as south of the Missouri Compromise line?"

A. I am impliedly, if not expressly, pledged to a belief in the *right* and *duty* of Congress to prohibit slavery in all the United States territories.

Q. 7. "I desire him to answer whether he is opposed to the acquisition of any new territory unless slavery is first prohibited therein."

A. I am not generally opposed to honest acquisition of territory; and, in any given case, I would or would not oppose such acquisition, accordingly as I might think such acquisition would or would not aggravate the slavery question among ourselves.

Now, my friends, it will be perceived upon an examination of these questions and answers, that so far I have only answered that I was not *pledged* to this, that or the other. The Judge has not framed his interrogatories to ask me anything more than this, and I have answered in strict accordance with the interrogatories, and have answered truly that I am not *pledged* at all upon any of the points to which I have answered. But I am not disposed to hang upon the exact form of his interrogatory. I am rather disposed to take up at least some of these questions, and state what I really think upon them.

In regard to the . . . question of whether I am pledged to the admission of any more slave states into the Union, I state to you very frankly that I would be exceedingly sorry ever to be put in a position of having to pass upon that question. I should be exceedingly glad to know that there would never be another slave state admitted into the Union; but I must add, that if slavery shall be kept out of the territories during the territorial existence of any one given territory, and then the people shall, having a fair chance and a clear field, when they come to adopt the constitution, do such an extraordinary thing as to adopt a slave constitution, uninfluenced by the actual presence of the institution among them, I see no alternative, if we own the country, but to admit them in the Union. . .

In regard to the abolition of slavery in the District of Columbia, I have my mind very distinctly made up. I should be exceedingly glad to see slavery abolished in the District of Columbia. I believe that Congress possesses the constitutional

power to abolish it. Yet as a member of Congress, I should
not with my present views, be in favor of *endeavoring* to
abolish slavery in the District of Columbia, unless it would
be upon these conditions. *First,* that the abolition should be
gradual. *Second,* that it should be on a vote of the majority
of qualified voters in the District, and *third,* that compensation should be made to unwilling owners. With these three
conditions, I confess I would be exceedingly glad to see Congress abolish slavery in the District of Columbia, and, in the
language of Henry Clay, "sweep from our Capital that foul
blot upon our nation."[9]

Lincoln's answers thus revealed not only his precise lawyer's
approach to a question, but also his cautious conservatism. At
the same time, in pointing out that if he went beyond the scope
of the platforms he alone was responsible, he demonstrated
that independence of opinion which, once arrived at, no one
could shake. Whatever position he took had to be based on
solid legal or constitutional ground, and no one could stampede
him from it. This he made clear in his next statement:

Now in all this, the Judge . . . has me on the record. I suppose he had flattered himself that I was really entertaining
one set of opinions for one place and another set for another
place — that I was afraid to say at one place what I uttered
at another. What I am saying here I suppose I say to a vast
audience as strongly tending to Abolitionism as any audience
in the state of Illinois, and I believe I am saying that which,
if it would be offensive to any persons and render them
enemies to myself, would be offensive to persons in this
audience.[10]

THE FREEPORT QUESTION

Lincoln now propounded his own interrogatories. The second was the "Asbury" question, and the third dealt with the
possibility of another and more sweeping Dred Scott decision:

Q. 2. Can the people of a United States territory, in any
lawful way, against the wish of any citizen of the United
States, exclude slavery from its limits prior to the formation
of a state constitution?
Q. 3. If the Supreme Court of the United States shall
decide that states can not exclude slavery from their limits,

are you in favor of acquiescing in adopting and following such decision as a rule of political action?[11]

Leaving the interrogatories, Lincoln addressed himself to the "Springfield" resolutions which investigation had disclosed as having been drawn up in Kane County. Since this showed that he had nothing to do with them, he took Douglas to task on the issue:

> When we consider who Judge Douglas is — that he is a distinguished Senator of the United States — . . . that his name has become of world-wide renown — it is *most extraordinary* that he should so far forget all the suggestions of justice to an adversary, or of prudence to himself, as to venture upon the assertion of that which the slightest investigation would have shown him to be wholly false. I can only account for his having done so upon the supposition that that evil genius which has attended him through his life, giving to him an apparent astonishing prosperity, such as to lead very many good men to doubt there being any advantage in virtue over vice — I say I can only account for it on the supposition that that evil genius has at last made up its mind to forsake him.
>
> And I may add that another extraordinary feature of the Judge's conduct in this canvass — made more extraordinary by this incident — is that he is in the habit, in almost all the speeches he makes, of charging falsehood upon his adversaries — myself and others. I now ask whether he is able to find anything that Judge Trumbull, for instance, has said, or in anything that I have said, a justification at all compared with what we have, in this instance, for that sort of vulgarity.[12]

These were harsh words, indeed, for Lincoln to use. It is one of the rare instances when he betrays a "streak of jealousy," as well as extreme annoyance with his adversary's methods.

Lincoln closed his presentation with a refutation of Douglas' *"ipse dixit"* answer to the conspiracy charge:

> Judge Douglas recurs again, as he did upon one or two other occasions, to the enormity of Lincoln — an insignificant individual like Lincoln — upon his *ipse dixit* charging a conspiracy upon a large number of members of Congress, the Supreme Court and two Presidents, to nationalize slavery. I want to say that, in the first place, I have made no charge of this sort upon my *ipse dixit*. I have only arrayed the evi-

dence tending to prove it, and presented it to the understanding of others, saying what I think proves it or not. This
is precisely what I have done. I have not placed it upon my
ipse dixit at all. . .

I wish to recall his attention to a piece of evidence which
I brought forward at Ottawa on Saturday, showing that he
had made substantially the *same charge* against substantially
the *same persons,* excluding his dear self from the category.
I ask him to give some attention to the evidence. . . that he
himself had discovered a "fatal blow being struck" against the
right of the people to exclude slavery from their limits . . . in
an article in the Washington *Union,* published "by authority,". . .

He pointed it not at a newspaper editor merely, but at the
President and his Cabinet and the members of Congress
advocating the Lecompton Constitution and those framing
that instrument. I must again be permitted to remind him,
that although my *ipse dixit* may not be as great as his, yet it
somewhat reduces the force of his calling my attention to
the *enormity* of my making a like charge against him.[13]

It was then the Little Giant's turn to speak. To the second
interrogatory he made the reply anticipated by Lincoln:

I answer emphatically, as Mr. Lincoln has heard me answer
a hundred times from every stump in Illinois, that in my
opinion the people of a territory can, by lawful means, exclude slavery from their limits prior to the formation of a
state constitution. Mr. Lincoln knew that I had answered that
question over and over again. He heard me argue the Nebraska Bill on that principle all over the state in 1854, in 1855
and in 1856, and he has no excuse for pretending to be in
doubt as to my position on that question.

It matters not what way the Supreme Court may hereafter
decide as to the abstract question whether slavery may or
may not go into a territory under the Constitution, the people
have the lawful means to introduce it or exclude it as they
please, for the reason that slavery cannot exist a day or an
hour anywhere, unless it is supported by local police regulations. Those police regulations can only be established by the
local legislature, and if the people are opposed to slavery
they will elect representatives to that body who will by
unfriendly legislation effectually prevent the introduction of
it into their midst. If, on the contrary, they are for it, their
legislation will favor its extension. Hence, no matter what

the decision of the Supreme Court may be on that abstract question, still the right of the people to make a slave territory or a free territory is perfect and complete under the Nebraska Bill.[14]

In answering the third interrogatory, the Little Giant also repudiated the charge that the Washington *Union* article implicated anyone in high authority in a conspiracy to nationalize slavery:

> The third question which Mr. Lincoln presented is, if the Supreme Court of the United States shall decide that a state of this Union cannot exclude slavery from its own limits will I submit to it? I am amazed that Lincoln should ask such a question. . . Mr. Lincoln's object is to cast an imputation upon the Supreme Court. . .
>
> It is true that the Washington *Union,* in an article published on the 17th of last December, did put forth that doctrine, and I denounced the article on the floor of the Senate, in a speech which Mr. Lincoln now pretends was against the President. The *Union* had claimed that slavery had a right to go into the free states and that any provision in the Constitution or laws of the free states to the contrary were null and void. I denounced it in the Senate, as I said before, and I was the first man who did. Lincoln's friends, Trumbull, and Seward . . . and the whole Black Republican side of the Senate were silent.
>
> They left it to me to denounce it. And what was the reply made to me on that occasion? Mr. Toombs, of Georgia, got up and undertook to lecture me on the ground that I ought not to have deemed the article worthy of notice, and ought not to have replied to it; that there was not one man, woman or child south of the Potomac, in any slave state, who did not repudiate any such pretension.
>
> Mr. Lincoln knows that that reply was made . . . and yet now he asks this question. He might as well ask me, suppose Mr. Lincoln should steal a horse would I sanction it (Laughter.) . . . He cast an imputation upon the Supreme Court of the United States by supposing that they would violate the Constitution of the United States. I tell him that such a thing is not possible. (Cheers.) It would be an act of moral treason that no man on the bench could ever descend to.[15]

The Little Giant finished his reply to the four interrogatories with the following barb:

I trust now that Mr. Lincoln will deem himself answered on his four points. He racked his brain so much in devising these four questions that he exhausted himself, and had not strength enough to invent the others. (Laughter.) As soon as he is able to hold a council with his advisers, Lovejoy, Farnsworth, and Fred. Douglass, he will frame and propound others.[16]

To this sally the largely Republican crowd shouted: "Good, good!" Douglas, who had demonstrated on so many fields his ability to handle heckling crowds, retorted with a gibe designed to cut deep into the pride of the audience:

You Black Republicans who say good, I have no doubt think that they are all good men. ("White, white.") I have reason to recollect that some people in this country think that Fred. Douglass is a very good man. The last time I came here to make a speech, while talking from the stand to you people of Freeport, as I am to-day, I saw a carriage and a magnificent one it was, drive up and take a position on the outside of the crowd; a beautiful young lady was sitting on the box seat, whilst Fred. Douglass and her mother reclined inside, and the owner of the carriage acted as driver. (Laughter, cheers, cries of "Right, what have you to say against it," etc.) I saw this in your own town. ("What of it?")

All I have to say of it is this, that if you, Black Republicans, think that the negro ought to be on a social equality with your wives and daughters, you have a perfect right to do so. ("Good, good," and cheers, mingled with hooting and cries of "White, white.") I am told that one of Fred. Douglass' kinsmen, another rich black negro, is now traveling in this part of the state making speeches for his friend Lincoln as the champion of black men. ("White men, white men," and "What have you got to say against it?" "That's right," etc.)

All I have to say on that subject is that those of you who believe that the negro is your equal and ought to be on an equality with you socially, politically, and legally, have a right to entertain those opinions, and of course will vote for Mr. Lincoln. ("Down with the negro," "No, no," etc.)[17]

ON THE SPOT

Douglas then went on to attack Lincoln's answers to his own interrogatories:

I have a word to say on Mr. Lincoln's answer to the interrogatories contained in my speech at Ottawa, and which
he has pretended to reply to here to-day. Mr. Lincoln makes
a great parade of the fact that I quoted a platform as
having been adopted by the Black Republican party at Springfield in 1854, which, it turns out, was adopted at another
place.

Mr. Lincoln loses sight of the thing itself in his ecstasies
over the mistake I made in stating the place where it was
done. He thinks that that platform was not adopted on the
right "spot". . . Lincoln and his political friends are great
on "*spots.*" In Congress, as a representative of this state, he
declared the Mexican war to be unjust and infamous, and
would not support it, or acknowledge his own country to be
right in the contest, because he said that American blood
was not shed on American soil in the "*right spot.*" And now
he cannot answer the questions I put to him at Ottawa because the resolutions I read were not adopted at the "*right
spot.*"

It may be possible that I was led into error as to the *spot*
on which the resolutions I then read were proclaimed, but I
was not, and am not in error as to the fact of their forming
the basis of the creed of the Republican party when that
party was first organized.[18]

At this point, Douglas had another exchange with the
crowd. When he read a set of resolutions from another district
to show their similarity to the Springfield resolutions, the crowd
yelled: "Good, good. That's the doctrine." To which Douglas
retorted:

I am glad to find that you are more honest in your abolitionism than your leaders, by avowing that it is your platform, and right in your opinion. . . What do you think of
Mr. Lincoln, your candidate for the U. S. Senate, who is
attempting to dodge the responsibility of the platform, because it was not adopted in the right spot?[19]

When Tom Turner interrupted to say proudly that he had
drawn the resolutions, and the crowd began to cheer, Douglas
boomed: "That is right, give Turner cheers for drawing the
resolutions if you approve them. If he drew those resolutions
he will not deny that they are the creed of the Black Republican
party."

"They are our creed exactly," said Turner.

"And yet Lincoln denies that he stands on them," returned Douglas. "Mr. Turner says that the creed of the Black Republican party is the admission of no more slave states, and yet Mr. Lincoln declares that he would not like to be placed in a position where he would have to vote for them." And then to the laughter of the crowd he continued, "As Mr. Lincoln would be very sorry to be placed in such an embarrassing position as to be obliged to vote on the admission of any more slave states, I propose, out of mere kindness, to relieve him from any such necessity."[20]

Shortly thereafter when Douglas charged Lincoln and Trumbull with having made a deal to divide the state's two Senate seats between them, the crowd became uproarious. The Little Giant's fury was aroused. He began to berate the crowd: "I wish to remind you that while Mr. Lincoln was speaking there was not a Democrat vulgar and blackguard enough to interrupt him. But I know that the shoe is pinching you. I am clinching Lincoln now and you are scared to death for the result. I have seen this thing before. I have seen men make appointments for joint discussions, and the moment their man has been heard, try to interrupt and to prevent a fair hearing of the other side. I have seen your mobs before, and defy your wrath."[21]

His scrappy outburst brought forth cheers and applause. "My friends," he barked, "do not cheer, for I need my whole time. The object of the opposition is to occupy my attention in order to prevent me from giving the whole evidence and nailing this double dealing on the Black Republican party."[22]

There were subsequent occasional interruptions as Douglas continued his speech, but no more than were customary in those rough-and-tumble days of the stump debate, or than were to be expected and handled effectively by the speaker. Many of the interruptions were encouraging shouts by Democratic partisans in support of Douglas.

The Little Giant addressed himself once more to Lincoln's "house divided" statement. This time, on the basis of Lincoln's reply, he was able to use it to attack his position on the admission of new slave states. "If he believes this Union cannot endure divided into free and slave states," he said, "that they must all become free in order to save the Union, he is bound, as an honest man, to vote against any more slave states. Show me that it is my duty in order to save the Union to do a particular act, and I will do it if the Constitution does not prohibit it."[23]

Knowing the strong attachment of his auditors to the Union and giving voice to his own strong convictions on the subject, he continued:

> I am not for the dissolution of the Union under any circumstances. I will pursue no course of conduct that will give just cause for the dissolution of the Union. The hope of the friends of freedom throughout the world rests upon the perpetuity of this Union. The down-trodden and oppressed people who are suffering under European despotism all look with hope and anxiety to the American Union as the only resting place and permanent home of freedom and self-government.[24]

With heavy sarcasm, he used this issue to contrast once again his open espousal of principle with Lincoln's:

> Mr. Lincoln says that he believes that this Union cannot continue to endure with slave states in it, and yet he will not tell you distinctly whether he will vote for or against the admission of any more slave states, but says he would not like to be put to the test. . . I do not think that the people of Illinois desire a man to represent them who would not like to be put to the test on the performance of a high constitutional duty. I will retire in shame from the Senate of the United States when I am not willing to be put to the test in the performance of my duty.
>
> I have been put to severe tests. I have stood by my principles in fair weather and in foul, in the sunshine and in the rain. I have defended the great principles of self-government here among you when Northern sentiment ran in a torrent against me, and I have defended that same great principle when Southern sentiment came down like an avalanche upon me. I was not afraid of any test they put to me. I knew I was right — I knew my principles were sound — I knew that the people would see in the end that I had done right.[25]

When Lincoln rose for his rejoinder, he gave a brief demonstration of his own competence in the art of forensic infighting. "The first thing I have to say," he began, "is a word in regard to Judge Douglas' declaration about the 'vulgarity and blackguardism' in the audience — that no such thing, as he says, was shown by any Democrat while I was speaking. Now, I only wish, by way of reply on this subject, to say that while I was speaking *I* used no 'vulgarity or blackguardism' towards any Democrat."[26]

Then turning once more to the charge, because of Douglas' heavy emphasis on it, that his position was different from that of the Republican platform, he tried to clear up the confusing elements between the various resolutions of 1854–1855 and those of the 1856 platform of the newly organized Republican Party, and at the same time to clarify his own stand:

> It is true that many of these resolutions are at variance with the positions I have assumed. . . The Judge's opinion to the contrary notwithstanding, I have never tried to conceal my opinions, nor tried to deceive anyone in reference to them.
>
> At the introduction of the Nebraska policy, we believed there was a new era being introduced in the history of the Republic, which tended to the spread and perpetuation of slavery. But in our opposition to that measure we did not agree with one another in everything. The people in the north end of the state were for stronger measures of opposition than we of the central and southern portions of the state, but we were all opposed to the Nebraska doctrine. We had that one feeling and that one sentiment in common. You at the north end met in your conventions and passed your resolutions. We in the middle of the state and further south did not hold such conventions and pass the same resolutions, although we had in general a common view and a common sentiment. So that these meetings which the Judge has alluded to, and the resolutions he has read from were local and did not spread over the whole state.
>
> We at last met together from all parts of the state, and we agreed upon a common platform. You, who held more extreme notions either yielded those notions, or if not wholly yielding them, agreed to yield them practically, for the sake of embodying the opposition to the measures which the opposite party were pushing forward at that time. . . We agreed then upon a platform for the party throughout the entire state of Illinois, and now we are all bound as a party, *to that platform*.
>
> And I say here to you, if any one expects of me — in the case of my election — that I will do anything not signified by our Republican platform and my answers here to-day, I

tell you frankly that person will be deceived. I do not ask
for the vote of any one who supposed that I have secret
purposes or pledges that I dare not speak out. . . I hope to
deal in all things fairly with Judge Douglas, and with the
people of the state, in this contest. And if I should never be
elected to any office, I trust I may go down with no stain of
falsehood upon my reputation, — notwithstanding the hard
opinions Judge Douglas chooses to entertain of me.[27]

Lincoln next defended against the charge that he did not
fully answer Douglas' interrogatories, especially on the admission of new slave states and their effect on the Union:

If I have been fairly reported he will see that I did give
an explicit answer to his interrogatories. I did not merely say
that I would dislike to be put to the test; but I said clearly,
if I were put to the test, and a territory from which slavery
had been excluded should present herself with a state constitution sanctioning slavery — a most extraordinary thing and
wholly unlikely ever to happen — I did not see how I could
avoid voting for her admission. But he refused to understand
that I said so, and he wants this audience to understand that
I did not say so. Yet it will be so reported in the printed
speech that he cannot help seeing it.

He says if I should vote for the admission of a slave state
I would be voting for a dissolution of the Union, because I
hold that the Union can not permanently exist half slave
and half free. I repeat that I do not believe this government
can endure permanently half slave and half free, yet I do
not admit, nor does it at all follow, that the admission of a
single slave state will permanently fix the character and
establish this as a universal slave nation. The Judge is very
happy indeed at working up these quibbles.[28]

In the remaining time left him, Lincoln went back to be-
laboring Douglas on the implications of his attack on the
Washington *Union,* charging the Little Giant with seeking to
win Republican support:

Judge Douglas says he made a charge upon the editor of
the Washington *Union, alone,* of entertaining a purpose to
rob the states of their power to exclude slavery from their
limits. . . I will undertake to prove by the record here, that
he made that charge against more and higher dignitaries
than the editor of the Washington *Union.* . .

The Judge says that though he made this charge Toombs

got up and declared there was not a man in the United
States, except the editor of the *Union,* who was in favor of
the doctrines put forth in that article. And thereupon, I
understand that the Judge withdrew the charge. Although he
had taken extracts from the newspaper, and then from the
Lecompton Constitution, to show the existence of a conspiracy to bring about a "fatal blow," by which the states
were to be deprived of the right of excluding slavery, it all
went to pot as soon as Toombs got up and told him it was
not true.[29]

To ridicule Douglas' change of position, he told one of his
humorous stories reminiscent of the days when he was a young
surveyor, which provoked the audience to roars of laughter:

> It reminds me of the story that John Phoenix, the Califor-
> nia railroad surveyor, tells. He says they started out from the
> Plaza to the Mission of Dolores. They had two ways of deter-
> mining distances. One was by a chain and pins taken over
> the ground. The other was by a "go-it-ometer" — an inven-
> tion of his own — a three-legged instrument, with which he
> computed a series of triangles between the points.
>
>   At night he turned to the chain-man to ascertain what
> distance they had come, and found that by some mistake he
> had merely dragged the chain over the ground without keep-
> ing any record. By the "go-it-ometer" he found he had made
> ten miles. Being skeptical about this, he asked a drayman
> who was passing how far it was to the Plaza. The drayman
> replied it was just half a mile, and the surveyor put it down
> in his book — just as Judge Douglas says, after he had made
> his calculations and computations, he took Toombs' state-
> ment. I have no doubt that after Judge Douglas had made
> his charge, he was as easily satisfied about its truth as the
> surveyor was of the drayman's statement of the distance to
> the Plaza.[30]

His parting shot taunted the Little Giant with the failure
of his maneuvers to win Republican votes:

> His hope rested on the idea of visiting the great "Black
> Republican" party, and making it the tail of his new kite.
> He knows he was then expecting from day to day to turn
> Republican and place himself at the head of our organiza-
> tion. He has found that these despised "Black Republicans"
> estimate him by a standard which he has taught them none
> too well. Hence he is crawling back into his old camp, and

you will find him eventually installed in full fellowship among those whom he was then battling, and with whom he now pretends to be at such fearful variance.[31]

The Republican crowd enjoyed the verbal lashing which their hero was administering to the Little Giant and applauded loudly. "Go on, go on," they yelled, but Lincoln's time had expired and the second debate was over.

WAS DOUGLAS DRIVEN INTO A CORNER?

What reaction did Lincoln's questions evoke? According to Joseph Medill and Horace White, the Republican leaders privately were none too happy.[32] They felt that Douglas had been given an opportunity to reiterate in a forthright and direct manner a position which carried weight with many voters. The rabid Republican press, however, expressed elation at Lincoln's showing. The *Chicago Press and Tribune* spoke of "his cornering Douglas."[33] It was in this way that the legend started that Lincoln trapped Douglas on the Dred Scott decision and thus secured the presidency for himself.[34]

The accounts by Medill and White reveal Lincoln as using the second question against the advice of his friends, and add to the story that Lincoln was aiming at something beyond the local 1858 campaign.

Writing in the *Chicago Tribune* in 1895, Medill says that he was on the train from Amboy with Lincoln, and that the latter showed him the questions and asked what he thought of them. Medill responded that he did not like the second question. He felt that it would permit Douglas to wiggle out of the "tight place" he was in by giving the answer which would appeal to the voters of Illinois — popular sovereignty through unfriendly local legislation would nullify the implementation of the Dred Scott decision. Lincoln, however, was unmoved. He said he intended "to spear the question at Douglas that afternoon." Medill was so concerned that he sought out Elihu B. Washburne, the Congressman from the district, and Norman B. Judd, the Republican State Chairman, and informed them of Lincoln's plans. They, too, tried to change Lincoln's mind, but were unsuccessful.

Medill climaxes his narrative by telling how he met Lincoln shortly after his election to the presidency in 1860. Lincoln asked: "Do you recollect the argument we had on the way up to Freeport two years ago over my question that I was going to ask Judge Douglas about the power of squatters to exclude slavery from territories?" When Medill replied that he recollected very well, Lincoln continued: "Now don't you think I was right in putting that question to him?" Medill answered: "Yes, Mr. Lincoln, you were, and we were both right. Douglas' reply to that question undoubtedly hurt him badly for the presidency but it re-elected him to the Senate at that time as I feared it would." Lincoln then smiled broadly and said: "Now I have won the place that he was playing for."[35]

The second account is from a memoir written in 1890 by Horace White of his travels with Lincoln during the 1858 campaign. White repeats a story told him by his editor, Dr. Charles H. Ray. It seems that Ray and Judd and other friends discussed the questions with Lincoln the night before, and tried to dissuade him from using the second question. They argued that Douglas should not be "driven into a corner." He could not give a negative answer because that would cost him the election. If he answered affirmatively, he might possibly lose favor in the South, but he would defeat Lincoln for the senatorship. Lincoln is said to have replied that an affirmative answer was what he wanted, remarking: "I am after larger game; the battle of 1860 is worth a hundred of this."[36]

Did these incidents really happen? Was Lincoln really looking beyond the senatorial election to 1860? Or was the term "Freeport Doctrine," merely the unforeseen result of the publicity attendant upon the debates, with Lincoln the accidental beneficiary two years later?

Albert Beveridge is of the opinion that Lincoln had no ulterior motive in mind. He was merely playing good politics and trying to win the senatorial election. He bases this on Lincoln's statement in the Asbury letter that Douglas "cares nothing for the South; he knows he is already dead there." He therefore considers the stories apocryphal — just another legend to be added to the fable of Lincoln's political prescience.[37]

The first to attack these stories was Clark E. Carr, a lawyer of Galesburg, Illinois. Carr knew and was an admirer of both Lincoln and Douglas. Though a Republican, Carr wrote a biography of Douglas because he felt that the Little Giant was misunderstood and unappreciated. He was particularly incensed by the implications of the statement that Douglas was driven into a corner. He considered it a canard upon Lincoln as well as Douglas. In a speech before the Illinois Bar Association in 1907, he said:

> Can anyone believe that he [Lincoln] thought he was driving his adversary into a corner and forcing him to say what he did in order to save himself from defeat? Can anyone believe Abraham Lincoln to have been so insincere as to have pretended, when talking with friends upon a railway train, or at Freeport, that he was in doubt as to Senator Douglas's position or that he could drive him into a corner?
>
> Senator Douglas was never driven into a corner during all his long career of public life. In all his debates with the greatest American statesmen, running through a quarter of a century, he was never driven into a corner. His views in regard to slavery were wrong, radically wrong, as we Republicans then believed and as we still believe, but there was no concealment of them. He was always outspoken and it is an unwarrantable and an outrageous imputation against him to say that he was forced to take a position through being "driven into a corner."[38]

However, two problems remained unanswered: Why Lincoln should ask the questions at all, and whether his friends and advisers tried to dissuade him from asking the second question. The veracity of Joseph Medill and Dr. Ray was also involved. Carr addressed himself to these problems in an article in the Chicago *Record-Herald* in 1909:

> With Senator Douglas' Bloomington and Springfield speeches before us, to say that such a conference as is alleged, was held on the day before the Freeport debate, is a reflection upon Joseph Medill, C. A. Ray, Norman B. Judd, Robert R. Hitt and others — the ablest men in Illinois of that day. . .
> That some of them, years after the death of both Lincoln and Douglas, thought they could recall such a conference simply shows a defective memory in having forgotten the speeches at Bloomington and Springfield.
> But why . . . did Mr. Lincoln propound the second interrogatory?
> The same question might be asked in regard to either of the three other interrogatories. . . Mr. Lincoln made and

arranged those interrogatories, following one another in logical sequence, each relating directly to and necessary to the
other, in order to attain the result for which they were intended, which was to make up and so plainly define the
issues of the campaign that they would be clear to everybody. . . It was in the quality of mind that enabled him to
marshal, combine and make the most of interrogatories, syl-
logisms, metaphors, anecdotes, and, indeed, every kind and
form of reasoning and illustration, that Mr. Lincoln excelled
Senator Douglas.[39]

As one considers the facts one must conclude that Carr was
justified in coming to Douglas' defense. The public's wrong
impression had to be corrected. One may also agree with Carr's
delineation of the reasons why Lincoln posed the four questions. But it is difficult to accept his conclusion that men like
Medill, White and Ray had defective memories. All of these
men were journalists, accustomed to taking notes. White, in
particular, at the close of his narrative, stated that everything
he wrote was taken from memoranda made at the time of the
occurrence.

It seems certain, therefore, that Lincoln consulted his advisers on the questions. The strategy of the campaign had been
planned in close association with them. They accompanied him
from town to town, and undoubtedly discussed daily developments with him. Slow to make up his mind, he liked to get the
opinions of others, though once having reached a conclusion,
he could not be argued out of it, as was illustrated in the case
of the "house divided" portion of his Springfield speech. It is
very unlikely, therefore, that in this instance Lincoln kept the
questions to himself.

Assuming then that conferences took place, did his friends
advise against the use of the second question? If one agrees
with Carr's reasons for asking all of the questions, Judd and
the Republican campaign committee could have no objections
to any of them. It is quite possible, however, that they could
have found objections to the second question alone, based on
misgivings like those expressed by Medill and White. If we
put credence in the narratives of both men, then Lincoln
stuck to his guns, and refused to be budged, as was characteristic of him. In that case he must be credited with greater insight and farsight than the politicians who surrounded him.

Stephen A. Douglas in 1858.

The Little Giant in 1859.

The "Cooper Union portrait" which, Lincoln said, helped make him President.

Photograph of Abraham Lincoln taken on May 7, 1858.

Library of Congress

Illinois State Historical Society

Little Giant and Tall Sucker.

Adele Cutts Douglas, the Little Giant's second wife, who accompanied him during the debates.

Probably taken in 1870, this is the earliest known photograph of Lincoln's junior law partner and biographer William H. (Billy) Herndon.

Lyman Trumbull, who played an exciting role in the 1858 campaign.

An artist's conception of the Galesburg debate. *Library of Congress*

Quincy at the time of the Lincoln-Douglas debates. The speaker's platform was erected in front of the white-pillared courthouse in the center of the street. Washington Park is at the left.

ᖰ ᖰ ᖰ ᖰ ᖰ ᖰ ᖰ ᖰ ᖰ
Last Great Discussion.

Let all take notice, that on Friday next, Hon. S. A. Douglas and Hon. A. Lincoln, will hold the seventh and closing joint debate of the canvass at this place. We hope the country will turn out, to a man, to hear these gentlemen.

The following programme for the discussion has been decided upon by the Joint Committee appointed by the People's Party Club and the Democratic Club for that purpose.

Arrangements for the 15th inst.

The two Committees—one from each party—heretofore appointed to make arrangements for the public speaking on the 15th inst., met in joint Committee, and the following programme of proceedings was adopted, viz :

1st. The place for said speaking shall be on the east side of City Hall.

2d. The time shall be 1½ o'clock, P. M. on said day.

3d. That Messes. C. Stigleman and W. T. Miller be a Committee to erect a platform; also, seats to accommodate ladies.

4th. That Messrs. B. F. Barry and William Post superintend music and salutes.

5th. Messrs. H. G. McPike and W. C. Quigley be a committee having charge of the platform, and reception of ladies, and have power to appoint assistants.

6th. That the reception of Messrs. Douglas and Lincoln shall be a quiet one, and no public display.

7th. That no banner or motto, except national colors, shall be allowed on the speakers' stand.

On motion, a committee, consisting of Messrs. W. C. Quigley and H. G. McPike, be appointed to publish this programme of proceedings.   W. C. QUIGLEY,
                                                H. G. McPIKE.

Alton, Oct. 13, 1858.

To the above it should be added that the C. A. & St. Louis Railroad, will, on Friday, carry passengers to and from this city at half its usual rates. Persons can come in on the 10:40 a. m. train, and go out at 6:20 in the evening.

Clipping from the Alton *Daily Whig* announcing the last of the seven debates.

This is believed to be the first public announcement in behalf of Lincoln for President.

Commercial Register

Published Daily, Tri-Weekly & Weekly
BY HENRY D. COOKE AND C. C. BILL.

SANDUSKY, OHIO,

SATURDAY MORNING, NOV. 6, 1858.

Lincoln for President.

We are indebted to a friend at Mansfield for the following special dispatch :

"Mansfield, Nov. 5th, 1858.

"Editor Sandusky Register :—An enthusiastic meeting is in progress here to-night in favor of Lincoln for the next Republican candidate for President.   Reporter."

As a practical politician, however, he would not wish to prejudice his chances in the current election for the questionable and remote possibilities that might be offered in two years.[40] One must therefore conclude that Lincoln was convinced that the second question would not hurt, but help his candidacy, at the same time that it accentuated the split between the northern and southern Democrats.[41] The result could be a Republican victory in 1860. It is doubtful that Lincoln thought of himself as the beneficiary of such a victory.[42] As a good and shrewd party man, he was interested merely in a defeat for the Democrats and their probable standard-bearer.

In any event, because the debates were followed by a national audience, what Douglas said at Freeport caught the attention of the country, and emphasized his stand for the southern radicals plainly to see, thus helping to shape the presidential race in 1860. In this connection it is interesting to know what Asbury himself later thought of the effect of his question. On the back of Lincoln's reply he wrote as follows:

July 1883

The main question I had urged Mr. Lincoln to put to Judge Douglas — as may be perceived from his letter to me was the question 2 at Freeport "Can the people of a United States territory in any lawful way against the wish of any citizen of the United States exclude Slavery from its limits prior to the formation of a state constitution."

The Judge answered that they could, and went on to state how, but the answer I think lapped over and went further than Mr. Lincoln expected it would, when he answered my letter of the 31 of July. I have always thought that the Judge's answer whilst it probably secured his reelection to the Senate laid the foundation of his defeat for the Presidency. Whilst on the other hand it made a large factor in securing to Mr. Lincoln his own nomination & election in 1860.[43]

CHAPTER 9

Trotted Down to Egypt: The Jonesboro Debate

If the Republican leaders were worried about the progress of the campaign, Douglas had his troubles, too. Not only was he being hard pressed by the Republicans in the northern part of the state, but the Danites were waging a bitter campaign in Egypt. Trumbull, Lovejoy, John Palmer and other Republican stalwarts were joined by powerful speakers from outside the state, like Senator Chase of Ohio and Fred Douglass, the Negro orator. Last-ditch Administration men, including Ex-Governor John Reynolds, Ex-Senator Sidney Breese, Colonel John Dougherty and Dr. Charles Leib were hurting Douglas in the recognized Democratic strongholds. To worsen the picture, the crafty John Slidell, one of the chiefs of the southern clique, appeared with large sums of money to bolster the Buchaneers, and also spread malicious rumors of the mistreatment of the slaves on the plantations owned by Douglas' sons.

The Little Giant needed help. What he wished most was aid from Old Line Whigs. When Usher F. Linder let it be known that he would be glad to take the stump, Douglas telegraphed him: "The Hell-hounds are on my track. For God's sake, Linder, come and help me fight them."[1] The Republicans got the contents of the message from a venal telegrapher, and their press had a merry time with it. They rarely missed an opportunity to take a dig at "For God's Sake Linder," as he was known thereafter.

Other Whigs rallied to the cause of the Little Giant, many of them from out of state, like Henry Clay's son, James, and the brilliant Alexander H. Stephens. A major triumph for Douglas and a severe blow to Lincoln, however, was the news that John T. Stuart, Lincoln's first law partner and Douglas' rival in the Congressional race twenty years before, opposed the Republican Party and favored Douglas' position on the slavery question. Out of regard for his personal relation with Lincoln, however, Stuart did not take an active part in the campaign.

A surprising development was the unexpected support Douglas received from some southern leaders. Governor Henry A. Wise of Virginia wrote to Buchanan that Douglas' "success in Illinois without the aid of the Administration will be its rebuke; his defeat with its opposition will be the death of the Administration; and his success with the aid of the Administration might save it and the Democratic party."[2] Even Vice-President Breckinridge wrote a letter in behalf of Douglas which was used with such good effect in Egypt that, as second in command, he was accused by some stalwarts of treachery to the Administration.

But one of the greatest sources of strength and satisfaction to the Little Giant was the amazing news that Jefferson Davis, the recognized leader of the pro-slavery forces, had delivered a speech in Maine in which he took exactly the same stand as Douglas. Davis was in Maine for reasons of health, and was called upon by the Democrats of Portland to reassure the North that the South had no intention of trying to force slavery into the free states.[3] He was reported as saying:

> If the inhabitants of any territory should refuse to enact such laws and police regulations as would give security to property . . . it would be rendered more or less valueless in proportion to the difficulties of holding it without such protection. In the case of property in the labor of man, or what is usually called slave property, the insecurity would be so great that the owner could not ordinarily retain it. Therefore, though the right would remain, the remedy being withheld, it would follow that the owner would be practically debarred, by the circumstances of the case, from taking slave property into a territory where the sense of the inhabitants

was opposed to its introduction. So much for the oft repeated
fallacy of forcing slavery upon any community.[4]

When the text of the remarks subsequently reached him,
Douglas quoted them in the Alton debate. However, only a
short time would elapse thereafter before Davis would repudiate them. Actually he and Douglas had opposite concepts on
the protection to be offered to slavery, and when the full im-
port of Douglas' Freeport heresy reached the South, Davis'
opposition to the Little Giant hardened to outright hostility.

With the heat of the campaign rapidly mounting, the candidates toured the crucial central parts of the state before their
next meeting at Jonesboro in deepest Egypt on September 15.
Each was able to intersperse his heavy schedule with a little rest.

On August 31 the Little Giant was at Joliet. Ignoring Lincoln's answers at Freeport, he told the crowd how he had read
the Republican platform at Ottawa, and asked Lincoln whether
he concurred in its principles. Lincoln refused to answer my
questions, he gibed. "At last I said frankly, I wish you to
answer them, because when I get them up here where the color
of your principles is a little darker than in Egypt, I intend
to trot you down to Jonesboro." And then the Little Giant
cockily asserted:

> The very notice that I was going to take him down to
> Egypt made him tremble in the knees so that he had to be
> carried from the platform. He laid up seven days, and in the
> meantime held a consultation with his political physicians . . .
> and at last Lincoln came to the conclusion that he would
> answer, so he came up to Freeport last Friday.[5]

At Pontiac, the town's entire population of 1,200 inhabitants
responded to the booming of Douglas' cannon from the flat
car and turned out to greet him. At the courthouse he spoke
for three hours, after which he invited questions from the
audience. A spirited session followed:

Questioner: Do you believe in the right of the state of Illinois to give up a fugitive slave?

Mr. Douglas: I will answer you upon that point. I hold that
by the Constitution of the United States a fugitive from labor
is required to be delivered up, and I hold that Congress is
the proper legislative body to pass laws for that purpose. I

hold further, that it is the duty of every member of Congress to vote for a law which will be efficient in securing the rendition of fugitives. . . So long as I am your representative and take an oath to support the Constitution of the United States, I will do all in my power to carry it out in good faith. ("That's right," and intense enthusiasm.) I want to know whether your candidate would vote in favor of rendering up a fugitive slave?

Questioner: I am a radical Abolitionist and have no candidate. (Laughter and cries of "Don't Abe suit you? What's wrong with him?")

Mr. Douglas: I wish to say a word about that. I admire your candor in saying that you are a radical Abolitionist. For that reason you would not surrender a fugitive slave, and yet you will vote for Mr. Lincoln, who says that he will, and support his election to the United States Senate.

Questioner: (fervently) — No, never!

Mr. Douglas: Then you are a more honest man than I thought you were. (Great laughter and cheers.)[6]

While Douglas was holding forth at Pontiac, Lincoln was speaking at Clinton. This was the town where he is recorded as making his famous remark: "You can fool all the people some of the time, and some of the people all of the time, but you cannot fool all the people all the time."[7]

On the way to Clinton an incident occurred which afforded Lincoln much amusement and which he loved to recall when he was President. Horace White and he boarded the train at night from Springfield east to Decatur, where they had to change trains for Clinton. White was very tired, and curled up to take a nap, first asking Lincoln to awaken him when they reached Decatur. But Lincoln was tired, too, and fell asleep, awaking just as the train was pulling out of the station. In the excitement of getting out, he forgot to awaken his companion. White slept on until the train reached the Indiana border, and he had to take another train back. He got to Clinton too late for Lincoln's speech. Much as he was put out by the experience, White could not help joining in Lincoln's laughter, because Long Abe thought it was so funny.

At Lincoln, a town named after his rival, Douglas struck exceptionally windy weather and had to speak in the tent of the Spalding and Rogers circus. From here the *Chicago Times* correspondent reported a conversation he had with a "Black Republican" who acknowledged that he was disappointed with Lincoln's showing thus far, but said: "Get Old Abe before a town-meeting, where every once in a while he can get off a smutty joke and raise a laugh, he'll take the crowd, and there's no man can beat him." On which the correspondent commented that if Lincoln's popularity consisted in smutty jokes, his friends had much to be proud of.[8]

DOUGLAS VERSUS TRUMBULL

The Little Giant received a tremendous welcome at Jacksonville, his former home town. Trumbull had preceded him there, and then had gone on to Alton where he attacked Douglas for his vituperative reply at Beardstown to the charges he had made in Chicago in connection with the Toombs Bill. At Alton he had lashed out at the Little Giant:

> After indulging in language which would disgrace a loafer in the filthiest purlieus of a fish-market, he winds up by saying that he will not make a blackguard of himself, that he has no charges to make against me. So I suppose he considers that to say of another that he knew a thing to be false when he uttered it, that he was a "miserable cravenhearted wretch," does not amount to a personal assault, and does not make a man a blackguard. A discriminating public will judge of that for themselves. . .
> At the risk of offending this mighty man of war, and losing something more than my ears, I shall have the audacity to again read the record upon him. . . My colleague says that he is willing to stand on his public record. By that he shall be tried; and if he had been able to discriminate between the exposure of a public act by the record, and a personal attack upon the individual, he would have discovered that there was nothing personal in my Chicago remarks, unless the condemnation of himself by his own public record is personal. . .
> As an individual, I care very little about Judge Douglas . . .
> It is with his public acts with which I have to do, and if they condemn, disgrace, and consign him to oblivion, he has only himself, not me, to blame.[9]

Trumbull then went on to explain why he kept silent during the Senate debate the previous December, when Douglas was under attack by the Democrats for his Lecompton stand, and the Toombs Bill had figured in the discussion:

> Do you ask why I did not expose him at the time? I will tell you; Mr. Douglas was then doing good service against the Lecompton iniquity. The Republicans were then engaged in a hand to hand fight with the National Democracy to prevent the bringing of Kansas into the Union as a Slave State against the wishes of its inhabitants, and of course I was unwilling to turn our guns from the common enemy to strike down an ally.
>
> The facts ... establish beyond the power of controversy all the charges I have made and show Judge Douglas was made use of as an instrument by others, or else knowingly was a party to the scheme to have a government put in force over the people of Kansas without giving them an opportunity to pass upon it. That others high in position in the so-called Democratic party were parties to such a scheme is confessed by Governor Bigler; and the only reason why the scheme was not carried, and Kansas long ago forced into the Union as a Slave State, is the fact that Republicans were sufficiently strong in the House of Representatives to defeat the measure.[10]

In his speech to the admiring Jacksonville crowd, Douglas included a reply to Trumbull:

> Why did he deem it necessary to make a threat in advance that he would "cram the lie" down the throat of any man that should deny it? I have no doubt that the entire Abolition party consider it very polite for Mr. Trumbull to go around uttering calumnies of that kind, bullying, and talking of cramming lies down men's throats; but if I deny any of his lies by calling him a liar, they are shocked at the indecency of the language; hence, today, instead of calling him a liar I intend to prove that he is one. . .
>
> In Congress he declared the bill to be silent on the subject, and a few days since, at Alton, he ... said that there was a provision in the bill prohibiting submission.
>
> I had two answers to make to that. In the first place, the amendment which he quotes as depriving the people of an opportunity to vote upon the constitution *was stricken out on my motion!* ... In the second place, in lieu of it, a provision was voted in, authorizing the Convention to order an election whenever it pleased. . .

Mr. Trumbull when he made that speech knew these facts.
He forged the evidence from beginning to end, and by falsifying the record he endeavors to bolster up his false charge.
I ask you what you think of Trumbull thus going around the
country, falsifying and garbling the public records. I ask you
whether you will sustain a man who will descend to the in-
famy of such conduct.[11]

Douglas then went on to say that he would not thereafter
occupy his time refuting charges made by Trumbull, but
would hold Lincoln responsible for any slanders, inasmuch
as he had indorsed the character of Trumbull. Lincoln took
up this challenge at the Charleston debate.

After Jacksonville, Douglas proceeded to Carlinville and
Alton, and from there via boat to St. Louis, Missouri, where
he visited the State Fair. Returning, he went to Belleville,
Waterloo and Chester, reaching the last-named town on the
Mississippi on September 13. He then proceeded by boat to
Cairo at the southern tip of the state where the Ohio River
joins the Mississippi. Arriving on the morning of the 14,
he spoke to the crowd in the afternoon, and at night attended
a ball with his wife. The next day he covered the thirty miles
north to Jonesboro by train accompanied by the ubiquitous
cannon.

Lincoln was even busier than Douglas, stopping at more
places and making more speeches. At Carlinville he was joined
by John M. Palmer and at Paris by Owen Lovejoy. On September 11 he came to Edwardsville, where, in answer to a
question put to him, he delineated the differences between the
Democratic and Republican parties. In doing so, he stressed
the moral issues, to which he would give more emphasis in
the course of the campaign.

Lincoln had also given much thought to refuting Douglas'
position on the Dred Scott decision as expressed at Freeport.
He planned to subject it to severe analysis at Jonesboro. At
Edwardsville he dealt with its implications on a moral level
with an eloquence which stirred echoes of Clay:

When . . . you have succeeded in dehumanizing the negro;
when you have put him down and made it forever impossible
for him to be but as the beasts of the field; when you have
extinguished his soul, and placed him where the ray of hope

is blown out . . . are you quite sure the demon which you
have roused *will not turn and rend you?*

What constitutes the bulwark of our own liberty and independence? It is not our frowning battlements, our bristling
sea coasts, the guns of our war steamers, or the strength of
our gallant and disciplined army. These are not our reliance
against a resumption of tyranny in our fair land. All of them
may be turned against our liberties. . .

Our reliance is in *the love of liberty* which God has planted
in our bosoms. Our defense is in the preservation of the spirit
which prizes liberty as the heritage of all men, in all lands,
everywhere. Destroy this spirit, and you have planted the
seeds of despotism around your own doors. Familiarize yourselves with the chains of bondage, and you are preparing
your own limbs to wear them. Accustomed to trample on the
rights of those around you, you have lost the genius of your
own independence, and become the fit subjects of the first
cunning tyrant who rises. And let me tell you, all these things
are prepared for you with the logic of history, if the elections
shall promise that the next Dred Scott decision and all future
decisions will be quietly acquiesced in by the people.[12]

Meantime, Herndon was busy looking up records and newspaper files and sending them to his partner. Lincoln wanted
to give Douglas a taste of his own medicine of identifying a
candidate with inconsistent platforms and opposite commitments. It was part of the necessary infighting in a tough campaign, even though it had little to do with the real issues.

From Edwardsville, Lincoln proceeded south to Jonesboro,
stopping overnight at Centralia where the Illinois State Fair
was in progress. He reached Jonesboro on the evening of the
14 and stayed at the little hotel on the town square. During
the evening he sat with friends in front of the hotel watching
the splendor of Donati's comet in the sky.

Jonesboro was a tiny spot on the map with a population of
eight hundred. Slow-moving and lazy, it resembled a small
southern town. This was indeed the county center to which
Douglas said he would trot Lincoln down and bring him to his
milk. It had missed its chance to amount to anything when the
Illinois Central Railroad passed it by and erected a station a
mile and a half away which it called Anna in honor of the wife
of one of its officers. Within a few years Anna was as large as
Jonesboro and gave promise of outstripping it entirely.

The crowd that turned out was small, numbering between 1,200 to 1,500. In addition to the local people, there were a few carloads of auditors brought in by special train from the State Fair at Centralia, and a large group of Douglas supporters from Cairo. Some country folk also came in, mostly with ox teams which looked "stunted," pulling old-fashioned wagons which seemed "as though they were ready to fall in pieces."[13] In spite of the fact that this was supposedly Danite territory, Douglas men outnumbered the Buchananites by two to one. The sprinkling of Republicans present came from Anna.

It was a typical dog day, characteristic of the region, as the crowd gathered at the grove where the speaking was to take place. There was little outward enthusiasm, and in an attempt to awaken a semblance of festivity, the Douglas cannon worked overtime, filling the atmosphere with "a loud noise and a bad smell."[14] Several Douglas banners were distributed around the stand, and on the principal one, which the Danites complained had been stolen from them, was inscribed a biblical paraphrase:

MY SON, IF BOLTERS ENTICE THEE,
CONSENT THOU NOT.

CHANGE OF NAME AND PRINCIPLES

It was Douglas' turn to speak first and at two o'clock he was introduced to the audience. He spent considerable time tracing the development of the Republican Party at the hands of Lincoln and Trumbull, whose mission, he said, was to abolitionize Whigs and Democrats by guile. They employed different principles and different language in different parts of the state in order to trap the unwary:

> They were Republicans or Abolitionists in the north, anti-Nebraska men down about Springfield, and in this neighborhood they contented themselves with talking about the inexpediency of the repeal of the Missouri Compromise. . . . In the northern counties, you find that all the conventions are called in the name of the Black Republican party; at Springfield, they dare not call a Republican convention, but invite all the enemies of the Democracy to unite, and when they get down into Egypt, Trumbull issues notices calling upon the *"free democracy"* to assemble and hear him speak.
> What is the name of "free Democrats" put forth for unless

to deceive the people, and make them believe that Trumbull and his followers are not the same party as that which raises the black flag of Abolitionism in the northern part of this state, and makes war upon the Democratic party throughout the state. When I put that question to them at Waterloo on Saturday last, one of them rose and stated that they had changed their name for political effect in order to get votes. There was a candid admission.... Why cannot a political party that is conscious of the rectitude of its purposes and the soundness of its principles declare them everywhere alike? I would disdain to hold any political principles that I could not avow in the same terms in Kentucky that I declared in Illinois, in Charleston as well as in Chicago, in New Orleans as well as in New York.[15]

He also heaped scorn on the "bargain" between Lincoln and Trumbull to deprive him of his Senate seat. When he had had his fill of castigating his opponents, he turned to Lincoln's "house divided" speech which, he felt, served so admirable a text for his arguments in support of the Union, half-slave and half-free. When he touched on the moral aspect involved, there were echoes of his brilliant Chicago speech of October 23, 1850 when he defended the omnibus Compromise and swayed a hostile audience to his side:

> Mr. Lincoln says that a house divided against itself cannot stand, and pretends that this scriptural quotation, this language of our Lord and Master, is applicable to the American Union and the American Constitution? . . .
> Mr. Lincoln . . . says that it is contrary to the law of God, and cannot stand. It has stood thus divided into free and slave states from its organization up to this day. During that period we have increased from four millions to thirty millions of people; we have extended our territory from the Mississippi to the Pacific Ocean; we have acquired the Floridas and Texas and other territory sufficient to double our geographical extent; we have increased in population, in wealth, and in power beyond any example on earth; we have risen from a weak and feeble power to become the terror and admiration of the civilized world; and all this has been done under a constitution which Mr. Lincoln, in substance, says is in violation of the law of God, and under a union divided into free and slave states, which Mr. Lincoln thinks, because of such

division, cannot stand. Surely, Mr. Lincoln is a wiser man than those who framed the government.[16]

CUBA, MEXICO, CANADA

The Little Giant then turned to the Dred Scott decision. "I am content to take that decision as it stands delivered by the highest judicial tribunal on earth," he said sarcastically. "Hence, I do not choose to go into any argument . . . whether or not Chief Justice Taney understood the law better than Abraham Lincoln." In support of the decision, he continued:

> The signers of the Declaration had no reference to the negro whatever when they declared all men to be created equal. . . One great evidence that such was their understanding, is to be found in the fact that at that time every one of the thirteen colonies was a slaveholding colony, every signer of the Declaration represented a slaveholding constituency, and we know that no one of them emancipated his slaves, much less offered citizenship to them when they signed the Declaration, and yet, if they had intended to declare that the negro was the equal of the white man, and entitled by divine right to an equality with him, they were bound, as honest men, that day and hour to have put their negroes on an equality with themselves.[17]

Toward the close of his speech he returned to his favorite theme of the permanent existence of the Union, as it was. But this time he salted it with a plea for expansion as well as with the doctrine of popular sovereignty:

> Why cannot this Union exist forever divided into free and slave states as our fathers made it? It can thus exist if each state will carry out the principles upon which our institutions were founded, to wit: the right of each state to do as it pleases, without meddling with its neighbors. . .
> We are yet a young nation growing with a rapidity unequalled in the history of the world . . . and . . . the emigration from the old world is increasing, requiring us to expand and acquire new territory from time to time in order to give our people land to live upon. If we live upon the principle of state rights and state sovereignty, each state regulating its own affairs and minding its own business, we can go on and extend indefinitely, just as fast and as far as we need the territory.

The time may come, indeed has now come, when our interests would be advanced by the acquisition of the island of Cuba. When we get Cuba we must take it as we find it, leaving the people to decide the question of slavery for themselves, without interference on the part of the Federal government, or of any state of this Union. So, when it becomes necessary to acquire any portion of Mexico or Canada or of this continent or the adjoining islands, we must take them as we find them, leaving the people free to do as they please, to have slavery or not, as they choose.[18]

Lincoln's reply revealed the skills of the tough stump-speaker which had prompted Douglas to characterize him as so difficult an opponent to face. He rephrased Douglas' position of a Union permanently half-slave and half-free as: "Why can't we let slavery stand as our fathers placed it?":

Judge Douglas and his friends have changed the position in which our fathers originally placed it. . . The way they left the slavery question, [it] was in the course of ultimate extinction.

Brooks, the man who assaulted Senator Sumner on the floor of the Senate, and who was complimented with dinners and silver pitchers, and gold-headed canes, and a good many other things for that feat, in one of his speeches declared that when this government was originally established nobody expected that the institution of slavery would last until this day.

That was but the opinion of one man, but it was such an opinion as we can never get from Judge Douglas or anybody in favor of slavery in the North at all. You *can* sometimes get it from a Southern man. He said at the same time that the framers of our government did not have the knowledge that experience has taught us — that experience and the invention of the cotton-gin have taught us that the perpetuation of slavery is a necessity. He insisted, therefore, upon its being changed from the basis upon which the fathers of the government left it to the basis of its perpetuation and nationalization.

I insist that this is the difference between Judge Douglas and myself — that Judge Douglas is helping that change along. I insist upon this government being placed where our fathers originally placed it.[19]

Lincoln now switched to the little surprise he had prepared.

With a view to giving Douglas a taste of his own medicine on the conflicting statements of his supporters and the Democratic platforms, he called on the material furnished him by Billy Herndon. Referring to the Democratic Convention of the previous April which supported Douglas for Senator and which drew up resolutions acknowledged by Douglas as his platform, he said:

> On the 16th of June the Republicans had their convention and published their platform, which is as clear and distinct as Judge Douglas'. In it they spoke their principles as plainly and as definitely to the world. What is the reason that Judge Douglas is not willing I should stand upon that platform? Why must he go around hunting for some one who is supporting me, or has supported me at some time in his life, and who has said something at some time contrary to that platform? Does the Judge regard that rule as a good one? If it turn out that the rule is a good one for me — that I am responsible for any and every opinion that any man has expressed who is my friend — then it is a good rule for him. In my opinion, it is not a good rule for either of us.

Then turning to Douglas, he asked, "Do you think differently, Judge?"

"I do not," was the reply:

> Judge Douglas says he does not think differently. I am glad of it. Then can he tell me why he is looking up resolutions of five or six years ago, and insisting that they were my platform, notwithstanding my protest that they are not, and never were my platform, and my pointing out the platform of the state convention which ... nominated me for the Senate? I cannot see what he means by parading these resolutions, if it is not to hold me responsible for them in some way...
>
> At Freeport Judge Douglas occupied a large part of his time in producing resolutions and documents of various sorts ... to make me somehow responsible for them; and I propose now doing a little of the same sort of thing for him.[20]

Lincoln then went on to quote from statements of two of Douglas' supporters, Thompson Campbell and R. S. Molony, made when they were Democratic candidates for Congress in 1850. The statements opposed slavery in the territories and in the District of Columbia, opposed the admission of new slave

states, and advocated the repeal of the Fugitive Slave Law. Both
men had been elected. Both were now participating in the
campaign in behalf of Douglas. He also quoted the resolutions
of a radical Democratic state convention in Vermont, Douglas'
home state, which were distinctly abolitionist in tone. For more
recent evidence, he quoted a current editorial by a Judge Mayo
in a newspaper backing Douglas, which advocated "the equality
of the blacks; that is, that they should enjoy all the privileges
of the whites where they reside."[21]

Next Lincoln addressed himself to Douglas' Freeport Doctrine as embodied in his answer to the second interrogatory.
His analysis illustrates his habit of reaching past superficialities
to the root of a problem. It gave a new twist to the Dred Scott
issue:

> In the Senate of the United States, in 1856 ... the Judge
> said that whether the people could exclude slavery prior to
> the formation of a constitution or not *was a question to be
> decided by the Supreme Court.* . . I maintain that when he
> says, after the Supreme Court have decided the question, that
> the people may yet exclude slavery by any means whatever, he
> does virtually say, that it is *not* a question for the Supreme
> Court. Has not the Supreme Court decided that question?
> When he now says the people *may* exclude slavery, does he
> not shift his ground and say that it is *not* a question for the
> Court, but for the people? ... He did not tell us that what-
> ever the Supreme Court decides the people can by withhold-
> ing necessary "police regulations" keep slavery out...
>
> I hold that the proposition that slavery cannot enter a new
> country without police regulations is historically false. . . I
> hold that the history of this country shows that the institution
> of slavery was originally planted upon this continent *without
> these* "police regulations" which the Judge now thinks neces-
> sary for the actual establishment of it. Not only so, but is
> there not another fact — how came this Dred Scott decision
> to be made? It was made upon the case of a negro being taken
> and actually held in slavery in Minnesota Territory ... not
> only without police regulations, but in the teeth of congres-
> sional legislation supposed to be valid at the time. This
> shows that there is vigor enough in slavery to plant itself in
> a new country even against unfriendly legislation. It takes
> not only law but the *enforcement* of law to keep it out. That
> is the history of this country upon the subject.

I wish to ask one other question. It being understood that the Constitution of the United States guarantees property in slaves in the territories, if there is any infringement of the right of that property, would not the United States courts, organized for the government of the territory, apply such remedy as might be necessary in that case? . . .

I will ask you my friends, if you were elected members of the legislature, what would be the first thing you would have to do before entering upon your duties? *Swear to support the Constitution of the United States.* Suppose you believe, as Judge Douglas does, that the Constitution of the United States guarantees to your neighbor the right to hold slaves in that territory — that they are his property — how can you clear your oaths unless you give him such legislation as is necessary to enable him to enjoy that property? . . . How could you, having sworn to support the Constitution, and believing it guaranteed the right to hold slaves in the territories, assist in legislation *intended* to defeat that right? That would be violating your own view of the Constitution. Not only so, but if you were to do so, how long would it take the courts to hold your votes unconstitutional and void? Not a moment. . .

Let me ask you why many of us who are opposed to slavery upon principle give our acquiescence to a Fugitive Slave Law? Why do we hold ourselves under obligations to pass such a law, and abide by it when it is passed? Because the Constitution makes provision that the owners of slaves shall have the right to reclaim them. It gives the right to reclaim slaves, and that right is, as Judge Douglas says, a barren right, unless there is legislation that will enforce it. . .

Is the right to have fugitive slaves reclaimed any better fixed in the Constitution than the right to hold slaves in the territories? For this decision is a just exposition of the Constitution as Judge Douglas thinks. . . If I acknowledge with Judge Douglas that this decision properly construes the Constitution, I cannot conceive that I would be less than a perjured man if I should refuse in Congress to give such protection to that property as in its nature is needed.[22]

On the basis of this analysis, Lincoln now proceeded to propound a fifth interrogatory to Douglas:

If the slaveholding citizens of a United States territory should need and demand congressional legislation for the protection of their slave property in such territory, would you, as a member of Congress, vote for or against such legislation?[23]

CRAZY

During the remainder of his time Lincoln took up Douglas' taunt which he had made at Joliet about his knees trembling and his being carried off the platform. He had a merry time with it, and so did the crowd. After reading Douglas' statement, he said:

> Now that statement altogether furnished a subject for philosophical contemplation. (Laughter.) I have been treating it in that way, and I have really come to the conclusion that I can explain it in no other way than by believing the Judge is crazy. (Renewed laughter.) If he was in his right mind, I cannot conceive how he would have risked disgusting the four or five thousand of his own friends who stood there, and knew, as to my having been carried from the platform, that there was not a word of truth in it.

"Didn't they carry you off?" interposed Douglas:

> There, that question illustrates the character of this man Douglas, exactly. He smiles now and says, "Didn't they carry you off?" But he says then, *"He had to be carried off;"* and he said it to convince the country that he had so completely broken me down by his speech that I had to be carried away. Now he seeks to dodge it, and asks, "Didn't they carry you off?" Yes, they did. *But, Judge Douglas, why didn't you tell the truth?* (Great laughter and cheers.) I would like to know why you didn't tell the truth about it. (Continued laughter.)
>
> And then again "He laid up seven days." He puts this in print for the people of the country to read as a serious document. I think if he had been in his sober senses he would not have risked that barefacedness in the presence of thousands of his own friends, who knew that I made speeches within six of the seven days ... including all the necessary travel to meet him again at Freeport at the end of the six days. Now, I say, there is no charitable way to look at that statement, except to conclude that he is actually crazy. (Laughter.)
>
> There is another thing in that statement that alarmed me very greatly as he states it, that he was going to "trot me down to Egypt." Thereby he would have you to infer that I would not come to Egypt unless he forced me — that I could not be got here, unless he, giant-like, had hauled me down here. (Laughter.) That statement he makes, too, in the teeth of the knowledge that I had made the stipulation to come down here, *and that he himself had been very reluctant to*

enter into the stipulation. (Cheers and laughter.) More than all this, Judge Douglas, when he made that statement must have been crazy, and wholly out of his sober senses, or else he would have known that when he got me down here — that promise — that windy promise — of his powers to annihilate me, wouldn't amount to anything. Now, how little do I look like being carried away trembling? Let the Judge go on, and after he is done with his half hour I want you all, if I can't go home myself, to let me stay and rot here; and if anything happens to the Judge, if I cannot carry him to the hotel and put him to bed, let me stay here and rot. (Great laughter.) . . .

I ask you if you know any other living man who would make such a statement? . . . Did the Judge talk of trotting me down to Egypt to scare me to death? Why, I know this people better than he does. I was raised further north, and perhaps he has some horrid idea of what this people might be induced to do. (Roars of laughter and cheers.) But really I have talked about this matter perhaps longer than I ought, for it is no great thing, and yet the smallest are often the most difficult things to deal with. The Judge has set about seriously trying to make the impression that when we meet at different places I am literally in his clutches — that I am a poor helpless, decrepit, mouse, and that I can do nothing at all. This is one of the ways he has taken to create that impression. I don't know any other way to meet it, except this. I don't want to quarrel with him — to call him a liar — but when I come square up to him I don't know what else to call him, if I must tell the truth out. (Cheers and laughter.) . . . My time, now, is very nearly out, and I give up the trifle that is left to the Judge to let him set my knees trembling again, if he can.[24]

Douglas' rejoinder was an excellent demonstration of his skill in defending against attacks. He started off where Lincoln concluded:

I will commence where Mr. Lincoln left off, and make a remark upon this serious complaint of his about my speech at Joliet. I did say there in a playful manner that when I put these questions to Mr. Lincoln at Ottawa he failed to answer, and that he trembled and had to be carried off the stand, and required seven days to get up his reply. (Laughter.) That he did not walk off from that stand he will not deny. That when the crowd went away from the stand with me, a few persons carried him home on their shoulders and laid him down, he will admit. (Shouts of laughter.) I wish to say to you that whenever I degrade my friends and myself by allowing them to carry me on their backs along through the public streets when I am able to walk I am willing to be deemed crazy. (Laughter and applause.)[25]

He countered Lincoln's surprise maneuver by saying:

It is true that Tom Campbell, when a candidate for Congress in 1850, published the letter which Lincoln read . . . If he will take the trouble to examine, he will find that the letter was published only two days before the election, and was never seen until after it, except in one county. Tom Campbell would have been beat to death by the Democratic party if that letter had been made public in his district. As to Molony, it is true he uttered sentiments of the kind referred to by Mr. Lincoln, and the best Democrats would not vote for him for that reason. I returned from Washington after the passage of the compromise measures in 1850, and when I found Molony running under John Wentworth's tutelage, and on his platform, I denounced him, and declared that he was no Democrat.[26]

He went on to show how single-handedly he had changed the attitude of his party by his Chicago speech of 1850 and concluded with: "These facts are well known, and Mr. Lincoln can only get up individual instances, dating back to 1849, '50, which are contradicted by the whole tenor of the Democratic creed."[27]

He made no mention, however, of Judge Mayo's editorial nor of the Vermont Democratic platform. Instead, he came right back to the attack with an attempt to turn Lincoln's celebrated metaphor against him:

I now bring down upon him the vengeance of his own scriptural quotation, and give it a more appropriate application than he did, when I say to him that his party, abolition in one end of the state and opposed to it in the other, is a house divided against itself, and cannot stand, and ought not to stand, for it attempts to cheat the American people out of their votes by disguising its sentiments.[28]

Then, in order to overcome whatever favorable impression Lincoln might have made by referring to his kinship with the people of Egypt, Douglas in humorous and confidential vein said:

   Mr. Lincoln attempts to cover up and get over his Abolitionism by telling you that he was raised a little east of you,
(Laughter.) beyond the Wabash in Indiana, and he thinks
that makes a mighty sound and good man of him on all
these questions. . . True, I was not born out west here. I
was born away down in Yankee land, ("Good.") I was born
in a valley in Vermont, ("All right.") with the high mountains around me. I love the old green mountains and valleys
of Vermont, where I was born, and where I played in my
childhood.
   I went up to visit them some seven or eight years ago, for
the first time for twenty odd years. When I got there they
treated me very kindly. They invited me to the commencement of their college, placed me on the seats with their distinguished guests, and conferred upon me the degree LL.D.
in Latin, (doctor of laws,) the same as they did on Old
Hickory, at Cambridge, many years ago, and I give you my
word and honor I understood just as much of the Latin as he
did. (Laughter.)
   When they got through conferring the honorary degree,
they called upon me for a speech, and I got up with my
heart full and swelling with gratitude for their kindness, and
I said to them, "My friends, Vermont is the most glorious
spot on the face of this globe for a man to be born in,
provided he emigrates when he is very young." (Uproarious
shouts of laughter.)
   I emigrated when I was very young, I came out here when
I was a boy, and I found my mind liberalized, and my
opinions enlarged when I got on these broad prairies, with
only the Heavens to bound my vision, instead of having them
circumscribed by the little narrow ridges that surrounded
the valley where I was born. But, I discard all flings of the
land where a man was born. I wish to be judged by my
principles upon which the peace, the happiness and the perpetuity of this republic now rest.[29]

   Toward the close of his speech Douglas answered Lincoln's
fifth interrogatory. He took sharp issue with him on the nature
of slave property, which the South was beginning to regard as
a special species requiring preferential treatment under the
Constitution. To Lincoln, this conclusion was inevitable from
the Dred Scott decision, but to Douglas, slaves were the same
as any other kind of merchandise — a position which, equally
with his Freeport Doctrine, was to earn him the enmity of the
South:

My doctrine is, that even taking Mr. Lincoln's view that the decision recognized the right of a man to carry his slaves into the territories of the United States, if he pleases, yet after he gets there he needs affirmative law to make that right of any value. The same doctrine not only applies to slave property, but all other kinds of property.

Chief Justice Taney places it upon the ground that slave property is on an equal footing with other property. Suppose one of your merchants should move to Kansas and open a liquor store; he has a right to take groceries and liquors there, but the mode of selling them, and the circumstances under which they shall be sold, and all the remedies must be prescribed by local legislation, and if that is unfriendly it will drive him out just as effectually as if there was a constitutional provision against the sale of liquor. So the absence of local legislation to encourage and support slave property in a territory excludes it practically just as effectually as if there was a positive constitutional provision against it. Hence, I assert that under the Dred Scott decision you cannot maintain slavery a day in a territory where there is an unwilling people and unfriendly legislation.[30]

Press reports of the debate followed the usual exuberant pattern. Typical were the headlines:
(From the *Chicago Press and Tribune*)

GREAT DEBATE BETWEEN LINCOLN AND DOUGLAS AT JONESBORO
Fourteen Hundred Persons Present. — Douglas Rehearses the Same Old Speech. — He "Comes To His Milk" Voluntarily, and Old Abe Takes What He Has to Spare. — Lincoln Pulverizes His Freeport Answers on the Dred Scott Decision. — Douglas Impeaches the Democracy of His Friends Thompson Campbell and R. S. Molony. — Was He Drunk When He Made His Joliet Speech or Was He Only "Playful?" — Concluding Speeches by Hon. "For-God's-Sake Linder" and Hon. John Dougherty.[31]

(From the *Chicago Times*)

THE CAMPAIGN — DOUGLAS AT JONESBORO
Lincoln in Egypt. — Lincoln "Trotted Out." His "Points" Displayed. His Wind Fails Him. — Douglas Triumphs Over All![32]

CHAPTER 10

Brawl for Crucial Votes: The Charleston Debate

Three days intervened between Jonesboro and the next meeting at Charleston on Saturday, September 18. Lincoln used this time to relax and to prepare for the debate which it was now his turn to open. Returning to Centralia, he spent the afternoon of the 16 at the State Fair, where he was the object of much attention. At night he took the Illinois Central train to Mattoon, a town ten miles west of Charleston, where he remained until the morning of the debate.

Douglas, however, kept right on campaigning. On the 16th he spoke at Benton, a town halfway between Jonesboro and Centralia, and on the 17 he was in Centralia itself, to reply to the attacks of Reynolds, Breese, and Dougherty, the Danites who had preceded him the previous evening. But the occasion must have been one of conviviality as well as forensics, because Douglas is reported as "keeping spirits up by pouring spirits down."[1] In any event, the Little Giant arrived at Mattoon at three o'clock of the morning of the debate.

At eight o'clock, however, he was on the road to Charleston. A procession of wagon and carriage teams filled with men and women accompanied him across the wide stretch of prairie road, new teams and riders on horseback attaching themselves to the parade at every crossroad and farmhouse. The procession kept spreading out until it was two miles long. Flags, banners and bunting added sparkle and gaiety. Particular attention centered on thirty-two girls on horseback, each bearing the stars and stripes and the American eagle to represent the thirty-two states of the Union.

It was a dusty cavalcade that entered Charleston, to be greeted by noisy and milling citizens of the town and delegations from adjoining counties. The marchers proceeded to the Union Hotel, where Douglas was welcomed by Orlando B. Ficklin who had served in Congress with Lincoln and had also opposed him in the Matson slave case several years back. As he started to speak, a Republican band stationed close by tried to drown him out. A near riot ensued before the band could be made to desist and Ficklin could continue his speech and Douglas could reply to his welcome. Things were certainly livelier than they had been at Jonesboro — even livelier than they had been in Ottawa and Freeport.

Lincoln too had a procession just as long and as enthusiastic as Douglas'. It also had thirty-two young ladies to represent the states of the Union, but these came in a wagon following Lincoln's carriage. The wagon bore a motto:

"Westward the star of Empire takes its way,
The girls *link-on* to Lincoln, as their mothers did to Clay."[2]

Each girl waved a white banner with the name of a state upon it. Behind the wagon rode another pretty girl on horseback, representing Kansas and bearing a banner reading "Kansas — I will be free." Leading the entire procession was the Bowling Green Band of Terre Haute, Indiana, come from forty miles across the border. The marchers reached the Capitol House, where Lincoln was to stay, and there he, too, received a welcoming speech, to which he responded with thanks for the "flattering reception" and, referring to the young ladies in the wagon, "for this beautiful basket of flowers."[3]

DISPUTED TERRITORY

Charleston was a warm and friendly little town in Coles County at the northeastern extremity of Egypt. The county was regarded as one of the wealthiest and most progressive in the state. It was strong with Old Line Whigs.

To Long Abe it was familiar territory. His father had settled in Goose Nest Prairie which was only eight miles away, and his stepmother still lived in the vicinity. The inhabitants round about knew the Lincoln family. It was expected that Abe would get plenty of votes here. To express their sentiments the Republicans had spread a gigantic white banner eighty feet long across the court house square. On one side was inscribed:

"COLES COUNTY
FOUR HUNDRED MAJORITY FOR LINCOLN"

On the reverse side a lifesize painting depicted Lincoln as he looked thirty years earlier driving an ox team.

But this was, indeed, disputed territory. It was the Whig vote that both sides were trying to capture and the question of Negro equality assumed importance here. To emphasize this point, the Douglasites had displayed a caricature of a white man standing with a Negro woman followed by a colored boy, bearing the inscription "NEGRO EQUALITY." This maneuver caused the *Chicago Journal* to deprecate such a practice as characteristic of "low-lived politicians."[4]

Lincoln knew that he had to clarify his position on the equality issue in such a way as to overcome Whig prejudice, but he was also determined to hit Douglas again with Trumbull's charge that popular sovereignty was a sham because of the attempt to foist a constitution on Kansas without a vote of the people, by means of the Toombs Bill. He saw how sensitive Douglas was on this point and how angrily he reacted to the charge. Besides, it was no longer a quarrel between Douglas and Trumbull. Douglas had definitely brought Lincoln into the picture by saying that he held him responsible for Trumbull's alleged slanders. Accordingly, since he had the opening speech, he prepared to take the initiative by obtaining the necessary data and documents to prove the charges beyond refutation and thus nail his opponent to the wall.

Interest in the encounter was so keen that visitors poured into Charleston not only from the surrounding areas but also, like the Bowling Green Band, from Indiana by special train. By Friday evening the hotels were jammed. On Saturday morning "the streets and sidewalks around the public square were almost impassable."[5] When the crowd gathered at the county fair grounds a quarter of a mile from the town, over 12,000 people were estimated to be present. In the excitement of the occasion the debate was late in getting started. It was not until

2:45 that Lincoln was introduced and stepped to the front of the platform to make the opening speech.

He plunged immediately into the question of Negro equality. For the benefit of the Whigs, he repeated substantially what he had said a month before in the opening debate at Ottawa:

> I am not nor ever have been in favor of making voters or jurors of negroes, nor of qualifying them to hold office, nor to intermarry with white people; and I will say in addition to this that there is a physical difference between the white and black races which I believe will forever forbid the two races living together on terms of social and political equality. And inasmuch as they cannot so live, while they do remain together there must be the position of superior and inferior, and I as much as any other man am in favor of having the superior position assigned to the white race. I say upon this occasion I do not perceive that because the white man is to have the superior position the negro should be denied everything.[6]

He followed by ridiculing Douglas' charges, bringing laughter from the crowd with his sallies:

> It seems to me quite possible for us to get along without making either slaves or wives of negroes. . . I have never had the least apprehension that I or my friends would marry negroes if there was no law to keep them from it, (Laughter.) but as Judge Douglas and his friends seem to be in great apprehension that they might, if there were no law to keep them from it, (Roars of laughter.) I give him the most solemn pledge that I will to the very last stand by the law of this state, which forbids the marrying of white people with negroes (Continued laughter and applause.) . . .
>
> I do not understand there is any place where an alteration of the social and political relations of the negro and the white man can be made except in the state legislature — not in the Congress of the United States — and as I do not really apprehend the approach of any such thing myself, and as Judge Douglas seems to be in constant horror that some such danger is rapidly approaching, I propose as the best means to prevent it that the Judge be kept at home and placed in the state legislature to fight the measure. (Uproarious laughter and applause.)[7]

THE TOOMBS BILL AGAIN

After this brief opening Lincoln devoted the rest of his time to the Trumbull charges. He had not wished to enter the controversy, he said, but since Douglas asserted that he was holding him responsible for Trumbull's statements, he had no choice but to accept the responsibility and substantiate the charges. He referred to the various changes in the Toombs Bill and the statement of Senator Bigler. In answer to Douglas' defense that the bill as finally presented to the Senate was no different from previous territorial bills, he said:

> It is true, as Judge Douglas states, that many territorial bills have passed without having such a provision for them. I believe it is true, though I am not certain, that in some instances, constitutions framed under such bills have been submitted to a vote of the people, with the law silent upon the subject, but it does not appear that they once had their enabling acts framed with an express provision *for* submitting the constitution to a vote of the people, and then that they were stricken out. . .[8]

Lincoln next took up the clause designed to prevent a referendum which had been inserted in place of the original Toombs provision:

> The question is, what did he [Douglas] put it in for? In the first place what did he take the other provision out of the bill for? — the provision which Trumbull argued was necessary for submitting the constitution to a vote of the people? What did he take that out for, and having taken it out, what did he put this in for? . . . The question that Trumbull has made is that Judge Douglas put it in, and he don't meet Trumbull at all unless he denies that.[9]

He ridiculed Douglas' cry of forgery by asking whether the copies of the original and final bill shown to the audience by Trumbull and the quotations of Douglas' own words from the official records of the *Congressional Globe* were forgeries:

> What is a forgery? It is the bringing forward of something in writing or in print purporting to be of certain effect when it is altogether untrue. If you come forward with my note for one hundred dollars when I have never given such a note, there is a forgery. If you come forward with a letter purporting to be written by me which I never wrote, there is

another forgery. If you produce anything in writing or print saying it is so and so, the document not being genuine, a forgery has been committed. How do you make this a forgery when every piece of evidence is genuine?[10]

With only three minutes left him, he concluded:

The point upon Judge Douglas is this. The bill that went into his hands had the provision in it for a submission of the constitution to the people; and I say its language amounts to an express provision for a submission, and that he took the provision out. He says it was known that the bill was silent in this particular; *but I say, Judge Douglas, it was not silent when you got it.* It was vocal with the declaration when you got it, for a submission of the constitution to the people. And now, my direct question to Judge Douglas is, to answer why, if he deemed the bill silent on this point, he found it necessary to strike out those particular words...

How could he infer that a submission was still implied, after its express provision had been stricken from the bill? ... He took it out, and although he took out the other provision preventing a submission to a vote of the people, I ask, *why did you first put it in?* I ask him whether he took the original provision out, which Trumbull alleges was in the bill? If he admits that he did take it, *I ask him what he did it for?* It looks to us as if he had altered the bill. If it looks differently to him — if he has a different reason for his action from the one we assign him — he can tell it.[11]

When Lincoln finished, it looked as though he had cornered Douglas at last. It seemed impossible for Douglas to disprove that he, the champion of popular sovereignty, had been instrumental in stifling a popular vote. But such tight situations only served to test the Little Giant's mettle and to offer him opportunities of demonstrating his brilliance on the stump.

In choosing to emphasize a mere political maneuver above the essential moral issues Lincoln had entered dangerous ground. In the bruising give-and-take and dodges and twists of ordinary debate, Douglas had no peer. An out-and-out political brawl was what he loved. Though Lincoln, too, knew all the tricks of the hustings, it was in the realm of the ethical that his genius and strength lay. Only by taking Douglas to higher ground could Lincoln demonstrate his superiority. There, like Antaeus who was lifted into the air and defeated by Hercules, Douglas seemed weak in comparison with Lincoln. Now, on ground that was familiar to him, Douglas saw his chance and took full advantage of it. He attacked immediately and effectively:

> I had supposed that we assembled here to-day for the purpose of a joint discussion between Mr. Lincoln and myself upon the political questions that now agitate the whole country. . . Let me ask you what questions of public policy relating to the welfare of this state or the Union has Mr. Lincoln discussed before you? . . .
>
> He spent his whole hour in retailing a charge made by Senator Trumbull against me. The circumstances out of which that charge was manufactured, occurred prior to the last presidential election, over two years ago. If the charge was true, why did Trumbull not make it in 1856, when I was discussing the questions of that day all over this state with Lincoln and him, and when it was pertinent to the then issue? He was then as silent as the grave on the subject. If that charge was true, the time to have brought it forward was the canvas of 1856, the year when the Toombs Bill passed the Senate. When the facts were fresh in the public mind, when the Kansas question was the paramount question of the day, and when such a charge would have had a material bearing on the election. . . Were they not false to you and false to the country in going through that entire campaign, concealing their knowledge of this enormous conspiracy which, Mr. Trumbull says, he then knew and would not tell? . . .
>
> I am amazed that Mr. Lincoln should now come forward and endorse that charge, occupying his whole hour in reading Mr. Trumbull's speech in support of it. Why, I ask, does not Mr. Lincoln make a speech of his own instead of taking up his time reading Trumbull's speech at Alton? I supposed that Mr. Lincoln was capable of making a public speech on his own account, or I should not have accepted the banter from him for a joint discussion. . .
>
> Mr. Lincoln asks you to elect him to the United States Senate to-day solely because he and Trumbull can slander me. Has he given any other reason? Has he avowed what he was desirous to do in Congress on any one question? He desires to ride into office not on his own merits, not upon the merits and soundness of his principles, but upon his success in fastening a stale old slander upon me. . .
>
> Are you going to elect Mr. Trumbull's colleague upon an

issue between Mr. Trumbull and me? I thought I was running against Abraham Lincoln, that he claimed to be my
opponent, had challenged me to a discussion of the public
questions of the day with him, and was discussing these
questions with me; but it turns out that his only hope is to
ride into office on Trumbull's back, who will carry him by
falsehood.[12]

Going specifically into the Toombs Bill, he repeated his
defense against the charge of preventing ratification of the
Kansas Constitution:

> Up to the time of the introduction of the Toombs Bill,
> and after its introduction, there had never been an act of
> Congress for the admission of a new state which contained a
> clause requiring its constitution to be submitted to the people.
> The general rule made the law silent on the subject, taking
> it for granted that the people would demand and compel a
> popular vote on the ratification of their constitution. Such
> was the general rule under Washington, Jefferson, Madison,
> Jackson and Polk, under the Whig Presidents and the Demo-
> cratic Presidents from the beginning of the government down,
> and nobody dreamed that an effort would ever be made to
> abuse the power thus confided to the people of a territory.
> For this reason . . . whether there was or was not a clause
> in the Toombs Bill compelling submission . . . it was taken
> for granted that the constitution would be submitted to the
> people. . .
> Are Mr. Lincoln and Mr. Trumbull prepared to charge
> upon all those eminent men from the beginning of the gov-
> ernment down to the present day, that the absence of a
> provision compelling submission, in the various bills passed
> by them authorizing the people of territories to form state
> constitutions, is evidence of a corrupt design on their part to
> force a constitution upon an unwilling people?[13]

Taking up the charge that he had put in the offending
clause against submission of the constitution to the people,
he said:

> The Committee on Territories overruled me in commit-
> tee and put the clause in, but as soon as I got the bill back
> into the Senate I moved to strike it out and put another
> clause in its place. On the same page you will find that my
> amendment was agreed to *unanimously*. . . Trumbull con-

cealed in his Alton speech the fact that the clause he quoted
had been stricken out in my motion. . .

On this record that I have produced before you, I repeat
my charge that Trumbull did falsify the public records of
the country, in order to make his charge against me, and I
tell Mr. Abraham Lincoln that if he will examine these
records, he will then know that what I state is true.

He dismissed the matter cavalierly:

I regret the necessity of occupying my time with these
petty personal matters. It is unbecoming the dignity of a
canvass for an office of the character for which we are candidates. When I commenced the canvass at Chicago, I spoke
of Mr. Lincoln in terms of kindness as an old friend — I said
that he was a good citizen, of unblemished character, against
whom I had nothing to say. I repeated these complimentary
remarks about him in my successive speeches, until he became the endorser for these and other slanders against me.
If there is anything personally disagreeable, uncourteous, or
disreputable in these personalities, the sole responsibility
rests on Mr. Lincoln, Mr. Trumbull and their backers.[14]

Douglas now turned his attention to the Old Line Whigs,
whose votes he was so anxious to capture. His manner changed
and he followed a different tack:

You know that prior to 1854 this country was divided into
two great political parties, one the Whig, the other the
Democratic. I, as a Democrat for twenty years prior to that
time, had been in public discussions in this state as an advocate of Democratic principles, and I can appeal with confidence to every Old Line Whig within the hearing of my
voice to bear testimony that during all that period I fought
you Whigs like a man on every question that separated the
two parties. I had the highest respect for Henry Clay as a
gallant party leader, as an eminent statesman, and as one of
the bright ornaments of this country; but I conscientiously
believed that the Democratic party was right on the questions
which separated the Democrats from the Whigs. The man
does not live who can say that I ever personally assailed
Henry Clay or Daniel Webster, or any one of the leaders of
that great party, whilst I combatted with all my energy the
measures they advocated.

He attempted to identify the Whigs and Democrats in common opposition to the Republicans:

What did we differ about in those days? Did Whigs and Democrats differ about this slavery question? On the contrary, did we not, in 1850, unite to a man in favor of that system of compromise measures which Mr. Clay introduced, Webster defended, Cass supported, and Fillmore approved and made the law of the land by his signature? While we agreed on those compromise measures we differed about a bank, the tariff, distribution, the specie circular, the sub-treasury, and other questions of that description. Now let me ask you which one of those questions on which Whigs and Democrats then differed now remains to divide two great parties. Every one of those questions which divide Whigs and Democrats has passed away, the country has out-grown them, they have passed into history. Hence it is immaterial whether you were right or I was right on the bank, the sub-treasury, and other questions, because they no longer continue living issues.

What then has taken the place of those questions about which we once differed? The slavery question has now become the leading and controlling issue; that question on which you and I agreed, on which the Whigs and Democrats united, has now become the leading issue between the national Democracy on the one side, and the Republican or Abolition party on the other...

When the Whig party assembled in 1852 at Baltimore in national convention for the last time, to nominate Scott for the Presidency, they adopted as a part of their platform the compromise measures of 1850 as the cardinal plank upon which every Whig would stand and by which he would regulate his future conduct. When the Democratic party assembled at the same place one month after to nominate General Pierce, we adopted the same platform so far as those compromise measures were concerned, agreeing that we would stand by those glorious measures as a cardinal article in the Democratic faith. Thus you see that in 1852 all the old Whigs and all the old Democrats stood on a common plank so far as this slavery question was concerned, differing on other questions.[15]

THE LINCOLN-TRUMBULL "BARGAIN"

At this point Douglas led into the familiar charge that Trumbull was seeking to abolitionize the Democrats and Lincoln the Whigs, and to unite them under the Republican banner. Bringing up the election of 1855 in which Lincoln narrowly missed becoming United States Senator and finally threw his votes to Trumbull, Douglas charged that there had been a bargain between them which Trumbull broke. To substantiate the charge, Douglas quoted from a reported speech by Lincoln's close friend, James Matheny, who was alleged to have said: "In the most perfidious manner, they [Trumbull's supporters] refused to elect Mr. Lincoln; . . . and thus it has ever been, that an honest man makes a bad bargain when he conspires or contracts with rogues." Douglas had a lot of fun with this statement, taunting Lincoln with it to the amusement of the crowd:

> Lincoln's confidential friend, Matheny, thought that Lincoln made a bad bargain when he conspired with such rogues as Trumbull and the Abolitionists. (Great laughter.) I would like to know whether Lincoln has as high an opinion of Trumbull's veracity when the latter agreed to support him for the Senate, and then cheated him as he does now, (Renewed laughter.) when Trumbull comes forward and makes charges against me. . .
>
> And now I will explain to you what has been a mystery all over the state and union, the reason why Lincoln was nominated for the United States Senate by the Black Republican convention. You know it has never been usual for any party, or any convention to nominate a candidate for United States Senator. Probably this was the first time that such a thing was ever done. The Black Republican convention had not been called for that purpose, but to nominate a state ticket, and every man was surprised and many disgusted when Lincoln was nominated. . .
>
> Not only that, but he received the nomination unanimously, by a resolution declaring that Abraham Lincoln was "the first, last, and only choice" of the Republican party. How did this occur? Why, because they could not get Lincoln's friends to make another bargain with "rogues," (Laughter.) unless the whole party would come up as one man and pledge their honor that they would stand by Lincoln first, last and all the time, and that he should not be cheated by Lovejoy this time, as he was by Trumbull before. . . He would not go into the arrangement until he got their bond for it, and Trumbull is compelled now to take the stump, get up false charges against me, and travel all over the state to try and elect Lincoln, in order to keep Lincoln's friends quiet about

the bargain in which Trumbull cheated them four years ago. You see, now, why it is that Lincoln and Trumbull are so mighty fond of each other. (Tremendous laughter.)[16]

Climaxing his speech by hitting once more the sensitive side of the Whigs — Negro equality — Douglas demanded of Lincoln:

> Everywhere up north he has declared that he was not in favor of the social and political equality of the negro, but he would not say whether or not he was opposed to negroes voting and negro citizenship. I want to know whether he is for or against negro citizenship? He declared his utter opposition to the Dred Scott decision, and advanced as a reason that the court had decided that it was not possible for a negro to be a citizen under the Constitution of the United States. If he is opposed to the Dred Scott decision for that reason he must be in favor of conferring the right and privilege of citizenship upon the negro! I have been trying to get an answer from him on that point, but have never yet obtained one.[17]

The Little Giant closed with his usual attack on the "house divided" statement, making his customary plea for the perpetuation of the Union half-slave and half-free.

NO PEACE ON SLAVERY

In his rebuttal Lincoln tackled the matter of Negro citizenship first:

> Judge Douglas has said to you that he has not been able to get from me an answer to the question whether I am in favor of negro citizenship. So far as I know, the Judge never asked me the question before. He shall have no occasion to ever ask it again, for I tell him very frankly that I am not in favor of negro citizenship. . . Now my opinion is that the different states have the power to make a negro a citizen under the Constitution of the United States if they choose. The Dred Scott decision decides that they have not that power. If the state of Illinois had that power I should be opposed to the exercise of it. That is all I have to say about it.[18]

Next he turned to the question of slavery and the Union:

> Have we ever had any peace on this slavery question? When

are we to have peace upon it if it is kept in the position it now occupies? . . . This was the trouble which was quieted by the Compromise of 1850, when it was settled "forever," as both the great political parties declared in their national conventions. That "forever" turned out to be just four years, *when Judge Douglas himself re-opened it.* When is it likely to come to an end? He introduced the Nebraska Bill in 1854 to put *another end* to the slavery agitation. . .

Now, at this day in the history of the world we can no more foretell where the end of this slavery agitation will be than we can see the end of the world itself. The Nebraska-Kansas Bill was introduced four and a half years ago, and if the agitation is ever to come to an end, we may say we are four years and a half nearer the end of the world; and we can just as clearly see the end of the world as we can see the end of this agitation. The Kansas settlement did not conclude it. If Kansas should sink to-day, and leave a great vacant space in the earth's surface, this vexed question would still be among us.

I say, then, there is no way of putting an end to the slavery agitation amongst us but to put it back upon the basis where our fathers placed it, no way but to keep it out of our new territories — to restrict it forever to the old states where it now exists. Then the public mind *will* rest in the belief that it is in the course of ultimate extinction. That is one way to put an end to the slavery agitation. . .

I do not mean that when it takes a turn towards ultimate extinction it will be in a day, nor in a year, nor in two years. I do not suppose that in the most peaceful way ultimate extinction would occur in less than a hundred years at the least; but that it will occur in the best way for both races in God's own good time, I have no doubt.[19]

Taking up Douglas' charge of a bargain with Trumbull, Old Abe stirred up the crowd a little himself:

Now, in regard to this matter about Trumbull and myself having made a bargain to sell out the entire Whig and Democratic parties in 1854 — Judge Douglas brings forward no evidence to sustain his charge, except the speech Matheny is said to have made in 1856, in which he told a cock-and-bull story. . . I have twice told Judge Douglas to his face, that from beginning to end there is not one word of truth in it. (Thunders of applause.) I have called upon him for the proof, and he does not at all meet me as Trumbull met him upon that of which we were just talking, by producing the

record. He didn't bring the record, because there was no
record for him to bring. (Cheers and laughter.) When he asks
if I am ready to indorse Trumbull's veracity after he has
broken a bargain with me, I reply that if Trumbull *had*
broken a bargain with me, I would not be likely to indorse
his veracity because *neither in that thing, nor in any other,
in all the years that I have known Lyman Trumbull, have I
known him to fail of his word or to tell a falsehood, large or
small.* (Great cheering.)[20]

The rest of his rebuttal Lincoln devoted to Trumbull's
charges against Douglas in the matter of the Toombs Bill. He
was ready to meet the formidable Little Giant on his own
ground, and approached the subject by bringing up the Mexican War, even though Douglas had not mentioned this sore
subject in his speech:

Judge Douglas complains, at considerable length, about a
disposition on the part of Trumbull and myself to attack
him personally. I want to attend to that suggestion a moment. . . Judge Douglas, in a general way, without putting
it in a direct shape, revives the old charge against me, in
reference to the Mexican war. . . That charge is more than
ten years old. He complains of Trumbull and myself, because
he says we bring charges against him one or two years old.
He knows, too, that in regard to the Mexican war story, the
more respectable papers of his own party throughout the
state have been compelled to take back and acknowledge that
it was a lie.[21]

Here a dramatic incident took place. Lincoln strode over
to Orlando B. Ficklin, who was seated on the platform, and led
him to the speaker's stand. Since Ficklin, as a former colleague,
supposedly knew Lincoln's record in Congress, Long Abe saw
an opportunity to destroy Douglas' canard by first-hand evidence. Was Ficklin a willing witness who was glad to have
Lincoln lead him forward to testify, or was he a prisoner in
Long Abe's iron grip from which he could not free himself?
The official newspaper accounts report that Lincoln took him
by the hand, but other observers state that he held him by the
collar or the neck. In later years, in commenting on his experience, Ficklin himself said that he had had the democracy
shaken out of him. In any event, the crowd appreciated the
situation, especially when Lincoln stated:

I do not mean to do anything with Mr. Ficklin except to present his face and tell you that *he personally knows it to be a lie!* He was a member of Congress at the only time I was in Congress, and he knows that whenever there was an attempt to procure a vote of mine which would indorse the origin and justice of the war, I refused to give such indorsement, and voted against it; but I never voted against the supplies for the army, and he knows, as well as Judge Douglas, that whenever a dollar was asked by way of compensation or otherwise, for the benefit of the soldiers, *I gave all the votes that Ficklin or Douglas did, and perhaps more.*

The crowd applauded, but before Lincoln could continue, the unfortunate Ficklin got in a thrust of his own. He called out:

My friends, I wish to say this in reference to the matter. Mr. Lincoln and myself are just as good personal friends as Judge Douglas and myself. In reference to this Mexican war, my recollection is that when Ashmun's resolution was offered by Mr. Ashmun of Massachusetts, in which he declared that the Mexican war was unnecessarily and unconstitutionally commenced by the President — my recollection is that Mr. Lincoln voted for that resolution.

"That is the truth," Lincoln shot back, unshaken by Ficklin's remark:

Now you all remember that was a resolution censuring the President for the manner in which the war was *begun.* You know they have charged that I voted against the supplies, by which I starved the soldiers who were out fighting the battles of their country. I say that Ficklin knows it is false. . . If the Judge now says that he offers this as a sort of a set-off to what I said to-day in reference to Trumbull's charge, then I remind him that he made this charge before I said a word about Trumbull's. He brought this forward at Ottawa, the first time we met face to face; and in the opening speech that Judge Douglas made, he attacked me in regard to a matter ten years old. Isn't he a pretty man to be whining about people making charges against him only *two* years old.[22]

Pursuing the matter of the Toombs Bill, Lincoln continued:

I ask the attention of this audience to the question whether I have succeeded in sustaining the charge, and whether Judge Douglas has at all succeeded in rebutting it? You all heard me call upon him to say *which of these pieces of evidence*

was a forgery? Does he say that what I present as a copy of
the bill reported by himself is a forgery? Or what is presented
as a transcript from the *Globe,* of the quotations from Bigler's
speech is a forgery? Does he say the quotations from his own
speech are forgeries? *I would then like to know how it comes
about, that when each piece of a story is true, the whole story
turns out false?*[23]

Employing one of the homely analogies which the crowd
loved to hear, Lincoln drove his point home:

> I take it these people have some sense; they see plainly that
> Judge Douglas is playing cuttlefish (Laughter.), a small
> species of fish that has no mode of defending itself when pur-
> sued except by throwing out a black liquid, which makes the
> water so dark the enemy cannot see it and thus it escapes.
> (Roars of laughter.) Ain't the Judge playing the cuttlefish?
> ("Yes, yes," and cheers.)[24]

In order to leave no room for Douglas to disclaim personal
responsibility for the changes in the Toombs Bill, he said:

> Not only is this the evidence, but when he comes in with
> the bill having the provision stricken out, he tells us in a
> speech . . . that these alterations and modifications in the bill
> *had been made by him in consultation with Toombs, the
> originator of the bill. . .* We have his own word that these
> alterations were made *by him* and not by the committee.[25]

As his time drew to a close, Lincoln got in an unusual parting shot:

> Until he gives a better or more plausible reason than he
> has offered against the evidence in the case — *I suggest to him
> it will not avail him at all that he swells himself up, takes
> on dignity, and calls people liars.* (Great applause and laugh-
> ter.) Why, sir, there is not a word in Trumbull's speech that
> depends on Trumbull's veracity at all. He has only arrayed
> the evidence and told you what follows as a matter of reason-
> ing. . . . If you have ever studied geometry, you remember
> that by a course of reasoning Euclid proves that all the angles
> in a triangle are equal to two right angles. Euclid has shown
> you how to work it out. Now, if you undertake to disprove
> that proposition, and to show that it is erroneous, would you
> prove it to be false by calling Euclid a liar? (Roars of laughter
> and enthusiastic cheers.) They tell me my time is out, and
> therefore I close.[26]

PRESS ECHOES, POETRY, AND SONG

In addition to the laudatory or derogatory comments made in the partisan newspapers, the Administration press lost few opportunities to declare a plague on both candidates. Typical was the blast in the Washington *Union*:

> We cordially join . . . in the wish . . . that "Douglas may whip Lincoln out of his boots;" but we go further. After Lincoln receives his drubbing, we want him to return the compliment and larrup Douglas. And then, by way of making honors easy and ridding the country entirely of a pair of depraved, blustering, mischievous, lowdown demagogues, we would have them make a Kilkenny cat fight of it, and eat each other up. We have no choice to express between them; because it is like choosing between Punch and the devil.[27]

The *Cincinnati Commercial* expressed its opinion as follows:

> Few debates less dignified in their external manifestations, or containing so little that was worthy to be remembered, have fallen under our observation; and it is scarcely probable that this one will come to an end and not leave both parties in a worse condition, in the esteem of the judicious, than they were in the beginning. Falsehood and personal vituperation are among the most common of the offenses committed, upon one side at least, usurping the place of principle, and the merest sophistry offered, and it would seem received, as a worthy substitute for argument. In short, *the reports represent the debate to be little more than a strife for victory between two political pettifoggers, neither of whom occupies a doctrinal position, that he can sustain against a serious attack; while each is only able to continue in the field, through the weakness of his adversary.*[28]

With all the excitement and interest that was stirred up, however, it was not surprising that some readers should be moved to contribute verses that passed for poetry or that were meant to be sung to popular tunes, such as the following one by a Douglas, and the other by a Lincoln partisan:

EQUALIZE THE NATIONS
To be sung at the close of every speech delivered by Abe Lincoln during the present campaign. Air — "Black Bird."

Come, equalize the nations, Abe Lincoln does proclaim;
Let Cuffee have the freedom the white man has attained;
Our platform's broad and ample, the noblest and the best —
It extends from north to south, from the east unto the west.

Come, equalize the nations — our party will be great! —
Let Cuffee have the privilege with us to 'malgamate;
We have damsels white as lilies, whom we can sacrifice,
And raise motley plants, that will the world surprise...

Come, equalize the nations, ere a century shall come,
We'll rule this mighty nation with a Mustee or quadroon;
Then that harmony and union will reign throughout the land,
That has long been advocated by the black republican.[29]

LINCOLN AND DOUGLAS
Written on Reading their Speeches, by James Lewis, of
Lewisburg, Pa.

In Lincoln's hand see Freedom's torch of light,
Flashing its radiance o'er "Egyptian" night;
While little Douglas on his tip-toe stands,
And holds th' extinguisher in both his hands.
Too short to reach, he tried with many a groan,
To quench the light with his dark, hollow cone,
By that o'd tinker, Roger Taney, made
For James Buchanan in the way of trade.

'Tis label'd "Law decision," in the case
Of one Dred Scott, whose long-time dwelling place
Was on free soil, by his own master's act —
He claimed his freedom by that very fact —
All former precedents sustain his plea;
In law, and right, poor old Dred Scott was free...

This law, says Taney, its firm grapple holds,
Where'er our flag displays its shining folds;
The greatest boon our Constitution yields,
Is chattel slaves to till our fertile fields.
When our flag floats in conquest, anywhere,
Champions our Freedom! bring your niggers there,
And buy, and sell, and discipline, and feed,
And try by all means to improve the breed.
The Constitution, in its power of might,
To hold a nigger guarantees your right.[30]

CHAPTER 11

Mudsills of Society:
The Galesburg Debate

Though three weeks were to elapse before the next scheduled meeting of the rivals at Galesburg, they unexpectedly found themselves confronting each other on September 20, just two days after their last joint debate. The circumstances led to brawls between their followers.

How did it happen? Sensitive to the earlier charge that Lincoln was following closely at Douglas' heels because he could get no crowds of his own, the Republican campaign committee had tried to arrange an itinerary for the latter part of the campaign which would avoid Lincoln's speaking at any point on the same day that Douglas was there. It was impossible to do so, however, in the case of the little town of Sullivan, located about forty miles west of Charleston. After the fourth debate it was logical for both Lincoln and Douglas to canvass the area in Charleston's vicinity. Thus each was scheduled to speak in Danville and Urbana on successive days, after which Douglas was to travel north and Lincoln west. It was only at Sullivan that their trails met.

Douglas was scheduled to speak at ten o'clock in the morning and Lincoln at two in the afternoon. Everything would have been fine if Douglas had adhered to schedule, but by the time the Little Giant had driven the thirty miles or so across the prairie from Mattoon, and the bands had played, and the processions and delegations had marched, it was one o'clock before he started to speak. Lincoln, who had arrived in the meantime and sized up the situation, sent the following note by messenger to Douglas' hotel:

> Understanding that Judge Douglas would speak before dinner, I announced that I would address our friends at Freeland's Grove at 2 P.M. As he does not begin till 1 o'clock, if he will announce the fact, so that I can understand it, I will postpone to 3 o'clock.[1]

Douglas duly made the announcement to the crowds but could not at the same time resist taking a dig at his rival:

> I will remark, however, that I regret that our appointments, when we have not a joint discussion, should have come in collision, due in one place on the same day. My appointment for to-day was made as long ago as the 29th July, and it has been published in the newspapers ever since. Mr. Lincoln has his appointment here to-day, to speak after I get through; tomorrow I have to speak at Danville and he makes his appointment to speak the day after me there, and he follows me in like manner at Urbana. He has a great fancy for getting behind me and I have concluded that I will keep him behind me, especially about next November.[2]

In spite of this attempt to avoid collision, trouble developed. Shortly before 2:30 P.M., the Lincoln partisans, impatient to get started and desirous of publicizing their hero's appearance, began their parade, and with their band "blowing their mightiest," passed around the square where Douglas was speaking. Unrattled the Little Giant boomed out, "I can speak louder than their noise."[3] Some of Douglas' supporters, however, jumped on the bandwagon and pulled the driver from his seat. Fists began to fly and a general melee seemed likely to ensue, but somehow order was restored.

The Lincoln parade turned away from the square and the Douglas meeting continued. According to the *Chicago Times,* the melee was averted because Douglas left the stand and quieted his followers. Subsequently the press of both sides published their conflicting versions of the incident, with the Democratic papers charging that Lincoln himself was in a buggy that formed part of the disruptive procession, and left the scene only when he saw that a fight was about to start.

The reverberations of the incident echoed throughout the

remainder of the campaign. The Lincoln forces had supplied free ammunition for Douglas and he knew how to use it. When he resumed his speech, the Little Giant said:

> Ladies and Gentlemen: Now that this unpleasant scene which has disturbed our meeting somewhat has passed by, it is well that I should call your attention to the facts of the case, so that there can be no dispute about the truth of it in the future.
>
> You all know that in the month of July I made an appointment to speak today, and the gentlemen who brought the notice of that appointment to you is now by my side. Some weeks after that appointment had been made and published in the newspapers, Mr. Lincoln made an appointment here for the same day...
>
> Today one of his friends... came to my room at the hotel with this memorandum... [Douglas proceeded to read Lincoln's message.]
>
> I call upon you thousands now, to bear testimony, that before I uttered one word of my speech, I did, in a distinct and loud tone of voice, announce that I had been requested by Mr. Lincoln to give notice that he would speak at... 3 o'clock. Hence I complied with this compact on my part. . . At twenty-five minutes past 2 o'clock he, with his friends and a band of music, drove around the stand and came right up within forty feet of where I am now speaking, driving in the midst of some of my friends, beating their drum so as to break up this meeting...
>
> The fact that that procession organized and drove up here to break up this meeting, in violation of the written agreement which I hold in my hand, signed and written by Mr. Lincoln, no honest man will deny. Hence, I say, that this disturbance is in violation of Mr. Lincoln's word.... it was a deliberate attempt on the part of his friends to break up a Democratic meeting... and therefore I say that I am warranted, under this state of facts, in charging that Mr. Lincoln, as well as his friends, has been a party this day to break up this meeting, in order to prevent me from exposing his alliance with the Abolitionists.[4]

Following the brush at Sullivan, the contestants appeared at Danville and Urbana, a day apart. On Lincoln's train into Danville was Mrs. Douglas whose "queenly face and figure," (this was Horace White's description of her)[5] were capturing hearts and winning votes for her husband's cause. Lincoln

and she had an amiable conversation, until the train pulled
into Danville at 7:00 P.M. This was probably the occasion
recalled by Mrs. Douglas many years later when Lincoln, in
handing her over to her husband on the platform, said gallantly, "Judge Douglas, here's your old 'oman that I brought
along. She can do more with you than I can."[6]

Danville put on quite a show for Lincoln. In addition to
the Reynolds' Brass Band, and the usual banners and slogans,
prominent among which was one reading "Free Territory for
White Men," the procession contained four separate groups
of young ladies from outlying towns and villages, one group
of thirty-two representing the states of the Union and the
other three groups of thirty-seven representing the states and
territories. This was followed by a barbecued dinner spread
out on three 300-foot-long tables. After the festivities came
Lincoln's speech.

At Urbana, destined to become the site of the University
of Illinois, Douglas spoke to a very large audience. It was the
last day of the Champaign County Agricultural Fair, and there
was plenty of excitement, color and noise. Douglas' speech
from the grandstand made it a memorable occasion for his
auditors. Though Lincoln missed the fair crowd the next day,
the reception he received made up for it. The evening before
he was serenaded by three brass bands, and on the following
day there was another barbecue spread. Lincoln spoke after
the meal and again in the evening at the Evart House.

From this point the contestants went their separate ways.
Before proceeding on his itinerary, Lincoln stopped off at
Springfield for a two-day rest at home. Douglas, however, con-
tinued without respite.

Some idea of the strenuous nature of the campaign may be
seen from the itineraries of both men. Lincoln's route west
took him by the Great Western Railroad for a speech at Jacksonville, Douglas' home town. From there he proceeded by
carriage to Winchester, where he spent two days. Then crossing
the Illinois River, he spoke at Pittsfield. On October 2 he
boarded a packet steamer for an eighteen-hour 116-mile trip
upstream to Peoria, taking a stage from that point to Metamora, where Douglas had preceded him on September 30.
Returning to Peoria to spend the night, he once more took
a steamer for Pekin a few miles down river. Back again at

Peoria, he spent the night in the famous Peoria House where
he occupied Room 16, which had been used by Douglas only
a few nights before. The next afternoon, October 6, he boarded
a train on the Peoria and Oquawka Railroad for Knoxville,
nine miles distant from Galesburg, from where he proceeded
the next day to the debate.

Lincoln was in the habit of jotting down notes, and we have
a fragment of something he wrote somewhere along the way
during this period:

> Suppose it is true, that the negro is inferior to the white,
> in the gifts of nature; is it not the exact reverse justice that
> the white should for that reason, take from the negro any
> part of the little which has been given him? *"Give* to him that
> is needy" is the Christian rule of charity; but *"Take* from
> him that is needy" is the rule of slavery. . .
>
> But, slavery is good for some people!!! As a *good* thing,
> slavery is strikingly peculiar in this, that it is the only good
> thing which no man ever seeks the good of, for *himself.*
>
> Nonsense! Wolves devouring lambs, not because it is good
> for their own greedy maws, but because it is good for the
> lambs!!![7]

Douglas meanwhile had gone by the Illinois Central Railroad to Onarga on September 24 and Kankakee on the 25th.
Thence he traveled the short distance on the railroad to spend
the weekend in Chicago. September 28 found him at Henne-
pin, a town on the northernmost end of the Illinois River. He
was greeted enthusiastically, but the crowd was small, because
this was abolitionist territory.

The Little Giant now proceeded downstream for speeches
at Henry, Washington, Metamora and Pekin, stopping off at
Peoria between engagements to spend the nights of September
29 and 30 in Room 16 of the Peoria House. At Henry, a large
banner strung across the street proclaimed: "Our Senator,
Now, Our President in 1860," while four anvils clanged a re-
sounding iron welcome. At Pekin two young men were killed
while firing salutes from their six-pounder cannon.

From Pekin, Douglas took the Peoria and Oquawka train
for Galesburg where he spent Sunday, October 3, resting. The
next day in heavy rain, he set out for Oquawka, situated on
the Mississippi River, where he addressed a crowd of almost
1,000. Late in the afternoon he boarded the steamer *Keokuk*

for the short trip to Burlington, Iowa, for an evening speech. Up early the next morning, he was on the train at 6:55 for a short speech and then a rest at Monmouth, about twenty miles west of Galesburg, preparatory to the debate the following day.

By this time raw autumn weather had hit the prairies of Illinois. Strong winds and gusts of rain alternated with fits of sunshine. While Lincoln, toughened by his early pioneer life, was standing up well to the strain of campaigning and to the vagaries of the weather, the Little Giant needed constant reinforcement for the fires of his energy. Abetted by his natural conviviality, his drinking became heavier, and its effects more noticeable. Financial worries were also gnawing at his strength. In order to meet campaign expenses he had been forced to mortgage his real estate holdings in Chicago. It was at Charleston that Lincoln was reported as saying, "I flatter myself that thus far my wife has not found it necessary to follow me around from place to place to keep me from getting drunk."[8]

That keen observer, Billy Herndon, a convivialist himself, who had undoubtedly clinked glasses with Douglas on many occasions, wrote to his friend Parker on October 4: "Douglas is bloated as I ever saw him; he drinks very hard indeed; his look is awful to me, when I compare him as he now looks with what he was in February, 1858."[9]

GREELEY STANDS ALOOF

In the same letter he was bitter about Greeley, who, convinced that the Republicans should have supported Douglas against the Administration and not have entered a candidate against him, was silent during the campaign. Billy's irritation seethed through his words:

> Greeley is acting a great dog, is he not? Just look at the power of his great paper, with its world-wide circulation, and does he state who he is for, what he wants, what Illinois is doing, what freedom is struggling for, and how? . . . Nothing of the kind. He does not seem to know there is such a man as Lincoln, such a struggle as 1858–9, and such a State as Illinois. Does he keep his own people "posted?" Who would know by Greeley's paper that a great race for weal or woe was being fought all over the wide prairies of Illinois?[10]

He went so far as to write Greeley himself about it. As a

Republican, the editor of the *New York Tribune* could not
allow himself to hinder his party's candidate, but he would
not help either. He wanted to stay out of it, and so he told
Herndon in a letter of October 6:

> It seems to me that my name ought not to be used to
> distract and disorganize the Republicans of your State. . .
> Senator Douglas . . . *in his present position* I could not, of
> course, support, but he *need not have been in this position*
> had the Republicans of Illinois been as wise and far-seeing
> as they are earnest and true. . . Seeing that things are as they
> are, I would not wish to be quoted as authority for making
> trouble and division among our friends.[11]

That Lincoln needed all the help he could get was becoming obvious from the way Douglas was hammering away at
the Negro equality issue. This was the bugaboo which was
frightening the conservatives and the Old Line Whigs, whose
vote would tip the election. To reassure this element and convince the waverers, Lincoln had conceded all that he could
on the issue by granting the inferiority of the Negro. However,
with his precise logic of pinpointing issues and keeping them
clear, he was trying to show that superiority did not confer
the right to impose slavery as was Douglas' contention.

In spite of all that he had said, he knew that Douglas, in his
attacks on the interpretation of the Declaration of Independence, would continue to ignore the question of liberty and
emphasize that of equality, the ultimate implications of which
were certain to be abhorred and rejected by the voters. To
Lincoln the practical aspects of the abstract rights of both liberty and equality would "follow as fast as circumstances should
permit" and "in God's own good time." But would the electorate really comprehend the distinctions? He was hopeful that
they would. He realized that he would have to utilize his speaking time much better than he had at Charleston, devoting more
to the moral issues and less to petty questions of fact and veracity on minor issues, ground on which Douglas was able to more
than hold his own.

HOTBED OF ABOLITIONISM

Thursday, October 7, broke raw, chilly and damp over the
little town of Galesburg. It had rained heavily the day before,

and during the night the weather had changed. The cold was aggravated by a "fiercely blowing, cutting wind" which ripped banners and sent signs scattering all over town.[12]

Galesburg, founded only twenty-one years before by the Reverend George W. Gale, was a thriving community of 5,500 souls. Its chief ethnic group was Swedish, the immigrants having arrived throughout the 1840's and early 1850's. It was already a miniature railroad center, with two lines passing through it, which reached to Chicago, Peoria, Quincy and Burlington, Iowa. A foundry and a farm implement factory lent a hum to its busy activities.

But its chief pride was Knox College which was established with the founding of the city and was indeed the motive for its settlement. The college imparted the stamp of culture and intellectualism to the town. Its faculty and students were Free Soilers, and its president, Jonathan Blanchard, was an active anti-slavery worker of extremist views. In 1854, when Douglas was touring the state trying to repair the damage to his political fortunes as a result of the Nebraska Bill, Blanchard had engaged him in formal debate at Knoxville, and created a sensation by a vigorous and intemperate attack on the Little Giant.[13]

For many years, Galesburg had also been one of the principal depots of the Underground Railroad. At one time four Negroes had been kept for a day in the belfry of the First Congregational Church, whose pastor was Edward Beecher, brother to the famous Henry Ward Beecher and Harriet Beecher Stowe.[14] The town therefore had the reputation of being the "chief city of the abolitionists."

Galesburg was not bereft of Democrats, however. Federal posts in town, like that of Postmaster, were held by Democrats. In fact, as an act of revenge, Buchanan had recently removed the Galesburg Postmaster because he was a Douglas man and replaced him with a Danite. Not far from Knox College, a new college had sprung up, chartered in 1851 as Lombard College, which harbored a number of students with Democratic leanings.

Despite the unfavorable weather, crowds poured in from all sides to attend the debate. The railroads again offered half-fare excursion rates, and the trains were filled to overflowing. The Peoria *Transcript* warned its readers that the Democrats

were seeking to overcome Lincoln's advantage by attracting
as large a crowd of their partisans as possible:

> We urge our Republican friends to be on hand. An extra-
> ordinary effort will be made by the Douglas-worshipers to
> get out the largest crowd for the occasion. The decided ad-
> vantage which Mr. Lincoln has heretofore gained over his
> antagonist in these joint debates, has exasperated them to
> such an extent that no pains will be spared at Galesburg to
> regain their lost ground by giving Douglas as large a number
> of sympathizers in the audience as possible, who will be
> desperate in their enthusiasm to the last degree. But the
> Republican party throughout this section is confident and
> spirited, and Old Abe will meet with a reception next Thurs-
> day, which, in point of zeal and magnificence will far excel
> anything of the kind ever before witnessed in the west.[15]

Unfortunately, however, the train out of Peoria, jammed
with people in twenty-two cars, developed engine trouble on
the way and did not arrive until the closing minutes of the
debate.

There was, of course, the usual stream of people from nearby
areas who came by wagon, on horseback and on foot. Altogether it was the largest crowd of the debates, exceeding even
the throng at Freeport. Between 15,000 and 20,000 people,
depending on the bias of the estimator, braved the cold and
the wind to listen for three hours to the contestants.

The debate was to be held on the Knox College grounds,
and the platform had been erected on an open section of its
campus. On the morning of the debate, however, the platform
was moved to the east end of the college's main building, in
order to afford the speakers some shelter from the icy northwest
wind. It was erected on a level with the tall windows on the
main floor, and there is a tradition that the speakers entered
the building and stepped on to the platform through the
windows.[16] Lincoln, as he did so, is supposed to have quipped:
"Well, at last I have gone through college."

The committee on arrangements, however, had the usual
problems and difficulties attendant on the use of the platform.
The *Chicago Press and Tribune* appealed to the committee
two days before the debate in this vein:

> At none of the previous discussions have there been any
> adequate accommodations for reporters. . . . We request that

arrangements be made for at least six reporters — that the chairs and tables be placed where they will not be jarred or overthrown by the people on the platform and where there will be no room for persons to crowd between the reporters and the speakers — and that somebody with authority and physical strength enough to secure obedience, be appointed to keep loafers out of the reporting corner. These things are absolutely essential to the accuracy of the reports.[17]

BATTLE OF THE SLOGANS

Stretched across the entire side of the building high above the platform was a huge streamer reading "Knox College for Lincoln." Banners and sketches and cartoons were all over town. Each delegation paraded the streets proudly displaying its banners. The reporter for the *Chicago Press and Tribune* gave excellent descriptions of some of them:

A crayon sketch of Douglas and Toombs *"modifying"* in which Douglas with pen in hand is erasing the clause referring the Kansas Constitution back to the people.

"Dug at Freeport," "my platform" in which Douglas stands *"reversed"* upon the Dred Scott platform, one leg of which is giving way beneath.

"Coming from Egypt," in which Douglas, roaring with rage, is being punched up with Lincoln's cane.

A representation of the Capitol, and over the Senate room door Douglas' complaint, "He's got my place." Douglas is turning away while Lincoln is coming in.

A representation of a two donkey act, or Douglas attempting to ride Popular Sovereignty and Dred Scott. His straddle is remarkable but not equal to the task as both animals kicking up their heels send him sprawling.

"ABE LINCOLN THE CHAMPION OF FREEDOM." Upon this banner was also a portrait of "Long Abe."

Three figures, one taking a chair from beneath Mr. Douglas and dropping him plump upon the floor, at which he exclaims, "Oh my place!" Mr. Lincoln standing by blandly remarks, "The people say it." The *"place"* Mr. Douglas referred to was doubtless the portion which came in contact with the floor.

Upon a four-sided banner the following: "Macomb Lincoln Club." "We honor the man who brands the Traitor and Nullifier." "Small-fisted Farmers, Musills of Society, Greasy

Mechanics, for A. Lincoln." "The dose of milk Abe gave Dug down in Egypt made him very sick."

A well-painted banner with a terrible Lion on one side and ditto Dog on the other, with the inscriptions "Douglas the dead Lion," "Lincoln the living Dog."

The best banner upon the ground was a painting of the locomotive "FREEDOM" with a long train of Free State cars rushing round a curve, with the warning, "Clear the track for Freedom," while sticking upon the track a little in advance of the train was Douglas' ox cart laden with cotton. His negro driver had just taken the alarm and springing up in terror exclaims, "Fore God, Massa, I bleves we's in danger!"

Another ludicrous banner had a representation upon one side of Douglas going down to Egypt, pail in hand, to bring Abe to his milk. On the other, "How he succeeded." — Like Mr. Sniggs, in his effort at milking a cow, he gave the customary command to *"histe"* the foot. Abe *histed,* and Douglas and his pail are seen "laying around loose."[18]

Though "lithographs of Douglas abounded" and there were many banners, among which was a large blue one with an inscription emblazoned "Douglas and Popular Sovereignty," the Democrats were clearly out-bannered and out-sloganed by the Republicans. Writing his description of the proceedings, the reporter of the St. Louis *Missouri Republican* — a Democratic paper despite its name — complained:

The Abolitionists, by their committee of arrangements, had published a secret circular to call upon their followers to make a great show of numbers and banners for this occasion, which, I take it, indicates the fact that they are badly weakened about the knees. They know that the battle has been already won by Douglas, and it is only by the most extraordinary exertions that they can whip in their crestfallen men. Without any such claptrap, the Democrats turned out "formidable as an army with banners." You could not only discover the proportion of each, as they entered the city in long processions, by the badges they wore, or by the shouts they gave, but you could more signally "spot" them by noting that the Abolitionists, obeying the behests of their leading men, paraded dirty designs and beastly caricatures, indicating their vexation at the way things are working, while the Democrats, having some respect for the feelings of their neighbors, bore no banners but such as served to decorate

the procession, and such as no living man could take exception to, unless it be some very radical Abolitionist.[19]

Douglas arrived at ten o'clock on the Burlington train from
Monmouth. He was welcomed by three military companies
and escorted to the Bancroft House, where he was presented
with a banner of white satin trimmed with blue and wreathed
with flowers, made by women students and carrying the legend
"The Democracy of Lombard University to Stephen A. Douglas." A carriage with six horses then took the Little Giant at
the head of a long procession to the Bonney House, affording
the Democratic crowds along the way an opportunity to cheer
their idol.

Lincoln approached Galesburg from Knoxville to the east.
At the Hebard House where he had spent the night, he had
been serenaded by a brass band, and when he stepped out on
the porch, a man held up a lantern to Lincoln's face. "My
friends," Old Abe had said, "the less you see of me the better
you will like me."[20]

In the morning a long line of wagons and buggies, in one
of which sat Lincoln, rode the prairie to Galesburg. As they
approached the town, they were met by another long procession of buggies, wagons, floats and hayracks, featured by a
hundred men and a hundred ladies on horseback. It was
described as "about long enough to reach around the town
and tie in a bowknot."[21] Old Abe was taken to the home of
Mayor Henry Sanderson, where he freshened up with a warm
bath. Sanderson saw Lincoln as he stripped, and subsequently
reminisced that he was "the strongest man I ever looked at."[22]

At Sanderson's house, it was the turn of the Republican students of Lombard to present a banner to Lincoln, and the
ladies of Galesburg offered a beautiful silk red-white-and-blue
shield and coat of arms, on one side of which was inscribed
in fine handwriting the entire Declaration of Independence.

Two four-horse carriages, driven abreast, escorted by the
military organizations of the town and a large body of citizens,
bore the contestants to the scene of the debate. It was 2:30
before the preliminaries were concluded, and then James
Knox, the chairman, introduced Douglas whose turn it was to
begin.

The Little Giant decided to play one of his strongest cards

first: his opposition to the Lecompton Constitution and to the bill which had led to his break with the Administration. This was the stand which had aroused so much admiration throughout the country and won back for him the esteem which he had lost by the Nebraska Bill. This was the stand which had served to confuse the Republicans, bringing Greeley and other high eastern Republicans to his support and leading to talk of the possible organization of a Constitutional Union Party with Douglas at its head. Douglas was sure he could get the sympathy of his hearers by recounting his persecution at the hands of the Administration, and if he could show that the Republicans were allied with the Buchaneers against him, it could help to undermine the Republican campaign.

> I led off in the fight against the Lecompton Constitution and conducted it until the effort to carry that constitution through Congress was abandoned.... When the Lecompton Constitution was defeated, the question arose in the minds of those who had advocated it what they should next resort to in order to carry out their views. They devised a measure known as the English Bill, and granted a general amnesty and political pardon to all men who had fought against the Lecompton Constitution, provided they would support that bill. I for one did not choose to accept the pardon or to avail myself of the amnesty granted on that condition. The fact that the supporters of Lecompton were willing to forgive all differences of opinion at that time in the event those who opposed it favored the English Bill, was an admission that they did not think that opposition to Lecompton impaired a man's standing in the Democratic party.
>
> Now the question arises, what was that English Bill which certain men are now attempting to make a test of political orthodoxy in this country?... By the English Bill, if the people of Kansas had only agreed to become a slave-holding state under the Lecompton Constitution, they could have done so with 35,000 people, but if they insisted on being a free state, as they had a right to do, then they were to be punished by being kept out of the Union until they had nearly three times that population. I then said in my place in the Senate, as I now say to you, that whenever Kansas has population enough for a slave state she has population enough for a free state. ("That's it," and cheers.) I have never yet given a vote, and I never intend to record one making an

odious and unjust distinction between the different states of this Union. (Applause.). . .

The effort has been and is now being made in this state by certain postmasters and other federal office holders, to make a test of faith on the support of the English Bill. These men are now making speeches all over the state against me and in favor of Lincoln, either directly or indirectly, because I would not sanction a discrimination between slave and free states by voting for the English Bill.

But while that bill is made a test in Illinois for the purpose of breaking up the Democratic organization in this state, how is it in the other states? Go to Indiana, and there you find English himself, the author of the English Bill, who is a candidate for re-election to Congress, has been forced by public opinion to abandon his own darling project, and to give a promise that he will vote for the admission of Kansas at once, whenever she forms a constitution in pursuance of law, and ratifies it by a majority vote of her people. . .

Pass to Ohio, and there you find that . . . all the other anti-Lecompton men who stood shoulder to shoulder with me against the Lecompton Constitution, but voted for the English Bill, now repudiate it and take the same ground that I do on that question. . .

And yet, notwithstanding the fact, that every Lecompton and anti-Lecompton Democrat in the free states has abandoned the English Bill, you are told that it is to be made a test upon me. . .

I now submit the question to you as my constituency, whether I was not right, first, in resisting the adoption of the Lecompton Constitution; and secondly, in resisting the English Bill. (An universal "Yes," from the crowd.) . . . I submit the question to you whether or not if it had not been for me that constitution would have been crammed down the throats of the people of Kansas against their consent. ("It would, it would." "Hurrah for Douglas;" "Three cheers for Douglas," etc.)

While at least ninety-nine of every hundred people here agree that I was right in defeating that project, yet my enemies use the fact that I did defeat it by doing right, to break me down and put another man in the U.S. Senate in my place. ("No, no, you'll be returned;" "Three cheers," etc.) My political opponent, Mr. Lincoln, has no hope on earth, and has never dreamed that he had a chance of success, were it not for the aid he is receiving from federal office holders,

who are using their influence and the patronage of the government against me in revenge for my having defeated the
Lecompton Constitution. ("Hear him;" and applause.)

What do you Republicans think of a political organization
that will try to make an unholy and unnatural combination
with its professed foes to beat a man merely because he has
done right? ("Shame on it.") You know such is the fact with
regard to your own party. You know that the axe of decapi-
tation is suspended over every man in office in Illinois, and
the terror of proscription is threatened every Democrat by
the present administration unless he supports the Republican ticket in preference to my Democratic associates and myself. ("The people are with you." "Let them threaten," etc.)

I could find an instance in the postmaster of the city of
Galesburg and in every other postmaster in this vicinity, all
of whom have been stricken down simply because they discharged the duties of their offices honestly, and supported
the regular Democratic ticket in this state. . . The Republican party is availing itself of every unworthy means in the
present contest to carry the election, because its leaders
know that if they let this chance slip they will never have
another, and their hopes of making this a Republican state
will be blasted forever.[23]

TOUCHE

The Little Giant then asserted his familiar argument, that
the Republican Party was hurting the nation because it was
a sectional party, and furthermore that Lincoln was taking
different positions in different parts of the state to conform
with the prejudices of his audiences. To prove his point he
brought out his trump card: the question of Negro equality.

He quoted from Lincoln's former speeches to demonstrate
this inconsistency. He contrasted his words at Chicago at the
opening of the campaign with what he had said at Charleston
three weeks before. At Chicago Lincoln had deplored "all this
quibbling about . . . this race and that race, and the other
race being inferior and therefore they must be placed in an
inferior position," while at Charleston he had emphasized the
"physical difference between the white and black races, which,
I suppose, will forever forbid . . . social and political equality."

At this stage, however, the crowd which had received Douglas' opening statements with sympathy began to heckle. In

abolitionist territory, his appeal to fears and prejudices could not sway the audience as it would in the central part of the state among the former Whigs. Douglas responded to the comments of the crowd in his usual vigorous fashion:

> Fellow-citizens, here you find men hurrahing for Lincoln and saying that he did right, when in one part of the state he stood up for negro equality, and in another part for political effect, discarded the doctrine and declared that there always must be a superior and inferior race. Abolitionists up north are expected and required to vote for Lincoln because he goes for the equality of the races, holding that by the Declaration of Independence the white man and the negro were created equal and endowed by the Divine law with that equality, and down south he tells the Old Whigs, the Kentuckians, Virginians, and Tennesseeans, that there is a physical difference in the races, making one superior and the other inferior, and that he is in favor of maintaining the superiority of the white race over the negro. Now, how can you reconcile those two positions of Mr. Lincoln? He is to be voted for in the south as a pro-slavery man, and he is to be voted for in the north as an Abolitionist.[24]

The comparison tended to put Lincoln in a bad light. To the average listener there seemed no doubt that he was guilty of equivocation.

Douglas used the remainder of his time expounding his own opinion of the Negro's status, defending the Dred Scott decision and popular sovereignty, and calling for the right of each state to do as it pleased without interference from any other state. When he finished, he put on his overcoat and broad-brimmed white hat for protection against the cold, sat down, took out a cigar, and began to smoke.

It had been very noticeable during the Little Giant's speech that his effort had taxed his sorely-tried voice, which was already deep and hoarse. Many of his words had been spent in the wind, and sections of his speech had come over indistinctly to the audience.

RIPOSTE

Lincoln removed his shawl and stood up slowly. His manner seemed to be even more deliberate than usual. His opening words indicated that he was unworried by Douglas' attack.

Across the cold air his high-pitched voice rang out: "A very large portion of the speech which Judge Douglas has addressed to you has previously been delivered and put in print." A burst of laughter greeted this sentence. "I do not mean that for a hit upon the judge at all," he continued:

> If I had not been interrupted, I was going to say that such an answer as I was able to make to a very large portion of it, had already been more than once made and published. There has been an opportunity afforded to the public to see our respective views upon the topics discussed in a large portion of the speech which he has just delivered. . . I however desire to take up some of the points that he has attended to, and ask your attention to them.[25]

Lincoln's voice grew fuller and more penetrating:

> He asks you: Is it possible to believe that Mr. Jefferson, who penned the immortal paper, could have supposed himself applying the language of that instrument to the negro race, and yet hold a portion of that race in slavery? Would he not at once have freed them? . . .
>
> I believe the entire records of the world, from the date of the Declaration of Independence up to within three years ago, may be searched in vain for one single affirmation, from one single man, that the negro was not included in the Declaration of Independence. I think I may defy Judge Douglas to show that he ever said so, that Washington ever said so, that any President ever said so, that any member of Congress ever said so, or that any living man upon the whole earth ever said so, until the necessities of the present policy of the Democratic party, in regard to slavery, had to invent that affirmation.
>
> And I will remind Judge Douglas and this audience, that while Mr. Jefferson was the owner of slaves, as undoubtedly he was, in speaking upon this very subject, he used the strong language that "he trembled for his country when he remembered that God was just;" and I will offer the highest premium in my power to Judge Douglas if he will show that he, in all his life, ever uttered a sentiment at all akin to that of Jefferson. . . .[26]
>
> [Those] speeches of mine, which Judge Douglas had to read to you, and which he supposes are in very great contrast to each other . . . have been before the public for a considerable time, and if they have any inconsistency in them, . . . the

public have been able to detect it. When the Judge says, in speaking on this subject, that I make speeches of one sort for the people of the northern end of the state, and of a different sort for the southern people, he assumes that I do not understand that my speeches will be put in print and read north and south. I knew all the while that the speech that I made at Chicago and the one I made at Jonesboro and the one at Charleston, would all be put in print and all the reading and intelligent men in the community would see them and know all about my opinions. And I have not supposed, and do not now suppose, that there is any conflict whatever between them.

But the Judge will have it that if we do not confess that there is a sort of inequality between the white and black races, which justifies us in making them slaves, we must, then insist that there is a degree of equality that requires us to make them our wives. . .

I have all the while maintained, that in so far as it should be insisted that there was an equality between the white and black races that should produce a perfect social and political equality, it was an impossibility. This you have seen in my printed speeches, and with it I have said, that in their right to "life, liberty and the pursuit of happiness, as proclaimed in that old Declaration, the inferior races are our equals." And these declarations I have constantly made in reference to the abstract moral question, to contemplate and consider when we are legislating about any new country which is not already cursed with the actual presence of the evil — slavery.

I take it that I have to address an intelligent and reading community, who will peruse what I say, weigh it, and then judge whether I advance improper or unsound views, or whether I advance hypocritical, and deceptive, and contrary views in different portions of the country. I believe myself to be guilty of no such thing as the latter, though, of course, I cannot claim that I am entirely free from all error in the opinions I advance.

The Judge has also detained us a while in regard to the distinction between his party and our party. His, he assumes to be a national party — ours, a sectional one. . . The argument is, that no party can be a rightful party . . . unless it can announce its principles everywhere.

I presume that Judge Douglas could not go into Russia and announce the doctrine of our national democracy; he could not denounce the doctrine of kings, and emperors, and

monarchies, in Russia; and it may be true of this country,
that in some places we may not be able to proclaim a doctrine
as clearly true as the truth of democracy, because there is a
section so directly opposed to it that they will not tolerate
us in doing so. Is it the true test of the soundness of a doctrine, that in some places people won't let you proclaim it? . . .

Why, I understood that at one time the people of Chicago
would not let Judge Douglas preach a certain favorite doctrine of his. I commend to his consideration the question,
whether he takes that as a test of the unsoundness of what
he wanted to preach.

What has always been the evidence brought forward to
prove that the Republican party is a sectional party? The
main one was that in the southern portion of the Union the
people did not let the Republicans proclaim their doctrine
amongst them.[27]

With shrewd insight and keen political sagacity, he read
Douglas' fate for him in the South:

I ask his attention also to the fact that by the rule of
nationality he is himself fast becoming sectional. I ask his
attention to the fact that his speeches would not go as current
now south of the Ohio River as they have formerly gone
there. I ask his attention to the fact that he felicitates himself
to-day that all the Democrats of the free states are agreeing
with him, while he omits to tell us that the Democrats of
any slave state agree with him. . . Whatever may be the result
of this ephemeral contest between Judge Douglas and myself,
I see the day rapidly approaching when his pill of sectionalism, which he has been thrusting down the throats of Republicans for years past, will be crowded down his own throat.[28]

THE RIGHT TO DO WRONG

Lincoln now exposed Douglas to the moral issue; the Little
Giant's vulnerable point:

The Judge tells [us] that he is opposed to making any
odious distinctions between free and slave states. I am altogether unaware that the Republicans are in favor of making
any odious distinctions between the free and slave states.
But there still is a difference, I think, between Judge Douglas
and the Republicans in this . . . that the Judge is not in favor
of making any difference between slavery and liberty — that
he is in favor of eradicating, of pressing out of view, the

questions of preference in this country for free over slave institutions; and consequently every sentiment he utters discards the idea that there is any wrong in slavery. Everything that emanates from him or his coadjutors in their course of policy, carefully excludes the thought that there is anything wrong in slavery. . .

If you will take the Judge's speeches, and select the short and pointed sentences expressed by him — as his declaration that he "don't care whether slavery is voted up or down" — you will see at once that this is perfectly logical, if you do not admit that slavery is wrong. If you do admit that it is wrong, Judge Douglas cannot logically say that he don't care whether a wrong is voted up or voted down. Judge Douglas declares that if any community want slavery they have a right to have it. He can say that logically, if he says that there is no wrong in slavery; but if you admit that there is a wrong in it, he cannot logically say that anybody has a right to do wrong. . .

And from this difference of sentiment . . . arises the real difference between Judge Douglas and his friends, on the one hand, and the Republicans on the other. Now, I confess myself as belonging to that class in the country who contemplate slavery as a moral, social and political evil, having due regard for its actual existence amongst us and the difficulties of getting rid of it in any satisfactory way, and to all the constitutional obligations which have been thrown about it; but, nevertheless, desire a policy that looks to the prevention of it as a wrong, and looks hopefully to the time when as a wrong it may come to an end.[29]

Douglas' stand on Lecompton and his break with Buchanan, on which he counted to split the Republican Party, he belittled with a touch of sarcasm:

Judge Douglas has again, for, I believe, the fifth time, if not the seventh, in my presence, reiterated his charge of a conspiracy or combination between the National Democrats and Republicans. What evidence Judge Douglas has upon this subject I know not, inasmuch as he never favors us with any. I have said upon a former occasion, and I do not choose to suppress it now, that I have no objection to the division in the Judge's party. He got it up himself. It was all his and their work. He had, I think, a great deal more to do with the steps that led to the Lecompton Constitution than Mr. Buchanan had; though at last, when they reached it, they

> quarrelled over it, and their friends divided upon it . . . but I
> defy the Judge to show any evidence that I have in any way
> promoted that division. . .[30]

Lincoln then charged that Douglas had shown that he was
not to be regarded as a competent witness. As proof, he could
not resist bringing up the Codding resolutions and illustrated
his point with one of his stories that brought hilarious laughter
from the crowd:

> So apparent had it become that the resolutions which he
> read had not been passed at Springfield at all, or by a state
> convention in which I had taken part, that seven days after-
> wards, at Freeport, Judge Douglas declared that he had been
> misled by Charles H. Lanphier, editor of the *State Register*,
> and Thomas L. Harris, member of Congress in that district,
> and he promised in that speech that when he went to Spring-
> field he would investigate the matter. Since then Judge Doug-
> las has been to Springfield, and I presume has made the
> investigation. I have waited as I think sufficient time for the
> report of that investigation, and I have some curiosity to see
> and hear it. A fraud — an absolute forgery was committed,
> and the perpetration of it was traced to the three — Lanphier,
> Harris and Douglas. . . The main object of that forgery at
> that time was to . . . elect Harris to Congress. . .
>
> The fraud having been apparently successful upon the
> occasion, both Harris and Douglas have more than once since
> then been attempting to put it to new uses. As the fisher-
> man's wife, whose drowned husband was brought home with
> his body full of eels, said when she was asked, "What was to
> be done with him?" *"Take the eels out and set him again,"* so
> Harris and Douglas have shown a disposition to take the eels
> out of that stale fraud by which they gained Harris' election,
> and set the fraud again more than once.[31]

Turning to the implications of the Dred Scott decision,
which had been the subject of the third interrogatory he had
put to Douglas at Freeport, Lincoln gave a new twist to his
previous arguments:

> To this interrogatory Judge Douglas made no answer in
> any sense of the word. He contented himself with sneering
> at the thought that it was possible for the Supreme Court
> ever to make such a decision. He sneered at me for propound-
> ing the interrogatory. . .

The essence of the Dred Scott case is compressed into the sentence which I will now read: . . . "*The right of property in a slave is distinctly and expressly affirmed in the constitution!*" . . . What follows as a short and even syllogistic argument from it? I think it follows, and I submit to the consideration of men capable of arguing, whether as I state it in syllogistic form the argument has any fault in it:

Nothing in the Constitution or laws of any state can destroy a right distinctly affirmed in the Constitution of the United States;

The right of property in a slave is distinctly and expressly affirmed in the Constitution of the United States;

Therefore, nothing in the Constitution or laws of any state can destroy the right of property in a slave.

I believe that no fault can be pointed out in that argument; assuming the truth of the premises, the conclusion, so far as I have capacity at all to understand it, follows inevitably. There is a fault in it as I think, but the fault is not in the reasoning; but the falsehood in fact is a fault of the premises. I believe that the right of property in a slave *is not* distinctly and expressly affirmed in the Constitution, and Judge Douglas thinks it *is*. I believe that the Supreme Court and the advocates of that decision may search in vain for the place in the Constitution where the right of property in a slave is distinctly and expressly affirmed. I say, therefore, that I think one of the premises is not true in fact. But it is true with Judge Douglas. It is true with the Supreme Court who pronounced it.[32]

Lincoln went on to show how Douglas' pronouncements and actions were preparing the public mind to accept slavery on a nationwide basis:

I have said, upon a former occasion, and I repeat it now, that the course of argument that Judge Douglas makes use of upon this subject, . . is preparing the public mind for that new Dred Scott decision. . . He swells himself up and says, "All of us who stand by the decision of the Supreme Court are the friends of the Constitution; all you fellows that dare question it, in any way, are the enemies of the Constitution". . . He does not investigate it, and won't inquire whether this opinion is right or wrong. So he takes the next one without inquiring whether *it* is right or wrong. He teaches men this doctrine, and in so doing prepares the public mind to take the next decision when it comes, without any inquiry. . .

He is preparing (whether purposely or not), the way for making the institution of slavery national![33]

As his time drew to a close, Lincoln compared his own position with that of Douglas on the admission of new states into the Union:

He was in favor of the acquisition of further territory, as fast as we might need it, in disregard of how it might affect the slavery question. . . If Judge Douglas' policy upon this question succeeds, and gets fairly settled down, until all opposition is crushed out, the next thing will be a grab for the territory of poor Mexico, and invasion of the rich lands of South America, then the adjoining islands will follow, each one of which promises additional slave fields.

And this question is to be left to the people of those countries for settlement. When we shall get Mexico, I don't know whether the Judge will be in favor of the Mexican people that we get with it settling that question for themselves and all others; because we know the Judge has a great horror for mongrels, and I understand that the people of Mexico are most decidedly a race of mongrels. I understand that there is not more than one person there out of eight who is pure white, and I suppose from the Judge's previous declaration that when we get Mexico or any considerable portion of it, that he will be in favor of these mongrels settling the question, which would bring him somewhat into collision with his horror of an inferior race. . .

You will bear in mind that it [territory] is to be acquired, according to the Judge's view, as fast as it is needed, and the indefinite part of this proposition is that we have only Judge Douglas and his class of men to decide how fast it is needed. We have no clear and certain way of determining or demonstrating how fast territory is needed as slave territory. . . Whatever motive a man or set of men may have for making annexation of property or territory, it is very easy to assert, but much less easy to disprove, that it is necessary for the wants of the country. . .

I think it is a very grave question for the people of this Union to consider, whether, in view of the fact that this slavery question has been the only one that has ever endangered our republican institutions — the only one that has ever threatened or menaced a dissolution of the Union — that

has ever disturbed us in such a way as to make us fear for
the perpetuity of our liberty — . . . whether we shall engage in
the policy of acquiring additional territory, discarding altogether from our consideration . . . the question how it may
affect us in regard to this, the only endangering element to
our liberties and national greatness . . . I think it will become
an important practical question.[34]

The applause and shouts of approval that followed from the
partisan audience after Lincoln finished were so prolonged
that Douglas had to wait until there was sufficient quiet for
him to begin. That doughty warrior correctly sized up the
situation. "The highest compliment you can pay me," he began, "is by observing a strict silence. I desire to be heard rather
than to be applauded."

Attempting to convert Lincoln's slur about the sameness of
his speeches into a virtue, he declared: "The first criticism that
Mr. Lincoln makes on my speech was that it was in substance
what I have said everywhere else in the state where I have addressed the people. I wish I could say the same of his speech."

Then waving aside Lincoln's proof of consistency on the
issue of Negro equality, he endeavored to show that his statements could not be reconciled. "He tells you today that the
negro was included in the Declaration of Independence when
it asserted that all men are created equal," he started to say
and was interrupted by shouts of "We believe it," from the
crowd. This was followed by catcalls, groans and other noises
which put the audience into an uproar.

"Gentlemen," bellowed Douglas, "I ask you to remember
that Mr. Lincoln was listened to respectfully, and I have the
right to insist that I shall not be interrupted during my reply."

The situation got so out of hand that Lincoln, too, felt impelled to quiet the crowd. "I hope that silence will be preserved," he called out.

The noises subsided, but an obvious restlessness prevailed
as Douglas continued. He sought to show that even from the
moral viewpoint Lincoln's position was untenable:

> If the negro was made his equal and mine, if that equality
> was established by Divine law, and was the negro's inalienable
> right, how came he to say at Charleston to the Kentuckians
> residing in that section of our state, that the negro was
> physically inferior to the white man, belonged to an inferior

race, and he was for keeping him always in that inferior
condition? . . . There he gave the people to understand that
there was no moral question involved, because the inferiority
being established, it was only a question of degree and not a
question of right; here, to-day, instead of making it a question
of degree, he makes it a moral question, says that it is a great
crime to hold the negro in that inferior condition.

"He's right," interrupted a voice.
"Is he right now or was he right in Charleston?"
"Both," came the answer.
"He is right then, sir, in your estimation, not because he is
consistent, but because he can trim his principles any way in
any section, so as to secure votes."[35]

From this point on, Douglas' arguments seemed trite and
specious, lacking the depth necessary to meet Lincoln's minute
analysis of an issue. The best he could do on the test of the
soundness of political principles, which Lincoln had examined
so logically, was the following:

> But did you notice how he answered my position that a
> man should hold the same doctrines throughout the length
> and breadth of this republic? He said, "Would Judge Douglas
> go to Russia and proclaim the same principles he does here?"
> I would remind him that Russia is not under the American
> Constitution. If Russia was a part of the American republic,
> under our federal Constitution, and I was sworn to support
> that Constitution, I would maintain the same doctrine in
> Russia that I do in Illinois.
>
> The slaveholding states are governed by the same federal
> Constitution as ourselves, and hence a man's principles, in
> order to be in harmony with the Constitution, must be the
> same in the South as they are in the North, the same in the
> free states as they are in the slave states. . . When Mr. Lincoln
> went to Congress in 1847, and laying his hand upon the holy
> evangelists, made a solemn vow in the presence of high
> Heaven that he would be faithful to the Constitution, —
> what did he mean? the Constitution as he expounds it in
> Galesburg, or the Constitution as he expounds it in Charle-
> ston?[36]

POINT OF PERSONAL DIFFICULTIES

However, Douglas had an opportunity to fight again on solid
ground for him on the Codding resolutions. In bringing this

matter up, Lincoln had dealt, not with essential issues, but with political maneuvering. By thus descending from the rarefied atmosphere which was so difficult for Douglas' political breathing, he had put the Little Giant on even terms with himself. Nevertheless, Lincoln's blows had evidently taken effect, for the Little Giant appeared irritated, and his argument sounded defensive and apologetic:

> Mr. Lincoln . . . has used hard names; has dared to talk about fraud, about forgery, and has insinuated that there was a conspiracy between Mr. Lanphier, Mr. Harris, and myself to perpetuate a forgery. Now, bear in mind that he does not deny that these resolutions were adopted in a majority of all the Republican counties of this state in that year; . . . he does not deny the truthfulness of the resolutions, but takes exceptions to the *spot* on which they were adopted. . . He tries very hard to make out that there is something very extraordinary in the place where the thing was done, and not in the thing itself. . .
>
> The moment it was intimated to me that they had been adopted at Aurora and Rockford instead of Springfield, I did not wait for him to call my attention to the fact, but led off and explained in my first meeting after the Ottawa debate, what the mistake was, and how it had been made. I supposed that for an honest man, conscious of his own rectitude, that explanation would be sufficient. . .
>
> I did not think there was an honest man in the state of Illinois who doubted that I had been led into the error, if it was such, innocently . . . and I will now say that I do not now believe that there is an honest man on the face of the globe who will not regard with abhorrence and disgust Mr. Lincoln's insinuations of my complicity in that forgery, if it was a forgery.

As Douglas proceeded, his annoyance mounted and he could not refrain from expressing his pugnaciousness:

> Does Mr. Lincoln wish to push these things to the point of personal difficulties here? I commenced this contest by treating him courteously and kindly; I always spoke of him in words of respect, and in return he has sought, and is now seeking, to divert public attention from the enormity of his revolutionary principles by impeaching men's sincerity and integrity, and inviting personal quarrels.[37]

Having relieved his feelings, he continued:

> These resolutions were the platform of this Republican
> party of Mr. Lincoln's of that year. . . One cardinal point in
> that platform which he shrinks from is this — that there shall
> be no more slave states admitted into the Union, even if the
> people want them. Lovejoy stands pledged against the ad-
> mission of any more slave states.

"Right, so do we," yelled someone in the crowd.

"So do you, you say," the Little Giant answered, "and I
am informed that your candidate for the legislature here is
also pledged."

"Hurrah for him, good, good," came the shouts from the
crowd.

The Little Giant strained his hoarse voice a little higher:

> Now, you Republicans all hurrah for him, and for the
> doctrine of "no more slave states," and yet Lincoln tells you
> that his conscience will not permit him to sanction that doc-
> trine. . . You are one way, you confess, and he is or pretends
> to be the other, and yet you are both governed by *principle*
> in supporting one another. If it be true, as I have shown it is,
> that the whole Republican party in the northern part of
> the state stands committed to the doctrine of no more slave
> states, and that this same doctrine is repudiated by the Re-
> publicans in the other part of the state, I wonder whether
> Mr. Lincoln and his party do not present the case which he
> cited from the Scriptures, of a house divided against itself
> which cannot stand! I desire to know what are Mr. Lincoln's
> principles and the principles of his party?

This gave Douglas the opportunity to defend his slavery
position without committing himself on the moral aspects as
Lincoln had challenged him to:

> When I used the remark that I did not care whether slavery
> was voted up or down I used it in the connection that I was
> for allowing Kansas to do just as she pleased on the slavery
> question. I said that I did not care whether they voted slavery
> up or down, because they had the right to do as they pleased
> on the question.[38]

Turning to the Dred Scott decision, Douglas avoided answering Lincoln's legal and constitutional arguments, by flatly
denying that the decision meant what Lincoln said it did. Nor
did he consider it worthwhile to become involved with the

problem of unsound court decisions. There was nothing to do but obey them:

> I have a few words to say upon the Dred Scott decision, which has troubled the brain of Mr. Lincoln so much. He insists that the decision would carry slavery into the free states, notwithstanding that the decision says directly the opposite; and goes into a long argument to make you believe that I am in favor of, and would sanction the doctrine that would allow slaves to be brought here and held as slaves contrary to our constitution and laws. Mr. Lincoln knew better when he asserted this; ... Mr. Lincoln knows that there is not a member of the Supreme Court who holds that doctrine; he knows that every one of them, as shown by their opinions, holds the reverse.
>
> Why this attempt, then, to bring the Supreme Court into disrepute among the people? ... The Constitution has created that court to decide all constitutional questions in the last resort, and when such decisions have been made, they become the law of the land. . . It is possible that you Republicans have the right to raise your mobs and oppose the laws of the land and the constitutional authorities, and yet hold us Democrats bound to obey them? My time is within half a minute of expiring, and all I have to say is that I stand by the laws of the land. I stand by the Constitution as our fathers made it, by the laws as they are enacted, and by the decisions of the court upon all points within their jurisdiction as they are pronounced by the highest tribunal on earth; and any man who resists these must resort to mob law and violence to overturn the government of laws.[39]

With these words, the Little Giant closed the debate. He put on his hat and reached for his coat, while the admirers of both contestants surged to the platform to offer congratulations.

JOURNALISM AGOG

In reporting the debate the partisan press went to the usual extremes, oblivious of reality and incompetent of perspective. The headlines of the *Chicago Times* blared: "Black Republicanism Beaten In Its Stronghold and Outnumbered by the Democracy — Lincoln Again Defeated Before the People," while its columns contained choice gems like the following:

Mr. Lincoln experienced one of the most complete defeats which he has made during the campaign. His argument was lamentably weak, and as usual he confined himself to petty personal charges and insinuations.

In 1854 it was as much as a man's life was worth, in Galesburg, to advocate Democratic principles; but now owing to the wonderful change in popular sentiment within the past year or two, Democracy has hosts of friends and supporters in this abolition stronghold, and on Thursday last had possession of the town.

But the choicest of them all were those dealing with descriptions of Lincoln:

The cold was intense. Mr. Lincoln, when he mounted the stand, was nervous and trembling; whether from cold, or through fear of what was in store for him, we are unable to say; but before the close of the debate, he was the most abject picture of wretchedness we have ever witnessed. His knees knocked together, and the chattering of his teeth could be heard all over the stand. When Senator Douglas replied to his charge that he had forced a set of resolutions at Ottawa, he looked pitiful beyond expression, and curled himself up in a corner to avoid facing the bitter denunciation of the Senator and the scorn and derision with which he was treated by the crowd.

When Senator Douglas concluded, the applause was perfectly furious and overwhelming, he was surrounded by an immense mass of people who accompanied him to his hotel, which, during the whole evening, was thronged with people going and coming to congratulate him upon his great success; whilst Lincoln entirely forgotten, was taken care of by a few friends, who wrapped him in flannels and tried to restore the circulation of blood in his almost inanimate body. Poor Lincoln! he was not even *visible* to the friends who came to weep over him.[40]

On the Republican side, the level of journalism rose no higher. Typical was the reporting of the Quincy *Daily Whig* whose headlines proclaimed: " 'Old Abe' Skins the 'Little Giant,' " and whose columns matched those of the *Times* with the following comments:

About 3 o'clock JUDGE DOUGLAS was introduced to the audience by Hon. Jos. Knox, and was received with such a faint cheer by his few friends in attendance, that it caused universal laughter. He spoke for one hour; and in the spirit of a man who was suffering martyrdom.

Douglas actually foamed at the mouth, during his speech. It *may* have been the *milk* that he imbibed while sojourning in Egypt; but the general belief was that it was *foam*. It should be borne in mind that hydrophobia is not confined to dog-days. We don't wish to lull the people here into any false security by stating that it was *milk* that whitened the corners of Douglas' mouth, when it might actually be the saliva of incipient madness. Forewarned is to be forearmed.

When Douglas concluded, "Old Abe" mounted the stand, and was received with three such tremendous cheers as made the welkin ring again. His happy, good-humored countenance — in such marked contrast with that of Douglas, which is black and repulsive enough to turn all the milk in Egypt sour — at once cheered and animated the immense crowd. They pressed forward to the stand.[41]

CHAPTER 12

Drama in the Face of the World: The Quincy Debate

The campaign was rapidly drawing to a close. Only three weeks remained for the orators to carry their battle to the public. As the days went by, tensions mounted, excitement increased, and the tones of the partisan press became shriller.

By this time the arguments of the candidates were fairly familiar, but their repetition around the state, reaching into the corners of the small communities, was necessary in order to crystallize opinion among the voters. This was difficult in view of the emotional, and often hysterical, clamor of the press.

As Lincoln had foreseen more than a year before, the crux of the campaign lay in the issue of Negro equality which Douglas interpreted as synonymous with amalgamation. In his reply to Douglas' defense of the Dred Scott decision at Springfield in June 1857, he had said, "If he [Douglas] can, by much drumming and repeating, fasten the odium of that idea upon his adversaries, he thinks he can struggle through the storm."

Now the Democratic papers were concentrating on this issue and hammering away at it without let-up. The *Illinois State Register* began running a daily scarehead which read:

PEOPLE OF SANGAMON
Remember
A Vote for Cook and Brown
is a Vote for
LINCOLN AND NEGRO EQUALITY

Cook and Brown were running for the legislature in Lincoln's home county and, if elected, would cast two votes for

Lincoln for the senatorship. Both men were former Kentuckians. Captain James N. Brown's family had been slaveholders. His father had served in Congress with Henry Clay, and he himself, as a Whig, had had four terms in the House of Representatives, one of them as a colleague of Lincoln.

The circumstances under which Brown was nominated were revealing of the predicament of the Whigs. There were few sections of Illinois where prejudice against the Negro was stronger than in Sangamon County, which had been settled chiefly by Kentuckians. With the collapse of their party, the Old Line Whigs were politically stranded. Though anti-slavery in sentiment, only a few like Lincoln joined the Republican Party, whose platform was regarded by most conservatives as too radical.

Captain Brown, a personal friend of Lincoln's, was one of these conservatives. Driven by the necessity of deciding how to vote in the coming election, a number of prominent Whigs of Sangamon met early in the year to take counsel. Among those present were Judge Logan and Major Stuart, Lincoln's former law partners, as well as Brown. Everyone expressed his views freely and frankly. Stuart declared that the Whigs, although not yet prepared to align themselves with the Democrats, could never be Republicans. To this Brown replied, "My friends, I have been a Whig all my life. I cannot be a Democrat. From this time on, I am a Lincoln Republican."

Lincoln knew of this meeting and was fully aware of the Whigs' dilemma. It strengthened his determination to try to draw them into the Republican ranks by divesting his party of the specter of abolitionism. Accordingly, at a subsequent meeting of Sangamon Republicans for the purpose of drawing up a local ticket, at which Brown was present, Lincoln talked at length about the necessity of a policy which would set at rest the qualms of the Old Line Whigs who still remained without a party. They would not fear the new party if it stood only for the conservative doctrine of restricting slavery to its existing boundaries.

He then urged the nomination of Brown for the legislature. Brown wished to decline, but in line with the plan he had presented, Lincoln said: "You must run. We cannot, must not, nominate an eastern man; he would be beaten. We must have the votes of the Old Line Whigs. You have been a Whig; you are a Kentuckian; you have been a slaveholder. You will get the support of the large conservative element — the Old Line Whigs and the men of southern birth and sympathies who, while willing to let slavery remain where it is, are with us against its further extension, but who would be afraid to trust an eastern man." He then proceeded to call off the names of fifty Old Line Whigs of local prominence who would vote for such a man as Brown.

Brown succumbed to Lincoln's persuasiveness and, much as he was averse to further public service, reluctantly accepted the nomination. However, he began to feel his uncomfortable position fully when he was assailed by old friends for his support of Lincoln. "Why, Brown!" they would say in astonishment and reproach, "How can you, a Kentuckian, yourself once a slaveholder, stand for a black Abolitionist — a man who says the negro is your equal and mine." Thus the specter of radicalism continued to haunt Lincoln's efforts, and before the end of the canvass Brown was to find it necessary to appeal to Lincoln for help in combating the misstatements and misinterpretations which he was encountering in the course of his campaigning.[1]

ACTION ON THE MISSISSIPPI

During the five days that intervened between the Galesburg and Quincy debates, both contestants busied themselves in the areas adjoining the two towns. On Friday, October 8, Lincoln went north to Toulon while Douglas went south to Macomb. The next day Lincoln appeared at Oquawka, and then crossed the Mississippi River to address a capacity crowd at Burlington, Iowa. Douglas left Macomb for Plymouth, a town further south on the way to Quincy, where the entire population of 1,000 turned out, regardless of party, to hear him.

Both men rested on Sunday, which was marred by a dreary, all-day rain. It turned the country roads and the unpaved streets of the towns into heavy mud, which like,

> "Aunt Jemima's plaster,
> The more you try to scrape it off
> The more it sticks the faster."[2]

Despite the mud, large crowds gathered on Monday to hear

Lincoln at Monmouth and Douglas at Carthage. Lincoln had no speaking engagement for the next day, but the tireless Douglas, working his way down to the site of the debate, spoke at Augusta in the afternoon. Later his train entered the little town of Camp Point where it was greeted by people bearing torches, by a military company with fifes and drums, and by bonfires, rockets, a lighted flagpole and fireballs. In acknowledgement, he made the crowd a little speech from the platform of his car That night his train entered Quincy where he was to spend the night.

Quincy was a thriving town attractively situated on a bluff overlooking the Mississippi River. Fifteen miles downstream on the Missouri side was the town of Hannibal, where Mark Twain lived as a boy. Missourians interested in the debates availed themselves of the opportunity to hear this one which was being held so close to home. A correspondent for the *Chicago Press and Tribune,* under the pseudonym of "Old Pike," wrote:

> I had occasion to go over into Missouri, and there I found large handbills up calling on the Democrats of the State to turn out at Quincy. Several steamers have been engaged by the Missourians to convey them up the river. I was told by several of them that they intended to make Lincoln "dry up." What they meant by it I do not know. Douglas' friends in Quincy are looking to that State for their crowd on the 13th. Now I write you this for the purpose of having you urge the Republicans to turn out their strength, and sustain and cheer our noble champion by their presence.[3]

The Republicans were just as zealous. About thirty miles up river was the town of Keokuk, Iowa. The Republican Committee arranged to provide excursions for its followers on the steamers *Keokuk* and *St. Louis Packet.* The latter boat was scheduled to leave at 6:30 on the morning of the 13th from Keokuk and at 6:00 in the evening from Quincy. The fare for the round trip, supper included, was $1.50. Other boats with picturesque names, like *Hamilton Belle, Colonel Morgan* and *City of Louisiana,* brought spectators from various points along the river.

With excitement rising to a high pitch, both sides were determined to avoid the kind of conflict which had occurred at Sullivan. Each, therefore, published its order of procession in

its own press, with a request to rival papers to "please copy."
And so it was arranged that, while the bands and carriages and
marchers and horseback riders of one faction were parading
up one street, those of the other would be coming down an
adjacent street. While the noise and music might occasionally
mingle, there was no chance of the processions colliding.

Fortunately, the weather was favorable. After a series of
cold, dismal storms, a clear sky smiled on the bustle and scurry
of the preparations. The parades and preliminary ceremonies
were scheduled for the morning with time out for dinner
before the commencement of the debate. The Democrats,
however, got off to a better start than the Republicans. They
began their celebration the evening before with the arrival
of Douglas from Augusta and Camp Point. A huge torchlight
procession greeted the Little Giant at the railroad depot to
the booming of cannon and the blare of music, and escorted
him to his quarters at the Quincy House.

In the morning the Republicans had their opportunity with
the arrival of Lincoln on the train of the Burlington line. In
addition to the usual cannon and music and banners and transparencies, and girls on horseback representing the states, the
principal attraction was a model ship on wheels, drawn by
four horses and labelled "Constitution." It was filled with
sailors, and at the helm was a live raccoon, the symbol of the
dead Whig Party, which called to mind the days of Henry
Clay. A special section of the procession was devoted to private carriages containing ladies. The parade escorted Lincoln
to the home of Orville Browning, where the ladies presented
him with a bouquet, and a mixed choir sang "Columbia, the
Gem of the Ocean."

Douglas remained in his hotel as the Democrats paraded
through town. They carried a huge likeness of their hero at
the head of the procession, which one partisan reporter boasted
was at least two miles in length while the Republican procession was only "probably half a mile in length."[4] Among the
displays was a large number of flags on hickory poles, designed
to characterize Douglas in the popular mind as "Young Hickory" as Andrew Jackson had been "Old Hickory." And suspended by its tail to the top of a pole was a dead raccoon, meant
to serve as a gibe to the Republicans and as a symbol of triumph
of the Democracy. The *Chicago Press and Tribune*, however,
considered the display an insult to the Old Line Whigs.[5]

As the procession passed the Quincy House, Douglas stood at a second floor window, where he was cheered by the waves of marchers as they passed. By twelve o'clock the excitement died down, and the inhabitants dispersed to dinner preparatory to gathering again for the debate in front of the impressive Grecian-columned courthouse facing Washington Public Square.

The old public square is Washington Park today, and the old courthouse with its white columns still stands; its former impressiveness lost as it huddles between the taller buildings on each side. A large stone boulder containing the simple legend "Lincoln-Douglas Debate October 13, 1858," painted in white letters, lies near one of the paths in the park, an obscure reminder that on that day more than 12,000 people sat or stood before the wooden platform erected in front of the courthouse.

The crowd gathered early. Provision had been made for special seats accommodating 800 to be placed in front of the speaker's stand for the exclusive use of ladies. As had happened on other occasions, in the milling and pushing that preceded the arrival of the speakers, the railing of the crude platform broke and several people fell to the ground. Such incidents had become an accepted concomitant of the forensic exhibitions of the time and did not mar the proceedings, for after a brief flurry of excitement, Lincoln was introduced for the opening speech at 2:30 P.M.

Mindful of the way a crowd could get out of hand, his opening words were: "I have had no immediate conference with Judge Douglas, but I will venture to say he and I will perfectly agree that your entire silence both when I speak and when he speaks will be most agreeable to us."[6]

Next, after referring briefly to the much-wrangled-over Springfield resolutions, he devoted time to the charge that he was double dealing on the Negro equality issue. He traced his stand through his statements at Charleston, Ottawa and Chicago back to his speech at Peoria four years earlier to show that there had been no change in position, but merely in the form of expression. He quoted the words of his Ottawa statement and said:

> I have chiefly introduced this for the purpose of meeting
> the Judge's charge that the quotation he took from my

Charleston speech was what I would say down south among the Kentuckians, the Virginians, &c., but would not say in the regions in which was supposed to be more of the Abolition element.

I now make this comment: That speech from which I have now read the quotation ... was made away up north in the Abolition district of this state *par excellence* — in the Lovejoy district — in the personal presence of Lovejoy, for he was on the stand with us when I made it. It had been made and put in print in that region ... a month before the speech made at Charleston, the like of which Judge Douglas thinks I would not make where there was any Abolition element.

I only refer to this matter to say that I am altogether unconscious of having attempted any double dealing anywhere — ... but that I have said anything on one occasion that is inconsistent with what I have said elsewhere, I deny — at least I deny it so far as the intention is concerned."[7]

A THIRD CHANCE

By this summary, he hoped to silence Douglas or, at least, to render ineffective the charge that he favored Negro equality. He now proceeded to catch the Little Giant up on a statement he had made at Galesburg on the Dred Scott decision that was palpably untrue and in any event irresponsible. It was the kind of statement that had prompted Lincoln to tell Clifton H. Moore, of Clinton, that "Douglas will tell a lie to ten thousand people one day, even though he may have to deny it to five thousand the next."[8] Douglas had said, "He [Lincoln] insists that the Dred Scott decision would carry slavery into the free states, notwithstanding the decision itself says the contrary ... No member of the Supreme Court holds that doctrine. Every one of them in their opinions held the reverse."

Lincoln held up a copy of the Dred Scott decision:

I have the Dred Scott decision here, and I will thank Judge Douglas to lay his finger upon the place in the entire opinions of the court where any one of them "says the contrary" ... I have examined that decision with a good deal of care, as a lawyer examines a decision, and so far as I have been able to do so, the Court has no where in its opinions said that the states have the power to exclude slavery, nor have they used other language substantially that. I also say, so far as I can find, not one of the concurring Judges has said that the states can exclude slavery, nor said anything that was substantially that.[9]

Pointing out that he had asked the Judge twice before whether he would support a decision which denied the states the power to exclude slavery, he said, to the amusement of the crowd: "He gave me no direct answer as to whether he would or would not sustain such a decision if made. I give him this third chance to say yes or no. He is not obliged to do either — probably he will not do either — but I give him the third chance."[10]

Lincoln's manner exuded poise and confidence. He seemed to give the impression that he had his adversary in his grasp. It was as though two boxers had been fighting bitterly, and after the bruising infighting and long-range exchanges of the early rounds, one had solved the other's style and revealed himself the master, able to block his opponent's blows with ease and to strike back at will. This was further revealed as he reverted to the Springfield resolutions: "Among other expressions he used toward me was that I dared to say forgery." He repeated the words, "I had *dared* to say forgery." Then to the accompaniment of laughter and applause from the crowd, he turned to Douglas:

> Yes, Judge, I did dare to say forgery. But in this political canvass, the Judge ought to remember that I was not the first who *dared* to say forgery. At Jacksonville Judge Douglas made a speech in answer to something said by Judge Trumbull, and at the close of what he said upon that subject, he *dared* to say that Trumbull had forged his evidence. He said, too, that he should not concern himself with Trumbull any more, but thereafter he should hold Lincoln responsible for the slanders upon him.
>
> When I met him at Charleston after that, although I think that I should not have noticed the subject if he had not said he would hold me responsible for it, I spread out before him the statements of the evidence that Judge Trumbull had used, and I asked Judge Douglas, piece by piece, to put his finger upon one piece of all that evidence that he would say was a forgery! When I went through with each and every piece, Judge Douglas did not *dare* then to say that any piece of it was a forgery. So it seems that there are some things that Judge Douglas dares to do, and some that he dares not to do.[10]

He was interrupted by one of Douglas' supporters, who called out, "It's the same thing with you."

"Yes sir," returned Lincoln quickly, "it's the same thing with me. I do dare to say forgery, when it's true, and I don't dare to say forgery when it's false."

This retort was greeted by thunders of applause and cries of "Hit him again," "Give it to him, Lincoln." Then to the laughter of the audience, he added, "I am not a very daring man, but I dared that much, Judge, and I am not much scared about it yet."[11]

Lincoln, in perfect control of the situation, continued almost sadistically to bait the Little Giant:

> As soon as I learned that Judge Douglas was disposed to treat me in this way, I signified in one of my speeches that I should be driven to draw upon whatever of humble resources I might have — to adopt a new course with him. I was not entirely sure that I should be able to hold my own with him, but I at least had the purpose made to do as well as I could upon him; and now I say that I will not be the first to cry "hold." I think it originated with the Judge, and when he quits, I probably will. (Roars of laughter.)
>
> But I shall not ask any favors at all. He asks me, or he asks the audience, if I wish to push this matter to the point of personal difficulty. I tell him, no. He did not make a mistake, in one of his early speeches, when he called me an "amiable" man, though perhaps he did when he called me an "intelligent" man. (Laughter.) It really hurts me very much to suppose that I have wronged anybody on earth. I again tell him, no! I very much prefer, when this canvass shall be over, however it may result, that we at least part without any bitter recollections of personal difficulties.[12]

The last words softened the blows. It was not in Lincoln's nature to press an advantage too far. Besides, he fully sensed the far-reaching importance that the debates would assume and the wide publicity that would be given to the words that both he and Douglas spoke. It was essential that he hold in check his acknowledged superiority in wit and anecdote, so that his arguments on the issues might not be obscured and could withstand subsequent calm examination and objective scrutiny. This sensitivity he revealed in the following words:

> I was aware, when it was first agreed that Judge Douglas

and I were to have these seven joint discussions, that they were the successive acts of a drama — perhaps I should say, to be enacted not merely in the face of audiences like this, but in the face of the nation, and to some extent, by my relation to him, and not from anything in myself, in the face of the world; and I am anxious that they should be conducted with dignity and in the good temper which would be befitting the vast audience before which it was conducted.[13]

Having spoken thus, Lincoln now addressed himself to the moral issue of the slavery question:

We keep up a controversy in regard to it [slavery]. That controversy necessarily springs from difference of opinion, and if we can learn exactly . . . what that difference of opinion is, we perhaps shall be better prepared for discussing the different systems of policy that we would propose in regard to that disturbing element. I suggest that the difference of opinion, reduced to its lowest terms, is no other than the difference between the men who think slavery a wrong and those who do not think it wrong. . .

Because we think it wrong, we propose a course of policy that shall deal with it as a wrong. We deal with it as with any other wrong, in so far as we can prevent its growing any larger, and so deal with it that in the run of time there may be some promise of an end to it. . .[14]

The cautious, conservative character of Lincoln's position was revealed in his next words:

We go further than that; we don't propose to disturb it where, in one instance, we think the Constitution would permit us. We think the Constitution would permit us to disturb it in the District of Columbia. Still we do not propose to do that, unless it should be in terms which I don't suppose the nation is very likely soon to agree to — the terms of making the emancipation gradual and compensating the unwilling owners.[15]

The statement of this position prompted Lincoln to answer Douglas' assertion that anyone who opposed the Dred Scott decision was advocating revolution and the overthrow of the courts.

We oppose the Dred Scott decision in a certain way, upon which I ought perhaps to address you a few words. We do not propose that when Dred Scott has been decided to be a slave by the court, we, as a mob, will decide him to be free. We do not propose that, when any other one, or one thousand, shall be decided by that court to be slaves, we will in any violent way disturb the rights of property thus settled; but we nevertheless do oppose that decision as a political rule which shall be binding on the voter, to vote for nobody who thinks it wrong, which shall be binding on the members of Congress or the President to favor no measure that does not actually concur with the principles of that decision. We do not propose to be bound by it as a political rule in that way, because we think it lays the foundation not merely of enlarging and spreading out what we consider an evil, but it lays the foundation for spreading that evil into the states themselves. We propose so resisting it as to have it reversed if we can, and a new judicial rule established upon this subject.[16]

At this juncture he summarized the platform of the Republican Party, a platform of which he was one of the chief architects, and which, being free of the taint of extreme abolitionism, would attract hesitant voters to its standard:

I will add this, that if there be any man who does not believe that slavery is wrong ... that man is misplaced, and ought to leave us. While, on the other hand, if there be any man in the Republican party who is impatient over the necessity springing from its actual presence, and is impatient of the constitutional guarantees thrown around it, and would act in disregard of these, he too is misplaced standing with us. He will find his place somewhere else; for we have a due regard, so far as we are capable of understanding them, for all these things. This, gentlemen, as well as I can give it, is a plain statement of our principles in all their enormity.[17]

Pursuing the theme that the kind of policy adopted toward slavery stemmed from the moral attitude toward it, he analyzed the Democratic position:

I will say now that there is a sentiment in the country contrary to me — a sentiment which holds that slavery is not wrong, and therefore it goes for policy that does not propose dealing with it as a wrong. That policy is the Democratic policy, and that sentiment is the Democratic sentiment. . . The leading man — I think I may do my friend Judge Douglas the honor of calling him such — advocating the present Democratic policy, never himself says it is wrong. He has the high distinction, so far as I know, of never having said slavery is either right or wrong. (Laughter.) Almost everybody else says one or the other, but the Judge never does. If there be a man in the Democratic party who thinks it is wrong, and yet clings to that party, I suggest to him ... that his leader don't talk as he does, for he never says that it is wrong.[18]

He pointed out the anomalous position of those Democrats who thought slavery wrong, but still opposed Republican policy:

You say it is wrong; but don't you constantly object to anybody else saying so? Do you not constantly argue that this is not the right place to oppose it? You say it must not be opposed in the free states, because slavery is not here; it must not be opposed in the slave states, because it is there; it must not be opposed in politics, because that will make a fuss; it must not be opposed in the pulpit because it is not religion. (Loud cheers.) Then where is the place to oppose it?[19]

As his time drew to a close, Lincoln clinched his point with a concluding statement so crystal clear that it could not be misunderstood:

Let us understand this. I am not, just here, trying to prove that we are right and they are wrong. I have been stating where we and they stand, and trying to show what is the real difference between us; and I now say that whenever we can get the question distinctly stated — can get all these men who believe that slavery is ... wrong, to stand and act with us in treating it as a wrong — then, and not till then, I think we will in some way come to an end of this slavery agitation.[20]

When Douglas arose to make his reply, the horizontal wrinkle between his eyes, as Carl Schurz described it, seemed "unusually dark and scowling." The seasoned combatant, toughened by his many campaigns, was prepared to return the blows he had received with all the strength he could command. His deep voice, a range lower now because of its hoarseness, boomed out: "Permit me to say that unless silence is observed it will be impossible for me to be heard by this immense crowd, and my friends can confer no higher favor upon me than by omitting all expressions of applause or approbation."

"We cannot help it, Douglas," came the cries from the huge number of Democrats, who had come from every surrounding

area to cheer their idol, and were impatient to hear the Little
Giant strike his opponent down. But Douglas held up his
hand. "I desire to be heard rather than to be applauded," he
said, and then, aiming his first blow at Lincoln, he continued,
"I wish to address myself to your reason, your judgment, your
sense of justice, and not to your passions."

Immediately he sprang to the attack on the Springfield resolutions with which Lincoln had badgered him:

> I regret that Mr. Lincoln should have deemed it proper
> for him to again indulge in gross personalities and base in-
> sinuations in regard to the Springfield resolutions. It has
> imposed upon me the necessity of using some portion of my
> time for the purpose of calling your attention to the facts
> of the case, and it will then be for you to say what you think
> of a man who can predicate such a charge upon the circum-
> stances he has this.[21]

Then, after giving a resume of the matter, he made his own
thrust at Lincoln:

> He knows, in his heart, that I quoted them in good faith,
> believing, at the time, that they had been adopted at Spring-
> field. I would consider myself an infamous wretch, if, under
> such circumstances, I could charge any man with being a
> party to a trick or a fraud. (Great applause.) And I will tell
> him, too, that it will not do to charge a forgery on Charles
> H. Lanphier or Thomas L. Harris. No man on earth, who
> knows them, and knows Lincoln, would take his oath against
> their word. (Cheers.) There are not two men in the state of
> Illinois, who have higher characters for truth, for integrity,
> for moral character, and for elevation of tone, as gentlemen,
> than Mr. Lanphier and Mr. Harris. Any man who attempts
> to make such charges as Mr. Lincoln has indulged in against
> them, only proclaims himself a slanderer. (Vociferous ap-
> plause.)[22]

To the cheers of the crowd, and cries of "Hit him again" and
"Give it to him," he continued his attack:

> I will now show you that I stated with entire frankness,
> as soon as it was made known to me, that there was a mistake
> about the spot where the resolutions had been adopted,
> although their truthfulness, as a declaration of the principles
> of the Republican party, had not, and could not be ques-

tioned. I did not wait for Lincoln to point out the mistake. . .
I corrected it myself, as a gentleman, and an honest man,
and as I always feel proud to do when I have made a mistake.
I wish Mr. Lincoln could show that he has acted with equal
fairness, and truthfulness, when I have convinced him that
he has been mistaken.

I will give you an illustration to show you how he acts in
a similar case: In a speech at Springfield, he charged Chief
Justice Taney, and his associates, President Pierce, President
Buchanan, and myself, with having entered into a conspiracy
at the time the Nebraska Bill was introduced, by which the
Dred Scott decision was to be made by the Supreme Court, in
order to carry slavery everywhere under the Constitution. I
called his attention to the fact, that at the time alluded to,
to wit: the introduction of the Nebraska Bill, it was not
possible that such a conspiracy could have been entered into,
for the reason that the Dred Scott case had never been taken
before the Supreme Court and was not taken before it for a
year after; and I asked him to take back that charge. Did he
do it?

I showed him that it was impossible that the charge could
be true, I proved it by the record, and I then called upon
him to retract his false charge. What was his answer? Instead
of coming out like an honest man and doing so, he reiterated
the charge, and said that if the case had not gone up to the
Supreme Court from the courts of Missouri at the time he
charged that the Judges of the Supreme Court entered into
the conspiracy, yet, that there was an understanding with
the Democratic owners of Dred Scott, that they would take
it up. I have since asked him who the Democratic owners of
Dred Scott were, but he could not tell, and why? Because
there were no such Democratic owners in existence. Dred
Scott at the time was owned by the Reverend Dr. Chaffee, an
Abolition member of Congress, of Springfield, Massachusetts,
in right of his wife. He was owned by one of Lincoln's friends,
and not by Democrats at all; his case was conducted in court
by Abolition lawyers, so that both the prosecution and the
defense were in the hands of the Abolition political friends
of Mr. Lincoln. . .

Yet, I never could get Mr. Lincoln to take back his false
charge, although I have called upon him over and over
again. He refuses to do it, and either remains silent, or, resorts
to other tricks to try and palm his slander off on the country.
Therein you will find the difference between Mr. Lincoln

and myself. When I make a mistake, as an honest man, I correct it without being asked to do so, but when he makes a false charge he sticks to it, and never corrects it.[23]

By this time the Little Giant's supporters were shouting with glee. Their hero was not disappointing them. However, their cheers and applause were making it difficult for Douglas to be heard, and he paused to admonish them: "My friends, if you are my friends, you will be silent, instead of interrupting me by your applause."

The Little Giant now proceeded to give Lincoln a taste of the baiting he had received at his hands. Referring to his rival's answer to the interrogatory on the admission of slave states, he turned to Lincoln and said:

> I ask you, will you vote to admit Kansas into the Union, with just such a constitution as her people want, with slavery or without as they shall determine? He will not answer. ("He's afraid," and cheers.) I have put that question to him time and time again, and have not been able to get an answer out of him. I ask you again, Lincoln, will you vote to admit New Mexico when she has the requisite population with such a constitution as her people adopt, either recognizing slavery or not as they shall determine? He will not answer. . .
>
> He will not answer these questions in reference to any territory now in existence; but says, that if Congress should prohibit slavery in a territory, and when its people asked for admission as a state, they should adopt slavery as one of their institutions, that he supposes he would have to let it come in. . . I ask you whether there is an intelligent man in America who does not believe, that that answer was made for the purpose of concealing what he intended to do.[24]

This tactic brought out delighted laughter and, in spite of Douglas' request for silence, repeated cheers from the Democrats in the audience. But there was more in store. There was the Negro equality issue, the Little Giant's trump card. This he now played with even greater effect than previously. Lincoln, in his opening speech, had traced his stand on the equality issue, but had quoted only from his Ottawa statements as substantiation of his position.

Douglas now quoted from Lincoln's Chicago speech, emphasizing such statements as: "I should like to know, if taking this old Declaration of Independence, which declares that all men are equal upon principle, and making exceptions to it, where will it stop?" and "Let us discard all this quibbling about this man and the other man — this race and that race and the other race being inferior, and therefore they must be placed in an inferior position." Douglas asked: "Did old Giddings, when he came down among you four years ago, preach more radical Abolitionism than that? Did Lovejoy, or Lloyd Garrison, or Wendell Phillips, or Fred. Douglass, ever take higher Abolition grounds than that?"[25]

After this, Douglas began to touch on the moral aspects of slavery, attempting to turn the tables on Lincoln by showing that the practical result of the latter's policy would be the genocide of the Negro race:

> Mr. Lincoln thinks that it is his duty to preach a crusade in the free states, against slavery, because it is a crime, as he believes, and ought to be extinguished; and because the people of the slave states will never abolish it. How is he going to abolish it? Down in the southern part of the state he takes the ground openly that he will not interfere with slavery where it exists, and says that he is not now and never was in favor of interfering with slavery where it exists in the states. Well, if he is not in favor of that, how does he expect to bring slavery in a course of ultimate extinction? . . .
>
> He first tells you that he would prohibit slavery everywhere in the territories. He would thus confine slavery within its present limits. When he thus gets it confined, and surrounded, so that it cannot spread, the natural laws of increase will go on until the negroes will be so plenty that they cannot live on the soil. He will hem them in until starvation seizes them, and by starving them to death, he will put slavery in the course of ultimate extinction. If he is not going to interfere with slavery in the states, but intends to interfere and prohibit it in the territories, and thus smother slavery out, it naturally follows, that he can extinguish it only by extinguishing the negro race, for his policy would drive them to starvation. This is the humane and Christian remedy that he proposes for the great crime of slavery.[26]

He followed this amazing argument with his reasons for not committing himself on the morality of slavery:

> He tells you that I will not argue the question of whether slavery is right or wrong. I tell you why I will not do it. I

hold that under the Constitution of the United States, each
state of this Union has a right to do as it pleases on the
subject of slavery. In Illinois we have exercised the sovereign
right by prohibiting slavery within our own limits. I approve
of that line of policy. We have performed our whole duty in
Illinois. We have gone as far as we have a right to go under
the Constitution of our common country. It is none of our
business whether slavery exists in Missouri or not. . . Hence
I do not choose to occupy the time allotted to me in discussing a question that we have no right to act upon.[27]

Using this argument as a point of departure he took the
position that Lincoln was concerning himself with irremediable
irrelevancies and not with important issues:

I thought that you desired to hear us upon those questions
coming within our constitutional power of action. Lincoln
will not discuss these. What one question has he discussed
that comes within the power or calls for the action or interference of an United States Senator? He is going to discuss
the rightfulness of slavery when Congress cannot act upon it
either way. He wishes to discuss the merits of the Dred Scott
decision when, under the Constitution, a Senator has no
right to interfere with the decision of judicial tribunals. . .
From that decision there is no appeal this side of Heaven.

Yet, Mr. Lincoln says he is going to reverse that decision.
By what tribunal will he reverse it? Will he appeal to a
mob? . . . He . . . keeps appealing each day from the Supreme
Court of the United States to political meetings in the country. (Laughter.)[28]

He rounded off this argument by ridiculing Lincoln to the
further laughter and amusement of the crowd:

When I used to practice law with Lincoln, I never knew
him to be beat in a case that he did not get mad at the Judge
and talk about appealing; and when I got beat I generally
thought the court was wrong, but I never dreamed of going
out of the court house and making a stump speech to the
people against the Judge, merely because I had found out
that I did not know the law as well as he did.[29]

Turning again to his theory that popular sovereignty was
not incompatible with the Dred Scott decision, he cast Lincoln
and the Washington *Union* into the roles of partners seeking
his defeat. From the tenor of his argument, we are made aware

that his Freeport Doctrine was already beginning to stir up unfavorable repercussions:

> Neither Mr. Lincoln or the Washington *Union* like my Freeport speech on that subject. The *Union,* in a late number, has been reading me out of the Democratic party. . .
>
> It says that my Freeport speech is not Democratic, and that I was not a Democrat in 1854 or in 1850! Now, is not that funny? Think that the author of the Kansas and Nebraska Bill was not a Democrat when he introduced it. The *Union* says I was not a sound Democrat in 1850, nor in 1854, nor in 1856, nor am I in 1858. . .
>
> The *Union,* in advocating the claims of Lincoln over me to the Senate, lays down two unpardonable heresies which it says I advocate. The first, is the right of the people of a territory, the same as a state, to decide for themselves the question whether slavery shall exist within their limits . . . and the second is, that a constitution shall be submitted to the people of a territory for its adoption or rejection before their admission as a state under it. . . Thus you find this little corrupt gang who control the *Union,* wish to elect Lincoln in preference to me — because, as they say, of these two heresies which I support.[30]

FOREVER DIVIDED

As Douglas neared the end of his allotted time he offered his frequently-repeated solution for the maintenance of peace among the states:

> Let each state mind its own business and let its neighbors alone, and there will be no trouble on this question. If we will stand by that priniple, then Mr. Lincoln will find that this republic can exist forever divided into free and slave states, as our fathers made it.[31]

That word "forever" was the key to Douglas' outlook on the future of the Union. Although Douglas had used this expression in the Jonesboro debate, this was the first time that Lincoln took special note of it and would grasp the opportunity it offered to contrast their philosophies of free government. Continuing, Douglas closed his speech with another version of his moral principles:

> It does not become Mr. Lincoln, or anybody else, to tell

the people of Kentucky that they have no consciences, that they are living in a state of iniquity, and that they are cherishing an institution to their bosoms in violation of the law of God. Better for him to adopt the doctrine of "judge not lest ye be judged." Let him perform his own duty at home, and he will have a better fate in the future.

I think there are objects of charity enough in the free states to excite the sympathies and open the pockets of all the benevolence we have amongst us, without going abroad in search of negroes, of whose condition we know nothing. We have enough objects of charity at home, and it is our duty to take care of our own poor, and our own suffering, before we go abroad to intermeddle with other people's business.[32]

After the applause for Douglas died down, Lincoln began his rejoinder. His first blow was directed at the opening given him by Douglas' use of the word "forever":

I wish to return Judge Douglas my profound thanks for his public annunciation here to-day, to be put on record, that his system of policy in regard to the institution of slavery *contemplates that it shall last forever*. We are getting a little nearer the true issue of this controversy, and I am profoundly grateful for this one sentence.

Judge Douglas asks you "why cannot the institution of slavery, or rather, why cannot the nation, part slave and part free, continue as our fathers made it *forever*?" In the first place, I insist that our fathers *did not* make this nation half slave and half free, or part slave and part free. I insist that they found the institution of slavery existing here. They did not make it so, but they left it so because they knew of no way to get rid of it at that time. When Judge Douglas undertakes to say that as a matter of choice the fathers of the government made this nation part slave and part free, *he assumes what is historically a falsehood*.

More than that; when the fathers of the government cut off the source of slavery by the abolition of the slave trade, and adopted a system of restricting it from the new territories where it had not existed, I maintain that they placed it where they understood, and all sensible men understood, it was in the course of ultimate extinction; and when Judge Douglas asks me why it cannot continue as our fathers made it, I ask him why he and his friends could not let it remain as our fathers made it?[33]

Lincoln was in fine form now. He felt he had the situation well in hand, and proceeded to slash at Douglas' arguments with banter, wit and sarcasm. Sitting on the platform was William H. Carlin, whose father had served as Governor and who was running for the state Senate as an Administration man. Lincoln saw an opportunity to dramatize the quarrel between the Douglasites and the Danites, which the Little Giant had tried to turn in his favor, and gave the crowd a hilarious time with it:

> The Judge has informed me, or informed this audience, that the Washington *Union* is laboring for my election to the United States Senate. (Cheers and laughter.) That is news to me — not very ungrateful news either.

Then turning to Carlin he said: "I hope that Carlin will be elected to the State Senate and will vote for me." When Carlin shook his head negatively he continued:

> Carlin don't fall in, I perceive, and I suppose he will not do much for me (Laughter.), but I am glad of all the support I can get anywhere, if I can get it without practicing any deception to obtain it. In respect to this large portion of Judge Douglas' speech, in which he tries to show that in the controversy between himself and the administration party he is in the right, I do not feel myself at all competent or inclined to answer him. I say to him, "Give it to them (Laughter.) — give it to them just all you can" (Renewed laughter and cheers.) — and, on the other hand, I say to Carlin . . . "Give it to Douglas (Roars of laughter.) — just pour it into him." (Cheers and laughter — "good for you," "Hurrah for Lincoln.")[34]

As Lincoln proceeded, he seemed to give the impression that he held his opponent in his strong grasp and was shaking him and his arguments to shreds:

> Now in regard to this matter of the Dred Scott decision, I wish to say a word or two. . . the Judge will not say whether, if a decision is made holding that the people of the *states* cannot exclude slavery, he will support it or not. . . I reminded him that at Galesburg he had said the Judges had expressly declared the contrary, and you remember that in my opening speech I told him I had the book containing that decision here, and I would thank him to lay his finger

on the place where any such thing was said. He has occupied
his hour and a half, and he has not ventured to try to sustain
his assertion. *He never will.*

But he is desirous of knowing how we are going to reverse
the Dred Scott decision. Judge Douglas ought to know
how. . . Didn't Judge Douglas find a way to reverse the decision of our Supreme Court, when it decided that Carlin's
father — old Governor Carlin — had not the constitutional
power to remove a Secretary of State? (Great cheering and
laughter.) Did he not appeal to the "MOBS" as he calls them?
Did he not make speeches in the lobby to show how villainous
that decision was, and how it ought to be overthrown? Did
he not succeed too in getting an act passed by the legislature
to have it overthrown? And didn't he himself sit down on
that bench as one of the five added judges, who were to over-
slaugh the four old ones — getting his name of "Judge" in
that way and no other? (Thundering cheers and laughter.)

If there is a villainy in using disrespect or making opposition to Supreme Court decisions, I commend it to Judge
Douglas' earnest consideration. (Cheers and laughter.) I know
of no man in the state of Illinois who ought to know so well
about *how much* villainy it takes to oppose a decision of the
Supreme Court, as our honorable friend, Stephen A. Douglas.
(Long continued applause.)[35]

The crowd was enjoying itself immensely. The laughter and
cheers mounted, as Lincoln turned his fire from the Supreme
Court decision to the target of popular sovereignty:

Judge Douglas has sung paeans to his "popular sovereignty"
doctrine until his Supreme Court cooperating with him has
squatted his squatter sovereignty out. He has at last invented
this sort of *do nothing sovereignty* — (Renewed laughter.) —
that the people may exclude slavery by a sort of "sovereignty"
that is exercised by doing nothing at all. (Continued laughter.) Is not that running his popular sovereignty down aw-
fully? (Laughter.) Has it not got down as thin as the homoeo-
pathic soup that was made by boiling the shadow of a pigeon
that had starved to death? (Roars of laughter and cheering.)
But at last, when it is brought to the test of close reasoning, there is not even that thin decoction of it left. It is a
presumption impossible in the domain of thought. It is precisely no other than the putting of that most unphilosophi-
cal proposition, that two bodies may occupy the same space
at the same time. The Dred Scott decision covers the whole

ground, and while it occupies it, there is no room even for
the shadow of a starved pigeon to occupy the same ground.
(Great cheering and laughter.)[36]

At this point, some one on the platform called out: "Your
time is almost out." But voices from the crowd shouted back:
"Go on, go on; we'll listen all day."

Evidently pleased, Lincoln said, "Well, I'll talk to you a
little longer," and continued:

> Now, in relation to my not having said anything about
> the quotation from the Chicago speech: He thinks that it
> is a terrible subject for me to handle. Why, gentlemen, I
> can show you that — the substance of the Chicago speech I
> delivered two years ago in "Egypt," as he calls it. It was
> down at Springfield. That speech is here in this book, and
> I could turn to it and read it to you but for the lack of time.
> I have not now the time to read it.[37]

"Read it, read it," shouted the crowd. But Lincoln, taking
a leaf from Shakespeare's Mark Antony, replied, "No, gentlemen, I am obliged to use discretion in disposing most advan-
tageously of my brief time." He contented himself with saying, "I maintain that you may take Judge Douglas' quotations
from my Chicago speech, and from my Charleston speech, and
the Galesburg speech, — in his speech to-day, and compare
them over, and I am willing to trust them with you upon his
proposition that they show rascality or double dealing. I deny
that they do." Evidently this satisfied the crowd because it
broke into protracted applause.[38]

Lincoln was not disposed to leave any point untouched. He
had only five minutes left, but with terrier persistence he took
after Douglas on the "forgery" charge and the Little Giant's
defense to it:

> The Judge does not seem at all disposed to have peace, but
> I find he is disposed to have a personal warfare with me. He
> says that my oath would not be taken against the bare word
> of Charles H. Lanphier or Thomas L. Harris. Well, that is
> altogether a matter of opinion...
> He says, when he discovered there was a mistake in that
> case, he came forward magnanimously, without my calling
> his attention to it, and explained it. I will tell you how he
> became so magnanimous. When the newspapers of our side

had discovered and published it, and put it beyond his power
to deny it, then he came forward and made a virtue of necessity by acknowledging it.

Now he argues that all the point there was in those resolutions, although never passed at Springfield, is retained by
their being passed at other localities. Is that true? He said I
had a hand in passing them, in his opening speech — that I
was in the convention and helped to pass them. Do the resolutions touch me at all? It strikes me there is some difference
between holding a man responsible for an act which he *has
not* done, and holding him responsible for an act that he
has done. You will judge whether there is any difference in
the *"spots."* And he has taken credit for great magnanimity
in coming forward and acknowledging what is proved on him
beyond even the capacity of Judge Douglas to deny, and he
has more capacity in that way than any other living man.[39]

The reference to "spots," as well as to Douglas' reputation,
was fully appreciated by the crowd, and was greeted by laughter and cheers. This was the first time in the course of the
debates that Lincoln had used the odious word "spots" for his
own purposes.

Then he wants to know why I won't withdraw the charge
in regard to a conspiracy to make slavery national, as he has
withdrawn the one he made. May it please his worship, I will
withdraw it *when it is proven false on me as that was proved
false on him.* I will add a little more than that. I will withdraw it whenever a reasonable man shall be brought to believe that the charge is not true.[40]

Before closing, Lincoln touched on Douglas' charges on the
Dred Scott case. "He says that I say the *Democratic* owners of
Dred Scott got up the case. I never did say that. I defy Judge
Douglas to show that I ever said so for *I never uttered it.*"[41]

As he said this, one of Douglas' reporters gesticulated affirmatively at him. To this Lincoln answered, "I don't care
if your hireling does say I did, I tell you myself that *I never
said the 'Democratic' owners of Dred Scott got up* the case."
His handling of this incident was greeted with loud approval,
and Lincoln clinched his point as his time ended.

I have never pretended to know whether Dred Scott's
owners were Democrats or Abolitionists, or Free Soilers or
Border Ruffians. I have said that there is evidence about the

case tending to show that it was a made-up case, for the purpose of getting that decision. I have said that that evidence was very strong in the fact that when Dred Scott was declared to be a slave, the owner of him made him free, showing that he had had the case tried and the question settled for such use as could be made of that decision; he cared nothing about the property thus declared to be his by that decision. But my time is out and I can say no more.[42]

A CARL SCHURZ PERSPECTIVE

Though the debate was over, the excitement and festivities continued. Bands and parades, speechmaking and torchlight processions enlivened Quincy throughout the evening, and it was not until eleven o'clock that the streets of the little town became quiet.

One of the speechmakers was Carl Schurz, the brilliant young German from Wisconsin, who was to become famous in the political life of the country as a United States Senator and subsequently as Secretary of the Interior.

Schurz was in Illinois at the request of the Republican Central Committee in order to win over the German vote. Quincy had a sizable German population, and it crowded the courthouse to capacity to hear him speak. Schurz was only twenty-nine years of age, but he had already demonstrated that he was a powerful orator as well as a keen observer. A great admirer of Lincoln, he had met his idol on the train to Quincy. Lincoln had greeted him with such "off-hand cordiality" and "talked in so simple and familiar a strain," that Schurz felt "that I had known him all my life and we had long been close friends."[43]

In his *Reminiscences* he gives descriptions of Lincoln and Douglas, and of the general scene of the debate, that are vivid and striking. He was startled by Lincoln's height, and describes how, although he was over six feet tall himself, he had to throw his head backward in order to look into Lincoln's eyes when he stood near him. He portrays the scene on the train with the lank, skinny, ungainly Lincoln in his ill-fitting "store" clothes, carrying on his left arm his gray woolen shawl, and in his left hand his cotton umbrella and worn satchel, so that his right hand might be free for a round of handshaking that seemed to be unending. Though in Washington and in the West he had seen several public men of rough appearance, he had chanced upon "none whose look seemed quite so uncouth not to say grotesque, as Lincoln's."[44]

Schurz was seated on the platform during the debate and was able to observe things closely. He often turned to look at Douglas while Lincoln was speaking, and noticed that "a contemptuous smile now and then flitted across his lips." He then goes on to say: "When he arose, the tough parliamentary gladiator, he tossed his mane with an air of overbearing superiority, of threatening defiance, as if to say: 'How dare anyone stand up against me.' "[45]

Schurz also noticed that Douglas' face "seemed a little puffy" and repeated the common gossip that Douglas had been drinking. The Republican papers were not backward in carrying this "news." The reporter of the *Missouri Democrat*, a Republican paper despite its name, wrote: "Douglas looked very much the worse for wear. Bad whisky and the wear and tear of conscience have had their effect. . . Even in his manner of address a great difference is perceptible between Douglas four months ago and Douglas now. He speaks very slowly — making a distinct pause at the end of each word." Though he claimed that he did not like to accuse Lincoln of glorying in human misery, he was of the opinion that Old Abe "felt encouraged by the disconsolate appearance of his antagonist."[46]

The Republicans were highly satisfied with Lincoln's performance. One paper, the Quincy *Whig* wrote:

> The agent who sells photographic likenesses of Judge Douglas was in the City on Wednesday, hawking them through the crowd during the speeches. While Mr. Lincoln was closing the debate, a gentleman asked him if he was not willing to sell his pictures at a discount now? He said that he was — that the price was 75 cents when Douglas was speaking — that they had been reduced to 60 cents, and that he thought he would be compelled to reduce them to 25 cents before Lincoln got through!
>
> We don't believe there was a Douglasite in Quincy who had the remotest desire to buy a picture when Lincoln had concluded his half hour's speech.[47]

To the Democrats, of course, Douglas had overshadowed his opponent. The *Missouri Republican* (Democratic) characterized the Republicans present as a trained claque and compared their responses unfavorably with the spontaneous reactions of the Douglasites:

> The enthusiasm which greeted Douglas while he was speaking and when he had concluded, was so unlike the shouts of the Lincoln trained band that our hearts rejoiced at the discomfiture of the enemy. These latter, instructed to shout, did so at all times, with and without reason, so that during the closing half hour there was such a din and confusion that I think it very doubtful if even the tall Sucker was able to hear himself think.[48]

The partisan press contended with each other on even such trivialities as the size and impressiveness of the parades and the displays. The boast of the *Chicago Times* that Douglas had been "received by one of the most extensive and brilliant torch-light processions ever witnessed" was belittled by the *Whig* with the statement that "the thing was a fizzle; about fifty boys carried the torches."[49] But even the prejudiced Schurz was forced to admit that "on the whole, the Democratic displays were much more elaborate and gorgeous than those of the Republicans, because" — and he repeated another bit of gossip — "Douglas had plenty of money to spend for such things."[50]

CHAPTER 13

These Poor Tongues: The Alton Debate

With the final debate to be held at Alton only two days later, both candidates and their retinues boarded the steamboat *City of Louisiana* the next day for their destination. Alton was about 115 miles downstream from Quincy and only about twenty miles above St. Louis. Like Quincy, it was situated on a bluff, and like its sister city was a lively little place, with a newly-built town hall, which was to be the site of the debate. This was the town where, early in its history twenty-one years before, the abolitionist editor Elijah Lovejoy had been murdered by a mob and his press thrown into the Mississippi River. Madison County, in which it was situated, had a large population of Old Line Whigs, and was therefore one of the areas of crucial importance in the election.

The *City of Louisiana* docked at Alton at five o'clock in the morning after a slow and majestic trip. It was a lordly boat, 250 feet long, but not so fast as the *White Cloud,* a 200-footer, which brought a crowd of Missourians up from St. Louis in about two and a half hours. One can well imagine the excitement on board as the partisans of both men engaged in heated and uproarious controversy, fortifying their arguments with fuel from the ship's bar. It is doubtful that either Lincoln or Douglas got much sleep that night.

On their arrival, Lincoln repaired to the Franklin House and Douglas to the Alton House, where they received admirers and well-wishers.

A half-fare excursion train of the Chicago, Alton, and St. Louis Railroad, publicized by both the Democratic and Republican papers, left Springfield at 6:30 in the morning, and after picking up passengers along the way, arrived at Alton at 10:30 A.M. with eight fully-loaded cars. On the train were the Springfield cadets, of which Lincoln's eldest son Robert was a member, and Merritt's Cornet Band and also Mrs. Lincoln, to be present for the first time at one of the debates.

Mary Lincoln evidently was not too sanguine of her husband's prospects in the campaign, because Gustav Koerner, one of the leading German politicians of Illinois describes how he found Lincoln in despondent mood, and was greeted with "Let us go and see Mary." Koerner had known Mary Todd before she was married, and when Lincoln said, "Now, tell Mary what you think of our chances," he assured her that Abe would carry the state by popular vote, and also win in the Legislature despite the unequal apportionment of seats.[1]

While Lincoln and Douglas were receiving at their respective hotels, the noisy crowds were milling through the city. Both sides had agreed, in planning the arrangements, that "the reception of Messrs. Douglas and Lincoln shall be a quiet one, [with] no public display," and that "no banner or motto, except national colors, shall be allowed on the speakers' stand."[2] Despite these provisions the Springfield Cadets marched and Merritt's Cornet Band played, and although there was no Democratic or Republican procession as such, the crowds provided their own excitement, and mottoed banners flapped in the wind in front of stores and across the streets. The perceptive and literate reporter of the Alton *Daily Courier* described the crowd in vivid language:

> By the hour of 12, the great American people had taken possession of the city. It went up and down the streets — it hurrahed for Lincoln and hurrahed for Douglas — it crowded the auction rooms — it thronged the stores of our merchants — it gathered on the street corners and discussed politics — it shook its fists and talked loudly — it mounted boxes and cried the virtues of Pain Killer — it mustered to the eating saloons and did not forget the drinking saloons — it was here, there and everywhere, asserting its privileges and maintaining its rights.[3]

The Democrats climaxed their efforts on the field of slogan-
ning with "a grand, magnificent, superb right-royal banner,"
suspended across one of the principal streets, bearing the words:

"POPULAR SOVEREIGNTY!
STEPHEN A. DOUGLAS, THE PEOPLE'S CHOICE"

Two large Republican banners proclaimed: "LINCOLN NOT
TROTTED OUT YET!" and "TOO LATE FOR THE
MILKING," while another in rhymed doggerel read:

"FREE TERRITORIES AND FREE MEN,
FREE PULPITS AND FREE PREACHERS,
FREE PRESS AND FREE PEN,
FREE SCHOOLS AND FREE TEACHERS."

Douglas' cannon was also present, "blazing away in the most
obstreperous manner, to impress the Altonians with a proper
respect due the 'big gun' who was its master."

Long before the scheduled time of 1:30 P.M. the crowd
began to gather in front of the speakers' stand. Numbering
about 5,000, it was, except for the debate at Jonesboro, the
smallest gathering of the seven meetings, despite the influx
of visitors who had come from nearby areas and even from
Kentucky. But in contrast to the lethargic atmosphere of
Jonesboro, the spirit at Alton was enthusiastic and infectious.
The weather was pleasant, though the morning had started
cloudy and had threatened rain, and the crowd waited good-
humoredly for the proceedings to begin.

The speakers' platform had been erected on the south side
of the grand new city hall. This building, magnificent for such
a small town, no longer stands, having been razed by fire a few
years after the debate. Today its site is a small public square,
bordering on a parking lot. Only an obscure plaque commem-
orates the debate; there is no statue, no ambitious monument
to stir the citizens to pride in their city's glorious moment in
history.

DANITE HECKLER

Both debaters were on hand promptly; the Lincolns arriving after dining at the Franklin Hotel with Senator Trumbull
and reporters Horace White and Robert Hitt. It was close to
2:00, however, before the debate got under way, what with

the preliminary handshaking and the bustle of seating the officials and the guests. Douglas was the opening speaker, but no sooner had he been introduced than "a fat, burly-looking man, with frizzly-looking side-boards on his cheeks," sprang up to heckle him. He was Dr. Thomas Hope, the Danite candidate for Congress. A short colloquy followed, in which the Little Giant displayed his skill in disposing of a heckler with dispatch:

> DR. HOPE — Judge, before you commence speaking, allow me to ask you a question.
> SENATOR DOUGLAS — If you will not occupy too much of my time.
> DR. HOPE — Only an instant.
> SENATOR DOUGLAS — What is your question?
> DR. HOPE — Do you believe that the territorial legislatures ought to pass laws to protect slavery in the territories?
> SENATOR DOUGLAS — You will get an answer in the course of my remarks. (Applause.)[4]

Though his voice was in very bad shape, and the strain of the campaign could be read on his face, the Little Giant was determined to put forth a supreme effort in this final meeting. His plan called for emphasis on two major objectives: winning the Whigs, and destroying the effectiveness of Lincoln's appeal on the moral issues. Disturbed also by reports he was receiving of the reaction to his Freeport Doctrine in the South, and conscious of the presence of Missourians and Kentuckians in the audience, he decided to devote some attention to convincing the South of the rightness of his stand, and of recognizing his leadership as a solution to their problems.

With characteristic courage, he started off by reaffirming the position he had stated at Quincy. "First," he said, "in regard to his doctrine that this government was in violation of the law of God which says, that a house divided against itself cannot stand, I repudiated it as a slander upon the immortal framers of our Constitution. I then said, have often repeated, and now again assert, that in my opinion this government can endure forever, divided into free and slave states as our fathers made it."[5]

In the two days since Quincy he had devised an ingenious argument to justify his thesis:

> Suppose the doctrine advocated by Mr. Lincoln and the Abolitionists of this day had prevailed when the Constitu-

tion was made, what would have been the result? Imagine
for a moment that Mr. Lincoln had been a member of the
convention that framed the Constitution of the United States,
and that when its members were about to sign that wonderful document, he had arisen in that convention as he did at
Springfield this summer, and addressing himself to the President, had said "a house divided against itself cannot stand
(Laughter.); this government divided into free and slave states
cannot endure, they must all be free or all be slave, they must
all be one thing or all the other, otherwise, it is a violation
of the law of God, and cannot continue to exist. . ."

Suppose Mr. Lincoln had convinced that body of sages, that
that doctrine was sound, what would have been the result?
Remember that the Union was then composed of thirteen
states, twelve of which were slaveholding and one free. Do
you think that the one free state would have outvoted the
twelve slaveholding states, and thus have secured the abolition
of slavery? On the other hand, would not the twelve slaveholding states have outvoted the one free state, and thus have
fastened slavery, by a constitutional provision, on every foot
of the American Republic forever?

You see that if this Abolition doctrine of Mr. Lincoln had
prevailed when the government was made, it would have
established slavery as a permanent institution, in all the
states whether they wanted it or not, and the question for us
to determine in Illinois now as one of the free states is,
whether or not we are willing, having become the majority
section, to enforce a doctrine on the minority, which we
would have resisted with our heart's blood had it been attempted on us when we were in a minority.

This sally brought enthusiastic cheers from the audience,
and Douglas pursued the argument further:

How has the South lost her power as the majority section
in this Union, and how have the free states gained it, except
under the operation of that principle which declares the right
of the people of each state and each territory to form and
regulate their domestic institutions in their own way . . . It
was under that principle that one half of the slaveholding
states became free; it was under that principle that the number of free states increased until from being one out of
twelve states, we have grown to be the majority of states of
the whole Union, with the power to control the House of
Representatives and Senate, and the power, consequently, to

elect a President by Northern votes without the aid of a Southern state.

Having obtained this power under the operation of that great principle, are you now prepared to abandon the principle and declare that merely because we have the power you will wage a war against the Southern states and their institutions until you force them to abolish slavery everywhere. ("No, never," and great applause.)[6]

The Little Giant assailed Lincoln for asserting that he would vote for the admission of a state into the Union if it chose slavery provided it had been free from it as a territory. This was equivocation designed to fool the Old Line Whigs, shouted Douglas. Why did not Lincoln commit himself on the real instead of a hypothetical situation? "He invents a case which does not exist, and cannot exist under this government, and answers it," he barked, "but he will not answer the question I put to him in connection with any of the territories now in existence."[7]

Here Douglas led into the matter of the Lecompton Constitution and his successful opposition to it. "I repeat," he stated, "what I have said in every speech I have made in Illinois, that I fought the Lecompton Constitution to its death, not because of the slavery clause in it, but because it was not the act and deed of the people of Kansas." With an eye to its effect on the South, he analyzed his stand:

I hold that there is no power on earth, under our system of government, which has the right to force a constitution upon an unwilling people. Suppose there had been a majority of ten to one in favor of slavery in Kansas, and suppose there had been an Abolition President, and an Abolition administration, and by some means the Abolitionists succeeded in forcing an Abolition constitution on those slaveholding people, would the people of the South have submitted to that act for one instant? Well, if you of the South would not have submitted to it a day, how can you, as fair, honorable and honest men insist on putting a slave constitution on a people who desire a free state? Your safety and ours depend upon both of us acting in good faith, and living up to that great principle which asserts the right of every people to form and regulate their domestic institutions to suit themselves, subject only to the Constitution of the United States.

Most of the men who denounced my course on the Lecompton question, objected to it not because I was not right, but because they thought it expedient at that time, for the sake of keeping the party together, to do wrong. I never knew the Democratic party to violate any one of its principles out of policy or expediency, that it did not pay the debt with sorrow. There is no safety or success for our party unless we always do right, and trust the consequences to God and the people. I chose not to depart from principle for the sake of expediency in the Lecompton question, and I never intend to do it on that or any other question. . . .[8]

Douglas then proceeded to show that Buchanan and the southern extremists were hurting the Democratic Party, and really did not represent the true sentiment of the South. At the same time that he sought to awaken sympathy for being unjustly persecuted by the Administration, he endeavored to establish his image as the true leader of the South's aspirations:

In this state, every postmaster, every route agent, every collector of the ports, and every federal office holder, forfeits his head the moment he expresses a preference for the Democratic candidates against Lincoln and his Abolition associates. ("That's so," and cheers.) A Democratic administration which we helped to bring into power, deems it consistent with its fidelity to principle and its regard to duty, to wield its power in this state in behalf of the Republican Abolition candidates in every county and every congressional district against the Democratic party. . .

I have no personal difficulties with Mr. Buchanan or his cabinet. He chose to make certain recommendations to Congress as he had a right to do on the Lecompton question. I could not vote in favor of them. I had as much right to judge for myself how I should vote as he had how he should recommend. He undertook to say to me, if you do not vote as I tell you, I will take off the heads of your friends. (Laughter.) I replied to him, "You did not elect me, I represent Illinois and I am accountable to Illinois, as my constituency, and to God, but not to the President or to any other power on earth." ("Good, good," and vociferous applause.) . . .

I hold that an attempt to control the Senate on the part of the executive is subversive of the principles of our Constitution. ("That's right.") . . . In matters of legislation the President has a veto on the action of the Senate, and in appointments and treaties the Senate has a veto on the President. He has no more right to tell me how I shall vote on his appointments than I have to tell him whether he shall veto or approve a bill that the Senate has passed. Whenever you recognize the right of the executive to say to a Senator, "do this, or I will take off the heads of your friends," you convert this government from a republic into a depotism. . . I resisted this invasion of the constitutional rights of a Senator, and I intend to resist it as long as I have a voice to speak, or a vote to give.

Yet, Mr. Buchanan cannot provoke me to abandon one iota of Democratic principles out of revenge or hostility to his course. ("Good, good, three cheers for Douglas.") I stand by the platform of the Democratic party, and by its organization, and support its nominees. If there are any who choose to bolt, the fact only shows that they are not as good Democrats as I am. ("That's so," "good," and applause.)[9]

BUCHANAN AND JEFF DAVIS

The Washington *Union* was now reading him out of the Democratic Party, said the Little Giant. Why? Simply because he had introduced legislation which had incorporated a principle approved by great figures of both parties, Democratic and Whig, including Henry Clay. "Let me read what James Buchanan said on that point when he accepted the Democratic nomination for the Presidency in 1856," said Douglas, and he quoted Buchanan's support of "the recent legislation [which] declared that the people of a territory like those of a state, shall decide for themselves *whether slavery shall or shall not exist within their limits.*"

As he thundered out the last words, he turned to Dr. Hope — the Danite, the Administration man:

> Dr. Hope will there find my answer to the question he propounded to me before I commenced speaking. (Vociferous shouts of applause.) Of course no man will consider it an answer, who is outside of the Democratic organization, bolts Democratic nominations, and indirectly aids to put Abolitionists into power over Democrats. But whether Dr. Hope considers it an answer or not, every fair minded man will see that James Buchanan has answered the question.[10]

To show that this position was in harmony with his Freeport Doctrine, Douglas offered what he believed to be a crushing argument:

I . . . say that while under the decision of the Supreme
Court, as recorded in the opinion of Chief Justice Taney,
slaves are property like all other property and can be carried
into territory of the United States the same as any other
description of property, yet when you get them there they
are subject to the local law of the territory just like all other
property. You will find in a recent speech delivered by that
able and eloquent statesman, Hon. Jefferson Davis, at Bangor,
Maine, that he took the same view of this subject that I did
in my Freeport speech.[11]

Triumphantly the Little Giant quoted from the speech
which Jefferson Davis had delivered in Maine a few weeks
before, but the text of which he had only recently received. It
supported the theory of popular sovereignty completely. "The
whole South are rallying to the support of the doctrine," Douglas declared, little knowing that Davis would soon abandon
it:

It is the principle on which James Buchanan was made
President. . . I will never violate or abandon that doctrine
if I have to stand alone. . . ("Hurrah for Douglas.") I have
resisted the blandishments and threats of power . . . and have
stood immovably for that principle, fighting for it when
assailed by Northern mobs, or threatened by Southern hostility. ("That's the truth," and cheers.) I have defended it
against whoever assails it, and I will follow it wherever its
logical conclusions lead me. ("So will we allow," "Hurrah for
Douglas.")[12]

As his time began to run out, Douglas closed by posing as
the defender of the South against an encroaching Northern
sectionalism:

The moment the North obtained the majority in the House
and Senate by the admission of California, and could elect
a President without the aid of Southern votes, that moment
ambitious Northern men formed a scheme to excite the North
against the South, and make the people be governed in their
votes by geographical lines, thinking that the North, being
the stronger section, would outvote the South, and consequently they, the leaders, would ride into office on a sectional
hobby. I am told that my hour is out. It was very short.[13]

Lincoln began his reply by titillating the audience with a
humorous sally at Douglas' fight with the Administration. To

Long Abe this was a spurious issue, and the way to deflate it was to subject it to ridicule. Besides, he was now enjoying the debate with Douglas to the full. He felt he had mastered the Little Giant, and he could therefore afford to be expansive:

> I have been somewhat, in my own mind, complimented by a large portion of Judge Douglas' speech — I mean that portion which he devotes to the controversy between himself and the present administration. (Cheers and laughter.) This is the seventh time Judge Douglas and myself have met in these joint discussions, and he has been gradually improving in regard to his war with the administration. (Laughter, "That's so.")
>
> At Quincy, day before yesterday, he was a little more severe upon the administration than I had heard him upon any former occasion, and I took pains to compliment him for it. I then told him to "Give it to them with all the power he had;" and as some of them were present I told them I would be very much obliged if they would *give it to him* in about the same way. (Uproarious laughter and cheers.) I take it he has now vastly improved upon the attack he made then upon the administration. I flatter myself he has really taken my advice on this subject. All I can say now is to recommend to him and to them what I then commended — to prosecute the war against one another in the most vigorous manner. I say to them again — "Go it, husband! — Go it, bear!" (Great laughter.)[14]

Lincoln also could not resist taking a sharp dig at Douglas' reputation in Republican circles as an "artful dodger":

> There is one other thing I will mention before I leave this branch of the discussion — although I do not consider it much of my business, any way. He reads something from Mr. Buchanan, from which he undertakes to involve him in an inconsistency; and he gets something of a cheer for having done so. I would only remind the Judge that while he is very valiantly fighting for the Nebraska Bill and the repeal of the Missouri Compromise, it has been but a little while since he was the *valiant advocate* of the Missouri Compromise. (Cheers.) I want to know if Buchanan has not as much right to be inconsistent as Douglas has? (Loud applause and laughter; "Good, good!" "Hurrah for Lincoln!") Has Douglas the *exclusive right,* in this country, of being *on all sides of all questions?* Is nobody allowed that high privilege but him-

self? Is he to have an entire monopoly on that subject?
(Great laughter.)[15]

DEMOCRATIC CATCH-WORD

Getting down to the important issues, Lincoln addressed
himself to what he called Douglas' "beautiful fabrication" that
he wished "a perfect, social, and political equality between
the white and black races," — the charge that Douglas hoped
would cost Abe the votes of the former Whigs:

> Now . . . as Henry Clay has been alluded to, I desire to
> place myself, in connection with Mr. Clay, as nearly right
> before this people as may be. I am quite aware what the
> judge's object is here by all these allusions. He knows that
> we are before an audience having strong sympathies south-
> ward by relationship, place of birth and so on. He desires
> to place me in an extremely Abolition attitude.
>
> You have heard him frequently allude to my controversy
> with him in regard to the Declaration of Independence. I con-
> fess that I have had a struggle with Judge Douglas on that
> matter, and I will try briefly to place myself right in regard
> to it on this occasion. . .
>
> At Galesburg the other day, I said in answer to Judge
> Douglas, that three years ago there never had been a man,
> so far as I knew or believed, in the whole world, who had said
> that the Declaration of Independence did not include negroes
> in the term "all men." I re-assert it to-day. . .
>
> Do not let me be misunderstood. I know that more than
> three years ago there were men who, finding this assertion
> constantly in the way of their schemes to bring about the
> ascendancy and perpetuation of slavery, *denied the truth of
> it.* I know that Mr. Calhoun and all the politicians of his
> school denied the truth of the Declaration. I know that it
> ran along in the mouths of some Southern men for a period
> of years, ending at last in that shameful though rather forcible
> declaration of Pettit of Indiana, upon the floor of the United
> States Senate, that the Declaration of Independence was in
> that respect "a self-evident lie," rather than a self-evident
> truth.
>
> But I say, with a perfect knowledge of all this hawking
> at the Declaration without directly attacking it, that three
> years ago there never had lived a man who had ventured to
> assail it in the sneaking way of pretending to believe it and
> then asserting it did not include the negro. I believe the first

man who ever said it was Chief Justice Taney in the Dred Scott case, and the next to him was our friend Stephen A. Douglas. And now it has become the catch-word of the entire party.

When this new principle — this new proposition that no human being ever thought of three years ago, — is brought forward, *I combat* it as having an evil tendency, if not an evil design; I combat it as having a tendency to dehumanize the negro — to take away from him the right of ever striving to be a man. I combat it as being one of the thousand things constantly done in these days to prepare the public mind to make property, and nothing but property of the *negro in all the states of this Union*.[16]

Lincoln next took up Douglas' attack on the "house divided" issue. He quoted the words of his original statement, and said:

That extract and the sentiments expressed in it, have been extremely offensive to Judge Douglas. He has warred upon them as Satan does upon the Bible. (Laughter.) His perversions upon it are endless. Here now are my views upon it in brief.

I said we were now far into the fifth year since a policy was initiated with the avowed object and confident promise of putting an end to the slavery agitation. Is it not so? When that Nebraska Bill was brought forward four years ago last January, was it not for the "avowed object" of putting an end to the slavery agitation? . . . We were for a little while quiet on the troublesome thing and that very allaying plaster of Judge Douglas' stirred it up again. (Applause and laughter.) . . . In every speech you heard Judge Douglas make, until he got into this "imbroglio," as they call it, with the administration about the Lecompton Constitution, every speech on that Nebraska Bill was full of his felicitations that we were *just at the end* of the slavery agitation. The last tip of the last joint of the old serpent's tail was just drawing out of view. (Cheers and laughter.) But has it proved so? I have asserted that under that policy that agitation "has not only not ceased, but has constantly augmented". . .

It has been nothing but a living, creeping lie from the time of its introduction, till to-day. (Loud cheers.)[17]

Stop stirring things up, said Lincoln. Go back to the situation bequeathed by the founding fathers, who looked to slavery's eventual abolition. If there was any doubt about that, look at the Constitution. Where slavery was referred to, terminology other than "negro" or "slavery" was used.

To prove his point he quoted the three pertinent sections of the Constitution — prohibition of the slave trade, the three-fifths clause, and the reclamation of fugitive slaves:

> In all three of these places, covert language was used with a purpose, and that purpose was that in our Constitution, which it was hoped and is still hoped will endure forever — when it should be read by intelligent and patriotic men, after the institution of slavery had passed from among us — there should be nothing on the face of the great charter of liberty suggesting that such a thing as negro slavery had ever existed among us. This is part of the evidence that the fathers of the government expected and intended the institution of slavery to come to an end. . .
>
> It is not true that our fathers, as Judge Douglas assumes, made this government part slave and part free. Understand the sense in which he puts it. He assumes that slavery is a rightful thing within itself, — was introduced by the framers of the Constitution. The exact truth is, that they found the institution existing among us, and they left it as they found it. But in making the government they left this institution with many clear marks of disapprobation upon it. They found slavery among them and they left it among them because of the difficulty — the absolute impossibility of its immediate removal.
>
> And when Judge Douglas asks me why we cannot let it remain part slave and part free as the fathers of the government made [it], he asks a question based upon an assumption which is itself a falsehood. . . *I turn upon him and ask him why he could not let it alone?* I turn and ask him why was he driven to the necessity of introducing a *new policy* in regard to it? He has himself said he introduced a new policy. . . I ask you when he infers that I am in favor of setting the free and slave states at war, when the institution was placed in that attitude by those who made the Constitution, *did they make any war?* If we had no war out of it when thus placed, wherein is the ground of belief that we shall have war out of it if we return to that policy? Have we had any peace upon this matter springing from any other basis? I maintain that we have not. I have proposed nothing more than a return to the policy of the fathers.[18]

Turning from the serious for a moment, Lincoln injected a light note before proceeding to his next argument:

> You may say and Judge Douglas has intimated the same thing, that all this difficulty in regard to the institution of slavery is the mere agitation of office seekers and ambitious Northern politicians. He thinks we want to get "his place," I suppose. (Cheers and laughter.) I agree that there are office seekers amongst us. The Bible says somewhere that we are desperately selfish. I think we would have discovered that fact without the Bible. I do not claim that I am any less so than the average of men, but I do claim that I am not more selfish than Judge Douglas. (Roars of laughter and applause.)[19]

The laughter was short-lived, as Lincoln became serious again:

> But is it true that all the difficulty and agitation we have in regard to this institution of slavery springs from office-seeking — from the mere ambition of politicians? Does not this question make a disturbance outside of political circles? Does it not enter into the churches and rend them asunder? What divided the great Methodist Church into two parts, North and South? What has raised this constant disturbance in every Presbyterian General Assembly that meets? What disturbed the Unitarian Church in this very city two years ago? . . .
>
> Is this the work of politicians? Is that irresistible power which for fifty years has shaken the government and agitated the people to be stilled and subdued by pretending that it is an exceedingly simple thing, and we ought not to talk about it? If you will get everybody else to stop talking about it, I assure you I will quit before they have half done so.
>
> But where is the philosophy or statesmanship which assumes that you can quiet that disturbing element in our society which has disturbed us for more than half a century, which has been the only serious danger that has threatened our institutions — [and] . . . that we are to care nothing about it! I ask you if it is not a false philosophy? Is it not a false statesmanship that undertakes to build up a system of policy upon the basis of caring nothing about *the very thing that everybody does care the most about?*[20]

FREE WHITE SANCTUARY

Stating that Douglas was "but fighting a man of straw" on the issue that states could do as they pleased about slavery, Lincoln said:

> What I insist upon is, that the new territories shall be kept free from it while in the territorial condition. Judge Douglas assumes that we have no interest in them — that we have no right whatever to interfere. I think we have some interest. I think that as white men we have. Do we not wish for an outlet for our surplus population, if I may so express myself? Do we not feel an interest in getting to that outlet with such institutions as we would like to have prevail there?
>
> If *you* go to the territory opposed to slavery and another man comes upon the same ground with his slave, upon the assumption that the things are equal, it turns out that he has the equal right all his way and you have no part of it your way. If he goes in and makes it a slave territory, and by consequence a slave state, is it not time that those who desire to have it a free state were on equal ground?
>
> Let me suggest it in a different way. How many Democrats are there about here ("a thousand") who have left slave states and come into the free state of Illinois to get rid of the institution of slavery. (Another voice — "a thousand and one.") I reckon there are a thousand and one. (Laughter.) I will ask you, if the policy you are now advocating had prevailed when this country was in a territorial condition, where would you have gone to get rid of it? (Applause.) Where would you have found your free state or territory to go to? And when hereafter, for any cause, the people in this place shall desire to find new homes, if they wish to be rid of the institution, where will they find the place to go?
>
> Now irrespective of the moral aspect of this question as to whether there is a right or wrong in enslaving a negro, I am still in favor of our new territories being in such a condition that white men may find a home — may find some spot where they can better their condition — where they can settle upon new soil and better their condition in life. I am in favor of this not merely, for our own people who are born amongst us, but as an outlet for *free white people everywhere,* the world over — in which Hans and Baptiste and Patrick, and all other men from all the world, may find new homes and better their conditions in life.[21]

Having dealt with aspects of the problem which appealed to the practical interests of free whites, Lincoln turned to what he considered the important issue — the moral question:

> The real issue in this controversy — the one pressing upon every mind — is the sentiment on the part of one class that looks upon the institution of slavery *as a wrong,* and of another class that *does not* look upon it as a wrong. . . One of the methods of treating it as a wrong is to *make provision that it shall grow no larger. . .*
>
> You may have a wen or a cancer upon your person and not be able to cut it out lest you bleed to death; but surely it is no way to cure it, to engraft it and spread it over your whole body. That is no proper way of treating what you regard as a wrong.[22]

As Lincoln was swept along by his own earnestness, his words took on a simple eloquence:

> That is the real issue. That is the issue that will continue in this country when these poor tongues of Judge Douglas and myself shall be silent. It is the eternal struggle between these two principles — right and wrong — throughout the world. They are the two principles that have stood face to face from the beginning of time; and will ever continue to struggle. The one is the common right of humanity and the other the divine right of kings.
>
> It is the same principle in whatever shape it develops itself. It is the same spirit that says, "You work and toil and earn bread, and I'll eat it." No matter in what shape it comes, whether from the mouth of a king, who seeks to bestride the people of his own nation and live by the fruit of their labor, or from one race of men as an apology for enslaving another race, it is the same tyrannical principle.[23]

He closed this argument by saying:

> I was glad to express my gratitude at Quincy, and I re-express it here to Judge Douglas — *that he looks to no end of the institution of slavery.* That will help the people to see where the struggle really is. . . Whenever the issue can be distinctly made, and all extraneous matter thrown out so that men can fairly see the real difference between the parties, this controversy will soon be settled, and it will be done peaceably too.[24]

There were ten minutes left. Lincoln devoted them to a further scathing analysis of the theory that unfriendly local legislation could nullify the Dred Scott decision. This time he gave it a new twist, which applied the coup de grace to popular sovereignty:

> I believe the decision was improperly made and I go for reversing it. Judge Douglas is furious against those who go for reversing a decision. But he is for legislating it out of all force while the law itself stands. . . there has never been so monstrous a doctrine uttered from the mouth of a respectable man. (Loud cheers.) . . .
>
> Try it now. It is the strongest Abolition argument ever made. I say if that Dred Scott decision is correct then the right to hold slaves in a territory is equally a constitutional right with the right of a slaveholder to have his runaway returned. No one can show the distinction between them. The one is express, so that we cannot deny it. The other is construed to be in the Constitution. . .
>
> And the man who argues that by unfriendly legislation, in spite of that constitutional right, slavery may be driven from the territories, cannot avoid furnishing an argument by which Abolitionists may deny the obligation to return fugitives, and claim the power to pass laws unfriendly to the right of the slaveholder to reclaim his fugitive. . . Why there is not such an Abolitionist in the nation as Douglas, after all.[25]

A LION AROUSED

Loud and enthusiastic applause greeted the end of Lincoln's speech. But the note of overconfident banter on which it ended gave Douglas the opportunity to turn the jest against him. Harried and exhausted though he was, he manifested the soul of a lion. In the heat of battle he would not falter or flinch; it was his nature to rise to a challenge and to spring to the attack, seizing upon even the flimsiest opening to turn an opponent's argument to his own advantage. Thus he began his rejoinder by saying:

> Mr. Lincoln has concluded his remarks by saying that there is not such an Abolitionist as I am in all America. (Laughter.) If he could make the Abolitionists of Illinois believe that, he would not have much show for the Senate. (Great laughter and applause.) Let him make the Abolition-

ists believe the truth of that statement and his political back is broken. (Renewed laughter.)[26]

He made no attempt, however, to defend his favorite theory against Lincoln's new exposition of its demise as a result of the Dred Scott decision. Instead he played with insignificant side issues, raking up stale arguments with bite and sarcasm:

> His first criticism upon me is the expression of his hope that the war of the Administration will be prosecuted against me and the Democratic party of his state with vigor. . .
>
> There is something really refreshing in the thought that Mr. Lincoln is in favor of prosecuting one war vigorously. (Roars of laughter.) It is the first war I ever knew him to be in favor of prosecuting. (Renewed laughter.) It is the first war that the war of the Administration will be prosecuted against (Laughter and cheers.) When the Mexican war [was] being waged, and the American army was surrounded by the enemy in Mexico, he thought that war was unconstitutional, unnecessary and unjust. ("That's so," "you've got him," "he voted against it," &c.) He thought it was not commenced on the right *spot*. (Laughter.)
>
> When I made an incidental allusion of that kind in the joint discussion over at Charleston some weeks ago, Lincoln, in replying, said that I, Douglas, had charged him with voting against supplies for the Mexican war, and then he reared up, full length, and swore that he never voted against the supplies — that it was a slander — and caught hold of Ficklin, who sat on the stand, and said, "Here, Ficklin, tell the people that it is a lie." (Laughter and cheers.) Well, Ficklin, who served in Congress with him, stood up and told them all that he recollected about it.[27]

The Little Giant went on to rehearse Lincoln's role in the war, impeaching his patriotism and identifying his opposition to himself as of equal odium. "That a man who takes sides with the common enemy against his own country in time of war," roared the Little Giant, "should rejoice in a war being made on me now, is very natural. In my opinion, no other kind of man would rejoice in it."[28]

Douglas then set about to destroy Lincoln's position with the Whigs. This time it was he who introduced new points and new arguments which he had not raised before:

> Mr. Lincoln has told you a great deal to-day about his being

an Old Line Clay Whig. ("He never was.") Bear in mind
that there are a great many Old Clay Whigs down in this
region. It is more agreeable, therefore, for him to talk about
the Old Clay Whig party than it is for him to talk Abolitionism. We did not hear much about the Old Clay Whig party
up in the Abolition districts. How much of an Old Line
Henry Clay Whig was he?

Have you read Gen. Singleton's speech at Jacksonville?
("Yes, yes," and cheers.) You know that Gen. Singleton . . .
the confidential friend of Henry Clay, . . testified that in
1847, when the constitutional convention of this state was
in session, the Whig members were invited to a Whig caucus
at the house of Mr. Lincoln's brother-in-law, where Mr. Lincoln proposed to throw Henry Clay overboard, that the Whigs
had fought long enough for principle and ought to begin
to fight for success. Singleton also testifies that Lincoln's
speech did have the effect of cutting Clay's throat. . . Now,
Mr. Lincoln tells you that he is an Old Line Clay Whig!
(Laughter and cheers.) Gen. Singleton testifies to the facts I
have narrated in a public speech which has been printed and
circulated, broadcast over the state for weeks, yet not a lisp
have we heard from Mr. Lincoln on the subject, except that
he is an Old Clay Whig.[29]

Douglas was thoroughly embattled now and, once warmed
to his subject, he began to pour it on.

What part of Henry Clay's policy did Lincoln ever advocate? He was in Congress in 1848–9 when the Wilmot proviso warfare disturbed the peace and harmony of the country
until it shook the foundation of the republic from its centre
to its circumference. It was that agitation that brought Clay
forth from his retirement at Ashland again to occupy his seat
in the Senate of the United States. . .

Who got up that sectional strife that Clay had to be called
upon to quell? I have heard Lincoln boast that he voted
forty-two times for the Wilmot proviso, and that he would
have voted as many times more if he could. (Laughter.)
Lincoln is the man, in connection with Seward, Chase, Giddings, and other Abolitionists, who got up that strife that I
helped Clay to put down. (Tremendous applause.) Henry
Clay came back to the Senate in 1849, and saw that he must
do something to restore peace to the country. The Union
Whigs and Union Democrats welcomed him. . . We Democrats rallied under Clay then, as you Whigs in nullification

time rallied under the banner of old Jackson, forgetting
party when the country was in danger, in order that we
might have a country first, and parties afterwards. ("Three
cheers for Douglas.")[30]

ATTACK, ATTACK!

The Little Giant was magnificent as he slashed into Lincoln's position that slavery alone was the perpetual source of
trouble to the Union:

> Mr. Lincoln told you that the slavery question was the
> only thing that ever disturbed the peace and harmony of the
> Union. Did not Nullification once raise its head and disturb
> the peace of this Union in 1832? Was that the slavery ques-
> tion, Mr. Lincoln? The peace of this country has been dis-
> turbed three times, once during the war with Great Britain,
> once on the tariff questions, and once on the slavery ques-
> tion. His argument, therefore, that slavery is the only ques-
> tion that has ever created dissension in the Union falls to
> the ground.[31]

Douglas now adverted to the question of the attitude of the
fathers toward slavery. Undaunted by Lincoln's demolition of
his position that the framers of the government had made it
part slave and part free, he skillfully employed his opponent's
argument to substantiate his own theories of states' rights:

> It is true that they did not establish slavery in any of the
> states, or abolish it in any of them; but finding thirteen
> states, twelve of which were slave and one free, they agreed
> to form a government uniting them together, as they stood
> divided into free and slave states, and to guarantee forever to
> each state the right to do as it pleased on the slavery ques-
> tion. Having thus made the government, and conferred this
> right upon each state forever, I assert that this government
> can exist as they made it, divided into free and slave states,
> if any one state chooses to retain slavery.
>
> He says that he looks forward to a time when slavery shall
> be abolished everywhere. I look forward to a time when each
> state shall be allowed to do as it pleases. . . I care more for
> the great principle of self-government . . . than I do for all
> the negroes in Christendom. . .
>
> But Mr. Lincoln says that when our fathers made this
> government they did not look forward to the state of things

now existing; . . . that our fathers then thought that probably slavery would be abolished, by each state acting for itself before this time. Suppose they did; suppose they did not foresee what has occurred, — does that change the principles of our government? They did not probably foresee the telegraph that transmits intelligence by lightning, nor did they foresee the railroads that now form the bonds of union between the different states, or the thousand mechanical inventions that have elevated mankind. But do these things change the principles of the government?

Our fathers, I say, made this government on the principle of the right of each state to do as it pleases in its own domestic affairs, subject to the Constitution, and allowed the people of each to apply to every new change of circumstance such remedy as they may see fit to improve their condition. This right they have for all time to come.[32]

The Little Giant did not quail even from the moral issue, as he sought to blunt the effect of Lincoln's eloquence on the eternal clash between the two principles of right and wrong. Lincoln would "get rid of the terrible crime and sin entailed upon our fathers of holding slaves" by the genocide of the Negro race through starvation, he asserted. And this would be done in the name of humanity and Christianity!:

Mr. Lincoln appeals to the moral sense of justice, and to the Christian feeling of the community to sustain him. He says that any man who holds to the contrary doctrine is in the position of the king who claimed to govern by divine right.

Let us examine for a moment and see what principle it was that overthrew the divine right of George the Third to govern us. Did not these colonies rebel because the British Parliament had no right to pass laws concerning our property and domestic and private institutions without our consent? We demanded that the British government should not pass such laws unless they gave us representation in the body passing them, — and this the British government insisting on doing, — we went to war, on the principle that the home government should not control and govern distant colonies without giving them a representation.

Now, Mr. Lincoln proposes to govern the territories without giving the people a representation, and calls on Congress to pass laws controlling their property and domestic concerns without their consent and against their will. Thus, he asserts for his party the identical principle asserted by George III and the Tories of the Revolution.[33]

With time running against him, Douglas closed with an appeal to uphold the Constitution and the Supreme Court.

> Mr. Lincoln . . . says that this slavery question is now the bone of contention. Why? Simply because agitators have combined in all the free states to make war upon us. . . The only remedy and safety is that we shall stand by the Constitution as our fathers made it, obey the laws as they are passed, while they stand the proper test and sustain the decisions of the Supreme Court and the constituted authorities.[34]

When Douglas finished, Dr. Hope rushed to the stand and attempted to address the crowd, but he was shouted down by the Douglas partisans. An amusing scene ensued as Hope persisted in his harangue even though he could not be heard. When he finally gave up, the crowd began to disperse, thus closing the curtain on the final act of the formal debates.

CAPTAIN BROWN'S POCKET MEMORANDUM BOOK

There was much left for the antagonists to do, however. Newspaper comment pointed out that Lincoln still had twelve speeches to make and Douglas nine, "each to speak in sections where they deem it most necessary to exert a personal influence."[35]

The rivals made their tours in weather which was generally wretched, marked by cold and dampness or rains. Even Lincoln felt discouraged at times, especially when he spoke in the town of Vermont on October 27, standing under a large umbrella in a steady downpour. But for Douglas it was worse. When Gustav Koerner saw him at Alton after a period of four years, he was shocked by his haggard face, and the hoarseness and heaviness of his voice.[36] Newspaper accounts described the Little Giant's voice as extremely husky, his articulation thick and indistinct, so that only auditors close to the platform could understand what he was saying. Even Horace White commented that "to listen to him moved one's pity."[37] Nevertheless the undaunted Little Giant carried out his commitments to the end, continuing bravely to fire his cannon and harangue the crowds, while his beauteous wife won hearts and votes to his standard.

As for Lincoln, even though he was constantly on the move from town to town, traveling most of the time by carriage, his speaking engagements and social involvements did not prevent him from carrying on his political correspondence. From Captain Brown, the Old Line Whig whom he had induced to run for the legislature on the Republican ticket, he received a distress call. Brown was finding it increasingly difficult to meet Douglas' charge that Lincoln favored social and political equality for the Negro. He wanted a statement from Lincoln himself which he would be able to show on demand to refute the charge.

Lincoln sent Brown the statement in a letter dated October 18, written in a small pocket memorandum book approximately three-by-five inches in size, into which he had also pasted seven newspaper extracts from his speeches, dating from his Peoria speech of October 16, 1854 up to his debate with Douglas at Charleston. In the letter, in which he made sure to quote from Clay, he reaffirmed his views:

> I do not perceive how I can express myself, more plainly, than I have done in the foregoing extracts. In four of them I have expressly disclaimed all intention to bring about social and political equality between the white and black races, and, in all the rest, I have done the same thing by clear implication.
>
> I have made it equally plain that I think the negro is included in the word "men" used in the Declaration of Independence. . .
>
> I say, with Mr. Clay, it is desirable that the declaration of the equality of all men shall be kept in view, as a great fundamental principle. . .
>
> But it does not follow that social and political equality between whites and blacks, *must* be incorporated, because slavery must *not*. The declaration does not so require.[38]

Brown carried this interesting and curious little book around with him in his pocket for the remaining two weeks of the campaign, and when the occasion demanded, would produce Lincoln's own words to convince his Whig friends that Lincoln had not turned radical. However, it was either too late to be effective or a majority of the Old Line Whigs just could not bring themselves to vote the Republican ticket, because both Brown and his colleague, Cook, were defeated for election.

Lincoln had spoken in the town of Lincoln on October 16 and was in Springfield for a Sunday stopover when he gave this material to Brown. From here he took the Great Western railroad to Naples, whence he was scheduled to proceed by carriage to Meredosia for a speech. At Naples he observed something which disturbed him. It was a group of Irish laborers idling about the town.

This appeared to substantiate reports which had reached him that there had suddenly been a large influx of such laborers into Illinois, ostensibly for the purpose of looking for work on the railroads, but in reality to provide votes for the Democratic ticket. New immigrants, like the Irish and Germans, usually gravitated to the Democratic standard because of the magic of the term "democrat." They were repelled by the nativistic hostility of the Know-Nothings to the foreign-born, the taint of which in their eyes had rubbed off on the Whigs.

With the passage of the Kansas-Nebraska Bill, however, a great many Germans, like Koerner, switched their allegiance to the Republican Party, because of their antipathy to slavery. The efforts of the Republicans to win the stable German element to Lincoln were proving effective, thanks to such men as Schurz and Koerner. But the sudden appearance of a transient, mobile group like the Irish laborers, presented a different problem. Of all the population groupings in the North, the Irish had shown themselves most hostile to the free Negro. This was due to their own generally depressed economic condition, which classed them but a little higher than the free Negro by the standards of northern society. Their reaction, reflecting the desire to raise their status, was expressed in their newspapers which were leading defenders of slavery.

That Lincoln was not only disturbed, but also baffled by the sudden appearance of these laborers is revealed by a letter he wrote two days later to Norman Judd, the Republican chairman, in which he suggested a bizarre solution:

> On alighting from the cars and walking the square at Naples on Monday, I met about fifteen Celtic gentlemen, with black carpet sacks in their hands. I learned that they had crossed over from the railroad in Brown County, but where they were going no one could tell. They dropped in

about the doggeries, and were still hanging about when I
left. . .

What I most dread is that they will introduce into the
doubtful districts numbers of men who are legal voters in
all respects except residence and who will swear to *residence*
and thus put it beyond our powers to exclude them. They
can, and I fear will, swear falsely on that point because
they know it is next to impossible to convict them of perjury
upon it.

Now the great reassuring fact of the campaign is finding
a way to head this thing off. Can it be done at all?

I have a bare suggestion. When there is a known body of
these voters, could not a true man, of the *"detective"* class,
be introduced among them in disguise, who could, at the
nick of time, control their votes? Think this over. It would
be a great thing, when this trick is attempted upon us, to
have the saddle come up on the other horse. If we can head
off the fraudulent votes, we shall carry the day.[39]

In the meantime, Douglas had spoken in Gillespie and Decatur, and had arrived in Springfield, where on October 20
he addressed a crowd of 5,000 in front of the courthouse. The
planked streets of the public square offered refuge from the
mud which had been caused by two days of rain. The next
day, he left on a special train of the Chicago, Alton and
St. Louis line for the towns of Atlanta and Bloomington, and
thence across country to Peoria and Toulon. The last legs of
his trip brought him on October 28 and 29 to Geneseo and
Rock Island by train of the Chicago and Rock Island Railroad,
and then back to his home town of Chicago for his final speech
on November 1, the night before election. Despite inclement
weather, a tremendous crowd was on hand to hear him, while
bonfires blazed and lit up a brilliant display of banners and
transparencies.

Following his trip to Meredosia and Rushville, Lincoln's
itinerary obliged him to travel by carriage because of lack of
railroad communication. He covered Carthage, Dallas City
and La Harpe in Hancock county, writing to Judd: "Just out
of Hancock. Spoke three times in that county. *Tight,* with
chances slightly in our favor."[40] It turned out to be very tight
with the county eventually going to Douglas. At Carthage he
refuted charges which Douglas had made that he was "cozy"
with the Illinois Central Railroad Company.

On October 25, accompanied by a long escort of wagons,

Lincoln arrived in Macomb where he had spoken exactly two months before. It was raining, but despite the weather 4,000 turned out to hear him. Two days later he was in Vermont, speaking again in the rain under the large umbrella. Returning to Macomb, he took the train to Chicago, thus avoiding the rain and the muddy roads. From Chicago he took a second train home to Springfield where he was scheduled to close his campaign. However, on October 29 he drove twenty miles to Petersburg for another scheduled effort before making his final speech at Springfield the next day.

BILLY HERNDON'S BONES

October 30 was the Saturday before election, and the Republicans had prepared a giant rally. Shortly before the rally was to be held, Billy Herndon wrote a worried letter to his friend, Theodore Parker. Herndon had thrown himself into the campaign with all the impetuousness of youth, and had been highly optimistic about the outcome. The first note of doubt, however, crept into a letter of October 26 to Parker, who was ill in bed:

> Come, keep in good spirits and be merry. If you were in Illinois . . . you would thank God and take courage.
> The Republicans are full of hope and wild with enthusiasm. . . Do not understand me to say that all is surely and absolutely safe; but understand this — all looks well, *feels right in our bones*. If we are defeated it will be on this account: there are thousands of wild, roving, robbing, bloated, pock-marked Irish, who are thrown in on us by the Douglas Democracy for the purpose of outvoting us — robbing us of our "popular will."[41]

Now four days later, the feeling in his bones had changed. His letter to Parker seemed to shriek with concern:

> Today is Saturday and in a little while Mr. Lincoln opens on our square, close to the State House, on the great, vital, and dominant issues of the day and age. We feel, as usual, full of enthusiasm and of hope, and there is nothing which can well defeat us but the elements, and the wandering, roving, robbing Irish who have flooded over the State. This charge is no humbug cry: it is a real and solid and terrible reality, looking us right in the face, *with its thumb on its nose*. . . If blood is shed in Illinois to maintain the purity of the ballot box, and the rights of the popular will, do not

be at all surprised. We are roused and fired to fury. . . .

From all places and persons comes up this intelligence, "All is well." I, myself, fear and am scolded because I cannot feel as I should — as others do. My intuition — brute forecast, if you will — my bones tell me that all is not safe; yet I hope for the best.[42]

There was another reason for both Herndon and Lincoln to be concerned. Judge Dickey had begun circulating Crittenden's letter several days before election and it had finally found its way into print. At the very moment probably that Herndon was writing his letter to Parker on Saturday, October 30, Henry C. Whitney in Chicago saw it in a Democratic paper published in a nearby small town. Terribly agitated, he immediately sought out Norman Judd and editor Charles Ray of the *Chicago Press and Tribune* for an emergency council. The only way to save anything from the situation, they decided, was to send an emissary off to Frankfort, Kentucky, without delay, for the purpose of conferring with Crittenden and obtaining some sort of statement from him that could be published in a special edition of the *Press and Tribune* on Monday noon. The emissary was duly sent, but his mission was unsuccessful. Crittenden was away and could not be found.[43]

In the meantime the rally got under way and Lincoln made his speech. It was a tremendous rally in which the people ignored the marshals and expressed their spontaneous enthusiasm by marching and counter-marching, waving their banners and drowning out the music with their shouts. It took a long time for the tumult to subside, and then Lincoln addressed the crowd. During the debates he had spoken without notes, or with very few notes, but this time he wrote out his remarks. It is not clear whether they were the entire speech or served merely as the introduction or conclusion to an extemporaneous address, because what he said never was printed. The *Illinois State Journal* in its issue of Monday, November 1 commented: "We have neither time nor room to give even a sketch of his remarks. . . Suffice it to say, the speech was one of his very best efforts, distinguished for its clearness and force. . . The conclusion of this speech was one of the most eloquent appeals ever addressed to the American people."[44]

From this it would seem that Lincoln spoke at length and that his written remarks served as the conclusion of his address. For sixty-five years it remained a "lost speech" until the short written portion of the address was acquired by the great collector of Lincoln manuscripts, Oliver R. Barrett, and published in William E. Barton's biography of Lincoln:

> My friends, to-day closes the discussions of this canvass. The planting and the culture are over; and there remains but the preparation, and the harvest.
>
> I stand here surrounded by friends — some *political, all personal* friends, I trust. May I be indulged, in this closing scene, to say a few words of myself. I have borne a laborious, and, in some respect to myself, a painful part in the contest. Through all, I have neither assailed, nor wrestled with any part of the Constitution. The legal right of the Southern people to reclaim their fugitives I have constantly admitted. The legal right of Congress to interfere with their institution in the states, I have constantly denied.
>
> In resisting the spread of slavery to new territory, and with that, what appears to me to be a tendency to subvert the first principle of free government itself my whole effort has consisted. To the best of my judgment I have labored *for,* and not *against* the Union. As I have not felt, so I have not expressed any harsh sentiment towards our Southern brethren. I have constantly declared, as I really believed, the only difference between them and us, is the difference of circumstances.
>
> I have meant to assail the motives of no party, or individual; and if I have, in any instance (of which I am not conscious) departed from my purpose, I regret it.
>
> I have said that in some respects the contest had been painful to me. Myself, and those with whom I act have been constantly accused of a purpose to destroy the Union; and bespattered with every imaginable odious epithet; and some who were friends, as it were but yesterday have made themselves most active in this. I have cultivated patience, and made no attempt at a retort.
>
> Ambition has been ascribed to me. God knows how sincerely I prayed from the first that this field of ambition might not be opened. I claim no insensibility to political honors; but today could the Missouri restriction be restored, and the whole slavery question replaced on the old ground of "toleration" by *necessity* where it exists, with unyielding hostility to the spread of it, on principle, I would, in consideration, gladly agree, that Judge Douglas should never be *out,* and I never *in,* an office, so long as we both or either, live.[45]

PART IV
The Aftermath

While both Lincoln and Douglas had campaigned strenuously throughout the state, the seemingly tireless Little Giant had covered more ground and made more speeches.

Lincoln delivered 63 speeches, as well as numerous short, impromptu talks, while Douglas made a total of 130. In forty towns they both spoke, in twenty-three Douglas was the sole speaker, and in twelve Lincoln appeared alone. Douglas was estimated to have covered 5,227 miles in one hundred days, while Lincoln, in less than four months traveled 350 miles by boat, 600 by carriage, 3,400 by train, a total of 4,350 miles.

The immediate result — Douglas' election — was not so important as were the long-range consequences: the catapulting of Lincoln into the limelight and his subsequent election as President. For both the Tall Sucker and the Little Giant, the debates were the turning point of their careers, marking the rise of the one and the decline of the other.

The debates were also a turning point for the nation. Within three years it would undergo a bloody test of its ideals. Its subsequent history would be a struggle to bring to fruition the decision reached on the field of battle.

CHAPTER 14

Victory — Pyrrhic and Real

Lincoln proved to be as good a prophet as a debater. He had predicted that the Republicans would outvote the Democrats, but that the outmoded districting would give the latter the victory. And so it was.

To make matters worse, election day turned out cold and wet, a circumstance on which the Republicans blamed the loss of 10,000 votes. The final count stood Republicans 125,430, Democrats 121,609, Buchanan Democrats 5,079. Then the legislature met on January 5 to choose a Senator. The vote was: Douglas 54, Lincoln 41. Apprised in Washington of the result, Douglas wired exultingly to Lanphier and the *Illinois State Register*: "Let the voice of the people rule."[1]

Lincoln at first took his disappointment keenly. Again he had played political bridesmaid. When Horace White asked him how he felt, he said: "Well, it hurts too much to laugh, and I'm too big to cry."[2] He expressed his feeling in a gracious letter to Crittenden two days after the election:

> The emotions of defeat, at the close of a struggle in which I felt more than a merely selfish interest, and to which defeat the use of your name contributed largely, are fresh upon me; but even in this mood, I can not for a moment suspect you of anything dishonorable.[3]

However, his perspective gradually returned. After all, things had turned out just as he expected. This was merely

383

one battle in a war which the Republicans would eventually win. To Henry Asbury on November 19, he wrote:

> The fight must go on. The cause of civil liberty must not be surrendered at the end of *one* or even, one *hundred* defeats. Douglas had the ingenuity to be supported in the late contest both as the best means to *break down,* and to uphold the Slave interest. No ingenuity can keep those antagonistic elements in harmony long. Another explosion will soon come.[4]

And to Norman Judd four days earlier he had written in jocular vein:

> I have the pleasure to inform you that I am convalescent and hoping these lines may find you in the same improving state of health.[5]

Two other letters, written in early December, reveal how fully his perspective was restored. To H. D. Sharpe, a prominent New York anti-slavery man who had written expressing his appreciation of Lincoln's espousal of the rights of man, he said:

> While I desired the result of the late canvass to have been different, I still regard it as an exceeding small matter. I think we have fairly entered upon a durable struggle as to whether this nation is to ultimately become all slave or all free, and though I fall early in the contest, it is nothing if I shall have contributed, in the least degree, to the final rightful result.[6]

To Alexander Sympson, a friend and political associate, he wrote:

> I expect the result of the election went hard with you. So it did with me, too, perhaps not quite so hard as you may have supposed. I have an abiding faith that we shall beat them in the long run. Step by step the objects of the leaders will become too plain for the people to stand them. I write merely to let you know that I am neither dead nor dying.[7]

He even tried to cheer up his friends. To Editor Ray, he wrote:

> I believe, according to a letter of yours to Hatch, you are "feeling like h–ll yet." Quit that. You will soon feel better. Another "blow-up" is coming; and we shall have fun again.[8]

Lincoln's view of his role in the great political drama that had attracted national and world attention is illustrated in another letter to Dr. Anson G. Henry:

> Of course I wished, but I did not much expect, a better result. . . I am glad I made the late race. It gave me a hearing on the great and durable question of the age, which I could have had in no other way; and though I now sink out of view, and shall be forgotten, I believe I have made some marks which will tell for the cause of civil liberty long after I am gone.[9]

His personal ambitions were not entirely extinguished, however. That he hoped his contribution to the cause of liberty would be more than a few marks is illustrated by the following incident which he recalled on another election day six years later. November 7, 1864 was also a dismal and rainy day. To a small group of friends in the White House who had listened to the returns that announced his reelection to the presidency, Lincoln in reminiscent mood said:

> I remember the evening of the day in 1858 that decided the contest for the Senate between Mr. Douglas and myself, was something like this, dark, rainy and gloomy. I had been reading the returns, and had ascertained that we had lost the Legislature, and I started to go home. The path had been worn pigbacked and was slippery. My foot slipped from under me, knocking the other out of the way; but I recovered and said to myself, *"It's a slip and not a fall!"*[10]

BILLY HERNDON, SORE LOSER

Billy Herndon, however, could not take the turn of events quite so philosophically. In dejected mood, he wrote Parker a summary of the reasons for Lincoln's defeat:

> We are beaten in Illinois, as you are aware; but you may want to know the causes of our defeat. Firstly, then, I have more than once said our State presents three distinct phases of human development: the extreme north, the middle, and the extreme south. The first is intelligence, the second timidity, and the third ignorance on the special issue. . . . If a man spoke to suit the north — for freedom, justice — this killed him in the center and in the south. So in the center, it killed him north and south. So in the south, it surely killed

him north. Lincoln tried to stand high and elevated, so he fell deep.

Secondly, Greeley never gave us one single, solitary, manly lift. On the contrary, his silence was his opposition. This our people felt. We never got a smile or a word of encouragement outside of Illinois from any quarter during all this great canvass. The East was for Douglas *by silence*. . . Thirdly, Crittenden wrote letters to Illinois urging the Americans and Old Line Whigs to go for Douglas, and so they went "helter-skelter." Thousands of Whigs dropped us just on the eve of the election, through the influence of Crittenden.

Fourthly, all the pro-slavery men, north as well as south, went to a man for Douglas. They threw into this State money, and men, and speakers. . .

Fifthly, thousands of roving, robbing, bloated, pock-marked Catholic Irish were imported upon us from Philadelphia, New York, St. Louis, and other cities. I myself know of such, by their own confession. Some have been arrested, and are now in jail awaiting trial.

I want distinctly to say to *you* that no one of all of these causes defeated Lincoln; but I do want to say that it was the combination, with the power and influence of each, that "cleaned us out."[11]

To Lincoln and Douglas the canvass had meant more than a strenuous speaking campaign. It had also meant the expenditure of money. Douglas was estimated to have borrowed and disbursed between $50,000 and $80,000, incurring a debt which weighed him down to the grave.[12] While others, too, contributed to the Democratic campaign coffers, Douglas bore the lion's share.

Lincoln, on the other hand, spent less than $1,000. He was merely one of a large number of contributors. A letter to Judd on November 16 discloses the state of the party's and of Lincoln's own finances. Judd had evidently written asking Lincoln's help to raise money to cover the campaign deficit.

I am willing to pay according to my ability, but I am the poorest hand living to get others to pay. I have been on expenses so long without earning anything that I am absolutely without money now for even household purposes. Still if you can put in $250 for me towards discharging the debts of the committee, I will allow it when you and I settle the private matter between us. This, with what I have already

paid, and with an outstanding note of mine, will exceed my
subscription of $500. This, too, is exclusive of my ordinary
expenses during the campaign, all of which being added to
my loss of time and business, bears pretty heavily upon one
no better off in world's goods than I; but as I had the post
of honor, it is not for me to be overnice.[13]

Besides the expenditure of a large sum of money, the campaign exacted a heavy toll on the health of the Little Giant.
Not only had he suffered great voice strain, but physically he
was exhausted and required rest. He spent the weeks following
the canvass recuperating from his ordeal. Lincoln, on the other
hand, had thrived on the experience. It was like a tonic. His
voice not only grew stronger, but he himself put on some
weight.

POLITICAL FENCE-MENDING

Now that his tenure in Illinois was safe, Douglas contemplated recovering lost ground in the South. He was due back
in Washington for the Congressional session, but when his
doctor recommended the relaxation and salubrious effects of
a sea voyage, he decided to proceed to the capital by way of
the Mississippi River and Cuba. On the way he stopped off
for speeches in Memphis and New Orleans.[14]

At both places he was given grand receptions despite the
growing hostility toward him of the extremist group. Their
recognized leader, Jefferson Davis, back from New England,
had addressed the Mississippi legislature on November 16,
repudiating the unexpected words he had uttered in Maine
in support of popular sovereignty. He had labelled Douglas'
doctrine heresy. What the South needed, in his opinion, was
a Congressional code to support slavery in the territories in
accordance with the preferred status bestowed upon it by the
Dred Scott decision. Since Douglas insisted that slavery was
no different from any other property and must take its chances
with popular sovereignty, the cause of the South, according to
Davis, could not be furthered by Douglas' candidacy for the
presidency in 1860. If the Northern Democrats should support
Douglas, and a split in the Democratic ranks should result in
the election of a Black Republican, the only remedy for the
South was to secede.[15]

The Little Giant spoke at Memphis on November 29 and at New Orleans on December 6. In both speeches he attempted to counteract the influence of the extremists. Fearlessly and stubbornly he adhered to the doctrines which he had asserted in the recent debates. So long as we live under a common Constitution, binding on all the people of all the states, he said, any political creed which could not be proclaimed in Louisiana as boldly as in Illinois must be unsound and unsafe.[16]

Slavery had been the greatest disturbing element in the country's history, he declared, because the North insisted on "an exclusive right and interest to establish freedom for the territories, while the same delusion existed in the South with respect to her right and interest to establish slavery within them." And yet it was obvious that "the Constitution recognized no such distinction of sectional rights or interests." On the moral question he repeated his position that "the people have the right to decide the question of goodness or badness for themselves."[17]

The only solution was the doctrine he had propounded at Freeport. All property, including slaves, must be allowed into the territories, but once there, it was subject to local law. Congress had never yet passed a law providing a criminal code or furnishing protection to any kind of property. This was a slap at the demand of the extremists for a Congressional slave code. Congress simply organizes the territory and establishes a legislature, contended Douglas. Whatever jurisdiction the legislature possessed over other property, it had over slave property — no more, no less.

"It is visionary to talk of planting slavery where it is not wanted," he asserted, "and it is equally folly in the Northern fanatic to attempt to exclude it, where it is wanted."[18] It was essentially climate, soil and self-interest that would regulate the question, so why quarrel about it?

At Memphis he phrased his position in a way which would subsequently give Lincoln an opportunity not only to bare its moral nakedness, but also to reduce it to absurdity:

> You come right back to the principle of dollars and cents. If old Joshua R. Giddings should raise a colony in Ohio and settle down in Louisiana, he would be the strongest advocate of slavery in the whole South; he would find when he got there, his opinion would be very much modified; he

would find on those sugar plantations that it was not a question between the white man and the negro, but between the negro and the crocodile. . .

The Almighty has drawn the line on this continent on one side of which the soil must be cultivated by slave labor; on the other by white labor.[19]

At New Orleans, in order to convince the South that he truly represented their interests, he advocated the annexation of Cuba, Mexico and Central America. It was the "manifest destiny" of the nation.[20]

Further to insure that the South would not misunderstand his attitude toward slavery as an institution, he said:

It is a law of humanity, a law of civilization, that whenever a man or a race of men show themselves incapable of managing their own affairs, they must consent to be governed by those who are capable of performing the duty. . . In accordance with this principle, I assert that the negro race, under all circumstances, at all times, and in all countries, has shown itself incapable of self-government.[21]

But Douglas could not convince the Ultras. A great deal of water had flowed under the bridge in the four years since the Kansas-Nebraska Bill. Whereas at that time they had been willing to accept popular sovereignty in order to destroy the Missouri Compromise, now it was counterfeit coin. The Dred Scott decision had vindicated Calhoun. The Constitution must protect slavery as a distinct species of property, the only type of property, according to Taney, specifically mentioned in the Constitution.

Besides, had not Douglas in Democratic caucus at the time of the Kansas-Nebraska Bill agreed to abide by the decision of the Supreme Court on the status of slavery in the territories? And now that the decision had finally been made, what was he trying to do? Why, he was giving only lip service to the decision, while in reality he was negating its effects with his popular sovereignty doctrine. He had not honored the agreement he had made, and therefore he had forfeited their support.

A few moderates, like Alexander Stephens, who saw the full implications of the intransigence of the die-hards, sided with Douglas. They knew that the North could never accept a theory which might eventually foist slavery upon the free states. But their warnings fell on deaf ears.

We have a record of what Lincoln thought of Douglas' tour, and of his chances at the 1860 Democratic convention. It is revealing of the political insight which he had displayed on previous occasions. Writing to Trumbull on December 11, he said:

> Since you left, Douglas has gone South, making characteristic speeches, and seeking to re-instate himself in that section. The majority of the Democratic politicians of the nation mean to kill him; but I doubt whether they will adopt the aptest way to do it. Their true way is to present him with no new test, let him into the Charleston convention, and then outvote him, and nominate another. In that case, he will have no pretext for bolting the nomination, and will be as powerless as they can wish. On the other hand, if they push a Slave Code upon him, as a test, he will bolt at once, turn upon us, as in the case of Lecompton, and claim that all Northern men shall make common cause in electing him President as the best means of breaking down this Slave power.
>
> In that case, the Democratic party go into a minority inevitably; and the struggle in the whole North will be, as it was in Illinois last summer and fall, whether the Republican party can maintain its identity, or be broken up to form the tail of Douglas' new kite. Some of our great Republican doctors will then have a splendid chance to swallow the pills they so eagerly prescribed for us last Spring. Still I hope they will not swallow them; and although I do not feel that I owe the said doctors much, I will help them, to the best of my ability, to reject the said pills. The truth is, the Republican principle can, in no wise, live with Douglas; and it is arrant folly now, as it was last Spring, to waste time, and scatter labor already performed, in dallying with him.[22]

APPROACHING SHOWDOWN

The final break was not slow in coming. Douglas saw the first sign on his return to Washington in January 1859. In his absence he had been removed from the chairmanship of the Committee on Territories — a post which he had held for eleven years. Then events moved rapidly. In February, Senator Brown of Mississippi, long a friend and admirer of Douglas, called for the enactment of a slave code for the territories.

Brown pointed out the conflict between the Supreme Court decision and Douglas' theory. He asked the northern Democratic Senators whether they would uphold the Supreme Court: "If the Territorial Legislature refuse to act, will you act? If it pass unfriendly acts, will you pass friendly? If it pass laws hostile to slavery, will you annul them and substitute laws favoring slavery in their stead?" This was the very point that Lincoln had raised at Jonesboro. He then went on to say: "I would rather see the Democratic Party sunk, never to be resurrected, than to see it successful only that one portion of it might practice a fraud on another."[23]

To this Douglas replied:

> If you repudiate the doctrine of non-intervention, and form a slave code by act of Congress, where the people of a territory refuse it, you must step off the Democratic platform. I tell you gentlemen of the South, in all candor, I do not believe a Democratic candidate can ever carry any one Democratic State of the North on the platform that it is the duty of the Federal Government to force the people of a territory to have slavery when they do not want it.[24]

Thus the breach between the northern and southern Democracy widened. How broad the gulf was, was further revealed in May when the southerners held a convention at Vicksburg. By a vote of two to one they passed a resolution that "all laws State or Federal prohibiting the African slave trade ought to be repealed."[25]

These events were straws in the wind for the presidential convention at Charleston, South Carolina, in April 1860. There the fate of the Democratic Party would be decided. In order to clarify his position, Douglas wrote to a friend, J. B. Dorr, in response to an inquiry whether he would be a candidate for the nomination:

> If . . . it shall become the policy of the Democratic Party . . . to repudiate their time-honored principles, on which we have achieved so many patriotic triumphs, and in lieu of them the convention shall interpolate into the creed of the party such new issues as the revival of the African slave-trade, or a Congressional slave-code for the Territory, or the doctrine that the Constitution of the United States either establishes or prohibits slavery in the Territory beyond the

power of the people legally to control it, as other property —
it is due to candor to say that, in such an event, I could not
accept the nomination if tendered to me.[26]

The Little Giant went even further. He wrote a lengthy,
carefully documented article entitled "The Dividing Line
Between Federal and Local Authority" which appeared in
Harper's magazine for September 1859. Marshaling legal precedents and expounding political theory, he elucidated his
position with the hope of winning the southern leaders to a
policy of moderation and cooperation.

But while the article made a favorable impression in the
North where it consolidated Democratic opinion behind Douglas, it had an opposite effect in the South. To the southern
cabal, Douglas had further undermined the Dred Scott decision. He had substituted his own researches and legal opinion
for those of the Supreme Court. This was anathema to the
"Fire-Eaters." They were more determined than ever to deny
him the nomination at the Democratic Convention.

While events were thus moving against Douglas, Lincoln
was becoming the recipient of greater attention throughout the
North. He had retired to his much-neglected law practice, but
the profound impression he had created on the public mind
prevented his sinking into the oblivion he had anticipated.
Shortly before the start of the debates, Editor Ray, in initial
enthusiasm, had written to him:

> You are like Byron, who woke up one morning and found
> himself famous. People wish to know about you. You have
> sprung at once from the position of a capital fellow, and a
> leading lawyer of Illinois, to a national reputation.[27]

It was true. Even defeat did not lessen the national reputation which Ray had noted. Lincoln's name was even hinted
for the presidency. Republicans in Ohio had been tremen-
dously impressed with the debates. Reports filtering out of
Cincinnati favored him for the nomination, while a Sandusky
paper gave prominence to a purported meeting at Mansfield
which had announced support for his candidacy. At home,
papers like the *Chicago Press and Tribune* and the *Chicago
Democrat,* Wentworth's organ, suggested his name.[28]

But what was more important, political figures from all over
the country now turned to him for advice and counsel. Schuyler

Colfax, the Indiana Congressman, later to be Vice-President of the United States, was one of those Republicans, who like Greeley had been impressed with Douglas. Now, having received some sage pointers from Lincoln on the future course of the Republican Party,[29] he wrote to him: "Your counsel carries great weight with it; for, to be plain, there is not a political letter that falls from your pen which is not copied throughout the Union."[30]

He also pointed out the heterogeneity of elements in the Republican Party from strict conservatives to violent radicals, stating: "How this mass of mind shall be consolidated into a victorious phalanx in 1860 is the great problem . . . of our eventful times. . . . In this work, to achieve success, and to achieve it without sacrifice of essential principle, you can do far more than one like myself, so much younger."[31] A prescient comment on Lincoln's future role as the conserver of the party!

Demands for his services as a speaker came from various sections of the country: Iowa, Indiana, Wisconsin, Kansas and the East. In April, in declining an invitation to speak at a festival in Boston in honor of Jefferson's birthday, he wrote to the committee:

> It is now no child's play to save the principles of Jefferson from total overthrow in the nation. . . [They] are the definitions and axioms of free society. And yet they are denied and evaded, with no small show of success. One dashingly calls them "glittering generalities." Another bluntly calls them "self-evident lies." And others insidiously argue that they apply only to "superior races."
>
> These expressions, differing in form, are identical in object and effect — the supplanting of the principles of free government, and restoring those of classification, caste, and legitimacy. They would delight a convocation of crowned heads plotting against the people. They are the vanguard — the miners and sappers — of returning despotism. We must repulse them or they will subjugate us.
>
> This is a world of compensations; and he who would be no slave must consent to have no slave. Those who deny freedom to others deserve it not for themselves; and under a just God, cannot long retain it.
>
> All honor to Jefferson — to the man who, in the concrete pressure of a struggle for independence by a single people, had the coolness, forecast, and capacity to introduce into a

mere revolutionary document an abstract truth, applicable
to all men and all times, and so to embalm it there that
today and in all coming days it shall be a rebuke and a
stumbling-block to the very harbingers of re-appearing tyranny and oppression.[32]

During the various state elections of 1859, his speeches were
used as campaign material. In Ohio he was injected personally
into the campaign itself. The Democrats had scheduled Douglas to speak on behalf of the state ticket, with principal appearances at Columbus and Cincinnati. It was only natural, therefore, for the Republicans to invite Lincoln. As in the campaign
of the year before, Lincoln was scheduled to "follow Douglas
around" a few days later.

The result was a virtual continuation of their controversy of
the previous year. Douglas repeated his familiar arguments,
especially for the benefit of southerners who might be listening.
At Columbus, he said:

> In Ohio, it is a question only between the white man and
> the negro. But if you go further south, you will find that it
> is a question between the negro and the crocodile. The
> question then may be a different one under different cir-
> cumstances.
>
> Our fathers, when they framed this Government under
> which we live, understood this question just as well, and even
> better, than we do now.[33]

Lincoln found excellent targets for his speeches in Douglas'
recent utterances. At Columbus he challenged the historical
accuracy of Douglas' article in *Harper's*. It was faulty, he said,
in positive statement, but even more in "the suppression of
statements that really belong to history."[34] When all the chaff
was fanned out of Douglas' position, he asserted, "it was a bare
absurdity — no less than a thing may be lawfully driven away
from where it has a lawful right to be."[35]

He closed by saying:

> I ask attention to the fact that . . . these popular sovereigns
> are . . . blowing out the moral lights around us; teaching that
> the negro is no longer a man but a brute; that the Declaration
> has nothing to do with him; that he ranks with the crocodile
> and the reptile; that man, with body and soul, is a matter
> of dollars and cents. I suggest to this portion of the Ohio

Republicans, or Democrats if there be any present, the serious consideration of this fact, that there is now going on among you a steady process of debauching public opinion on this subject.[36]

At Cincinnati the next day he devoted more time to the new points advanced by Douglas since their previous encounter:

In a speech made at Memphis in Tennessee, shortly after the canvass in Illinois, last year . . . he distinctly told the people, that there was a "line drawn by the Almighty across this continent, on the one side of which the soil must always be cultivated by slaves," that he did not pretend to know exactly where that line was, (Laughter and applause,) but that there was such a line. . .

Whenever you can get these Northern audiences to adopt the opinion that Slavery is right on the other side of the Ohio . . . they will very readily make the other argument, which is perfectly logical, that that which is right on that side of the Ohio, cannot be wrong on this (Laughter.), and that if you have that property on that side of the Ohio, under the seal and stamp of the Almighty, when by any means it escapes over here, it is wrong to have constitutions and laws, "to devil" you about it. So Douglas is molding the public opinion of the North . . . that all laws and constitutions here, recognizing it as being wrong, are themselves wrong, and ought to be repealed and abrogated.

At this same meeting at Memphis, he declared that in all contests between the negro and the white man, he was for the white man, but that in all questions between the negro and the crocodile he was for the negro. (Laughter.) . . . I believe he repeated it at Columbus, and I should not wonder if he repeated it here. . . The first inference seems to be that if you do not enslave the negro you are wronging the white man in some way or other, and that whoever is opposed to the negro being enslaved is in some way or other against the white man.

Is not that a falsehood? If there was a necessary conflict between the white man and the negro, I should be for the white man as much as Judge Douglas; but I say there is no such necessary conflict. I say that there is room enough for us all to be free, and that it not only does not wrong the white man that the negro should be free, but it positively wrongs the mass of the white men that the negro should be enslaved — that the mass of white men are really injured by the effect of slave labor in the vicinity of the fields of their own labor. . .

The other branch of it is, that in a struggle between the negro and the crocodile, he is for the negro. Well, I don't know that there is any struggle between the negro and the crocodile, either. (Laughter.) I suppose that if a crocodile (or as we old Ohio River boatmen used to call them, alligators) should come across a white man, he would kill him if he could, and so he would a negro. But what, at last, is this proposition? I believe it is a sort of proposition in proportion, which may be stated thus: As the negro is to the white man, so is the crocodile to the negro, and as the negro may rightfully treat the crocodile as a beast or reptile, so the white man may rightfully treat the negro as a beast or a reptile. (Applause.) This is really the "knip" of all that argument of his.[37]

THE SCRAPBOOK

The elections proved so successful for the Ohio Republicans that they decided to publish the debates, including Lincoln's Columbus and Cincinnati speeches, in book form as campaign material for the following year. The committee therefore asked Lincoln for copies of the debates, writing as follows:

We regard them [the speeches] as luminous and triumphant expositions of the Republican party, successfully vindicated from the aspersions of its foes, and calculated to make a document of great practical service to the Republican party in the approaching Presidential contest.[38]

As if by some premonition of their value for future publication, Lincoln had already compiled a scrapbook of his and Douglas' speeches, starting with the "house divided" speech of June 16, 1858. In his letter to Charles H. Ray, editor of the *Chicago Press and Tribune* on November 20, 1858, he wrote:

I wish to preserve a set of the late debates . . . between Douglas and myself. To enable me to do so, please get two copies of each number of your paper containing the whole, and send them to me by express; and I will pay you for the papers and for your trouble. I wish the two sets, in order to lay one away in the raw, and to put the other in a scrap-book.[39]

At the same time Lincoln had requested other friends to obtain copies of the Douglas speeches as they had been reported in the *Chicago Times*. Securing the material evidently was not easy, because it took several weeks to get the scrapbook together. It was the manuscript of the only book that Lincoln wrote, edited or prepared for publication. In contrast to the little pocket notebook which he had prepared for Captain Brown to aid him in his campaigning, the scrapbook was quite large, being approximately fifteen-by-ten inches in size.

Early in 1859 a Lincoln partisan and a Springfield publishing house had shown an interest in publishing the speeches, using the scrapbook as a text, but negotiations fell through. Therefore, when the offer to publish came from the Ohio Republicans, Lincoln seized the opportunity.

On December 20 he sent his precious scrapbook to Columbus by courier. This was none other than John G. Nicolay, a young clerk in the office of the Secretary of State for Illinois, who was subsequently to become one of Lincoln's private secretaries after his election to the presidency, and who, together with John Hay, was to write a monumental biography of Lincoln. A letter went along with the scrapbook which said:

> The copies I send you are reported and printed, by the respective friends of Senator Douglas and myself, at the time — that is, his by his friends, and mine by mine. It would be an unwarrantable liberty for us to change a word or letter in his, and the changes I have made in mine, you perceive, are verbal only, and very few in number. I wish the reprint to be precisely as the copies I send, without any comment whatever.[40]

Within a month publication was in progress. By the end of March 1860 the book was due off the press, to sell for fifty cents a copy cloth-bound and thirty-five cents a copy paper-bound. It ran through several editions, reaching an estimated total of 30,000 to 50,000 copies.[41] This was a considerable number for a political tract, and it proved to be a potent factor in the nomination and election of Lincoln.

Despite Lincoln's scrupulous regard for the inviolability of his own text and that of Douglas, charges subsequently were made that the speeches were mutilated and changed solely for the purpose of defeating Douglas for the presidency. The Little Giant himself wrote to the publishers, Follet, Foster & Co., on June 9, 1860, protesting the publication and requesting that his letter of protest be included as a preface to all future editions.

To this the publishers replied that "the speeches of Mr. Lincoln were never 'revised, corrected or improved' in the sense you use those words." They asserted that they had merely omitted such reportorial comments as "cheers" and "applause" from the speeches of both men, and stated that "you will observe that nothing material has been omitted or added, and that the changes made by Mr. Lincoln are largely typographical." They offered to make similar corrections in Douglas' speeches if he would point them out, and expressed surprise that he should "call in question the accuracy of a reporter whom you had strongly commended." But they acceded to his request, and his letter was published as a preface in subsequent editions.[42]

Neither Lincoln nor Douglas received pecuniary remuneration for the publication of the speeches. However, Lincoln received a hundred copies for distribution to friends, while Douglas, as stated in his letter of protest to the publishers, "received by express one dozen copies . . . sent by order of the Hon. M. Cox, who will pay you the amount of your bill."[43]

Lincoln was delighted and gratified by the appearance of the speeches in book form. When Abraham Jonas, a friend and political associate, wrote him in February asking how he could get a copy, Lincoln wrote back: "As you are one of my most valued friends, and have complimented me by the expression of a wish for the book, I propose doing myself the honor of presenting you with one, so soon as I can. By the arrangement our Ohio friends have made with the publishers, I am to have one hundred copies gratis. When I shall receive them I will send you one by express."[44] The copy that went to Jonas was autographed. It is known that Lincoln inscribed the copies given to his friends. Two of such copies are extant.[45]

The great interest manifested in him finally brought Lincoln to New York. He had not been East since the presidential campaign of 1848 wnen he had made a speaking tour in behalf of Taylor. Easterners were curious to see and hear the picturesque Westerner. Henry Ward Beecher's church in Brooklyn was running a lecture series and Lincoln was invited to participate. However, when he indicated that he preferred a political speech to a lecture, the Young Men's Central Republican Union took over the arrangements and issued an invitation for a "political lecture." Provision was made to switch the site of the address to Cooper Union in Manhattan which had a hall sufficiently large to hold the anticipated audience.

"You are, I believe, an entire stranger to your Republican brethren here," said the letter of invitation, "but they have for you the highest esteem, and your celebrated contest with Judge Douglas awoke their warmest sympathy and admiration. Those of us who are in the ranks would regard your presence as of very material aid and as an honor and pleasure which I cannot sufficiently express."[46]

The letter also mentioned that his lecture was one of a series "contrived to call out our better but busier citizens who never attend political meetings."[47] The implication was clear that Lincoln was to have a distinguished and influential audience who would make a critical appraisal of the man from the prairies.

Lincoln made thorough preparations for this crucial appearance. In the course of the joint debates, Douglas had constantly referred to the intent of the founding fathers on the control of slavery. So had he. But no one had actually traced the votes of the original thirty-nine signers of the Constitution as the best indication of their attitude, nor of the seventy-six members of the first Congress which had framed the ten amendments as the Bill of Rights. To do so would require a formidable job of research, necessitating study of the preliminaries to the framing of the Constitution, as well as of the proceedings of Congress on acts pertaining to slavery. But Lincoln was determined to dig to the root of the matter and demolish Douglas' argument. He was also motivated by the desire to counteract the inaccuracies of Douglas' *Harper's* article by a thorough and irrefutable array of facts.

He therefore spent considerable time delving into the sources and accumulating the information which would establish beyond doubt that the founding fathers by their actions had put themselves on record as opposing the spread of slavery. The results of this painstaking research he intended to use on this occasion.

COOPER UNION

It was an elite and select audience that Lincoln faced when he stepped to the platform of Cooper Union Hall on the evening of February 27. Despite a snowstorm, 1,500 people crowded into the auditorium. William Cullen Bryant, celebrated poet and editor of the *New York Evening Post,* was chairman of the evening. Seated among the prominent personages on the platform were Horace Greeley, editor of the *Tribune,* and Henry J. Raymond, editor of the *Times.* Greeley stated in the *Tribune* the next morning: "Since the days of Clay and Webster no man has spoken to a larger assemblage of the intellect and mental culture of our city."[48]

Lincoln took as his text the statement which Douglas had made at Columbus, Ohio: "Our fathers, when they framed the Government under which we live, understood this question just as well, and even better, than we do now." He endorsed and accepted this statement, and then went on to demolish Douglas' interpretation of it by a careful statistical analysis, the fruit of his recent research.

Specifying them by name, he showed that twenty-three of the thirty-nine signers of the Constitution, who could properly be called the framers of the Government, had voted at various times from 1784 to 1820 on some aspect of the question of control of slavery in the federal territories. Twenty-one of them had voted for federal control and only two against. Sixteen of the thirty-nine had left no record of their position, but it was a reasonable assumption, said Lincoln, that if the opinion of these sixteen had been "manifested," it would have been no different as a group from that of their "compeers."[49]

Of the twenty-three whose votes were recorded, sixteen were among the seventy-six members of the first Congress, who could also be considered "fathers," because they added to the framework of government the ten amendments forming the Bill of Rights. This Congress unanimously passed the act to enforce the Ordinance of 1787 which prohibited slavery in the Northwest Territories. President George Washington, one of the original thirty-nine fathers, signed the act into law, and some years later wrote to Lafayette that he considered the measure a wise one, and hoped that in the future the nation would be a confederacy of free states.

Lincoln traced the votes of the twenty-three through other

stages of the country's early growth, pointing out that two of them were still around as members of Congress in 1820 and voted on the Missouri question. He then concluded:

> The sum of the whole is, that of our thirty-nine fathers who framed the original Constitution, twenty-one — a clear majority of the whole — certainly understood that no proper division of local from federal authority, nor any part of the Constitution, forbade the Federal Government to control slavery in the federal territories; while all the rest probably had the same understanding. Such, unquestionably, was the understanding of our fathers who framed the original Constitution; and the text affirms that they understood the question "better than we."[50]

There was still one other point to clinch. The advocates of slavery maintained that the Bill of Rights supported their position. Lincoln examined this argument:

> The Supreme Court, in the Dred Scott case, plant themselves upon the fifth amendment, which provides that no person shall be deprived of "life, liberty or property without due process of law;" while Senator Douglas and his peculiar adherents plant themselves upon the tenth amendment, providing that "the powers not delegated to the United States by the Constitution . . . are reserved to the States respectively, or to the people". . .
>
> These amendments were framed by the first Congress which sat under the Constitution — the identical Congress which passed the act enforcing the prohibition of slavery in the Northwestern Territory. . .
>
> Is it not a little presumptuous in any one at this day to affirm that the two things which that Congress deliberately framed . . . are absolutely inconsistent with each other? And does not such affirmation become impudently absurd when coupled with the other affirmation from the same mouth, that those who did the two things, alleged to be inconsistent, understood whether they really were inconsistent . . . better than he who affirms that they are inconsistent?[51]

Lincoln then tore all semblance of plausibility from Douglas' position:

> Let me guard a little against being misunderstood. I do not mean to say we are bound to follow implicitly in whatever our fathers did. To do so, would be to discard all the

lights of current experience — to reject all progress — all improvement. What I do say is, that if we would supplant the
opinions and policy of our fathers in any case, we should do
so upon evidence so conclusive, and argument so clear, that
even their great authority . . . cannot stand; and most surely
not in a case whereof we ourselves declare they understood
the question better than we.

If any man at this day sincerely believes [differently], he is
right to say so, and to enforce his position by all truthful
evidence and fair argument which he can. But he has no
right to mislead others, who have less access to history, and
less leisure to study it, into the false belief that "our fathers
who framed the Government under which we live" were of
the same opinion — thus substituting falsehood and deception
for truthful evidence and fair argument. . . . He should, at
the same time, brave the responsibility of declaring that, in
his opinion, he understands their principles better than they
did themselves.[52]

Throughout the presentation of Lincoln's argument the audience listened spellbound. Here was an original approach to
the vexing controversy over the powers of the federal government; one based on hard facts that led to a logical conclusion.
The gawky prairie lawyer with the high-pitched drawl was
giving the problem of slavery a new illumination. Sensing the
impact of this novel personality on the national scene, his auditors followed intently as he moved to another phase of his
speech.

RULE OR RUIN

He directed his words to the people of the South. You consider yourselves, he said, a "just and reasonable people," nevertheless you condemn the "Black Republicans" as worse than
"outlaws or murderers" who deserve no hearing. Is this just?
"Bring forward your charges and specifications," he challenged,
"and then be patient long enough to hear us deny or justify."[53]

One by one he held up to inspection the charges of sectionalism, radicalism and denial of constitutional rights leveled
against the Republicans, viewing each in the light of the policy
of the founding fathers. His constant referral to this premise
had a cumulative, telling effect:

> You say you are conservative, while we are revolutionary, destructive, or something of the sort. What is conservatism? Is it not adherence to the old and tried, against the new and untried? We stick to, contend for, the identical old policy... which was adopted by "our fathers who framed the Government under which we live;" while you with one accord reject, and scout, and spit upon that old policy, and insist upon substituting something new.
>
> True, you disagree among yourselves as to what that substitute shall be... but you are unanimous in rejecting and denouncing the old policy of the fathers. Some of you are for reviving the foreign slave trade; some for a Congressional Slave-Code for the Territories; some for Congress forbidding the Territories to prohibit Slavery within their limits; some for maintaining Slavery in the Territories through the judiciary; some for the "gur-reat pur-rinciple" that "if one man would enslave another, no third man should object," fantastically called "Popular Sovereignty;" but never a man among you is in favor of federal prohibition of slavery in federal territories, according to the practice of "our fathers who framed the Government under which we live."[54]

Having examined and refuted the charges, he drew the conclusion that the true purpose of the South was to "rule or ruin." "Plainly stated," he said, "you will destroy the government unless you be allowed to construe and enforce the Constitution as you please on all points in dispute between you and us."[55]

He referred to the oft-repeated threat of the South that it would not countenance the election of a Republican president:

> In that supposed event, you say, you will destroy the Union; and then, you say, the great crime of having destroyed it will be upon us! That is cool. A highwayman holds a pistol to my ear, and mutters through his teeth, "Stand and deliver, or I shall kill you, and then you will be a murderer!"
>
> To be sure, what the robber demanded of me — my money — was my own; and I had a clear right to keep it; but it was no more my own than my vote is my own; and the threat of death to me, to extort my money, and the threat of destruction to the Union, to extort my vote, can scarcely be distinguished in principle.[56]

In short, no matter how mild their platform, no matter how

they might try to find some mode of accommodation, there seemed to be nothing the Republicans could do to mollify the South. "What will satisfy them?" asked Lincoln:

> This, and this only: cease to call slavery *wrong*, and join them in calling it *right*. And this must be done thoroughly — done in *acts* as well as in *words*. Silence will not be tolerated — we must place ourselves avowedly with them. . . We must pull down our Free State constitutions. The whole atmosphere must be disinfected from all taint of opposition to slavery, before they will cease to believe that all their troubles proceed from us. . .
>
> Their thinking it right, and our thinking it wrong, is the precise fact upon which depends the whole controversy. Thinking it right, as they do, they are not to blame for desiring its full recognition, as being right; but, thinking it wrong, as we do, can we yield to them? . . .
>
> If our sense of duty forbids this, then let us stand by our duty, fearlessly and effectively. Let us be diverted by none of those sophistical contrivances wherewith we are so industriously plied and belabored — contrivances such as groping for some middle ground between the right and the wrong, vain as the search for a man who should be neither a living man nor a dead man — such a policy of "don't care" on a question about which all true men do care — such as Union appeals beseeching true Union men to yield to Disunionists, reversing the divine rule, and calling, not the sinners, but the righteous to repentance — such as invocations to Washington, imploring men to unsay what Washington said, and undo what Washington did.[57]

He concluded with a stirring peroration:

> Neither let us be slandered from our duty by false accusations against us, nor frightened from it by menaces of destruction to the Government nor of dungeons to ourselves. LET US HAVE FAITH THAT RIGHT MAKES MIGHT, AND IN THAT FAITH, LET US, TO THE END, DARE TO DO OUR DUTY AS WE UNDERSTAND IT.[58]

A tremendous ovation burst upon the speaker. The next day four New York newspapers printed the speech in full. There was no doubt of the profound impression the quaint, awkward figure from the West had made upon his hearers. It would stand him in good stead when the Republican nominating convention met in Chicago in May.

The Cooper Union speech was put out in pamphlet form. When, following Lincoln's nomination, the Young Republicans decided to publish a revised edition as a campaign document, Charles Nott, who was to do the editing with an associate, wrote to Lincoln: "You and your Western friends I think, underrate this speech. It has produced a greater effect than any other single speech. It is the real platform in the Eastern States, and must carry the conservative element in New York, New Jersey, and Pennsylvania."[59]

He then continued:

I cannot help adding that this speech is an extraordinary example of condensed English. After some experience in criticizing for Reviews, I find hardly anything to touch and nothing to omit. It is the only one I know of which I cannot shorten, and — like a good arch — moving one word tumbles a whole sentence down.[60]

When the revised edition appeared in September 1860, the preface contained the following comments:

From the first line to the last — from his premises to his conclusion, he travels with swift, unerring directness which no logician ever excelled — an argument complete and full, without the affectation of learning, and without the stiffness which usually accompanies dates and details. A single, easy, simple sentence of plain Anglo-Saxon words contains a chapter of history that, in some instances, has taken days of labor to verify and which must have cost the author months of investigation to acquire. . .

Commencing with this address as a political pamphlet, the reader will leave it as an historical work — brief, complete, profound, impartial, truthful — which will survive the time and the occasion that called it forth, and be esteemed hereafter, no less for its intrinsic worth than its unpretending modesty.[61]

Before he returned to Illinois, Lincoln made the most of his trip by visiting his son Robert, who was studying at Phillips Exeter Academy in New Hampshire, preparatory to taking the entrance examinations for Harvard. As his itinerary became known, demands for his appearance as a speaker mounted. He started with a speech at Providence, and followed with others in various towns of New Hampshire and Connecticut. He returned home to find a boom already initiated for him by the

Chicago Tribune, the flattering reports of his eastern trip enhancing his reputation as a "favorite son."

At the Republican Convention in Chicago, early in May, Abraham Lincoln, the dark horse from the prairies, outdistanced the preconvention favorites, Seward and Chase, and was nominated on the third ballot. With the signs pointing clearly to a Republican victory in the fall, the nomination was tantamount to election.

FINAL SPLIT

The signs could not be mistaken. Two weeks earlier the Democratic Convention had met in Charleston, and had broken up without naming a candidate. The Douglas men, forming a majority of the convention, had tried desperately to compromise with the insurgent southern leaders. By convention rules, a two-thirds vote was necessary for nomination, and they needed southern help to obtain the designation for their candidate. But when the Fire-Eaters brought in a plank demanding Congressional protection of slavery in the territories, the Douglasites had no choice but to reject it. The southern radicals bolted. Fifty-seven ballots were taken, but Douglas could not muster the necessary two-thirds. On May 3 the convention adjourned, to meet and try again in Baltimore in the middle of June.

The fate of the party, however, was already sealed. Alexander Stephens read the situation correctly. "The party is split forever," he said. "The Union will certainly be disrupted. Men will be cutting each other's throats in a little while. In less than twelve months we shall be in a war, and that the bloodiest in history."[62]

Douglas, however, would not entirely give up hope of winning the Ultras to his side. On May 16 in a speech in the Senate he tried to convince the South of the benefits it had received from popular sovereignty. He addressed himself particularly to Jefferson Davis of Mississippi. Davis' opposition made him experience to the full the hostile impact of the Freeport Doctrine. In reply to Davis' claim that southern rights were negated by Douglas' theories, the Little Giant paraded the blessings they had conferred, at the same time dangling future dazzling prizes to be won by the marriage of "manifest destiny" and popular sovereignty:

> We are told that the necessary result of this doctrine of non-intervention, which, gentlemen, by way of throwing ridicule upon it, call squatter sovereignty, is to deprive the South of all participation in what they call the common Territories of the United States. . . Has the South been excluded from all the territory acquired from Mexico? . . . It is part of the history of the country that under this doctrine of non-intervention, this doctrine that you delight to call squatter sovereignty, the people of New Mexico have introduced and protected Slavery in the whole of that Territory. Under this doctrine, they have converted a tract of Free Territory into Slave Territory, more than five times the size of the State of New York. Under this doctrine, Slavery has been extended from the Rio Grande to the Gulf of California, and from the line of the Republic of Mexico, not only up to 36 deg. 30 min., but up to 38 deg. — GIVING YOU A DEGREE AND A HALF MORE SLAVE TERRITORY THAN YOU EVER CLAIMED. . . and yet you say that this is a sacrifice of Southern rights!
>
> These are the fruits of this principle which the Senator from Mississippi regards as hostile to the rights of the South. Where did you ever get any other fruits that were more palatable to your taste or more refreshing to your strength? What other inch of Free Territory has been converted into Slave Territory on the American continent, since the Revolution, except in New Mexico and Arizona under the principle of non-intervention? . . .
>
> If it be true that this principle of non-intervention has given to Slavery all New Mexico, which was surrounded on nearly every side by Free Territory, will not the same principle protect you in the northern states of Mexico when they are acquired, since they are now surrounded by Slave Territory; are several hundred miles further South; have many degrees of greater heat; and have a climate and soil adapted to Southern products? Are you not satisfied with these practical results?[63]

But it was to no avail. On May 22 Judah P. Benjamin, the Senator from Louisiana, who was to be Secretary of War in the Confederate Cabinet, arose to speak on the floor of the Senate. In the grandiloquent and polished oratory for which he was distinguished, he proceeded to state the grievances of the South against Douglas, raking up the embers of the party caucus at which the Little Giant had agreed to abide by the decision of the Supreme Court on the status of slavery in the territories, and ridiculing his Pyrrhic victory over Lincoln:

> Up to the years 1857 and 1858 no man in this nation had a higher or more exalted opinion of the character, the services and the political integrity of the Senator from Illinois than I had. . . It has been with reluctance and sorrow that I have been obliged to pluck down my idol from his place on high, and to refuse him any more support or confidence as a member of the party. . . On what ground has that confidence been forfeited, and why is it that we now refuse him our support and fellowship? . . .
>
> We accuse him for this, to wit: that having bargained with us upon a point upon which we were at issue, that it should be considered a judicial point; that he would abide the decision; that he would act under the decision, and consider it a doctrine of the party; that having said that to us here in the Senate, he went home, and under the stress of a local election, his knees gave way; his whole person trembled.
>
> His adversary stood upon principle and was beaten; and lo! he is the candidate of a mighty party for the Presidency of the United States. The Senator from Illinois faltered. He got the prize for which he faltered; but lo! the grand prize of his ambition today slips from his grasp because of his faltering in his former contest, and his success in the canvass for the Senate, purchased for an ignoble price, has cost him the loss of the Presidency of the United States.[64]

When the Democratic delegates reconvened at Baltimore on June 18, with the Douglas men in full control of the convention, it was understood that the Little Giant would be nominated. There were still some southerners present, however, and hopeful that the unity of the party might be preserved, perhaps by his stepping aside in favor of another, Douglas sent a message to his lieutenants:

> If my enemies are determined to divide and destroy the Democratic party, and perhaps the country, rather than see me elected, and if the unity of the party can be preserved, and its ascendancy perpetuated by dropping my name and uniting upon a reliable non-intervention and Union-loving Democrat, I beseech you, in consultation with my friends,

to pursue that course which will save the country, without regard to my individual interests. I mean all this letter implies.[65]

However, there was no way of bringing the Ultras back into the fold. It was not only the Little Giant's head that the radicals wanted, but also complete capitulation of the party to their demands. In the judgment of the convention there was no other Democrat who had a chance of victory against Lincoln in the North, and accordingly, Douglas was nominated on the second ballot.

The bolters soon followed with the nomination of their own candidate, John C. Breckenridge of Kentucky. Earlier in May, remnants of the Whigs and Know-Nothings, mostly from the border states, had met as the Constitutional Union Party under the chairmanship of John J. Crittenden, and nominated John Bell of Tennessee.

With this division among his rivals, the stage was set for Lincoln's election.

CHAPTER 15

A Century's Perspective

"The inferior races are our equals."

In this statement in the fifth debate at Galesburg, Abraham Lincoln epitomized his interpretation of the Declaration of Independence.

In the previous debate at Charleston he had stated: "There is a physical difference between the white and black races which I believe will forever forbid their living together on terms of social and political equality."

On the surface there was no doubt that the two statements appeared contradictory. Douglas was quick to take advantage of this apparent inconsistency and to charge Lincoln with making conflicting statements in various sections of Illinois to suit the bias of his audiences.

Lincoln endeavored to disprove this charge. In the next debate at Quincy he pointed to the fact that he had made similar statements in such diverse parts of the state as Ottawa, Chicago and Peoria. He could therefore justifiably claim that he had not changed his position at all. But the point was: — Was there not something inconsistent in the position itself? For how can inferiority be equated with equality?

Lincoln's strongest characteristic was his ability to reason closely and carefully from sound premises. Accordingly, before he can be charged with inconsistency or unsoundness, we must subject his position to analysis.

410

Lincoln and Douglas differed over a simple issue: Was the Negro a man? This was, of course, more basic than whether the Negro was inferior. If he were not a man, there was no cause for quarrel between North and South. He could be treated as a beast or a tool. But if it was agreed that the Negro was a man, the question of inferiority would arise. In that case, what was society to do about it? The twin questions of the Negro's humanity and inferiority posed moral problems which were at the root of the conflict between North and South.

Despite its vaunted "progress," the sophisticated twentieth century has not advanced far beyond the times of Lincoln and Douglas. It was only short years ago that the Nazis created the most odious tyranny in history on the theory of Aryan superiority. They classified certain races and groups not merely as inferior but as sub-human. On the basis of their theory they felt justified in wiping out large populations.

We should be under no illusions that the destruction of the Nazis, any more than the destruction of the Southern slave power, has purged the human family of concepts of superiority and inferiority. We still hear these theories in the United States and throughout the world.

Lincoln's position was clear. He had stated it on many platforms. At Peoria he declared pointedly: "Why deny the humanity of the slave?" It followed logically that since the Negro was a man, the "unalienable rights" of "life, liberty, and the pursuit of happiness" which the Declaration of Independence applied to "all men" must of necessity apply also to the Negro.

Lincoln saw two immediate implications. Since the Negro had a right to be free, slavery must be placed in the course of ultimate extinction. In order to accomplish this, the first step was to keep slavery out of the territories. The ultimate consequence would be that slavery would be abolished in the states where it already existed, probably through compensated emancipation. In Lincoln's view this would occur in "God's own good time," but probably not "in a hundred years at the least," as he stated in the Charleston debate.

These premises and their immediate implications contrasted with those of Douglas. Judging from his comparison of the Negro with the crocodile, and from his statements on inferior races, the Little Giant held a position between the more ex-

treme and the more moderate views prevalent in the South.
The extremists asserted that the Negro was less than a man,
hence no moral question was involved in his enslavement. The
moderates viewed the Negro as human but inferior. In both
cases, however, the conclusion was the same: The Negro must
be enslaved for his own and society's good. The slave was a
chattel in which his master had valuable property rights assertable in any territory of the United States.

Considered from the perspective of the twentieth century,
Lincoln's position was, of course, morally superior. But this
was not obvious to the men of his generation. Tradition,
custom and religious controversy had blunted moral judgment.

The ultimate implication of the southern position was that
slavery must eventually be accepted in all the states of the
Union. This was an inevitable consequence of the Dred Scott
decision which invested slavery with a special property right.
If the right was assertable and protectable in the territories,
it would have to be equally so in the states. Carried to its conclusion, this meant that slavery would finally replace the "free
system." Ironically this result would fulfill Lincoln's prediction
in his "house divided" speech that "the Union . . . will become all one thing or all the other."

Douglas, of course, endeavored mightily to resist this implication. He could not win northern votes on such a platform.
He therefore tried to straddle the Dred Scott decision and
finally at Quincy took the stand that the republic "can exist
forever divided into free and slave states."

However, Douglas' position was less vulnerable than Lincoln's. The true implications of Lincoln's premises, whether
he liked it or not, were that the Negro, as a free man, should
take his place as an equal in society, entitled to suffrage, full
participation in civic and economic life, and equal opportunities for education and personal betterment. The end result
would be that there would be no bars to his mingling socially
with the whites. These were implications that most northern
whites were not prepared to accept. As we have seen, the legal
restrictions imposed on him in many states reflected the common attitude in the North toward the free Negro. Fear of the
practical consequences of general emancipation was a stronger
argument than moral principle or logic. Especially was this

true if the consequences could be interpreted as an immediate threat.

This was Lincoln's Achilles heel, and it was at this that Douglas struck. He employed every opportunity to identify Lincoln with the Abolitionists, those radicals who wanted the future now. To Illinois audiences, who had more experience with free Negroes than with slaves, the specter of civic and social equality was more real than the seemingly remote possibility of the free states of the North becoming slave. In the argument over ultimate implications, therefore, Douglas had the advantage over Lincoln.

How was Lincoln to deal with this situation? The only way was by emphasizing his major premises, and their immediate, practical application, while underplaying their ulitimate consequences. What he asked of his audiences was a moral commitment on the absolute right of freedom for even the most lowly and despised on the basis of sheer humanity. The only present action he called for was keeping slavery out of the territories. The future would take care of itself, in "God's own good time."[1] These were simple propositions which average people, conservative in their outlook, could readily accept.

This position was in consonance with Lincoln's cautious, carefully-reasoned "one step at a time" philosophy. He pinpointed the issue and emphasized it repeatedly: Universal freedom some day, but keep slavery out of the territories now.

But, pressed by Douglas, Lincoln had to face up to the implicit long-range issue: — equality. He endeavored to dispose of it briefly by his statements at Ottawa and Charleston that the physical difference between the two races would forever (at Ottawa he said *"probably* forever") forbid their living together on terms of social and political equality. Were these statements merely part of his strategy for campaign purposes or did they reflect his true views of the matter? For Lincoln to make a statement for political purposes only, or for partisan advantage, was entirely out of character. He was that rare breed, an honest politician. He said what he sincerely believed. We must therefore conclude that while his statement on physical differences helped to repel Douglas' attack, it also represented his convictions.

This brings us to our original query: How can such a view

accord with his Galesburg statement, "the inferior races are our equals," or his Chicago statement, "let us discard all this quibbling about this man and the other man — this race and that race and the other race being inferior, and therefore they must be placed in an inferior position?"

In answering this question one must bear in mind that Lincoln was free of racial prejudice. There is ample proof of this in the public display, when he was President, of his friendship for Fred Douglass, the Negro orator, who had aided his debating campaign, and to whom the Little Giant had referred in his speeches with scorn. Douglass said of Lincoln, "he was the first great man that I talked with in the United States freely, who in no single instance reminded me of the difference between himself and myself, of the difference of color."[2]

But Lincoln was aware that his attitude ran counter to the general feeling of the public. He expressed it at Peoria where, in speaking of granting equality to the freed slaves, he said: "My own feelings would not admit of this; and if mine would, we well know that those of the great mass of white people will not. . . . A universal feeling, whether well or ill-founded, cannot be safely disregarded."

What, then, was the solution? Lincoln disliked the thought that the freed Negroes "must be placed in an inferior position." Four years before, at Peoria, he had phased it in another way: "Free them all and keep them among us as underlings? Is it quite certain that this betters their condition?"

It is clear that his humanitarianism looked beyond mere physical liberation. If an improved and improving status for the Negro could not be achieved within a white society, there was only one solution: — removal. This was also the solution advanced by Jefferson who concluded that "the two races, equally free, cannot live in the same government" for the reason that "nature, habit, opinion had drawn indelible lines of distinction between them."

Lincoln recognized, however, that removal was a remote possibility, or at best, a long-range goal. At Peoria he said: "If all earthly power were given me, I should not know what to do, as to the existing institution. My first impulse would be to free all the slaves, and send them to Liberia. . . But a moment's reflection would convince me . . . that its sudden execution is impossible."

Lincoln's position may then be summarized as follows:

1. The Negro, as a member of the human family, was included in the benefits of the Declaration of Independence.
2. As an equal, therefore, he was entitled to the unalienable right of freedom.
3. The fact that he might be considered inferior was no bar to this right.
4. If, however, the Negro were kept in an inferior state, his condition would not improve. (He would be deprived of the opportunity for the "pursuit of happiness" set forth in the Declaration of Independence.)
5. Since the "universal feeling" of white prejudice would permit no other than an unfavorable position for him, it would be best for the Negro to be separated from the white population in order that he might be able to function elsewhere as a dignified human being.

Viewed in perspective, Lincoln's position was entirely consistent. The contradictions between his statements at Peoria, Ottawa and Charleston, and those at Chicago and Galesburg are apparent rather than real. They are elements in a well-reasoned and logical analysis whose premises are basically humanitarian.

Failure to understand and appreciate Lincoln's position has resulted in attempts to tarnish his image as a symbol of freedom. The twentieth century has tended to disparage and debunk our national heroes, and Lincoln has not escaped. Critics have seized upon his words on equality spoken at Ottawa and Charleston, and upon his cautious acts as President, to depict him as the opposite of the protagonist of freedom. He has been called the "Reluctant Emancipator."[3] A section of Negro opinion, aggressive in the pursuit of Negro rights, has expressed disenchantment with Lincoln's time-honored image as the great friend of the Negro. White supremacists have also quoted him as authority for their prejudices.[4]

But these interpretations take Lincoln's words out of context with his purposes. What appear as harmful statements must be judged in conjunction with such other statements as "the inferior races are our equals," "quibbling about inferiority," and "keeping [the Negroes] as underlings," as well as with his magnificent utterances on freedom. It is then that the un-

distorted picture emerges, and Lincoln's place with the im-
mortals remains secure.

If he can be faulted in any respect it is in his failure to see
that the solution to the race problem lay in both races eventually living together on terms of equality. But even here we must
hesitate to make an absolute judgment. Two clues in Lincoln's
position would seem to justify caution before arriving at such
a conclusion. First, Lincoln was a believer in the arbitrament
of time. With regard to universal freedom for the Negro he
spoke of "God's own good time." Is it unreasonable to assume
that he thought in the same terms with regard to equality for
the Negro?

One is led to the possibility of such a conclusion from the
second clue: At Ottawa he used the word "probably" to
qualify his opinion that it was forever impossible for the two
races to live together on terms of equality. Lincoln was very
careful and precise in his choice of words. Does his use of the
expression "probably forever" instead of the uncompromising
"forever" indicate that he could have entertained the idea that
at some time in the future both races could indeed live together on terms of equality, and that removal of the Negro was
not necessarily the solution?

LINCOLN'S SENSE OF HISTORY

Obviously there is no clear-cut answer to this question. The
two clues take on added significance when viewed in the light
of Lincoln's strong sense of history. We have already seen
several instances of this. In the fragment written in 1856, he
said of Douglas: "His name fills the nation; and is not unknown, even, in foreign lands. I affect no contempt for the
high eminence he has reached. So reached, that the oppressed
of my species, might have shared with me in the elevation, I
would rather stand on that eminence, than wear the richest
crown that ever pressed a monarch's brow." At Peoria in 1854
he expressed concern over the harm done by slavery to "our
republican example [and] its just influence in the world,"
while in the debate at Quincy he spoke of "drama in the face
of the world."

His conception of its ideals prompted him at Beardstown to
refer to the Declaration of Independence as "a beacon for the

farthest posterity." In his speech against the Dred Scott decision in June 1857 he described the Declaration as "augmenting the happiness and value of life to all people of all colors everywhere," and as "contemplating the progressive improvement in the conditions of all men everywhere."

In view of this evidence[5] can we say that Lincoln's perspective of history was long and broad enough to envision the eventual equality of the races living together and not separated? Before venturing an answer, we should give attention to Lincoln's place in the evolution of American society.

The American Revolution and the establishment of the United States have been regarded as a great political experiment. It has also been an experiment in human relations on a tremendous scale. From the time the first settlers came to these shores, the nation was destined to be a huge laboratory where man's age-old dreams of freedom, equality and dignity were to be tested and brought to reality.

This process has thus far gone through three stages. First, the period of preparation up to the American Revolution. Second, the period of the Declaration of Independence, the Revolution, and the establishment of the government of the United States. Third, the struggle, which ended in civil war, to achieve the most fundamental ideal of the Declaration: freedom from physical subjection for everyone no matter how lowly or despised. We are now in the fourth stage: the struggle to achieve equal opportunity in all spheres of life for all men, regardless of race, color or religion. There has never been anything in history comparable to this human experiment. Wave on wave of immigration has brought to America large groups of peoples of diverse backgrounds, and they have merged and been assimilated. But this has been the first instance in which exceptionally large numbers of a primitive people with different physical characteristics have been placed in intimate juxtaposition with a people at the opposite end of the scale of civilization. Thus integration has called for a process of adjustment unparalleled in human relations.

Did Lincoln see this? Did he look beyond the third stage of our history, of which he was the chief actor, to the fourth stage? A fairer question is: Can we or should we expect our great men to possess the powers of specific prophecy? Obviously not. Let us rather be satisfied that they are adequate for the problems of their times and that their influence serves as an inspiration for the future.

Of one thing there can be no doubt. Lincoln viewed the Declaration of Independence as a human, not as merely a political, document. Some who regard the American Revolution as a political expression consider it to be outmoded and ripe for replacement by movements supposedly more significant to the common man, such as Communism or, up to a few years ago, Fascism. Nothing can be more erroneous. The strength of the American Revolution, which Lincoln felt so keenly, lies in its emphasis on human values. This has been the true "wave of the future."

As the land whose genius gave expression to the visions of men in the Declaration of Independence, the United States seems destined to continue to serve as the chief experimental laboratory in which those visions will be worked out in practice. There seems little hope for mankind in the other misnamed "waves of the future." Fascism has already been discredited and destroyed. After many years of deception, Communism has shown its true face — an unabashed, brutal dictatorship, which disregards human values in the pursuit of material values. It is to the United States, therefore, that the newly-born nations of Africa and Asia will look for inspiration and guidance, because a concern for human values seems to bring material rewards, and not the other way around.

Lincoln may not have been a prophet, but he was a profound interpreter of the American Revolution. It is because the world has always sensed his humanitarianism and his understanding of the significance of the Declaration of Independence "for all men everywhere" that he will continue as the symbol of America's destiny, long after the fourth stage of American development has been completed, and an unforeseeable fifth stage has emerged.[6]

THE REHABILITATION OF DOUGLAS

Paralleling the detraction of Lincoln have been efforts to rehabilitate Douglas. There is no question that the Little Giant deserves reassessment of his place in history. Probably no other great figure has received more unmerited harsh treatment at the hands of historians. This is undoubtedly due to the human foible which insists upon finding a villain wherever we have a hero. Douglas has been cast in the role of the misguided statesman who pleaded a lost and dishonorable cause, the unscrupulous politician whose overweening ambition to become President caused him to straddle issues.

Over the last generation, however, several historians have endeavored to reevaluate the stature of the Little Giant. The most prominent is George Fort Milton, who in his exhaustive work, *The Eve of Conflict: Stephen A. Douglas and the Needless War,* advances the theory that if Douglas' doctrines had prevailed, the Union would have been preserved without war. Gerald Capers, in his perceptive biography, *Stephen A. Douglas, Defender of the Union,* voices a similar opinion.

The rehabilitators of Douglas base their theory on the following premises:

1. The doctrine of popular sovereignty is sound. Democracy is inconsistent with the unrestrained power of a strong central government. Local expression of the popular will is the key to freedom. The old conflict between the governmental theories of Jefferson and Hamilton is as vital today as it was in 1858, and will continue to be so in the future.

2. Douglas was sensible enough to recognize that slavery was doomed by changing economic conditions. He also envisioned an expanding West, where climate, soil and other natural factors would make slavery impossible. Hence, popular sovereignty was the only way to allow these conditions and factors political expression.

3. Douglas was personally opposed to slavery. His concessions to the South and his refusal to denounce slavery as a moral wrong merely reflected his efforts to prevent a sectional split and preserve the Union.

4. Douglas was the only national figure who could have held the South in line and prevented secession. While opposed by the extremist faction in 1860, he had the support of a large following of moderates like Alexander Stephens. This group, though crushed and silenced by the intransigents, were really in the majority in the South. If Douglas had been elected President, they would have been able to give expression to

their views and eventually to rally the South to his support.

Close examination reveals the invalidity of this theory. The conclusion is inescapable that the question of morality was the determinant in the slavery issue. Historians of the school of economic determinism may take issue with this, but on analysis, the points advanced above inevitably founder on this question.

First, the matter of popular sovereignty. In addition to the numerous political expositions of his doctrine, Douglas had very ably presented the legal case for local determinism in his *Harper's* article. The weakness of his position, however, was that he allowed popular sovereignty to be the determinant of right and wrong. At Memphis in November 1858 he stated that "the people have the right to decide the question of goodness or badness for themselves." In the same speech, he said, "I have never thought proper to disguise the fact that, if the people desire slavery, they are entitled to have it."[7] In 1848 he had stated to Senator Foote of Mississippi in a Senate debate:

> In the North it is not expected that we should take the position that slavery is a positive good — a positive blessing. If we did assume such a position, it would be a very pertinent inquiry, why do you not adopt this institution? We have moulded our institutions in the North as we have thought proper; and now we say to you of the South, if slavery be a blessing, it is your blessing; if it be a curse, it is your curse; enjoy it — on you rest all the responsibility.[8]

Douglas took the position that while he personally might not favor doing wrong, he had no objection if his neighbor did. He was not his brother's keeper, nor would he act as his moral censor. This was in keeping with the views he expressed when defending the Compromise of 1850 in his stirring speech to the populace at Chicago. It was equivalent to saying he would not commit murder, but it would be all right if the other fellow did. Any action was acceptable if it was voted by the people.

The untenability of this position was summarized by Hannis Taylor in an article entitled "The Lincoln-Douglas Debates and Their Application to Present Day Problems":

> Against the contention of Douglas that under the doctrine of "popular sovereignty" even a question so grave as human

> slavery might be localized stood Lincoln's contention that
> all local questions that affect all are the common concern of
> all. . . . When we consider the application of the basic prin-
> ciple involved in the famous debate of 1858 to present prob-
> lems, we should never for a moment forget that Lincoln's
> contention . . . has become the corner-stone of our new na-
> tional life. The first application of that principle by the
> reunited nation was in the destruction of a peculiar social
> institution [polygamy] within the Territory of Utah which
> conflicted with the general principles of our civilization.[9]

It is interesting to note that the question of popular sovereignty for the Mormons was raised in the encounter between
Douglas and Lincoln over the Dred Scott decision in June 1857.
The problem was: Could the Mormons in their territory vote
to have polygamy just as the people of Kansas could vote to
have slavery? Douglas skirted the question by holding that the
Mormons were in open rebellion against the United States and
that therefore they and their institutions, including polygamy,
should be suppressed. Lincoln, however, asked whether Douglas would favor the admission of the people of Utah into the
Union if they should "peacefully form a State Constitution
tolerating polygamy."[10] Douglas never answered this question,
and Lincoln concluded that the doctrine of popular sovereignty was "a mere deceitful pretense for the benefit of
slavery."[11]

LOCAL VERSUS FEDERAL LAW

A fatal flaw in Douglas' doctrine was his failure or unwilling-
ness to face up to the ultimate implications of the conflict of
local versus federal law. This was strikingly revealed in the
impasse between popular sovereignty and the Dred Scott decision. It was impossible to reconcile them; yet Douglas tried
to do it.

His conception of popular sovereignty was a narrower one
than Lincoln's. To Lincoln, popular sovereignty was expressed
on a nationwide as well as on a local scale. The national popular
will was just as important as local sentiment. Where there was
a conflict between them, the national will, freely expressed,
would have to be supreme. Lincoln, therefore, saw the nation
becoming "all one thing or all the other," as he said in his

"house divided" speech. In the conflict of views, one would
have to prevail. The nation could not exist as Douglas envisioned it, permanently split half-slave and half-free, or as two
separate nations side by side.

In support of the soundness of Douglas' popular sovereignty,
Milton in his article, "Douglas' Place in American History,"
cites the ineffectuality of the Fifteenth Amendment guaranteeing to the Negro the right to vote, because of southern opposition. He also points to the failure of the federal Prohibition
amendment.[12] His conclusion in the latter instance is faulty.
The opposition to prohibition was nationwide, not local, and
this is what brought about its repeal. As regards the Fifteenth
Amendment, it is sufficient to point out that the country is
now in the midst of a struggle to enforce the civil rights
guarantees of the Fourteenth and Fifteenth Amendments over
southern resistance.

The second premise — Douglas' belief that popular sovereignty would reflect economic and natural conditions, and
thus doom slavery — also does not withstand examination.
One of his statements on which his apologists base their contention is taken from the Senate debate on the Compromise of
1850. At that time Calhoun proposed a constitutional amendment to restore and preserve the original equilibrium between
the sections: an equal number of slave and free states,
Douglas opposed this. Speaking about the "laws of nature, of
climate and production," he said:

> We have a vast territory stretching from the Mississippi
> to the Pacific, which is rapidly filling up with a hardy, enter-
> prising, and industrious population, large enough to form at
> least seventeen new free States. . . I think I am safe in assum-
> ing that each of these will be free Territories and free States,
> whether Congress shall prohibit slavery or not. Now let me
> inquire where are you to find the slave Territory with which
> to balance these seventeen free Territories? . . . There is
> none — none at all.[13]

They also cite Douglas' belief that the Missouri Compromise
line was ineffectual and its repeal a step toward freedom. Support for this is found in what Douglas is said to have told
George Murray McConnell at the time of the Kansas-Nebraska
debate. This was the young man whose father had befriended

Douglas in his early days at Jacksonville. In his recollections of Douglas in 1900, McConnell recalls the statement of the Little Giant that with the repeal of the Missouri Compromise and the substitution of popular sovereignty, "slavery can no longer crouch behind a line which Freedom is cut off from crossing."[14]

Against these early statements stand Douglas' later ones — those which he repeated prior to, in the course of, and subsequent to the debates with Lincoln. In them he defended slavery as being in accord with the intent of the founding fathers, and finally in the Quincy debate committed himself to the position that the Union was designed to exist forever half-slave and half-free. He also repeatedly advocated the annexation of Cuba, as well as of Mexico and Central America, in order to provide the "natural conditions" where slavery could thrive and popular sovereignty could thus assert itself in favor of the institution.

That Douglas did not really conceive of popular sovereignty as a sound principle for the operation of freedom is thus an inescapable conclusion. The best its apologists can say for it is that it was a device to preserve the Union. But the emptiness of the doctrine as a principle or as a device was illustrated at the Democratic national convention at Charleston in 1860 where Douglas discarded it in favor of a plank which accepted the Dred Scott decision of the Supreme Court on the status of slavery in the territories.[15] Its hollowness was further revealed after Lincoln's election, when Douglas supported a compromise proposal by Senator Crittenden for the restoration of the Missouri line in order to halt the threatened secession of the southern states.[16]

By contrast, Lincoln, as President-elect and head of the Republican Party, set his face against any compromise which would open the territories to slavery, though there were many in the Republican ranks who wavered at the sight of the impending break-up of the Union. To insure adherence to this cardinal principle of the Republican Party, he wrote to Trumbull and other Republican leaders to "hold firm as with a chain of steel."[17]

On December 11, 1860 he wrote to William Kellogg, a member of the House of Representatives: "Entertain no proposition for a compromise in regard to the extension of slavery. The instant you do, they have us under again; all our labor is lost, and sooner or later must be done over. . . The tug has to come and better now than later."[18] To Elihu B. Washburne he wrote: "Whether it be a Missouri line or . . . popular sovereignty, it is all the same. Let either be done, and immediately filibustering and extending slavery recommences."[19]

Lincoln was probably convinced that economic and natural conditions were not the primary factors in determining the status of men of different skin color. Black men could work in cold and snow, and white men in torrid heat, as statistics of the time proved,[20] and white men might become subjected to slavery if the theories of a prominent Southern sociologist were to be followed.[21] Lincoln was more concerned with a philosophy of government, a relationship of man to man, based on freedom for all men everywhere, as he had said so often in his clashes with Douglas. He had a principle, and he stuck to it.

DOUGLAS AS AN ANTI-SLAVERY MAN

We turn now to the premise that Douglas was opposed to slavery, and that his refusal to denounce it as a moral wrong, and his concessions to the South, must be excused because of his desire to avoid a sectional split and thus preserve the Union.

The chief evidence to substantiate this premise is the account given by George Murray McConnell. Douglas met McConnell in a Washington hotel on the night that Chase's "Appeal of the Independent Democrats" attacking Douglas and the Kansas-Nebraska Act was published. Greatly wounded by this unexpected and vicious assault upon him, Douglas opened his heart to his young friend. It was forty-six years later that the story came to light in McConnell's account. McConnell recollects him as saying:

> I am not pro-slavery. I think it is a curse beyond computation, to both white and black. But we exist as a nation by virtue only of the Constitution, and under that there is no way to abolish it. I believe that the only power that can destroy slavery is the sword, and if the sword is once drawn, no one can see the end. . .[22]
> I am not willing to violate the Constitution to put an end to slavery. To violate it for one purpose will lead to violating it for other purposes. To "do evil that good may come" is false morality and worse policy, and I regard the integrity of

this political Union as worth more to humanity than the whole black race. Some time, without a doubt, slavery will be destroyed.[23]

McConnell's story offers the only clear-cut statement of Douglas' personal attitude toward slavery. It is open to challenge, however, because it was written so long after the event and trusts to the memory of its writer. There is also the evidence offered by Frank E. Stevens in his biography of Douglas. Stevens says that Douglas' sons, Robert M. and Stephen A. Jr. told him that their father was not pro-slavery.[24] The author also quotes a letter by the Reverend James Lemen, written to his son, Dr. Moses P. Lemen, on November 20, 1868:

> From his declarations I know that at heart, he [Douglas] was anti-slavery. . . Like Jefferson, who tolerated slavery, Douglas recognized it as a feature of the Constitution, but he believed that the southern people themselves, like Jefferson did, would eventually favor its extinction, and thus obviate all danger of war; but he held, that while the Constitution allowed the people in the states to hold slaves, if they would be of help to the people in the hardships of reclaiming a territory, and they wanted them, they should have them. I am aware that a good many people thought that Mr. Douglas was really pro-slavery at heart, but, in fact, he was opposed to it, just as Jefferson was. . .[25]

This evidence is also open to challenge. The statements of Douglas' sons may be considered as self-serving declarations to defend the reputation of their father. The letter by Reverend Lemen merely gives his unsubstantiated impression of what Douglas felt at heart, and it suffers from contradictions. Douglas cannot be compared with Jefferson, who unlike Douglas, proclaimed his hostility to slavery and took some measures, as we have seen, to effect its abolition. Furthermore, Douglas' belief that "the southern people would eventually favor its [slavery's] extinction" is negated by the statement that if "they wanted them [slaves], they should have them."

Other possible indications of an anti-slavery attitude on the part of Douglas are his replies to Foote in 1848 and to Calhoun in 1850, but the conclusion in these instances must be reached by implication. Further evidence is also offered in Douglas' refusal to accept a wedding gift of a Mississippi slave plantation from his father-in-law, Colonel Robert Martin.

All of Douglas' numerous public statements, however, not only upheld the morality of slavery, but interpreted the Declaration of Independence and the Constitution as approving it. He advocated the Union as a permanent association of free and slave states and favored southward expansion in order to provide more territory which would be conducive to slavery.

It was these pronouncements, rather than the hidden private feelings known supposedly only to McConnell or to a few intimate friends, that were influential in shaping the public mind and determining policy.

As for the slave plantation in Mississippi, Douglas continued to serve as its manager even after his wife's death, when the property devolved to his sons. One cannot escape the conclusion that, if slavery were abhorrent to him, Douglas would have found some way of ridding his sons of an odious benefit from slavery, and himself of the distasteful burden of managing the estate. In any event, if he could not emancipate his slaves, he could have sold the plantation and turned the proceeds into an investment more congenial to his feelings and those of his family.

Nor can the contention be accepted that Douglas subordinated his feelings because of his desire to preserve the Union. By his attack on the Republican Party as a sectional party whose principles were not merely radical but treasonable, he helped convince the South that it would be in great peril if a Republican President were elected. He constantly repeated that the Republicans meant to war upon the South and destroy it. In this way he contributed to the break-up of the Union, which he loved beyond any doubt.

It is true that he made these alarmist statements in the course of political embroilment. Yet only once did he essay the role of statesman instead of politician to emphasize to the South that adherence to the Constitution meant submission to majority rule. This occurred during the presidential campaign of 1860 when he sought to counteract the damage he had done by stumping the South to advise and warn against secession in the event of Lincoln's election. But by then it was too late.

As for concessions to the South for the sake of preserving the Union, those in the Nebraska Bill certainly do not belong in this category. The desire to open up the West, mingled with personal ambition, was probably his motive. Ironically, the concessions he made led directly to the fragmentation of the Democratic Party which Douglas regarded as the sole agency able to hold the Union together.

The most generous conclusion is that if Douglas was privately opposed to slavery, it was most regrettable that he permitted a dichotomy between his private and public expressions on a vital moral question. Not only he, but the country, was the loser.

NO CIVIL WAR?

The final premise of Douglas' rehabilitators is that if he had been elected President, the Union might have been preserved without civil war. This argument might have some validity if, as Professor Capers points out, his party had nominated him when it adopted his platform in 1856. At that time, before the Dred Scott decision and the destruction of the popular sovereignty doctrine, he might have had a good chance for election in spite of the furor aroused in the North by the Kansas-Nebraska Act.

But what kind of Union would have been saved? Assuming that Douglas could have influenced the course of the country, his program would have meant a Union which acknowledged the morality of slavery and engaged in southward expansion to increase the area of slavery; a Union whose Declaration of Independence had been reduced to ashes and whose Constitution was no longer a charter of free government. Instead of serving as a "beacon" of inspiration to millions throughout the world, the Union would have disappointed the hopes of mankind. An anomaly in a changing world, it would have forfeited its influence on the course of democracy.

Would economic conditions eventually have forced the southern states to abolish slavery? Perhaps. But the process would have been an exceedingly slow one. The snail's pace at which the rights of the freed Negro have been recognized and extended since the Civil War forces the conclusion that the rapid movement of world events would have outstripped any process of gradual emancipation, and trammeled the United States with an anachronistic institution. When we consider how America has been hampered in world affairs because of discrimination and segregation, it is easy to see how much worse its position would have been if emancipation had lagged, as it seems certain it would have.

It is doubtful, however, that the election of Douglas in 1856 would have had any result other than to postpone the eventual conflict. The root of controversy was too strong and too deep. The history of slavery shows clearly that the South was in the grip of a small clique of rabid slaveholders, who insisted on the perpetuation and the extension of slavery, and pursued a political course to attain these goals. They originally went along with the Missouri Compromise line because it guaranteed protection to slavery in some areas of the newly acquired Louisiana territory. Later they sought repeal of the Compromise, preferring the possibility of a foothold in formerly forbidden territory through popular sovereignty. Then the Dred Scott decision rendered dependence on popular sovereignty unnecessary by ruling that slavery could not be kept out of the territories. This led to a demand for enforcement of the decision through a Congressional slave code, which would have afforded federal protection to slavery in the territories.

The slaveholders used any political weapon to maintain their power and property. To them, democratic government with its emphasis on majority rule was of no consequence. They looked upon the expression of the popular will with contempt. Government was merely a vehicle for obtaining what they wanted, an instrument for imposing their policies on the country.

Lincoln recognized the calibre of this clique. He had indicated in the course of the debates what their grand strategy was: the nationalization of slavery. This was a necessary corollary to the Dred Scott decision. When he spoke of the conspiracy of Stephen, Franklin, Roger and James he had in mind the ultimate objectives of the slavocracy.

Douglas, of course, could not be accused of engaging in a conspiracy in the usual sense of a plot hatched under clandestine circumstances. Certainly there is no evidence to prove the charge, and considerable evidence to disprove it, such as his break with Buchanan and the southern radicals over Lecompton. But the charge of conspiracy was freely bandied about in those days of hysteria and tension, and as Lincoln pointed out in the Ottawa debate, Douglas himself levelled a similar charge against the Washington *Union* and the Buchanan administration when he termed their policies a "fatal blow being struck at the sovereignty of the states of this Union."

The kind of conspiracy Lincoln envisioned was a general cooperation in the interests of the slavocracy, arising out of a sympathy with those interests, and an understanding of the direction they were to take. It was a conspiracy in the sense that applied to the Nazis, Fascists and Japanese before the outbreak of the Second World War. Their general goals were the same and they complemented each other's efforts to destroy the democracies and impose dictatorship on the world. As Lincoln stated it in his "house divided" speech, the advocates of slavery would "push it forward till it will become alike lawful in all the states, old as well as new, North, as well as South." To Lincoln, Douglas' actions stamped him as one of those deliberately engaged in promoting the southern cause.

In his speech at Cooper Union, Lincoln bluntly characterized the nature of the southern clique. Addressing his words to them, he said:

> Your purpose, then, plainly stated, is that you will destroy the Government, unless you be allowed to construe and enforce the Constitution as you please, on all points in dispute between you and us. You will rule or ruin in all events. . .

The history of social change, as illustrated in the French and Russian revolutions, shows that the grip of an entrenched, willful, reactionary minority can be broken only by force and bloodshed. The historians who speculated that Douglas could have turned the tide of events and prevented civil war have indulged in wishful thinking, motivated no doubt by admiration of the man and by the desire to justify his policies. The slavocracy could be destroyed only by war.

Some speculation exists that Douglas' break with Buchanan and the Administration over Lecompton indicated his own disillusionment with the slavocrats.[26] If this is so, it is pertinent to ask why he continued to try to appease them right up to the time of the Democratic convention of 1860. Why did he not desert the Democratic Party and join the Republican ranks, as so many other prominent Democrats, such as Chase, Sumner and Trumbull, had done? We have seen that shortly after the break, there were rumors to that effect as well as to the possibility of his organizing a Constitutional Union Party, composed of Republicans and Union Democrats.[27]

But Douglas could not do this. By nature and training he was intensely loyal. Besides being a staunch party man, he held a position of foremost eminence and leadership within the party. He could not afford to jeopardize this position by quitting and leaving the field to his rivals. There was also much to be said for the party. It might be in the grip of the slaveholders, but it was still the party of Jefferson and Jackson, and therefore committed to the interests of the common man. It was opposed to such tendencies as Know-Nothingism, it favored the immigrant and his rights, and its economic policies had been designed originally to benefit the many, rather than the few.

It is possible that Douglas believed that the grip of the slaveholders could be broken and that he was the one to do it. He alone could rally the northern Democrats, whose preponderance of votes could control the party's destiny. United on a moderate program based on popular sovereignty (provided the Dred Scott decision could be reversed), the party could then unify the country and destroy the threat of secession.

This is also mere speculation. If Douglas was disillusioned with the southern clique, his actions did not show it. He did his best to demonstrate that he was a northern man with southern principles. We have seen how he supported the Dred Scott decision in the debates with Lincoln, and how he tried to convince the South in his post-debate trip through the area that his advocacy of popular sovereignty and of expansion in Latin America served the slavery interests. We have also seen how, on the floor of the Senate, he tried to appease Jefferson Davis and his Southern colleagues by reciting the great benefits that accrued to their section as a result of his efforts. And finally we have seen that the Democratic convention at Baltimore, which nominated him for the presidency, adopted a plank with his approval, supporting the decision of the Supreme Court on the status of slavery in the territories, and calling on all branches of the federal government to enforce it.[28] This meant final capitulation of popular sovereignty to the doctrine of Dred Scott. Certainly this was not the course of a man interested in breaking the hold of the slaveholders and uniting the party on northern terms.

DOUGLAS' PLACE IN AMERICAN HISTORY

Douglas' rehabilitation does not depend on these unsound premises. The reassessment of his place in history need not rest on vain speculation. His claim to distinction stands on more solid ground and his career has a significance beyond his own time.

Few public men have possessed to a greater degree his remarkable qualities: courage, energy, fairness, generosity and brilliance in debate. Few, also, have been so driven by ambition. These traits powered him to political eminence, but it was his passionate love of the Union that motivated his most lasting achievements. On this rests his claim to an honored place in history.

His greatest contribution was his part in the opening up of the western territories. The expansion of the United States was, for him, almost a fixation. No one had a more glorified concept of the nation's "manifest destiny." To him the Republic was a "young giant" whose limbs could not be "fettered," whether by treaties or timidity. Unlike Lincoln, who envisioned the Union in spiritual terms as a "beacon" of freedom and equality for all peoples, Douglas beheld it from the viewpoint of physical and material growth. He saw the country teeming with settlers from coast to coast, and in the debate on Oregon he looked to ascendancy in the Pacific Ocean in the competition with Britain for the trade with the Far East.

As Chairman of the Committee on Territories, first of the House and later of the Senate, he was intent on extinguishing Indian titles and facilitating the entry of settlers who would eventually bring the territories into the Union as states. It is true that his desire for expansion into Latin America betrayed an aggressive chauvinism which, undesirable in itself, was the more so in seeking to benefit the slavery interests. Nevertheless, the United States is indebted to him in large measure for the legislation which made the settlement of the West possible.

It was in the mistaken conviction that the states could be held together on the slaveholder's terms that Douglas' love of the Union was misguided. But during the campaign of 1860 and the inauguration of Lincoln this passion for the Union reached its finest expression. It was then that the Little Giant touched greatness. Contrary to the custom of the times which called for presidential candidates to remain at home, Douglas stumped the South to warn against secession. He need not have done this. His health was poor and he was almost bankrupt, but he taxed himself physically and financially because he saw the certainty of Lincoln's election and the possible danger- ous consequences to the Union if the South refused to accept the verdict. Courageously he toured hostile territory to call upon the South to abide by the result.

At Lincoln's inauguration he had a prominent place on the platform in order to symbolize the support of the northern Democracy for Lincoln's task of preserving the Union against the southern seceders. During the ceremonies he held his rival's hat as though to indicate openly the submergence of his dis- appointment and the bitterness of defeat in the greater cause of the country's welfare — a worthy example for politicians who cannot rise above their own petty ambitions.

Douglas merits recognition, therefore, as one of the country's most intriguing and important political figures. But what kept him from reaching the stature of statesmanship and greatness? Allan Nevins in his essay "Stephen A. Douglas: His Weaknesses and his Greatness," says he lacked "the long look ahead."[29] He terms Douglas a brilliant improviser, whose motto was, "For- ward, forward! Hurry, hurry! Improvise, improvise!"[30] This perceptive characterization explains many of the vagaries and contradictions in the Little Giant's career, such as the abandon- ment of the Missouri Compromise Line and the gyrations on the Kansas-Nebraska Bill.

But the cause lies deeper. The tragedy of the Little Giant was moral failure. This applies, of course, to his political career, and not to his personal life. On an issue of values so fundamental that it threatened to split the country, he was, by the most generous estimate, indifferent, if not hostile. There is a lesson in this for our times. Public life requires moral leadership. It is not so much the long look ahead as the ability to delineate and clarify the moral choices for a confused public and to provide the leadership toward attaining the chosen goals that distinguishes the statesman from the politician in a dem- ocratic society.

Had Douglas been "right" on the slavery issue, what would have been his place in history? He, instead of Lincoln, might have been the American hero of the nineteenth century. But, in the perspective of a century, it seems unlikely that the Little Giant will ever fully emerge from Lincoln's shadow, despite his substantial service to his country.

Perhaps he was born two generations too late. Had he lived at the time of the American Revolution, his extraordinary personality and powers would undoubtedly have won him a place among the great figures of the era. But the direction of his political genius was an anachronism in the third phase of our history — the struggle for freedom for all races in American society. He failed to comprehend the true nature of his country's destiny.

Lincoln and Douglas may be regarded as symbols of two forces, the spiritual and material, which have made America great. The nation's true strength, however, as revealed in times of crisis, lies in its spiritual heritage. This is expressed in the Declaration of Independence — the reflection of the conscience of America — of which Lincoln emerges as the foremost interpreter.

CHRONOLOGIES

THE LINCOLN-DOUGLAS CONFRONTATIONS

I. PRELIMINARY TO THE PRESIDENTIAL CAMPAIGN OF 1840

Douglas vs. Lincoln and Cyrus Walker   November 23, 1839

II. THE KANSAS-NEBRASKA ACT: 1854

Douglas at Chicago	September 1
Douglas at Springfield	October 3
Lincoln (Reply) at Springfield	October 4
Douglas (Rebuttal) at Springfield	October 4
Lincoln and Douglas at Peoria	October 16

III. THE DRED SCOTT DECISION: 1857

Douglas at Springfield	June 12
Lincoln at Springfield	June 26

IV. THE ILLINOIS SENATE CAMPAIGN OF 1858

Main Speeches Preliminary to the Formal Debates

Lincoln's Opening (House Divided) Speech	Springfield	June 16
Douglas' Opening Speech (Reply to Lincoln)	Chicago	July 9
Lincoln's Reply	Chicago	July 10
Douglas	Bloomington	July 16
	(afternoon) Springfield	July 17
Lincoln	(evening) Springfield	July 17

435

The Seven Formal Debates

Ottawa	Saturday, August 21
Freeport	Friday, August 27
Jonesboro	Wednesday, September 15
Charleston	Saturday, September 18
Galesburg	Thursday, October 7
Quincy	Wednesday, October 13
Alton	Friday, October 15

V. THE OHIO CAMPAIGN OF 1859

At Columbus, Douglas	September 7
Lincoln	September 16
At Cincinnati, Douglas	September 9
Lincoln	September 17

CHRONOLOGY OF THE LIVES OF
LINCOLN AND DOUGLAS

Douglas		*Lincoln*	
		1809	Born February 12 in Kentucky
1813	Born April 23 in Brandon, Vermont		
		1816	Family moves to Indiana
1828	Becomes apprentice cabinet-maker in Middlebury, Vt.	1828	Makes first flatboat trip to New Orleans
		1830	Family moves to Illinois
1831 -32	Student at Canandaigua Academy, New York Studies law	1831	Second flatboat trip to New Orleans Settles in New Salem, Illinois Clerk in store
		1832	Serves in Black Hawk War Defeated for Legislature Becomes partner in grocery store
1833	Goes west. Arrives in Jacksonville, Illinois Teaches school	1833	Appointed Postmaster at New Salem
1834	Admitted to bar	1834	Works as surveyor Studies law Elected to Legislature
1835	Elected State's Attorney by Legislature		
1836	Elected to Legislature	1836	Reelected to Legislature Admitted to bar
1837	Appointed Register of Federal Land Office at Springfield by President Van Buren	1837	Protests against pro-slavery action in Legislature Removes to Springfield Becomes law partner of John T. Stuart
1838	Defeated for Congress	1838	Reelected to Legislature
		1839	Meets Mary Todd
1840	Campaigns for Van Buren for President	1840	Reelected to Legislature Campaigns for Harrison for President
1841	Appointed Secretary of State of Illinois Elected Associate Justice of Supreme Court by Legislature	1841	Breaks off engagement with Mary Todd Enters law partnership with Stephen T. Logan Visits Joshua Speed's family at Louisville, Kentucky
		1842	Marries Mary Todd

Douglas	*Lincoln*
1842 Elected to Congress	
1844 Reelected to Congress	1844 Campaigns for Clay for President
-46 Becomes Chairman of Committee on Territories of House	Forms partnership with William H. Herndon
	1846 Elected to Congress
1847 Elected to United States Senate by Legislature	1847 Introduces "Spot Resolutions" in Congress
Becomes Chairman of Committee on Territories of Senate	
Marries Martha Denny Martin	
	1848 Campaigns for Taylor for President in New England
	1849 Presents bill to abolish slavery in the District of Columbia
1850 Effects Compromise of 1850	
1852 Seeks presidential nomination	
Reelected to Senate	
1853 Death of Mrs. Douglas	
Travels in Europe	
1854 Steers Kansas-Nebraska Act through Congress	1854 Delivers Springfield-Peoria speech
1856 Defeated for presidential nomination	1856 Joins Republican Party
Marries Adele Cutts	Makes famous "Lost Speech" at Bloomington
	Receives 110 votes for vice-presidential nomination
1857 Supports Dred Scott decision	1857 Opposes Dred Scott decision
Breaks with Buchanan over Lecompton Constitution	
1858 SENATORIAL CAMPAIGN: THE LINCOLN-DOUGLAS DEBATES	
1860 Nominated for President by northern Democrats	1860 Elected President
1861 Supports Union cause	
Death	
	1863 Emancipation Proclamation
	1865 Death

CHRONOLOGY OF SLAVERY

1619   Slaves introduced into Virginia
1776   Declaration of Independence
1787   Northwest Ordinance
1789   Constitution of the United States
1793   Invention of the Cotton Gin
1808   End of the Slave Trade
1817   Founding of the American Colonization Society
1820   Missouri Compromise
1823   Formation of the English Anti-Slavery Society
1831   William Lloyd Garrison and *The Liberator*
      Nat Turner's Insurrection
1833   Formation of American Anti-Slavery Society
1835   Attack on Garrison in Boston
1837   Elijah P. Lovejoy killed at Alton, Illinois
1840   Liberty Party formed — James G. Birney candidate for President
1844   Split in Methodist church
1846   Wilmot Proviso
1848   Free Soil Party formed
1849   Calhoun's "Address of the Southern Delegates in Congress to their Constituents"
1850   Compromise of 1850
1854   Kansas-Nebraska Act
      Republican Party formed
1855   Bleeding Kansas
1857   Dred Scott Decision
      Lecompton Constitution
1858   Lincoln-Douglas Debates

SLAVERY AND THE BALANCE OF POWER

How Admission of States into the Union
Affected Control of the Senate

	Free	Slave	Totals Free	Totals Slave
Original States	Massachusetts New Hampshire Connecticut Rhode Island New York New Jersey Pennsylvania	Delaware Maryland Virginia North Carolina South Carolina Georgia		
			7	6

Date			Free	Slave
1791	Vermont		8	6
1792		Kentucky	8	7
1796		Tennessee	8	8
1803	Ohio		9	8
1812		Louisiana	9	9
1816	Indiana		10	9
1817		Mississippi	10	10
1818	Illinois		11	10
1819		Alabama	11	11
1820	Maine		12	11
1821		Missouri	12	12
1836	Michigan	Arkansas	13	13
1845		Florida	13	14
		Texas	13	15
1846	Iowa		14	15
1848	Wisconsin		15	15
1850	California		16	15
1858	Minnesota		17	15
1859	Oregon		18	15

CHRONOLOGY OF "BLEEDING KANSAS" AND
THE LECOMPTON CONSTITUTION

1855

March	Election for territorial legislature. Border ruffians enter from Missouri and control election.
July-August	"Bogus Legislature" enacts "bogus laws."
October	Free State Constitution drawn up at Topeka.
November	"Law and Order" party formed by pro-slavery group.
December	Siege of Lawrence by pro-slavery "militia."

1856

January	President Pierce denounces the Topeka Constitution.
March	Investigating Committee appointed by the House of Representatives.
May	"Sack of Lawrence."
	John Brown at Pottawatomie Creek.
	Sumner's "Crime Against Kansas" speech.
June	Toombs Bill presented in Senate by Douglas.
July	Report of House Investigating Committee.
September	General Geary appointed Governor.

1857

January	Pro-slavery legislature provides for a constitutional convention. Delegates to be elected in June and to meet in September.
June	Election of delegates to the constitutional convention. Free-Staters boycott election. All elected delegates are pro-slavery.
September	Pro-Slavery Constitutional Convention meets in Lecompton. Adjourns until after October elections for legislature.
October	Election for legislature. Free-Staters win.
	Constitutional Convention meets.
November	The Lecompton Constitution. Convention provides for referendum on slavery provision on December 21, and election of a new legislature on January 4.
December 3	Douglas breaks with Buchanan over Lecompton.
7	Free-State legislature meets. Provides for January 4 referendum on entire constitution.
9	Douglas speaks against Lecompton.
21	First referendum on slavery provision of the Lecompton Constitution. Free-Staters abstain. Constitution with slavery voted.

1858

January 4	Second referendum. Pro-slaveryites abstain.
	Entire Lecompton Constitution voted down.
March	Senate passes Lecompton Bill. Crittenden substitute defeated.
April	House defeats Lecompton Bill. Passes Montgomery substitute.
	English Bill passes both Houses.
August	English Bill version of Lecompton Constitution defeated by people of Kansas.

DEBATE ITINERARIES OF
LINCOLN AND DOUGLAS

		Lincoln	*Douglas*
June	16	Springfield	
July	9		Chicago
	10	Chicago	
	16		Bloomington
	17	Springfield (evening)	Springfield (afternoon)
	27	Clinton (evening)	Clinton (afternoon)
	29	Monticello	Monticello
	30		Mattoon
	31		Paris
August	2		Hillsboro
	4		Greenville
	5		Highland
	6		Edwardsville
	7		Winchester
	9		Pittsfield
	11		Beardstown
	12	Beardstown	Walnut Hill
	13		Havana
	14	Havana	Lewistown
	16	Bath	Lewistown
	17	Lewistown	
	18		Peoria
	19	Peoria	Lacon
	21	*First Joint Debate at Ottawa*	
	23	Henry	
	24	Galesburg	
	25	Augusta (afternoon)	Galena
		Macomb (evening)	
	26	Amboy	
	27	*Second Joint Debate at Freeport*	
	28	El Paso	Turner Junction (now West Chicago)
	30	Tremont	
	31	Carlinville	Joliet
	2	Clinton	Pontiac
	4	Bloomington	Lincoln
			Springfield
	6	Monticello	Jacksonville
	7	Tolono	
		Mattoon	
		Paris	
	8		Carlinville
			St. Louis

	Lincoln	*Douglas*
9	Hillsboro	
10		Belleville
11	Edwardsville (afternoon)	Waterloo
	Highland (evening)	
13	Greenville	Chester
14		Cairo
15	*Third Joint Debate at Jonesboro*	
16		Benton
17		Centralia
18	*Fourth Joint Debate at Charleston*	
20	Sullivan (late afternoon)	Sullivan (early afternoon)
21		Danville
22	Danville	
23		Urbana
24	Urbana	
25	Springfield	Kankakee
27	Jacksonville	
28	Winchester	Hennepin
29	Winchester	Henry
30		Washington
		Metamora
October 1	Pittsfield	
2		Pekin
4	Metamora	Oquawka (afternoon)
		Burlington, Iowa (evening)
5	Pekin	Monmouth
7	*Fifth Joint Debate at Galesburg*	
8	Toulon	Macomb
9	Oquawka (afternoon)	Macomb (afternoon)
	Burlington, Iowa (evening)	Plymouth (evening)
11	Monmouth	Carthage
12		Augusta
		Camp Point
13	*Sixth Joint Debate at Quincy*	
15	*Last Joint Debate at Alton*	
16	Lincoln	Gillespie
18	Meredosia	Decatur
19	Mount Sterling	Springfield

		Lincoln	Douglas
	20	Rushville	Springfield
	21		Atlanta
	22	Carthage	Bloomington
	23	Dallas City	Peoria
		La Harpe	
	25	Macomb	
	26		Toulon
	27	Vermont	
	28		Geneseo
	29	Petersburg	Rock Island
	30	Springfield	
November	1		Chicago
	2	*Election Day*	

NOTES

CHAPTER 1: AMERICAN PARADOX

1. *Thomas Jefferson, Writings*, ed. by Paul Leicester Ford, Vol. III, 243–250. Jefferson wrote numerous private letters on the slavery problem, but most of his thinking is contained in his "Notes on Virginia," a sweeping analysis of the physical, economic and social features of his native state.

2. *Ibid.*, Vol. III, 267. See also *"The Jeffersonian Cyclopedia,"* ed. by John P. Foley, 812.

3. *Ibid.*, Vol. I, 440.

4. Ford, Paul Leicester, *Autobiography of Thomas Jefferson*, 76–77. See also Philip S. Foner, *Basic Writings of Thomas Jefferson*, 439–440. Also, Foley, *op. cit.*, 816.

5. Ford, *op. cit.*, Vol. III, 250.

6. Ford, *op. cit.*, 76–77; Foner, *op. cit.*, 439–440; Foley, *op. cit.*, 816.

7a. Meade, Robert D., *Patrick Henry, Patriot In The Making*, 299–300. Henry expressed these sentiments in a letter commenting on several pamphlets written by Anthony Benezet, a French-born Quaker. In the same vein he commented, "What adds to the wonder is that this abominable practice has been introduced in the most enlightened ages." "Would anyone believe that I am master of slaves of my own purchase?" "I lament . . . my want of conforming to [the precepts of virtue]."

   George Washington likewise found slavery "repugnant" to his feelings, a "powerful motive" to "liberate a certain species of property which [he] possessed" (Letter to Tobias Lear. *Writings of George Washington,* Vol. 33, p. 358). He was "principled against selling negroes as you would cattle in the market" (To Alexander Spottswood. Vol. 34, pp. 47–48), and "had resolved never to become the master of another slave by purchase" (To George Lewis. Vol. 36, p. 70). He

447

wished "sincerely to see a plan adopted for the abolition of slavery . . . by legislative authority" (To Robert Morris. Vol. 28, p. 408). This was "certain" to occur "at a period not remote" (To Sir John Sinclair. Vol. 35, p. 328), in order "to prevent future mischief" (To Lawrence Lewis. Vol. 36, p. 2). See also Padover, Saul K., *The Washington Papers*, p. 412.

In his will Washington provided for the manumission of all of his slaves.

8. Quoted in Helper, Hinton Rowan, *Compendium of the Impending Crisis of the South*, A. B. Burdick, New York, 1860, p. 131. John Wesley, the founder of Methodism, termed it "the sum of all villainies" Helper, 269.

9. Colonization was believed by some, especially in the South, to "pave the way for a general emancipation." Quoted in Jenkins, William S., *Pro-Slavery Thought In The Old South*, 57. The abolitionists were convinced, however, that it was merely "a plan to get rid of the free negroes [sic] in order to render slavery more secure." Quoted in Thomas, John L., *The Liberator, William Lloyd Garrison*, 116.

10. Calhoun, John C., *Works*, ed. by Richard K. Cralle, Vol. II, 629–633. See also *Slavery Defended, The Views of the Old South*, ed. by Eric L. McKitrick, 12–13. Calhoun expressed this sentiment in 1837, but Governors Miller and McDuffie of South Carolina enunciated it in 1829 and 1835 respectively. Jenkins, *op. cit.*, 76, 78.

11. Ford, *op. cit.*, Vol. X, 157.

12. *Ibid.*, Vol. VII, 158.

13. From Garrison's editorial "To The Public" in the first issue of *The Liberator*.

14. Garrison was fond of employing "Old Testament Hebraisms," according to one of his followers. In this case he took his text from Isaiah XXVIII, 15. Thomas, *op. cit.*, 330–331.

15. In 1842 this motto began to appear on the masthead of *The Liberator*. Thomas, *op. cit.*, 330, 332, 412.

16. Arnold, Isaac Newton, *The History of Abraham Lincoln and The Overthrow of Slavery*, 39. The governor was McDuffie of South Carolina.

17. This phrase was used as early as 1838, but Senator Charles Sumner gave prominence to it in his speech against the Kansas-Nebraska Bill on February 24, 1854. *Congressional Globe*, 33rd Cong., 1st Session, Append. p. 269. Beveridge, Albert J., *Abraham Lincoln*, Vol. II, 197 and note 2. In his answering speech of March 3, 1854, Douglas quoted Sumner and castigated him for use of the expression. Sheahan, James W., *The Life of Stephen A. Douglas*, 253; Flint, H. M., *Life of Stephen A. Douglas*, 135–136; *Life and Speeches of Stephen A. Douglas*, by A Member of the Western Bar, 135–136; Carr, Clark E., *Stephen A. Douglas*, 209.

18. *A Political Textbook for 1860*, ed. by Greeley and Cleveland, 179–181.

19. *Ibid.*, 17–18. The convention at which the platform was adopted was

known officially as the "Free Democratic" convention. For the Liberty Party platform, see p. 14. Designed as a Republican Party campaign instrument, the *Political Textbook* contains a compilation of information on national conventions, caucuses, platforms and election results from the beginning of the Republic to 1860, as well as significant speeches and documents on the slavery question.

20. Calhoun, *op. cit.*, Vol. VI, 290–313.

21. Nicolay and Hay, *Abraham Lincoln: A History*, Vol. I, 342. In his first annual message Pierce said, "The acquiescence of distinguished citizens . . . has restored a sense of repose and security to the public mind. . . . That this repose is to suffer no shock during my official term, if I have power to avert it, those who placed me here may be assured." *A Political Textbook for 1860*, p. 80.

22. Beveridge, *op. cit.*, Vol. II, 182 and note 3; Milton, George Fort, *The Eve of Conflict: Stephen A. Douglas and The Needless War*, 116. Nicolay and Hay, Vol. I, 350, state that Douglas showed the President's draft in his own writing to Hannibal Hamlin, later Vice-President of the United States. Douglas did not trust the vacillating Pierce and hence wanted evidence in the President's hand which he could not later disavow. For the language of the bill see *Congressional Globe*, 33rd Cong., 1st Session, Part 1, p. 421.

23. *History of the United States From the Compromise of 1850*, Vol. I, 490.

24. Senate speech, Feb. 3, 1854, page 28, printing of John T. and Lemuel Towers, Washington, 1854.

25. Sumner, Charles, *Works*, Vol. IV, 137–256.

26. Thomas Lanier Clingman, of North Carolina on December 22, 1847. *Congressional Globe*, 30th Cong., 1st Session, Append. p. 43.

27. Feb. 20, 1854 in the debate on the Kansas-Nebraska Bill. *Congressional Globe*, 33rd Cong., 1st Session, Append. p. 214.

28. *Congressional Globe*, 35th Cong., 1st Session, Append. p. 71. See also *Slavery Defended, The Views of the Old South*, ed. by Eric L. Mc Kitrick, 121–125, and Jenkins, *Pro-Slavery Thought In The Old South*, 286.

29. Calhoun, *op cit.*, VI, 290–313.

30. June 27, 1848. *Congressional Globe*, 30th Cong., 1st Session, Append. p. 872. See also Nevins, *Ordeal of the Union*, 419.

31. U. S. Supreme Court Reports, 19 Howard 393–633. These reports also appear in a special edition by Stephen K. Williams, published by The Lawyers' Cooperative Publishing Co., Newark, Wayne Co., N.Y., 1884, Vol. 60, pp. 691–795.

Channing, *A History of the United States*, VI, 186, points out that the name in the court report is incorrectly spelled Sandford.

For political aspects of the Dred Scott case see Warren's *The Supreme Court in United States History*, II, 279 ff; Rhodes' *History of the United States From The Compromise of 1850*, II, 252 ff; Nevins, Allan, *The Emergence of Lincoln*, Vol. II, 90–118.

32. Warren, *op. cit.*, 294 ff.

33. U. S. Supreme Court Reports, Williams' edition, 700–703.
34. *Ibid.*, 736.
35. *Ibid.*, 774.
36. *Ibid.*, 755–756.
37. Nevins, *op. cit.*, 96.
38. Seward, William H., *Works*, Vol. IV, 586. See also Nevins, *op. cit.*, 106.
39. Nevins, *op. cit.*, 83–84.
40. Johnson, Allen, *Life of Stephen A. Douglas*, 328; Stevens, Frank Everett, *Life of Stephen A. Douglas*, 519. See also Beveridge, *Op. Cit.*, II, 538; Milton, *Op. Cit.*, 273, Barton, William E., *The Life of Abraham Lincoln*, Vol. I, 365.
41. *Life of Stephen A. Douglas*, by A Member of the Western Bar, 123–125.
42. Milton, *op. cit.*, 280–283; Newton, Joseph Fort, *Lincoln and Herndon*, 145–149; Beveridge, *op. cit.*, II, 545–546, 592.
43. Rhodes, *op. cit.*, II, 296, cites the issue of February 26, 1858.

CHAPTER 2: "I NEVER DODGE A QUESTION": STEPHEN A. DOUGLAS

1. Douglas, *Autobiography*, 327. Frank E. Stevens, in his introduction to the autobiography, says it was "written in a little memorandum or pass book with a pencil."
2. Douglas takes his autobiography up to August 1836, the date of his election to the legislature.
3. Quoted in Milton, *The Eve of Conflict*, 25.
4. Sheahan, *The Life of Stephen A. Douglas*, 396–397. Milton, *op. cit.*, 303, note 48.
5. *Dictionary of American History*, James Truslow Adams, ed. The actual name of the band was "The Sons of Dan." For a full account of this secret organization, see Linn, *The Story of the Mormons*, 189–192.
6. Genesis XLIX, 17; Linn, *op. cit.*
7. Sheahan, *op. cit.*, 71. Sheahan gives a full account of the Jackson incident, together with Douglas' speech in the House, 60–71. See also Flint, *Life of Stephen A. Douglas,* 24, and the same title by A Member of the Western Bar, 28. (The latter book is an earlier edition by Flint. Both books are therefore almost identical except for pagination.) An abbreviated version of the Douglas speech is in Carr, *Stephen A. Douglas*, 145–155.
8. January 6, 1845. Quoted in Flint, 25, 27. See also Milton, *op. cit.*, 28 note 35.
9. May 13, 1846, given in Sheahan, *op. cit.*, 77.
10. Sheahan, *op. cit.*, 79.
11. *Ibid.*, 80.
12. Quoted in Carr, *op. cit.*, 58–59. See also Milton, *op. cit.*, 34.
13. Sheahan, *op. cit.*, 435–442, gives a full account of the matter, including Douglas' reply to the charge. See also Milton, *op. cit.*, 34–35.
14. Flint, *op. cit.*, and A Member of the Western Bar, *op. cit.*, Appendix 52. The full speech is given in both books, 31–54. See also Sheahan, *op. cit.*, 112–113.

15. *A Political Textbook For 1860,* ed. by Greeley and Cleveland, 215. See also Nevins, *Ordeal of the Union,* 101, note 55, quoting *Illinois State Register,* November 8, 1849.
16. Sheahan, *op. cit.,* 163–165.
17. Rhodes, *History of the United States From The Compromise of 1850,* I, 197. Milton, *op. cit.,* 81.
18. The full text of this speech is contained in both Flint, *op. cit.,* and A Member of the Western Bar, *op. cit.,* Appendix 3–30, and in Sheahan, *op. cit.,* 168–186. Douglas wrote out the speech from notes the next day: Sheahan, 186 and Milton, *op cit.,* 81, note 8.
19. Sheahan, *op. cit.,* 186; Flint, *op. cit.,* 46, Appendix 30; A Member of the Western Bar, *op. cit.,* 52, Appendix 30.
20. Sheahan, 184–185; Flint and A Member of the Western Bar, Appendix 27–29.
21. Sheahan, 169; Flint and A Member of the Western Bar, Appendix 4–5.
22. December 23, 1851. *Congressional Globe,* 32nd Congress, 1st Session, App. 66.
23. *Ibid.,* 68. See also Milton, *op. cit.,* 77, and Nicolay and Hay, *Abraham Lincoln: A History,* I, 334.
24. Sandburg, *Abraham Lincoln: The Prairie Years,* II, 126.
25. Sheahan, *op. cit.,* 443 ff. Gives a brief account of the European trip.
26. Nicolay and Hay, *op. cit.,* I, 357–358.
27. Beveridge, *Abraham Lincoln,* II, 182, note 2; Milton, *op. cit.,* 114; Nevins, *op. cit.,* II, 96; Milton, *op. cit.,* 114. All of the foregoing quote from *True History of the Missouri Compromise and its Repeal,* by Mrs. Archibald (Susan Bullett) Dixon, Cincinnati, 1899, p. 445.
28. Milton, *op. cit.,* 114, note 48; Rhodes, *op. cit.,* I, 434. These are also quoted from Dixon, *op. cit.,* 447–448.
29. *Congressional Globe,* 33rd Congress, 1st Session, Part I, 281–282. See also Beveridge II, 186; Rhodes I, 443; Milton, 120; Nevins II, 111–112.
30. Letter to Charles H. Lanphier, November 11, 1853. Johannsen, *The Letters of Stephen A. Douglas,* 267. See also Nevins, II, 81; Capers, *Stephen A. Douglas, Defender of the Union,* 85–86.
31. Flint, *op. cit.,* and A Member of the Western Bar, *op. cit.,* Appendix 85–86.
32. *Ibid.,* App. 75.
33. *Ibid.,* App. 89.
34. *Congressional Globe,* 33rd Cong., 1st Session, Appendix 325–338. See Beveridge, II, 215. The speech is also given and the above extracts are found in Sheahan 257, 258, 259–260; Flint and A Member of the Western Bar, Appendix 139, 140, 141–144.
35. Sheahan, 260, 261; Flint and A Member of the Western Bar, Appendix 144, 145.
36. June 3, 1854, as reported in the *New York Herald,* June 5, 1854. Quoted in Nicolay and Hay, *op. cit.,* I, 370.
37. Flint, 66–68; Beveridge, 232–233; Milton, 175–177.

38. *A Political Textbook For 1860*, ed. by Greeley and Cleveland, 155. Douglas' speech is given in full.
39. *Ibid.*
40. *Ibid.*, 155–157.
41. *Congressional Globe*, 35th Cong., 1st Session, Part I, 21–22. See also Sheahan, 322.
42. *Ibid.* See also Sheahan, 324; Milton, 278.

CHAPTER 3: "THERE IS NOT MUCH OF ME": ABRAHAM LINCOLN

1. Basler, Roy P., ed., *The Collected Works of Abraham Lincoln*, III, 511.
2. *Ibid.*, II, 268.
3. "Egypt," article in *Egyptian Key*, I, p. 1.
4. Nicolay and Hay, *Abraham Lincoln, A History*, I, 157, note 1.
5. Basler, *op. cit.*, I, 48.
6. *Ibid.*, II, 130.
7. *Ibid.*, II, 255.
8. From his response to Mendenhall's petition. Clay, *Works*, I, 219; Eaton, Clement, *Henry Clay and the Art of American Politics*, 122. On October 1, 1842, while on a political tour of Indiana, Clay rejected a petition, presented by a Quaker named Mendenhall, that he emancipate his slaves. Van Deusen, Glyndon G., *The Life of Henry Clay*, 361.
9. Clay, *Speeches*, I, 338; *Works*, V, 338.
10. Basler, *op. cit.*, II, 132.
11. Clay, *Speeches*, I, 339; *Works*, V, 339.
12. Basler, *op. cit.*, I, 74–75.
13. *Ibid.*, I, 108, 111, 112, 113.
14. *Ibid.*, I, 260. Letter dated September 27, 1841.
15. *Ibid.*, II, 320. Letter dated August 24, 1855.
16. *Ibid.*, II, 255, 256, 264, 265.
17. Herndon and Weik, *Abraham Lincoln: The True Story of a Great Life*, II, 31–32.
18. *Ibid.*, 40.
19. Basler, *op. cit.*, I, 347, 348.
20. Beveridge, *Abraham Lincoln*, I, 392–397. However, John J. Duff, in his illuminating work, *A. Lincoln, Prairie Lawyer*, 130–141, criticizes Beveridge for acceptance of an obviously apologetic version of Lincoln's conduct and of his argument before the court. He asserts that Lincoln was "most conscientious" in protecting the interests of clients and that his half-heartedness in this case was "pure hogwash."
21. Nicolay and Hay, *op. cit.*, I, 286, quoting Giddings' diary entry of January 11, 1849 as published in the *Cleveland Post*, March 31, 1878.
22. Thomas, John L., *The Liberator*, 399.
23. Basler, *op. cit.*, I, 420–421.
24. *Ibid.*, 446–447.
25. *Ibid.*, II, 222–223.
26. *Ibid.*, II, 229–230.

27. Nicolay and Hay, *op. cit.*, II, 378.
28. *Ibid.*, 379.
29. *Ibid.*
30. Basler, *op. cit.*, II, 247–248.
31. Quoted in Herndon and Weik, *op. cit.*, II, 91.
32. Basler, *op. cit.*, II, 257–258.
33. *Ibid.*, 259.
34. *Ibid.*, 260–261.
35. *Ibid.*, 268–270.
36. *Ibid.*, 262–263.
37. *Ibid.*, 271–272.
38. *Ibid.*, 266.
39. *Ibid.*, 274, 275.
40. *Ibid.*, 281–282.
41. *Ibid.*, 255.
42. *Ibid.*, 275–276.
43. *Ibid.*, 288.
44. *Ibid.*, 306. The letter is dated February 9, 1855.
45. *Ibid.*, 316.
46. *Ibid.*, 317.
47. *Ibid.*, 322–323.
48. Beveridge, *op. cit.*, II, 364.
49. Quoted in Tarbell, Ida, *The Life of Abraham Lincoln*, II, 441–442.
50. *Ibid.*, 443.
51. It is reproduced in Tarbell, *op. cit.*, II, 420–443. See also Lapsley, Arthur Brooks, ed., *The Writings of Abraham Lincoln*. It is not included in the authoritative *The Complete Works of Abraham Lincoln*, whose editor Roy P. Basler deemed it "not worthy of serious consideration."
52. Basler, *op. cit.*, II, 401, 402–403.
53. *Ibid.*, 404, 405.
54. *Ibid.*, 405–406.
55. *Ibid.*, 406–407.
56. *Ibid.*, 405.
57. *Ibid.*, 407–408.
58. *Ibid.*, 427.
59. *Ibid.*, 430.
60. Beveridge, *op. cit.*, II, 547, note 1.
61. Thomas, Benjamin P., *Abraham Lincoln*, 178.
62. *Ibid.*
63. *Ibid.*, 179.
64. Basler, *op. cit.*, II, 446.
65. *Ibid.*, 458.

CHAPTER 4: TALL SUCKER AND LITTLE GIANT

1. Rice, Allen Thorndike, ed., *Reminiscences of Abraham Lincoln by Distinguished Men of His Time*, 16. Elihu B. Washburne recalled that the appellation was first applied to Lincoln in 1847 when he

was only thirty-eight years old, because of his "dress and personal appearance." Washburne, one of Lincoln's intimate friends and political associates, served as Secretary of State and later as Minister to France under President Grant.

2.   There are two versions to the name. According to one, it was applied in the 1820's to the many workers who were accustomed to go up the Mississippi River during the summer to work in the mines of Galena and return downstream in the autumn, thus resembling the sucker fish in their seasonal migrations. Shankle, George Earlie, ed., *American Nicknames*, 260–261. The second version has it that travellers in the early days used long reeds as suckers to obtain water from craw·fish holes in the dry prairies. *Ibid.* See also *Illinois State Register*, Springfield, Ill., October 4, 1936 quoting this version by Dr. M. M. Mathews, assistant editor, *Dictionary of American English*.

3.   Milton, George Fort, *The Eve of Conflict*, 16.

4.   Sheahan, James W., *The Life of Stephen A. Douglas*, 19–20. See Douglas, Stephen Arnold, *Autobiography*, 336, for the footnote by editor Frank E. Stevens. See also Milton, *op. cit.*, 18–19; Beveridge, Albert, *Abraham Lincoln*, I, 182 and note 1.

5.   Quoted Sparks, Edwin Erle, ed., *The Lincoln-Douglas Debates,* 553.

6.   Barton, William E., *The Life of Abraham Lincoln*, I, 497–499. Sheahan, *op. cit.*, 41.

7.   Herndon, W. H., and Weik, J. W., *Abraham Lincoln*, original preface by Herndon, v, ix. (This book is also popularly known as *Herndon's Lincoln*).

8.   *Ibid.*, II, 294–297.

9   Rice, *op. cit.*, 479–480.

10.   Sparks, *op. cit.*, 201, quoting article in *N. Y. Tribune*, Oct. 9, 1858. See also McClure, Alexander K., *"Abe" Lincoln's Yarns and Stories*, 65.

11.   Karraker, I. O., *Talk to Members of the State Historical Society*. Mr. Karraker, president of the First National Bank of Jonesboro, and a member of a family long resident in Jonesboro, gave the author a copy of this talk in August 1957.

12.   Meserve, Frederick Hill, and Sandburg, Carl, *The Photographs of Abraham Lincoln*, 6. The introductory chapter of the book, entitled *The Face of Lincoln*, by Carl Sandburg, contains this and other descriptions.

13.   *Ibid.*, 8. See also Rice, *op. cit.*, 470 n.

14.   *Ibid.*, 9.

15.   Rice, *op. cit.*, 480.

16.   Herndon and Weik, *op. cit.*, Introduction, I, xxvi.

17.   *Ibid.*, II, 297 n.

18.   *Ibid.*

19.   Clark, L. P., *Lincoln, A Psycho-Biography*, 70.

20.   *Ibid.*, 62, 66.

21.   Shutes, M. H., *Lincoln's Emotional Life*, 108.

22.   Herndon and Weik, *op. cit.*, II, 232–233.

23. Meserve and Sandburg, *op. cit.*, 12–13.
24. Herndon and Weik, *op. cit.*, I, 310.
25. *Ibid.*
26. *Ibid.*
27. *Ibid.*, II, 101.
28. Flint, H. M., *Life of Stephen A. Douglas*, 14; Carr, Clark E., *Stephen A. Douglas*, 41–42.
29. Sparks, *op. cit.*, 538, quoting the *Louisville Democrat* of November 23, 1858.
30. Herndon and Weik, *op. cit.*, II, 105; Sparks, *op. cit.*, 129.
31. Schurz, Carl, *Reminiscences*, II, 91; Sparks, *op. cit.*, 448.
32. Carr, *op. cit.*, 46.
33. Rhodes, James Ford, *History of the United States from the Compromise of 1850*, II, 128.
34. Schurz, *op. cit.*, II, 94–95; Sparks, *op. cit.*, 448.
35. McConnell, George Murray, *Recollections of Stephen A. Douglas*, 41.
36. *Ibid.*, 42.
37. Carr, *op. cit.*, 42, 43.
38. McConnell, *op. cit.*, 42.
39. Carr, *op. cit.*, 42–43.
40. *Ibid.*, 44.
41. Rhodes, *op. cit.*, II, 128–129.
42. Sandburg, Carl, *Abraham Lincoln: The Prairie Years*, II, 148; Meserve and Sandburg, *op. cit.*, 2.
43. *Collected Works of Abraham Lincoln*, Basler, Roy P., ed., IV, 62.
44. Nicolay, John, and Hay, John, *Abraham Lincoln: A History*, I, 120.
45. Meserve and Sandburg, *op. cit.*, 5.
46. Herndon and Weik, *op. cit.*, I, 186–188.
47. Sheahan, *op. cit.*, 56.
48. Nevins, Allan, *The Emergence of Lincoln*, I, 277.
49. Sparks, *op. cit.*, 443, 499, 529.
50. Herndon and Weik, *op. cit.*, II, 76.
51. Rice, *op. cit.*, 16 (See note 1 above).
52. Herndon and Weik, *op. cit.*, II, 15–16.
53. *Ibid.*, II, 164n.
54. Carr, *op. cit.*, 46.
55. Sparks, *op. cit.*, 332.
56. Schurz, Carl, *Reminiscences*, II, 94. See also Sparks, *op. cit.*, 448.
57. Carr, *op. cit.*, 46, states: "He smoked incessantly. Even on the platform during the great debates, he smoked while Mr. Lincoln was speaking." For a newspaper description, see Sparks, *op. cit.*, 197. Douglas also chewed tobacco. Taft, Robert, *The Appearance and Personality of Stephen A. Douglas*, 11.
58. Weik, Jesse W., *The Real Lincoln: A Portrait*, 232.
59. Schurz, *op. cit.*, II, 94; Sparks, *op. cit.*, 448.
60. Sparks, *op. cit.*, 543.
61. Weik, *op. cit.*, 236.
62. Carr, *op. cit.*, 45–46.

63. Herndon and Weik, *op. cit.*, II, 74–77.
64. Quoted in Barton, *op. cit.*, I, 498.
65. Nicolay and Hay, *op. cit.*, I, 108.
66. Barton, *op. cit.*, I, 342.
67. Herndon and Weik, *op. cit.*, II, 91–92.
68. Schurz, *op. cit.*, 93; Sparks, *op. cit.*, 447.
69. Herndon and Weik, *op. cit.*, 292–293.
70. Putnam, George Haven, *Abraham Lincoln*, 44–45. See also Shaw, Albert, *Abraham Lincoln: His Path to the Presidency*, 253–254.
71. Flint, *op. cit.*, 13.
72. *The Diary of John Quincy Adams*, ed. by Allen Nevins, 566. See also Rhodes, *op. cit.*, I, 245.
73. Schurz, Carl, *Reminiscences*, II, 95. See also Beveridge, Albert J., *Abraham Lincoln*, II, 689.
74. *Ibid.*
75. Flint, *op. cit.*, 15.
76. Carr, *op. cit.*, 43.
77. Rhodes, *op. cit.*, II, 128.
78. McConnell, *op. cit.*, 41.
79. Herndon and Weik, *op. cit.*, II, 7–8.
80. *Ibid.*, II, 232.
81. *Ibid.*, II, 303–304.
82. *Ibid.*, II, 317.
83. *Ibid.*, II, 246–247.
84. Nicolay and Hay, *op. cit.*, I, 303, quoting Judge Drummond of the United States District Court for Illinois.
85. Herndon and Weik, *op. cit.*, I, 170.
86. Angle, Paul M., ed., *Herndon's Life of Lincoln*, 469n. (This book is a re-issue of the original book by Herndon and Weik, with special notes by the editor.) See also Weik, *The Real Lincoln*, 109–110.
87. Herndon and Weik, *op. cit.*, II, 73.
88. *Ibid.*, II, 73n.
89. Rhodes, *op. cit.*, II, 128.
90. Herndon and Weik, *op. cit.*, II, 93–94.
91. Nevins, Allan, *Stephen A. Douglas: His Weaknesses and His Greatness*, 397.
92. The incident occurred during Douglas' famous speech of March 3, 1854. Flint, *op. cit.*, App. 118, and Sheahan, *op. cit.*, 239. See also Rhodes, *op. cit.*, I, 474; Beveridge, *op. cit.*, II, 209, and Milton, *op. cit.*, 138.
93. Basler, ed., *Collected Works of Abraham Lincoln*, I, 209.
94. Greeley, Horace, *Autobiography*, 359; Johnson, Allen, *Life of Stephen A. Douglas*, 320; Capers, Gerald M., *Stephen A. Douglas, Defender of The Union*, 74.
95. Johnson, *op. cit.*, 352, quoting Forney, John W., *Anecdotes*, II, 79; Gardner, William, *Life of Stephen A. Douglas*, 169; Capers, *op. cit.*, 182.
96. Sandburg, *op. cit.*, II, 126.

97. Herndon and Weik, *op. cit.*, I, 154.

98. Nicolay and Hay, *op. cit.*, I, 162–163, in substantiation of Herndon's statement (see note 88 above).

99. Weik, *op. cit.*, 231.

100. Basler, *op. cit.*, 382–383.

101. Masters professes that he wrote his book *Lincoln: The Man* as an inquiry into Lincoln's mind and nature, rather than as a biography. However, his chief purpose seems to be to defame him. In this work and in his article, "Stephen A. Douglas," in the *American Mercury* of January 1931, he presumes to play the iconoclast, but emerges as a crackpot defender of southern institutions. His chapter on the Lincoln-Douglas debates is especially illustrative of a mad attempt to demolish Lincoln and exalt Douglas.

102. Sandburg, *op. cit.*, I, 422–423.

103. Barton, *op. cit.*, II, 428.

CHAPTER 5: LIVING DOG AND DEAD LION

1. According to Herndon, Lincoln first used the expression publicly in his "lost speech" at Bloomington in 1856. For the reaction to it, see Herndon and Weik, *Abraham Lincoln*, II, 67, 68n., 239. See also, Lamon, Ward H., *The Life of Abraham Lincoln*, 398.

    Four months later, on October 25, Senator Seward in his famous speech at Rochester, N.Y., would refer to the situation as an "irrepressible conflict."

2. *Ibid.*, II, 69.

3. *Ibid.*

4. Basler, Roy P., ed., *Collected Works of Abraham Lincoln*, II, 461–462.

5. *Ibid.*, 465–466.

6. *Ibid.*, 467.

7. *Ibid.*

8. Herndon and Weik, *op. cit.*, II, 70, 239; Lamon, *op. cit.*, 408.

9. Herndon and Weik, *op. cit.*, II 70.

10. Newton, Joseph Fort, *Lincoln and Herndon*, 177–178.

11. Basler, *op. cit.*, II, 471.

12. *Ibid.*, 483–484.

13. Sparks, Edwin Erle, *The Lincoln-Douglas Debates of 1858*, 141, quoting the *Chicago Times* of August 12, 1858.

14. *Ibid.*, 49, quoting the *Daily Herald* of Quincy, Ill., July 20, 1858.

15. Milton, George Fort, *The Eve of Conflict*, 303-304, and notes 46, 49; Beveridge, Albert J., *Abraham Lincoln*, II, 627. See also Lincoln's letter to Trumbull, Basler, *op. cit.*, II, 471–472.

16. Angle, Paul, *Created Equal? The Complete Lincoln-Douglas Debates of 1858*, 13–14.

17. *Ibid.*, 17–18.

18. *Ibid.*, 16.

19. *Ibid.*, 17.

20. *Ibid.*

21. *Ibid.*, 18.
22. *Ibid.*, 18–19.
23. *Ibid.*, 20–21.
24. *Ibid.*, 22, 23.
25. *Ibid.*, 24.
26. *Ibid.*, 25.
27. Sparks, *op. cit.*, 39, quoting the *Chicago Press and Tribune* of July 12, 1858; Miers, Earl Schenk, ed., *Lincoln Day by Day*, II, 221.
28. Angle, *op. cit.*, 26. Lincoln's speech is also given in full in Basler, *op. cit.*, II, 484–502.
29. *Ibid.*, 27.
30. *Ibid.*, 31.
31. *Ibid.*
32. *Ibid.*, 32–34.
33. *Ibid.*, 34–35.
34. *Ibid.*, 36.
35. *Ibid.*, 37, 38–39.
36. *Ibid.*, 41.
37. *Ibid.*, 42.
38. *The Illinois Political Campaign of 1858*, Facsimile of Abraham Lincoln's Scrapbook, 51.
39. *Ibid.*
40. *Ibid.*, 63, 65.
41. *Ibid.*, 67.
42. *Ibid.*
43. *Ibid.*
44. Sparks, *op. cit.*, 51, quoting the *Bloomington Pantograph*, of July 17, 1858; Beveridge, *op. cit.*, 614, note 2.
45. Angle, *op. cit.*, 56, 57, 58.
46. *Ibid.*, 58, 59.
47. *Ibid.*, 50.
48. *Ibid.*, 68. Basler, *op. cit.*, also gives the full speech, II, 504-521.
49. *Ibid.*, 69.
50. *Ibid.*, 71.
51. *Ibid.*, 72.
52. *Ibid.*, 72, 73.
53. *Ibid.*, 75.
54. *Ibid.*, 75–76.
55. *Ibid.*, 78, 79, 80.
56. *Ibid.*, 80, 81.
57. *Ibid.*, 81, 82.
58. Basler, *op. cit.*, II, 522.
59. Beveridge, *op. cit.*, II, 623–624. See also Donald, David, *Lincoln's Herndon*, 123. Both authors quote Herndon to Trumbull, July 22, 1858, Trumbull MSS.
60. Beveridge, *op. cit.*, II, 609; Milton, *op. cit.*, 320.

61. *Ibid.*, 623.
62. Newton, *op. cit.*, 186.

CHAPTER 6: CANVASS WESTERN-STYLE

1. Sparks, Edwin Erle, *The Lincoln-Douglas Debates of 1858*, 55.
2. *Ibid.*, 56.
3. Basler, Roy P., ed., *The Collected Works of Abraham Lincoln*, III, 84.
4. Beveridge, Albert J., *Abraham Lincoln*, II, 628, note 6.
5. *Ibid.*, 629.
6. Basler, *op. cit.*, II, 522.
7. Stevens, Frank Everett, *Life of Stephen A. Douglas*, 553.
8. Sparks, *op. cit.*, 59–60.
9. Beveridge, *op. cit.*, II, 631 and note 3.
10. Sparks, *op. cit.*, 61.
11. *Ibid.*, 62.
12. *Ibid.*, 65.
13. Beveridge, *op. cit.*, II, 635.
14. Sparks, *op. cit.*, 66–67.
15. Pratt, Harry E., *The Great Debates of 1858*, 11.
16. Basler, *op. cit.*, II, 528–530; Sparks, *op. cit.*, 68–69.
17. Sparks, *op. cit.*, 70.
18. *Ibid.* See also Basler, *op. cit.*, II, 531.
19. Sparks, *op. cit.*, 71.
20. *Ibid.*, 72.
21. *Ibid.*, 71.
22. Coleman, Mrs. Chapman, *The Life of John J. Crittenden*, II, 162–164. See also Milton, George Fort, *The Eve of Conflict*, 325. Crittenden's letter to Dickey is also given in full in Whitney, Henry C., *Lincoln, the Citizen*, 271–273.
23. Newton, Joseph Fort, *Lincoln and Herndon*, 231, and Herndon's letter to Parker, 234.
24. Basler, *op. cit.*, II, 532–534, for letters to Jediah F. Alexander, Joseph T. Eccles, Joseph Gillespie, and C. W. Michael and William Proctor.
25. Angle, Paul, *Created Equal?* 90.
26. *Ibid.*
27. Basler, *op. cit.*, II, 532.
28. *Ibid.*, 530.
29. *Political Debates Between Abraham Lincoln and Stephen A. Douglas*, 197. See also Milton, *op. cit.*, 334.
30. *Ibid.*, 192–193.
31. Basler, *op. cit.*, 540–541.
32. Herndon and Weik, *Abraham Lincoln*, II, 102, statement of Horace White.
33. *Ibid.*
34. *Ibid.*, 102–103; Basler, *op. cit.*, II, 541–542.
35. Basler, *op. cit.*, 542–543.

36. *Ibid.*, 544, note 1.
37. *Ibid.*, 546–547.
38. Milton, *op. cit.*, 336.

CHAPTER 7: "I WILL BRING HIM TO HIS MILK": THE OTTAWA DEBATE

 1. Sparks, Edwin Erle, *The Lincoln-Douglas Debates of 1858*, 128–129.
 2. *Ibid.*, 125.
 3. Angle, Paul, *Created Equal?* 107–108.
 4. *Ibid.*, 106–107.
 5. *Ibid.*, 114–115.
 6. *Ibid.*, 115.
 7. *Ibid.*, 115–116.
 8. *Ibid.*, 116.
 9. *Ibid.*, 118.
10. *Ibid.*, 117.
11. *Ibid.*, 125.
12. *Ibid.*, 127.
13. *Ibid.*, 128–129.
14. *Ibid.*, 129–130.
15. *Ibid.*, 130.
16. *Ibid.*, 131.
17. This colloquy between Lincoln and Douglas was reported differently
     by the press of both sides. The version used herein appeared in the
     Chicago Press and Tribune, a Lincoln supporter. The version of the
     Chicago Times, a Douglas supporter, omits the statement about milk.
     The *Press and Tribune* version is undoubtedly the true one, else the
     newspapers of the day would not have commented as they did upon
     the incident.

     The Angle, Sparks and all previous editions of the debates used the
     originally published text, which followed the *Press and Tribune* ver-
     sion for Lincoln's speeches, and the *Times* version for Douglas'
     speeches. Basler's *Collected Works,* however, includes in this case the
     Press and Tribune report of Douglas' remarks (Vol. III, page 31, note
     9). Without this version it is impossible to appreciate the newspaper
     comments quoted toward the end of the chapter.

     For an explanation of the editing of the debates, see Chapter 14.
     The different editions of the debates have a special listing in the
     bibliography.
18. Angle, *op. cit.*, 132–134.
19. *Ibid.*, 134–135.
20. *Ibid.*, 135–136.
21. *Ibid.*, 136–137.
22. *Ibid.*, 137.
23. Herndon and Weik, *Abraham Lincoln*, 108.
24. Sparks, *op. cit.*, 128.
25. *Ibid.*, 133.
26. *Ibid.*, 141.

27. *Ibid.,* 143.
28. *Ibid.*
29. *Ibid.,* 135.
30. *Ibid.,* 138.
31. *Ibid.,* 144.
32. *Ibid.,* 143.
33. *Ibid.,* 144–145.
34. *Ibid.,* 550.
35. *Ibid.,* 551.
36. Newton, Joseph Fort, *Lincoln and Herndon,* 208.

CHAPTER 8: A HERESY IS BROADCAST: THE FREEPORT DEBATE

1. Basler, Roy P., ed., *The Collected Works of Abraham Lincoln,* III, 37.
2. Angle, Paul M., ed., *created Equal?,* 138.
3. Sparks, Edwin Erle, *The Lincoln-Douglas Debates,* 147.
4. *Ibid.*
5. *Ibid.*
6. *Ibid.,* 192.
7. *Ibid.,* 193.
8. *Ibid.,* 189.
9. Angle, *op. cit.,* 140–142.
10. *Ibid.,* 143.
11. *Ibid.,* 143–144.
12. *Ibid.,* 145.
13. *Ibid.,* 149–150.
14. *Ibid.,* 152.
15. *Ibid.,* 154.
16. *Ibid.,* 156.
17. *Ibid.*
18. *Ibid.,* 157.
19. *Ibid.,* 160.
20. *Ibid.,* 162.
21. *Ibid.,* 163.
22. *Ibid.,* 164.
23. *Ibid.,* 168.
24. *Ibid.*
25. *Ibid.*
26. *Ibid.,* 171.
27. *Ibid.,* 171–172.
28. *Ibid.,* 173.
29. *Ibid.,* 173, 174.
30. *Ibid.,* 174.
31. *Ibid.,* 176.
32. Herndon and Weik, *Abraham Lincoln,* II, 110.
33. Angle, *op. cit.,* 177.
34. Horace White, in his account written in 1890 for the Herndon-Weik book, twice refers to Douglas being driven into a corner (*op. cit.,* II,

109, 132). Henry Clay Whitney, also a young contemporary of Lincoln, in *Lincoln, The Citizen*, page 276, writes (1907) of "the trap which Lincoln baited." Such statements helped perpetuate the legend.

35. Sparks, *op. cit.*, 203–206.

36. Herndon and Weik, *op. cit.*, II, 109. See also Lamon, Ward H., *The Life of Abraham Lincoln*, 406, 415; Hertz, Emanuel, *The Hidden Lincoln*, 255–256.

37. Beveridge, Albert J., *Abraham Lincoln*, II, 655–658.

38. Sparks, *op. cit.*, 208–209. See also Carr, Clark E., *Stephen A. Douglas*, 82.

39. Carr, *op. cit.*, 282–283.

40. Ida Tarbell in *The Life of Abraham Lincoln*, I, 368, thinks the opposite, however.

41. Barton, William E., *The Life of Abraham Lincoln*, I, 393; Thomas, Benjamin P., *Abraham Lincoln*, 189.

42. Villard, Henry, *Lincoln On The Eve of '61*, writes that at the Ottawa debate he spoke to both Lincoln and Douglas, and states (p. 5): "I had it from Lincoln's own lips, that the United States Senatorship was the greatest political height he at that time expected to climb."

43. Basler, Roy P., ed., *Abraham Lincoln, His Speeches and Writings*, 426.

CHAPTER 9: TROTTED DOWN TO EGYPT: THE JONESBORO DEBATE

1. Milton, George Fort, *The Eve of Conflict*, 346; Beveridge, Albert J., *Abraham Lincoln*, II, 654–655; Herndon and Weik, *Abraham Lincoln*, II, 123.

2. Milton, *op. cit.*, 348.

3. Rowland, Dunbar, ed., *Jefferson Davis, Constitutionalist*, III, 299; Milton, *op. cit.*, 347; Alfriend, Frank H., *Life of Jefferson Davis*, 212.

4. Portland *Daily Eastern Argus*, September 13, 1858. See Nevins, Allan *The Emergence of Lincoln*, I, 416–417; Angle, Paul M., *Created Equal?*, 373; Fehrenbacher, Don E., *Prelude to Greatness*, 138.

5. Angle, *op. cit.*, 221 (text taken from the *Missouri Republican* of September 9, and quoted by Lincoln in his speech).

6. *Ibid.*, 180–181.

7. Sandburg, Carl, *Abraham Lincoln: The Prairie Years*, II, 142. It has not been clearly established where, when and under what circumstances Lincoln uttered this aphorism. See McClure, Alexander K., *Abe Lincoln's Yarns and Stories*, Dodd, Mead & Co., New York, 1967, 184; *The Home Book of American Quotations*, ed. by Bruce Bohl, 112; *Dictionary of Best Known Quotations and Proverbs*, Garden City Publishing Co., New York, 1939, 9, footnote 4.

8. Angle, *op. cit.*, 182.

9. *Political Debates Between Abraham Lincoln and Stephen A. Douglas in the Celebrated Campaign of 1858 in Illinois*, The Burrows Bros. Co., 193. (See also the special bibliographical listing of editions of the text of the debates.)

10. *Ibid.*, 196, 197.

11. *Ibid.*, 198, 200, 201.
12. Basler, Roy P., *The Collected Works of Abraham Lincoln,* III, 95–96.
13. Herndon and Weik, *op. cit.,* II, 118.
14. Sparks, Edwin Erle, *The Lincoln-Douglas Debates,* 259.
15. Angle, *op. cit.,* 193, 194–195.
16. *Ibid.*, 199–200.
17. *Ibid.*, 200, 201.
18. *Ibid.*, 202–203.
19. *Ibid.*, 205–206.
20. *Ibid.*, 210, 211.
21. *Ibid.*, 214.
22. *Ibid.*, 217, 218, 219–220.
23. *Ibid.*, 220.
24. *Ibid.*, 221–223.
25. *Ibid.*, 223.
26. *Ibid.*, 226–227.
27. *Ibid.*, 227.
28. *Ibid.*, 228.
29. *Ibid.*, 228–229.
30. *Ibid.*, 230–231.
31. Sparks, *op. cit.,* 259.
32. *Ibid.*, 260.

CHAPTER 10: BRAWL FOR CRUCIAL VOTES: THE CHARLESTON DEBATE

1. Pratt, Harry E., *The Great Debates of 1858,* 19.
2. Herndon and Weik, *Abraham Lincoln,* 121; Sparks, Edwin Erle, *The Lincoln-Douglas Debates,* 317, 320, 324.
3. Angle, Paul M., ed., *Created Equal?,* 234.
4. Sparks, *op. cit.,* 324.
5. Angle, *op. cit.,* 233.
6. *Ibid.*, 235.
7. *Ibid.*, 235, 236.
8. *Ibid.*, 238.
9. *Ibid.*, 242–243.
10. *Ibid.*, 246.
11. *Ibid.*, 247.
12. *Ibid.*, 248, 249, 251, 252.
13. *Ibid.*, 251, 252.
14. *Ibid.*, 254, 255.
15. *Ibid.*, 257–258, 259.
16. *Ibid.*, 262–263.
17. *Ibid.*, 266.
18. *Ibid.*, 267–268.
19. *Ibid.*, 268, 269–270.
20. *Ibid.*, 270.
21. *Ibid.*, 271.

22. *Ibid.*, 271–272.
23. *Ibid.*, 272–273.
24. *Ibid.*, 273.
25. *Ibid.*, 274.
26. *Ibid.*, 275.
27. Sparks, *op. cit.*, 543.
28. *Ibid.*, 541.
29. *Ibid.*, 570.
30. *Ibid.*, 570–571.

CHAPTER 11: MUDSILLS OF SOCIETY: THE GALESBURG DEBATE

1. Basler, Roy, P., *The Collected Works of Abraham Lincoln*, III, 201.
2. Sparks, Edwin Erle, *The Lincoln-Douglas Debates*, 559.
3. Pratt, Harry E., *The Great Debates of 1858*, 20.
4. Angle, Paul M., *Created Equal?*, 278–280. In spite of the Sullivan incident, Horace White stated: "There was nothing of special interest between the Charleston debate and . . . Galesburg." Herndon and Weik, *Abraham Lincoln*, II, 123.
5. Herndon and Weik, *op. cit.*, II, 103–104. See also Sparks, *op. cit.*, 573. Newton, Joseph Fort, *Lincoln and Herndon*, 227, describes the incident of an editor of a Republican paper, who was so captivated by Mrs. Douglas that he turned Democrat and devoted his paper to advocating the election of Douglas.
6. Milton, George Fort, *The Eve of Conflict*, 332.
7. Basler, *op. cit.*, 204–205.
8. Weik, Jesse W., *The Real Lincoln: A Portrait*, 236.
9. Newton, *op. cit.*, 223.
10. *Ibid.*, 222–223.
11. *Ibid.*, 223–224.
12. Sparks, *op. cit.*, 372.
13. Newcombe, Alfred Watts, *The Galesburg Debate*, 3.
14. *Ibid.*, 2.
15. Sparks, *op. cit.*, 330.
16. Newcombe, *op. cit.*, 3.
17. Sparks, *op. cit.*, 330–331.
18. *Ibid.*, 374–375.
19. *Ibid.*, 376.
20. Sandburg, Carl, *Abraham Lincoln: The Prairie Years*, II, 147.
21. Sparks, *op. cit.*, 378.
22. Sandburg, *op. cit.*, II, 148.
23. Angle, *op. cit.*, 288–290.
24. *Ibid.*, 292–293.
25. *Ibid.*, 297–298.
26. *Ibid.*, 298.
27. *Ibid.*, 299–301.
28. *Ibid.*, 301–302.

29. *Ibid.*, 303–304.
30. *Ibid.*, 304.
31. *Ibid.*, 305, 306.
32. *Ibid.*, 308–309.
33. *Ibid.*, 310–311.
34. *Ibid.*, 311–314.
35. *Ibid.*, 315–316.
36. *Ibid.*, 316.
37. *Ibid.*, 316–317.
38. *Ibid.*, 317–319.
39. *Ibid.*, 319–321.
40. Sparks, *op. cit.*, 380, 381–382.
41. *Ibid.*, 384, 385.

CHAPTER 12: DRAMA IN THE FACE OF THE WORLD: THE QUINCY DEBATE

1. Davis, John McCan, *Abraham Lincoln: His Book*. The story of Brown's relationship with Lincoln is given in the explanatory notes by Mr. Davis, 1–11.
2. Pratt, Harry E., *The Great Debates of 1858*, 26.
3. Sparks, Edwin Erle, *The Lincoln-Douglas Debates*, 390.
4. *Ibid.*, 440.
5. *Ibid.*, 436.
6. Angle, Paul M., *Created Equal?*, 324.
7. *Ibid.*, 327–328.
8. Weik, Jesse W., *The Real Lincoln: A Portrait*, 231.
9. Angle, *op. cit.*, 329.
10. *Ibid.*, 328.
11. *Ibid.*, 329–330.
12. *Ibid.*, 331.
13. *Ibid.*, 330.
14. *Ibid.*, 332.
15. *Ibid.*
16. *Ibid.*, 333.
17. *Ibid.*
18. *Ibid.*, 333–334.
19. *Ibid.*
20. *Ibid.*, 335.
21. *Ibid.*
22. *Ibid.*, 336.
23. *Ibid.*, 336–337, 338.
24. *Ibid.*, 339.
25. *Ibid.*, 340, 341.
26. *Ibid.*, 342–343.
27. *Ibid.*, 343–344.
28. *Ibid.*, 344–345.
29. *Ibid.*, 345.

30. *Ibid.*, 347–348, 349–351.
31. *Ibid.*, 351–352.
32. *Ibid.*, 352.
33. *Ibid.*, 353–354.
34. *Ibid.*, 354–355.
35. *Ibid.*, 355.
36. *Ibid.*, 356–357.
37. See note #1 above. John McCan Davis' book is a facsimile reproduction of the original.
38. Angle, *op. cit.*, 357, 358.
39. *Ibid.*, 358, 359.
40. *Ibid.*, 359, 360.
41. *Ibid.*, 360.
42. *Ibid.*
43. Schurz, Carl, *Reminiscences*, II, 90, 91.
44. *Ibid.*
45. *Ibid.*, 94–95.
46. Sparks, *op. cit.*, 443.
47. *Ibid.*, 394.
48. *Ibid.*, 445.
49. *Ibid.*, 438, 439.
50. Schurz, *op. cit.*, II, 92.

CHAPTER 13: THESE POOR TONGUES: THE ALTON DEBATE

1. Koerner, Gustav, *Memoirs, 1809–1896*, II, 66.
2. Sparks, Edwin Erle, *The Lincoln-Douglas Debates*, 498, 509.
3. *Ibid.*, 500.
4. Angle, Paul M., *Created Equal?*, 362; Sparks, *op. cit.*, 506.
5. Angle, *op. cit.*, 364.
6. *Ibid.*, 364–366.
7. *Ibid.*, 367.
8. *Ibid.*, 368–369.
9. *Ibid.*, 370–371.
10. *Ibid.*, 373.
11. *Ibid.* Douglas was in error about Bangor. The speech was made in Portland.
12. *Ibid.*, 374.
13. *Ibid.*, 375.
14. *Ibid.*, 376.
15. *Ibid.*
16. *Ibid.*, 378, 379, 380, 382.
17. *Ibid.*, 383–384.
18. *Ibid.*, 385–386.
19. *Ibid.*, 387–388.
20. *Ibid.*, 388–389.
21. *Ibid.*, 389–390.
22. *Ibid.*, 390–391.

23. *Ibid.*, 393.
24. *Ibid.*
25. *Ibid.*, 394–396.
26. *Ibid.*, 396.
27. *Ibid.*, 396–397.
28. *Ibid.*, 397–398.
29. *Ibid.*
30. *Ibid.*, 398–399.
31. *Ibid.*
32. *Ibid.*, 399–400.
33. *Ibid.*, 401.
34. *Ibid.*, 402.
35. Sparks, *op. cit.*, 499.
36. Koerner, *op. cit.*, II, 67.
37. Herndon and Weik, II, 124.
38. Basler, Roy P., *The Collected Works of Abraham Lincoln*, III, 327.
39. *Ibid.*, 329.
40. *Ibid.*, 332.
41. Newton, Joseph Fort, *Lincoln and Herndon*, 231–232.
42. *Ibid.*, 232–233.
43. Whitney, Henry C., *Life On The Circuit With Lincoln*, 340–341; Newton, *op. cit.*, 231; Barton, William E., *The Life of Abraham Lincoln*, I, 397.
44. Basler, *op. cit.*, III, 334.
45. Barton, *op. cit.*, I, 400–401; Basler, *op. cit.*, III, 334.

CHAPTER 14: VICTORY — PYRRHIC AND REAL

1. Milton, George Fort, *The Eve of Conflict*, 352; Johnson, Allen, *Life of Stephen A. Douglas*, 392.
2. Herndon and Weik, *Abraham Lincoln*, II, 127.
3. Basler, Roy P., *The Collected Works of Abraham Lincoln*, III, 335.
4. *Ibid.*, 339.
5. *Ibid.*, 336.
6. *Ibid.*, 344.
7. *Ibid.*, 346.
8. *Ibid.*, 341.
9. *Ibid.*, 339.
10. Barton, William E., *The Life of Abraham Lincoln*, I, 403.
11. Newton, Joseph Fort, *Lincoln and Herndon*, 234–235.
12. Milton, *op. cit.*, 567; Stevens, Frank Everett, Life of *Stephen A. Douglas*, 589.
13. Basler, *op. cit.*, 337.
14. Capers, Gerald M., *Stephen A. Douglas, Defender of the Union*, 191; Milton, *op. cit.*, 358.
15. Milton, *op. cit.*, 359; Nevins, Allan, *The Emergence of Lincoln*, I, 414, 417.
16. Milton, *op. cit.*, 360.

17. Ibid., 360–361.

18. *Ibid.*, 361.

19. Johnson, Allen, *The Life of Stephen A. Douglas*, 394.

20. *Ibid.*, 396.

21. Nicolay and Hay, *Abraham Lincoln: A History*, II, 173.

22. Basler, *op. cit.*, III, 344–345.

23. Nicolay and Hay, *op. cit.*, II, 175.

24. *Congressional Globe*, 35th Cong., 2nd Sess., Part 2, pp. 1246, 1247; Flint, H. M., *Life of Stephen A. Douglas*, 167; Nicolay and Hay, *op. cit.*, II, 175; Johnson, *op. cit.*, 399.

25. Rhodes, James Ford, *History of the United States from the Compromise of 1850*, II, 371.

26. Flint, *op. cit.*, 168.

27. Letter dated July 27, 1858. Nicolay and Hay, op. cit., II, 176–177. For the complete letter, see Mearns, David C., *The Lincoln Papers*, I, 217.

28. Nevins, *op. cit.*, I, 398, and note 28.

29. Lincoln to Colfax, July 6, 1859. Basler, *op. cit.*, III, 390.

30. Nicolay and Hay, *op. cit.*, II, 180.

31. *Ibid.*

32. Basler, *op. cit.*, III, 375–376.

33. Jaffa, Harry V. and Johannsen, Robert W., *In The Name of The People: Speeches and Writings of Lincoln and Douglas in the Ohio Campaign of 1859*, p. 135.

34. e.g., Douglas had omitted mention of the Northwest Ordinance as illustrative of federal power. Basler, *op. cit.*, III, 413.

35. *Ibid.*, 417.

36. *Ibid.*, 425.

37. *Ibid.*, 443, 445–446.

38. Page 8 of the introduction to the facsimile of Lincoln's scrapbook, *The Illinois Political Campaign of 1858.*

39. Basler, *op. cit.*, III, 341.

40. *Ibid.*, 510.

41. McMurtry, R. Gerald, *Different Editions of the Debates of Lincoln and Douglas*, 106.

42. Scrapbook facsimile, *op. cit.*, 18–19.

43. *Ibid.*, 18.

44. Basler, *op. cit.*, III, 516.

45. Scrapbook facsimile, *op. cit.*, 22, n. 46; McMurtry, *op. cit.*, 106.

46. Mearns, David C., *The Lincoln Papers*, I, 229.

47. *Ibid.*

48. Freeman, Andrew, *Abraham Lincoln Goes To New York*, 95; Barton, William E., *The Life of Abraham Lincoln*, I, 408; Shaw, Albert, *Abraham Lincoln: His Path to the Presidency*, 252.

49. Basler, *op. cit.*, III, 531.

50. *Ibid.*, 532.

51. *Ibid.*, 533–534.

52. *Ibid.*, 534–535.

53. *Ibid.*, 535–536.
54. *Ibid.*, 537–538.
55. *Ibid.*, 543.
56. *Ibid.*, 546–547.
57. See note 7, Chapter 1.
58. Basler, *op. cit.*, III, 547–550.
59. Basler, Roy P., *Abraham Lincoln: His Speeches and Writings*, 538.
60. *Ibid.*, 538–539.
61. *Ibid.*, 537–538.
62. Johnston, Richard Malcolm, and Browne, William Hand, *Life of Alexander H. Stephens*, 355, 356; Milton, *op. cit.*, 468.
63. *A Political Text-Book for 1860*, compiled by Greeley and Cleveland, 159–160.
64. *Congressional Record*, 36th Congress, 1st Session, Part 3, page 2241.
65. Capers, *op. cit.*, 206; Milton, *op. cit.*, 473.

CHAPTER 15: A CENTURY'S PERSPECTIVE

1. For a similar expression, see the opening paragraph of Lincoln's second annual message to Congress, December 1, 1862. Basler, Roy P., ed., *The Collected Works of Abraham Lincoln*, V, 518.
2. Rice, Allen Thorndike, ed., *Reminiscences of Abraham Lincoln*, 193.
3. Current, Richard N., *The Lincoln Nobody Knows*, 220; Weyl, Nathaniel, *The Negro In American Civilization*, 74 ff.; See also Conrad, Earl, *The Invention of the Negro*.
4. In the early 1900's the most notorious was James K. Vardaman of Mississippi, who vilified even President Theodore Roosevelt for entertaining Negro educator Booker T. Washington at dinner in the White House. Current, *op. cit.*, 231–233.
5. Lincoln concluded his second annual message to Congress with the words: "We cannot escape history." Basler, *op. cit.*, V, 537.
6. Current, *op. cit.*, 236, concludes a stimulating analysis of Lincoln as "The Friend of Freedom" by stating: "Lincoln, as a symbol of man's ability to outgrow his prejudices, still serves the cause of human freedom."
7. Milton, George Fort, *The Eve of Conflict*, 361. Douglas used similar language on other occasions, e.g., see his Chicago speech of July 9, supra 199.
8. *Congressional Globe*, 30th Cong., 1st Session, App. 507, April 20, 1848; quoted Milton, *op. cit.*, 40, 150.
9. *North American Review*, 1909, p. 172. See Lincoln's expression of this concept in his Peoria speech of 1854.
10. Basler, *op. cit.*, II, 399.
11. *Ibid.*
12. *Journal of the Illinois State Historical Society*, Vol. 26, #4, 1934, pp. 344–45.
13. *Congressional Globe*, 30th Cong., 1st Session, App. Pt. 1, 371, March 13, 1850.

14. Milton, *op. cit.*, 121, 150.

15. *A Political Text-Book for 1860*, p. 48.

16. Milton, *op. cit.*, 523–525; Capers, Gerald M., *Stephen A. Douglas, Defender of the Union*, 215.

17. Basler, *op. cit.*, IV, 150, 151.

18. *Ibid.*, 150.

19. *Ibid.*, 151.

20. Helper, Hinton Rowan, *The Impending Crisis of the South*, 298–301.

21. Fitzhugh, George, *Cannibals All*, 324–325.

22. Milton, *op. cit.*, 150.

23. *Ibid.*, 121.

24. Stevens, Frank Everett, *Life of Stephen A. Douglas*, 668.

25. *Ibid.*

26. Milton, op. cit., 282; Nevins, Allan, *Stephen A. Douglas, His Weaknesses and His Greatness*, 405.

27. Milton, *op. cit.*, 280–283.

28. Supra and note 15. The Charleston plank was carried into the Baltimore Convention without any change.

29. Nevins, *op. cit.*, 410.

30. *Ibid.*, 392.

BIBLIOGRAPHY

Alfriend, Frank H., *Life of Jefferson Davis*, Caxton Publishing House, Cincinnati and Chicago, 1868.

Angle, Paul M., ed., *Created Equal? The Complete Lincoln-Douglas Debates of 1858*, The University of Chicago Press, Chicago, 1958.

————, ed., *Herndon's Life of Lincoln*, World Publishing Co., Cleveland, Ohio, 1949.

————, ed., *Lincoln 1854–1861: Being the Day-by-Day Activities of Abraham Lincoln*, Abraham Lincoln Association, Springfield, Ill., 1933.

A Political Text-Book for 1860, compiled by Horace Greeley and John F. Cleveland, The Tribune Association, New York, 1860.

Aptheker, Herbert, *American Negro Slave Revolts*, International Publishers, New York, 1963.

Arnold, Isaac Newton, *The History of Abraham Lincoln and the Overthrow of Slavery*, S. C. Griggs & Co., Chicago, 1871.

Barton, William E., *Abraham Lincoln and His Books*, Marshall Field & Co., Chicago, 1920.

————, *The Life of Abraham Lincoln*, Bobbs-Merrill Co., Indianapolis, 1925.

Basler, Roy P., ed., *Abraham Lincoln: His Speeches and Writings*, World Publishing Co., Cleveland, 1946.

————, ed., *The Collected Works of Abraham Lincoln*, The Abraham Lincoln Association, Springfield, Ill., Rutgers University Press, New Brunswick, N. J., 1953.

Beveridge, Albert J., *Abraham Lincoln*, Houghton Mifflin Co., Boston, 1928.

Brooks, Noah, *Abraham Lincoln and the Downfall of American Slavery*, G. P. Putnam's Sons, The Knickerbocker Press, New York, 1896.

Brown, William Garrott, *Stephen Arnold Douglas*, Houghton, Mifflin and Co., Boston, 1902.

Calhoun, John C., *Works*, ed. by Richard K. Cralle, D. Appleton & Co., New York, 1854–1856.

Capers, Gerald M., *Stephen A. Douglas, Defender of the Union*, Little, Brown & Co., Boston, 1959.

Carr, Clark E., *Stephen A. Douglas*, A. C. McClurg & Co., Chicago, 1909.

Channing, Edward, *A History of the United States*, MacMillan Company, New York, 1925.

Charnwood, Lord, *Abraham Lincoln*, Henry Holt & Co., New York, 1917.

Chase, Salmon Portland, *Speech In The Senate, February 3, 1854*, John T. and Lemuel Towers, Washington, D.C., 1854.

Clark, L. Pierce, *Lincoln: A Psycho-Biography*, Charles Scribner's Sons, New York, 1933.

Clay, Henry, *Speeches*, A. S. Barnes & Co., New York, 1857.

————, *Works*, Ed. by Calvin Colton, Henry Clay Publishing Co., New York, 1897.

Coit, Margaret L., *John C. Calhoun, American Portrait*, Houghton, Mifflin Co., Boston, 1950.

Cole, Arthur Charles, *Centennial History of Illinois*, Vol. 3, The Era of the Civil War 1848–1870, Springfield, 1919.

Coleman, Mrs. Chapman, *The Life of John J. Crittenden*, J. P. Lippincott & Co., Philadelphia, 1871.

Conrad, Earl, *The Invention of the Negro*, Paul S. Erickson, New York, 1967.

Congressional Globe, 30th to 36th Congresses.

Crocker, Lionel, *Analysis of Lincoln and Douglas as Public Speakers and Debaters*, C. C. Thomas, Springfield, Ill., 1968.

Current, Richard N., *The Lincoln Nobody Knows*, McGraw-Hill Co., New York, 1958.

————, *John C. Calhoun*, Washington Square Press, New York, 1966.

Davis, John McCan, *Abraham Lincoln: His Book*, A Facsimile Reproduction of the Original, McClure, Phillips & Co., New York, 1903.

Davis, Varina, *Jefferson Davis, A Memoir by his Wife*, Belford Co., New York, 1890.

(The) Diary of John Quincy Adams, ed. by Allan Nevins, Longmans, Green and Co., New York, 1928.

Dictionary of American Biography, Allen Johnson, ed., Charles Scribner's Sons, New York, 1928.

Dictionary of American History, ed. by James Truslow Adams, Charles Scribner's Sons, New York, 1940.

Dodd, William E., *The Cotton Kingdom*, Chronicles of America Series, Vol. 27, Yale University Press, New Haven, 1919.

Doherty, Allan James, *The Lincoln-Douglas Debates, A Critical Estimate*, (Thesis for M.A.), Boston College, Boston, 1932.

Donald, David, *Lincoln's Herndon*, Alfred A. Knopf, New York, 1948.

Douglas, Stephen Arnold, *Autobiography*, Journal Illinois State Historical Society, Springfield, Ill., Vol. V, 1912.

————, "The Dividing Line Between Federal and Local Authority," *Harper's* Magazine, September 1859.

Dred Scott vs. Sandford (sic), 19 Howard 393, United States Supreme Court Reports.

Duff, John J., *A. Lincoln, Prairie Lawyer*, Rinehart & Co., New York, 1960.

Eaton, Clement, *Henry Clay and the Art of American Politics*, Little, Brown and Co., Boston, 1957.

"Egypt," Article in *Egyptian Key*, Vol. I, No. I, April-May 1943.

Faulkner, Harold U., *American Economic History*, 8th ed., Harper and Bros., New York, 1960.

Fehrenbacher, Don E., *Prelude to Greatness*, Stanford University Press, Stanford, Cal., 1962.

Filler, Louis, *The Crusade Against Slavery, 1830–1860*, Harper and Row, The New American Nation Series, New York, 1960.

Fitzhugh, George, *Cannibals All! or, Slaves Without Masters*, A. Morris, Richmond, Va., 1857.

———, *Sociology for the South or the Failure of Free Society*, A. Morris, Richmond, Va., 1854.

Flint, H. M., *Life of Stephen A. Douglas*, John E. Potter, Philadelphia, 1863.

Foley, John P., ed., *The Jeffersonian Cyclopedia*, Funk and Wagnalls Co., New York, 1900.

Foner, Philip S., ed., *Basic Writings of Thomas Jefferson*, Willey Book Co., New York, 1944.

Ford, Paul Leicester, ed., *Autobiography of Thomas Jefferson*, G. P. Putnam's Sons, New York, 1914.

Freeman, Andrew A., *Abraham Lincoln Goes to New York*, Coward-McCann Inc., New York, 1960.

Gardner, William, *Life of Stephen A. Douglas*, Roxburgh Press, Boston, 1905.

Greeley, Horace, *Autobiography or Recollections of a Busy Life*, E. B. Treat, New York, 1872.

Helper, Hinton Rowan, *The Impending Crisis of the South: How to Meet It*, Burdick Bros., New York, 1857.

Herndon, William H. and Weik, Jesse W., *Abraham Lincoln: The True Story of a Great Life*, D. Appleton & Co., New York, 1892.

Hertz, Emanuel, *Abraham Lincoln: A New Portrait*, Horace Liveright Inc., New York, 1931.

———, *The Hidden Lincoln*, Viking Press, New York, 1938.

Howland, Louis, *Stephen A. Douglas*, Charles Scribner's Sons, New York, 1920.

Illinois Political Campaign of 1858, Facsimile of Abraham Lincoln's Scrapbook, Library of Congress, U.S. Government Printing Office, 1958.

Jaffa, Harry V., *Crisis Of The House Divided: An Interpretation of the Issues in the Lincoln-Douglas Debates*, Doubleday and Co., Garden City, New York, 1959.

——— and Johannsen, Robert W., *In the Name Of The People: Speeches and Writings of Lincoln and Douglas in the Ohio Campaign of 1859*, Ohio State University Press, Columbus, 1959.

Jefferson, Thomas, *Writings*, ed. by Paul Leicester Ford, G. P. Putnam's Sons, New York, 1894.

Jenkins, William Sumner, *Pro-Slavery Thought In The Old South*, University of North Carolina Press, Chapel Hill, 1935.

Johannsen, Robert W., *The Letters of Stephen A. Douglas*, University of Illinois Press, Urbana, 1961.

Johnson, Allen, *Stephen A. Douglas: A Study in American Politics*, MacMillan Co., New York, 1908.

Johnston, Richard Malcolm and Browne, William Hand, *Life of Alexander H. Stephens*, J. B. Lippincott & Co., Philadelphia, 1878.

Karraker, I. O., *Talk to Members of the State Historical Society*, (Monograph), Jonesboro, Ill., 1908.

Koerner, Gustav, *Memoirs, 1809–1896*, ed. by T. J. McCormack, Torch Press, Cedar Rapids, 1909.

Lamon, Ward H., *The Life of Abraham Lincoln*, James R. Osgood & Co., Boston, 1872.

Lapsley, Arthur Brooks, ed., *The Writings of Abraham Lincoln*, G. P. Putnam's Sons, New York, 1923.

Lincoln, Abraham, *Autobiography*, Robert Dale Richardson, ed., The Beacon Press, Boston, 1948.

———, *The Illinois Political Campaign of 1858*, Facsimile of Lincoln's Scrapbook, Library of Congress, Alfred Whital Stern Collection, 1958.

Lincoln-Douglas Debate, Centennial 1858-1958 (Pamphlet), Illinois Historical Society, Knox College, Galesburg, Ill., 1958.

Linn, William Alexander, *The Story of the Mormons*, The MacMillan Co., New York, 1902.

Lorant, Stefan, *Lincoln: A Picture Story of His Life*, Harper & Bros., New York, 1952.

Masters, Edgar Lee, *Lincoln The Man*, Dodd, Mead & Co., New York, 1931.

———, *Stephen A. Douglas*, American Mercury, Vol. 22, Jan. 1931.

McClure, Alexander K., *Abe Lincoln's Yarns and Stories*, Copyright by Henry Neil, 1901.

McConnell, George Murray, *Recollections of Stephen A. Douglas*, Illinois State Historical Society Transactions, Springfield, 1900.

McMaster, John B., *A History of the People of the United States*, D. Appleton & Co., New York, 1913.

McMurtry, R. Gerald, *Different Editions of the Debates of Lincoln and Douglas*, Illinois State Historical Society Journal, Vol. 27, April 1934.

———, *Lincoln's Friend, Douglas* (Pamphlet), A Lincoln Day Address before the Principia School of Government at Elsah, Ill., Feb. 12, 1946.

Meade, Robert D., *Patrick Henry, Patriot In The Making*, J. B. Lippincott Co., Philadelphia, 1957.

Mearns, David C., ed., *The Lincoln Papers*, Doubleday and Co., Garden City, New York, 1948.

A Member of the Western Bar, *Life and Speeches of Stephen A. Douglas*, Derby and Jackson, New York, 1860.

Mededith, Roy, *Mr. Lincoln's Camera Man, Mathew B. Brady*, Charles Scribner's Sons, New York, 1946.

Meserve, Frederick Hill and Sandburg, Carl, *The Photographs of Abraham Lincoln*, Harcourt, Brace and Co., New York, 1944.

Miers, Earl Schenk, ed., *Lincoln Day by Day, A Chronology, 1809–1865*, Lincoln Sesquicentennial Commission, Washington, 1960.

Miller, Marion Mills, ed., *Life and Works of Abraham Lincoln*, Centenary Edition, Current Literature Publishing Co., New York, 1907, 9 vol. (see Whitney, H. C., *Lincoln, The Citizen*, as vol. 1).

Milton, George Fort, *Douglas' Place in American History*, Journal of the Illinois State Historical Society, Springfield, Ill., Vol. 26, No. 4, 1934.

———, *The Eve of Conflict: Stephen A. Douglas and the Needless War*, Houghton Mifflin Co., Boston, 1934.

Myrdal, Gunnar, *An American Dilemma: The Negro Problem and American Democracy*, Harper and Row, New York, 1962.

Nevins, Allan, *The Emergence of Lincoln*, Charles Scribner's Sons, New York, 1950.

———, *Ordeal of the Union*, Charles Scribner's Sons, New York, 1947.

———, *Stephen A. Douglas: His Weaknesses and His Greatness*, Journal Illinois State Historical Society, Springfield, Ill., Vol. 42, No. 4, December, 1949.

Newcombe, Alfred Watts, *The Galesburg Debate*, Knox College, Galesburg, Ill., 1928.

Newton, Joseph Fort, *Lincoln and Herndon*, Torch Press, Cedar Rapids, Iowa, 1910.

Nicolay, John G. and Hay, John, *Abraham Lincoln: A History*, The Century Co., New York, 1917.

Padover, Saul K., *The Washington Papers*, Harper and Bros., New York, 1955.

Phillips, Ulrich Bonnell, *American Negro Slavery*, D. Appleton & Co., New York, 1918.

Political Debates Between Abraham Lincoln and Stephen A. Douglas in the Celebrated Campaign of 1858 in Illinois, The Burrows Bros., Cleveland, Ohio, 1894.

Pratt, Harry E., *Concerning Mr. Lincoln*, Abraham Lincoln Association, Springfield, Ill., 1944.

———, *The Great Debates of 1858*, (Pamphlet), Illinois State Historical Library, Springfield, Ill., 1956.

Pro-Slavery Argument, As Maintained by the Most Distinguished Writers of the Southern States, by Dew, Thomas R. and others, Lippincott, Grambo & Co., Philadelphia, 1853.

Putnam, George Haven, *Abraham Lincoln*, G. P. Putnam's Sons, The Knickerbocker Press, New York, 1909.

Quarles, Benjamin, *Lincoln and the Negro*, Oxford University Press, New York, 1962.

Randall, James G., *Lincoln the President*, Dodd, Mead & Co., New York, 1945.

———, *Mr. Lincoln*, Dodd, Mead & Co., New York 1957.

Rhodes, James Ford, *History of the United States From The Compromise of 1850*, MacMillan Co., New York, 1902.

Rice, Allen Thorndike, ed., *Reminiscences of Abraham Lincoln by Distinguished Men of His Time*, North American Review Publishing Co., New York, 1886.

Richardson, Robert Dale, *Abraham Lincoln's Autobiography*, Beacon Press, Boston, 1948.

Rowland, Dunbar, ed., *Jefferson Davis, Constitutionalist—His Letters, Papers and Speeches*, Mississippi Archives and History, Jackson, Miss., 1923.

Sandburg, Carl, *Abraham Lincoln: The Prairie Years*, Harcourt, Brace & Co., New York, 1926.

————, *The Face of Lincoln*, Introduction to Meserve and Sandburg, *The Photographs of Abraham Lincoln* (see above).

Schouler, James, *History of the United States of America Under the Constitution*, William H. Morrison, Washington, D.C., 1889.

Schurz, Carl, *Reminiscences*, McClure Co., New York, 1907.

Seward, William H., *Works*, ed. by George E. Baker, Houghton, Mifflin & Co., Boston, 1884.

Shankle, George Earlie, ed., *American Nicknames*, 2nd ed., H. W. Wilson Co., New York, 1955.

Shaw, Albert, *Abraham Lincoln: His Path to the Presidency—A Cartoon History*, Review of Reviews Corp., New York, 1929.

Sheahan, James W., *The Life of Stephen A. Douglas*, Harper Bros., New York, 1860.

Shutes, Milton H., *Lincoln and the Doctors, A Medical Narrative of the Life of A. L.*, Pioneer Press, New York, 1933.

————, *Lincoln's Emotional Life*, Dorrance & Co., Philadelphia, 1957.

Slavery Defended: The Views of the Old South, ed. by Eric L. McKittrick, Prentice-Hall, Englewood Cliffs, New Jersey, 1963.

Sparks, Edwin Erle, ed., *The Lincoln-Douglas Debates*, Illinois State Historical Library, Springfield, Ill., 1908.

Speeches in the House of Delegates of Virginia, by Bolling, Faulkner et al., Thomas W. White, Richmond, Va., 1832.

Stampp, Kenneth M., *The Peculiar Institution*, Alfred A. Knopf, New York, 1956.

Stephenson, Nathaniel Wright, *Lincoln, An Account of His Personal Life*, Bobbs-Merrill Co., Indianapolis, 1922.

Stevens, Frank Everett, *Life of Stephen A. Douglas*, Journal Illinois State Historical Society, Vol. 16, Springfield, Ill., 1924.

Stoddard, Henry Luther, *Horace Greeley*, G. P. Putnam's Sons, New York, 1946.

Sumner, Charles, *Works*, Lee and Shepard, Boston, 1875.

Taft, Robert, *The Appearance and Personality of Stephen A. Douglas*, Kansas Historical Quarterly, Vol. XXI, Springfield, Kansas State Historical Society, Topeka, 1954.

Tarbell, Ida M., *The Life of Abraham Lincoln*, Doubleday and McClure Co., New York, 1900.

Taylor, Hannis, *The Lincoln-Douglas Debates and Their Application to Present Day Problems,* North American Review, Feb. 1909.

Thomas, Benjamin P., *Abraham Lincoln,* Alfred A. Knopf, New York, 1952.

————, *Portrait for Posterity: Lincoln and His Biographers,* Rutgers University Press, New Jersey, 1947.

Thomas, John L., *The Liberator: William Lloyd Garrison,* Little, Brown and Co., Boston, 1963.

Tisler, C. C., *Lincoln's in Town* (Monograph), Tisler, Ottawa, Ill., 1940.

Tracy, Gilbert A., *Uncollected Letters of Abraham Lincoln,* Houghton, Mifflin Co., Boston, 1917.

Van Deusen, Glyndon G., *The Life of Henry Clay,* Little, Brown & Co., Boston, 1937.

Villard, Henry, *Lincoln On The Eve of '61,* Alfred A. Knopf, New York, 1941.

Warren, Charles, *The Supreme Court in United States History,* Little, Brown & Co., Boston, 1922–28.

Washington, George, *Writings of George Washington,* Geo. Washington Bicentennial Comm., John C. Fitzpatrick, ed., U.S. Gov't. Printing Office, 1931–44.

Weik, Jesse W., *The Real Lincoln: A Portrait,* Houghton Mifflin Co., Boston, 1922.

Weyl, Nathaniel, *The Negro in American Civilization,* Public Affairs Press, Washington, D.C., 1960.

White, Horace, *The Life of Lyman Trumbull,* Houghton, Mifflin Co., Boston, 1913.

Whitney, Henry Clay, *Life on the Circuit with Lincoln,* ed. by Paul M. Angle, The Caxton Printers, Caldwell, Idaho, 1940.

————, *Lincoln, The Citizen,* Vol. 1 of *Life and Works of Abraham Lincoln,* ed. by Marion Mills Miller (9 vols.), Current Literature Publishing Co., New York, 1907.

Willis, Henry Parker, *Stephen A. Douglas,* American Crisis Biographies, Geo. W. Jacobs & Co., Philadelphia, 1910.

Wilson, Henry, *History of the Rise and Fall of the Slave Power in America,* James R. Osgood Co., Boston, 1875.

Wiltse, Charles M., *John C. Calhoun,* Bobbs-Merrill Co., Indianapolis, 1951.

EDITIONS OF THE TEXT
OF THE DEBATES

Most editions of the debates have followed the pattern of the original published by Follet, Foster and Company in 1860, entitled *Political Debates between Hon. Abraham Lincoln and Hon. Stephen A. Douglas in the Celebrated Campaign of 1858 in Illinois.* This was based on Lincoln's scrapbook and contained the bare text minus the parenthetical notations on cheering and other interruptions as Lincoln had stipulated.

Some editions have added one or more of the following: Lincoln's Peoria speech of 1854 and his Springfield speech of 1857, the speeches of Lincoln and Douglas preliminary to the formal debates, and Lincoln's two speeches in Ohio in 1859. The Burrow Brothers' edition includes extracts of Trumbull's speech at Alton and Douglas' reply at Jacksonville because of their importance to the Charleston debate.

These are the best-known texts:

Burrows Bros., Cleveland, Ohio, 1887 and 1894.
International Tract Society, Battle Creek, Michigan 1895, edited by
    Alonzo T. Jones
O. S. Hubbell & Co., Cleveland, Ohio, 1895
Scott, Foresman & Co., Chicago, 1900
Putnam's Sons, Knickerbocker Press, New York, 1912

In 1908, for the fiftieth anniversary of the debates, the Illinois State Historical Library published an edition under the editorship of Edwin Erle Sparks, containing only the seven formal debates, but including a brief introduction and extensive quotations from newspapers of the time.

For the centennial of the debates in 1958, the Chicago Historical Society published an edition under the title *Created Equal?* edited with an introduction and notes by Paul M. Angle. This book includes the speeches of Lincoln and Douglas preliminary to the formal debates, as well as some extracts from minor speeches delivered at various times and places.

Volume III of *The Collected Works of Abraham Lincoln*, edited by
Roy P. Basler, published in 1953, contains the full text of the debates,
and also includes extracts of Trumbull's speech at Alton and Douglas' reply
at Jacksonville.

The editions of Sparks, Angle and Basler include the parenthetical remarks originally deleted by Lincoln.

Angle's is the text quoted in this book except where reference is made
for special purposes to other texts, e.g., to Basler on page 460 and Burrows
Bros. on pages 462 and 463.

In honor of the centennial, the Library of Congress published a facsimile
copy of Lincoln's scrapbook, under the title employed by Lincoln: *The
Illinois Political Campaign of 1858*. The original scrapbook was presented
to the library by Alfred Whital Stern who had purchased it from the estate
of Oliver R. Barrett. With an introduction and annotations by David C.
Mearns, the facsimile is a beautiful and impressive addition to Lincolniana.

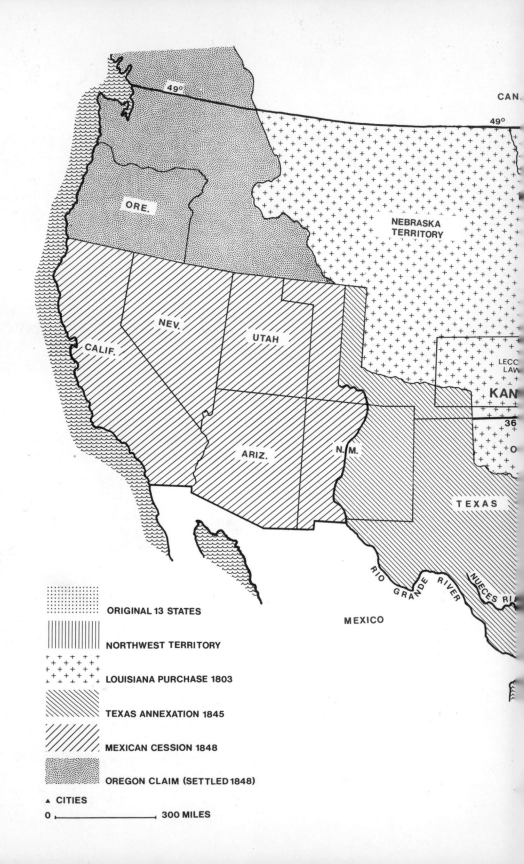

CAN.

49°

49°

ORE.

NEBRASKA
TERRITORY

NEV.

UTAH

CALIF.

LECC
LAW

KAN

36

ARIZ.

N. M.

O

TEXAS

RIO GRANDE RIVER

NUECES RI

MEXICO

ORIGINAL 13 STATES

NORTHWEST TERRITORY

LOUISIANA PURCHASE 1803

TEXAS ANNEXATION 1845

MEXICAN CESSION 1848

OREGON CLAIM (SETTLED 1848)

▲ CITIES

0 ⊢————————⊣ 300 MILES